GILLIAN COWLISHAW began life on a farm. After being a traveller, a mother and a teacher, she became a student, taking her doctorate in anthropology. Her academic interests are varied, though most of her research has been concerned with the position of Aborigines in relation to Australian society. She is currently a research scholar at the University of Technology, Sydney. Among her publications are *Black, White or Brindle* and *Race Matters: Indigenous Australians and 'our' society* (co-editor).

To Hal
and
The Bulman Mob

REDNECKS, EGGHEADS AND BLACKFELLAS

A study of racial power and intimacy in Australia

GILLIAN COWLISHAW

Routledge
Taylor & Francis Group

LONDON AND NEW YORK

Some of the material in Chapter 1 was published as part of 'Race at work' in the *Journal of the Royal Anthropological Institute*, 1997, 3(1). A version of Chapter 8 was published as 'Erasing culture and race' in *Oceania*, 1998, 68(3).

First published 1999 by Allen & Unwin

Published 2020 by Routledge
2 Park Square, Milton Park, Abingdon, Oxon OX14 4RN
605 Third Avenue, New York, NY 10017

Routledge is an imprint of the Taylor & Francis Group, an informa business

Copyright © Gillian Cowlishaw, 1999

National Library of Australia
Cataloguing-in-Publication entry:

Rednecks, eggheads and blackfellas: a study of racial power and intimacy in Australia.

Bibliography.
Includes index.
ISBN 1 86508 076 4.

1. Racism—Australia. 2. Aborigines, Australian—Civil rights.
3. Aborigines, Australian—Treatment. 4. Aborigines,
Australian—Public opinion. 5. Australia—Race relations. I. Title.

305.89915

Set in 11/13 pt Bembo by DOCUPRO, Sydney

ISBN-13: 9781865080765 (pbk)

Redneck: *colloq.* *(derog)* . . . uneducated prejudiced person . . . *adj.* especially in relation to political views
—*The Macquarie Dictionary*

Egghead: *colloq.* an intellectual; highbrow.
—*The Macquarie Dictionary*

Blackfellow: *(esp. in Aboriginal pidgin)* an Aborigine. Also **blackfella, blackfeller.**
—*The Macquarie Dictionary*

Contents

Maps and Figures

Foreword

What, in fact, is a foreword? Is it perhaps an invitation into the text that is to follow? If so, to what end? Is it, then, a preface or introduction to the author's *own* Preface and Introduction? Why would we need one? Is it, rather, a transcoding of the text into terms useful to a place or context different from the one in which it was written? That may be so. But who is to say that the foreword's writer is enough different from/ enough similar to the author of the book and *her* point of origin to accomplish this task? Who indeed is to say the forewordist is enough the 'master' of language in this 'new' space, whatever and wherever this 'new' space might be? Who is to say that in fact we are not in a situation of linguistic overlap, one in which polyglot meets polyglot?

Instead of, or perhaps as well as, some or all of the above, this foreword is in dialogue with the text at hand. It is an expression of why and how in this writer's opinion Gillian Cowlishaw's *Rednecks, Eggheads and Blackfellas: A Study of Racial Power and Intimacy in Australia* is essential reading.

To begin with a simple naming of this text, one might state that it examines 80-plus years of the history of relationships between indigenous Australians, white rancher settlers and more distant white administrators on the southern border of Australia's Arnhem Land. But part of Cowlishaw's challenge in this book is to complicate that naming, multiply the layers of mapping and historicising necessary in order to document, always incompletely, the spaces, the lives, the practices, and the people about which and about whom she is writing.

So, to come at this introduction from some other angles, one might add that Cowlishaw's *Rednecks, Eggheads and Blackfellas* is a study of racial formation and simultaneously of colonialist relations. It is also an ethnohistory, based both on Cowlishaw's own 23 years of fieldwork in the area under discussion, and on archival work in Darwin examining especially materials dealing with that which the state successively named 'native', 'aboriginal' and 'indigenous' affairs. The product is a painstaking examination of the gradual, inexorable remaking of meanings and lives through decades of colonial/racial domination. Both terms—colonial *and* racial—are crucial here.

This is also a text in which the voice of ethnographer and historian are examined and interrogated, but with a light hand, for this book is in no way simply a self-reflexive, confessional narrative. Rather it is one in which ethnography is understood to be deeply enmeshed in the history of colonial–racial domination. Further, it is a text wherein the author seeks to comprehend and work with her own positionings within changing racial formations, as ethnographer, as Australian and as white woman. Cowlishaw seeks in this book to position herself clearly, critically, and forcefully within contemporary Australian race relations. This is, then, a text whose author refuses to avoid taking controversial stands.

In any treatment of colonialism, racism and the discourses associated with these, the question of voice becomes crucial. Is it enough, for example, to hear only about and only from the colonisers, and from the critics that, inevitably, eventually emerge from among the descendants of those communities wherein the colonising effort first began? More crudely, can we be satisfied with hearing white folks commenting critically on white folks, and will such texts yield enough knowledge from or about the colonised themselves? Will such texts continue to occlude those very voices, spaces and meaning systems that they ostensibly set out to remind us had been occluded? These are the challenges that have for many years faced critics of colonial and racist discourses. On the other hand, what does it mean when white scholars draw upon the voices of the colonised within their own texts? What kinds of power relations are reinstantiated then? Further, what claims about authenticity, purity and restored originality might appropriately or erroneously be made, in those moments when the white historian, ethnographer or cultural critic seeks to draw into her text indigenous, colonised and/or 'subaltern' voices in order to document that which has been 'lost'?

Into this minefield enters the skilled hand of Gillian Cowlishaw. Cowlishaw is absolutely clear that indigenous voices must be heard, here. Thus early on and threaded through the text are voices of indigenous women and men, primarily of the Rembarrnga community. For example, Cowlishaw quotes a man, Ronnie Martin, speaking about Mainoru station, the pastoral lease (ranching area) around which she centered much of her historical analysis: 'Blackfella started that place . . . Mainoru is really on blackfella area'. Here, Cowlishaw reminds us that in the first *and* final analysis, the space under discussion was indigenous land. As she puts it, '[b]lack voices challenge the technical, moral and epistemological foundations on which conventional histories are based'. Towards the end of the text, Cowlishaw quotes Nelly Camfoo, a Rembarrnga woman who was key to Cowlishaw's coming to comprehension of the history about which she is writing. Camfoo sums up the contemporary situations thus:

> I will vote, but I'll never win. That's your law, we just vote, we don't get anything out of it . . . I vote because I'm in *mununga* [white] country now. I'm speaking *mununga* English now . . . So I have to vote while I'm here wearing your clothes and talking your English and smoking your tobacco, eating your sugar and tea, and talking in your tape recorder. It's not a blackfella thing that one. (p. 290)

These two quotes in a sense sum up the parameters of this book; its journey through the making and continuing reproduction of a white-dominated Australia.

But throughout, Cowlishaw reminds her readers that drawing upon indigenous voices to challenge that which is dominant is not a simple matter. For one thing, there are questions about language use itself, the degree to which hierarchisation of languages and language users may result in a kind of prefabricated ranking of the speech, the speaker and hence the validity of discourse. The language by means of which Rembarrnga speakers are in communication with 'whitefellas', that which is most often named 'Kriol', is widely viewed as childish, simplistic and/or the sign of essential inferiority. Thus, while Cowlishaw honored her interlocutors' wishes to transliterate/translate their speech into 'standardised "proper" English', she was simultaneously aware that she could not render the full contextual expression and meaning of their words, nor prevent their voices from being interpreted in negative, hostile ways. Cowlishaw also explains, transcoding for her readers, that the very intentionalities governing Rembarrnga and dominant 'whitefella' history telling are different, as are their ontologies and structures. Given all of this, it is utterly impractical to suppose that telling analogously constructed, yet substantively contradictory, dueling histories could lead to a definitive discursive overthrow of the oppressor by the oppressed.

Cowlishaw's text thus in no way attempts a simple 'overthrow' of one historical accounting, one sociocultural mapping, by means of another. Yet her juxtaposition of interlinked accounts of 'blackfella', 'redneck' and 'egghead' versions of the history of the same physical space does its own work—and without recourse to binary, overly simplified narrative resolutions to the tale. Reading *Rednecks, Eggheads and Blackfellas*, one witnesses the biracial yet tripartite investments of the three groups named in the book's title. One sees how ranchers—white, male, and for the most part not wealthy—arrived in southern Arnhem Land at the start of the twentieth century, seeking to establish new methods of interacting with land and resources in the area. In whitefella language the effort was to 'settle' the territory. In this project, they were dependent on Rembarrnga and other indigenous communities with whom they established material relationships somewhere between wage slavery and indenture. One sees how, for the Rembarrnga, new work relationships were simultaneously endured and resisted, even at times appreciated. Meanwhile one learns about the crucial part played by the introduction and provision of addictive substances—tea, alcohol, tobacco—in the cementing of these new economic relationships. Here, power and intimacy coexisted, in ways that were at times brutal, at times loving, and indeed at times both at once.

Perhaps even more startling is what happens after the achievement of so-called settlement of the territory—a project that succeeded in thoroughly altering Aboriginal and white relationships to the land even as it eventually 'failed' in local, economic terms. The second half of this book takes its readers through the transition from what Cowlishaw aptly names colonialism to what one might appropriately name neo-colonialism (there is no *post*colonialism here). Now, eggheads come into greater visibility.

From the beginnings of 'settlement' up to the present, those whom Cowlishaw calls 'eggheads' have been a continuous presence, arguably controlling the circumstances of rednecks' apparent yet partial control of land, resources and blackfellas. The investments and involvements of this category of whitefellas began as more distant and thus more abstract ones. They came closer into Rembarrnga life through the very same processes by which the Rembarrnga–redneck economic nexus was dissolved. In the egghead category Cowlishaw includes those able at times to exert control through the construction of knowledge (of some kind!) about indigenous people. Also part of this grouping are those whose power takes the form of the provision or withholding of money and material resources—whether, as in earlier days, with the ranchers as their intermediaries or, from the mid 1960s to the present, as functionaries of local, regional and national government.

Cowlishaw makes clear the interwovenness and also the relative autonomy of these three groupings. For the white population, this interweaving culminates in the emergence of an always-already present white Australia. For the indigenous people the harvest is a bitter one. The temporal and spatial mapping of this journey, through the pages of *Rednecks, Eggheads and Blackfellas*, is a remarkable one. First, Cowlishaw's narration moves with such care and precision that it almost feels as though it is taking place in 'real time'. Secondly, the 80-year lifespan of Mainoru station and the ongoing growth and transformation of the Bulman community to which many former Mainoru Rembarrnga relocated, instantiate many of the key stages of colonial settlement, disruption and transformation, compressed into a startlingly brief period. Thirdly, voices of whitefellas and blackfellas in all three categories, drawn into the text through interviews, observation and archival work place the text at times in the present, at other times in 'retrospect' from multiple standpoints. Throughout, Cowlishaw is able to demonstrate how it is that competing versions of history create equally discordant present experiences, with causal relationships at times known and at other times unknown to the actors involved.

Above, I noted that Cowlishaw is committed to a careful inter-weaving of the terms, 'race', 'racism', and 'colonialism'. I suggest that, for her, colonialism refers to the making and mapping of new material relations, simultaneously extractive and exploitative. It also designates the new forms of social organisation, new protocols and disciplinary processes, as well as the ontologies and epistemologies, that both make possible and are made possible by, the colonising process. *Rednecks, Eggheads and Blackfellas* details these throughout the period under consideration at Mainoru and Bulman, the two sites that are the main spatial foci of Cowlishaw's study.

Race, on the other hand, refers in this text to the naming and categorising of persons and communities that are in turn enabling of and made possible by the colonising processes just noted. The making of racialised persons and groups (or to put this differently, the imposition of racialised identities and identifications on persons and groups) is, of course, familiar to any scholar of colonisation and of (post)colonised spaces. Equally familiar is the minimal range of names and descriptions of colonised others available to the colonial imagination. Also well-known are the efforts to 'civilise, correct and assist' (or more correctly, discipline, control and assimilate) those persons, and the transition from culturalising to racialising languages when disciplinary efforts fail to work in the ways the coloniser would have hoped.

I would argue that the relative recentness of the history that Cowlishaw is documenting enables her to illustrate and examine in a compelling manner both the coimplication of colonial and racial discourses, and the mutation and displacement of the former into the latter. Also critical to note is the actuality that the transition from colonialism to racism is only partial in this instance. Cowlishaw's book maps the transitions from Aboriginal people seen as an alien, Other and less civilised (but perhaps civilisable) group; to constructions of them as intractable, recalcitrant, and racially Other; to, more recently, a culturally valuable group in relation to whom the white-initiated racial categorisation process has broken down; and as is often the case in the present period, simultaneously as all three of the above. By the end of *Rednecks, Eggheads and Blackfellas*, it would appear that indigenous Australians are now seen as perhaps culturally intransigent, perhaps injured, and certainly as a site of white confusion and anxiety. The signal role of the term 'culture' in this process is a crucial seam in Cowlishaw's argument.

Contemplating Cowlishaw's argument and building upon it, I would add that race and racialness only come to stand alone, conceptually, when the colonising process has established at least some manner of hegemony and has thus been (falsely) consigned to the past. Thus one aspect of the power of this text is that it shows us this transition process laid bare. Moreover its timeframe is within the living memory not only of her ethnographic subjects but of a good proportion of her readership, also. It is then challenging in a particularly beneficial way to audiences established within the frames of racialised hegemonic spaces grown all-too-familiar with time; and to those established in spaces wherein the term 'colonial' signals 'legacies' rather than present moments. By contrast the text may have especial familiarity and potency for audiences working from within and/or in relation to indigenous communities.

Cowlishaw is insistent that it is through the coexistence of all three groups—rednecks, eggheads and blackfellas—that new meanings, new actualities, have come into being and continue to be transformed. Yet for her the image of the palimpsest, 'the place where a text has been *overwritten or erased* in order to make way for another text' best describes the situation. And this is, of course, because of the blatantly power-laden relationships that mark the history under consideration. In opening her discussion, Cowlishaw says that this book should not be seen as a classic ethnography. It does not seek to mark or document a singular field site, nor does it map Rembarrnga life, practice, belief, religion or any other dimension of that which conventional ethno-graphy might name 'Rembarrnga culture'. I would not presume to dispute Cowlishaw's claim that this book leaves an enormous amount unsaid about Rembarrnga people. Yet to my mind, *Rednecks, Eggheads and Blackfellas* is in fact an ethnography, but one of a different kind; one that includes all participants, black and white, and is amoebic spatially and temporally. The ethnographer eschews the effort to construct and then document autochthonous culture-spaces. She also refuses the subject position of 'empathic yet non-implicated outsider' as well as that of her more recent counterpart, the 'ethnographer ethnographised'. In place of these, Cowlishaw offers us a complex, power-conscious, discontinuous, frankly partial account of the history that fashioned all three of the groups examined here and that continues to shape their individual and collective destinies. I would argue that *Rednecks, Eggheads and Blackfellas* demonstrates the power and potential of construing the palimpsest itself as the field site and as the worthy topos of anthropological investigation.

Ruth Frankenberg
Associate Professor of American Studies
University of California, Davis

Acknowledgments

This book represents years of work, and the working out of a series of ideas, many of which were generated from the work of others. I acknowledge especially the many contemporary scholars who have pioneered new ways of theorising and writing ethnography and history. I have made free with their ideas for my own purposes while limiting quotations and references so that the story can carry the ideas inside itself. What I brought to the task was a sense of disquiet, anger, disgust even, at misperception and myopia in the field which I entered in 1975. It seemed to me that in the Northern Territory of Australia there exists Kafka's Metamorphosis in reverse, an elaborate if unwitting pretence that already present difference, that is, Aboriginal culture, is not there, or not real, or at the very most, some kind of temporary aberration which can be erased or overcome with a little help. Otherness is an embarrassment. I began to conceive of the Northern Territory as a palimpsest where the overlay of a series of designs for modernity had concealed a dynamic Aboriginal story but not erased it. The task I undertook was not to reveal the precise nature of this living and changing text that is written underneath, but rather to reveal the art and effects of the palimpsest which has taken on a series of guises such as civilisation, colonial development, assimilation, and self-determination.

I am grateful to many people who, sometimes unknowingly, contributed to the long and often interrupted production of this book.

At Bulman, Nelly Camfoo, Lorna and Smiler Martin and their children, Dolly and Larry Murray and their family, Dorothy Murray, Florry and Chuckerduck Lindsay, Judy Farrar, Alma Gibbs and all the other Martins, Murrays, Lindsays and Forbes families and various other young and old people shared their lives with me when I first went there in 1975, and helped me understand certain things. Since then on numerous journeys north, many others, especially Tex Camfoo, Annette Murray and Jill Curtis, as well as people from Mt Catt, from Malyanganuk, Bulugadru and other Arnhem Land outstations and from Beswick and Barunga have contributed to my understanding of their history and their lives. I hope that this account of their experiences is satisfying to them. I want to particularly acknowledge the agreement that deceased people could be named and their photos reproduced in this book so that the children and grandchildren of the Bulman mob will know this story.

I am grateful also to the whitefellas who assisted me with their opinions and recollections, and sometimes with interviews. Over the 24 years of my engagement with the Northern Territory they have been many and various, including pastoralists, government officials, shopkeepers and stockmen. To those who have lived on the cultural frontier I owe the most thanks, though few of them realise it. One such was Heather Dodd, and I acknowledge her participation and regret her untimely death. While somewhat dubious about my project, she nonetheless wrote and spoke to me a number of times, and provided invaluable material.

Many anthropological colleagues and postgraduate students, mainly associated with the Department of Anthropology at the University of Sydney have provided a forum for critical discussion over many years and I thank them. Les Hiatt was my PhD supervisor, and his analytic interest in human emotion and sexuality, his understandings of Arnhem Land people, and the things I disagreed with him about, were early foundations for this work. Jeremy Beckett, who blazed the trail for a contemporary anthropology in Australia, has been a valuable commentator, colleague and critic. More recently I have been strengthened by debate with Franca Tamasari and with Sanjay Srivastava who made valuable suggestions. Others to whom I owe thanks are Michael Allen, Ghasan Hage, Michael Jackson, Vivienne Kondos, Neil McLean, Francesca Merlan, Jadran Mimeca and Alan Rumsay. The University of Technology, Sydney, also deserves thanks for welcoming me as a refugee from the University of Sydney in January 1998. The Faculty of Humanities and Social Sciences provided generous resources, and I was supported and encouraged by, among others, Liz Jacka, Sylvia Lawson, Meaghan Morris and Stephen Muecke as I was completing this work.

The most valued colleagues are those trusted friends who engage closely with one's work, and there are three whose inputs have been important and who share a faith in the radical potential of anthropology. Teresa Lea read versions the manuscript from its inception, and always insisted on the significance of my work when she was positioned outside the academy and since re-entering it. Over the years I have benefited enormously from interaction with my colleague and friend Barry Morris whose obsession with the living importance of ideas has always been a challenge and an inspiration. Andrew Lattas has also been an inspiration with his originality, urgency and endless fascination with the ingenuity and intelligence of the human imagination. His comments on earlier drafts encouraged me to develop ideas I had only hinted at.

I want also to acknowledge Bobbie Lea's hospitality in Darwin and her experience as a 'pen-pusher', and Anna Nolan's hospitality, swag and companionship at Barmedakola. I thank the staff at the Australian Archives, those at the Northern Territory Archives, and ATSIC for special permission to access DAA files. I thank the Australian Institute of Aboriginal and Torres Strait Islander Studies for funding several field trips since 1975.

My offspring Sally Dumbrell and Nick Cowlishaw and their families deserve appreciative mention for keeping me in mind of the vastly varied ways that knowledge and belief are absorbed, held and transmitted socially.

My husband Hal Wootten, though not present at the conception of this work, gave me unstinting support during its gestation. I benefited greatly from his strategic advice, generosity of spirit and misplaced humility in relation to intellectual work, and also from his sharing of his own experiences in the kinds of domains I am writing about. For this and for his presence at the birth I dedicate the book to him.

Introduction

Knowledge

In 1975 I noted in my field-work diary:

> Walked along the defunct railway line into Katherine with Alma Gibbs
> [plate 1]. She explained to me that a man was killed there. 'The train
> ran into him poor bugger,' she said softly. 'They stop the trains then.'
> She seems to assume that the trains no longer ran on this track because
> a man had been killed. Implies that it was the driver who had stopped
> the trains running due to his fear and shame.

I tell this to identify the personal forms that Aboriginal knowledge
takes, and also to show how strangely incongruous this emphasis on
a human tragedy seems beside 'our' western commonsense knowledge.
For we all know, after a certain age, that it is an *economic* logic which
determines whether a railway line will continue to operate. Who is
this 'we' which shares this knowledge? Both 'eggheads' (such as
anthropologists who keep field-work diaries), and 'rednecks' (including
perhaps the train driver), for a start, and certainly the 'pen-pushers',
those government officials who make decisions about railways, and
also about many things that will be dealt with in this work. The
pervasive consequences of the shared knowledge of literate whitefellas
in relation to 'bush' blackfellas is one focus of the story which properly
begins in Chapter 1 where some readers may also want to begin.

Another theme is the knowledge blackfellas have of whitefellas as well as the assertion and resurgence of that other domain; that is, the 'blackfella way'. The knowledge, in each case, is not merely of facts or events but is a lived understanding of causes, categories and values through which the world comes to make sense to a community of people. What is usually named as knowledge is formalised and authoritative, but knowledge also exists in less systematised forms, residing in tacit assumptions, commonsense homilies and in the meanings accorded to everyday interactions. Such knowledge is usually rendered as 'belief', 'discourse' or 'culture'.

I will follow the developing relationship between a group of mainly Rembarrnga[1] people and the cattle stations of Mainoru and Gulperan on the southern border of Arnhem Land in the Northern Territory (map 1) in order to explore how the society which developed in pastoral Australia as an extension of modern, enlightened and progressive European culture, could generate a savage regime which was so unintentionally destructive in its effects. What were the historical imperatives driving the insistent desire to bring 'the natives' into the nation, and how did the particular relationships between the black and white people[2] reflect or challenge the trajectory of this nation? What was the response of 'the natives' as they were caught up in the momentum of the great flywheel of modernity? This work traces the genealogy and duality of government policy and its impact at a particular site in the production of black subjects and white subjects. Links are made between intellectual currents, academic concerns and the varied experiences of people at one site on the racial frontiers where lives were being reformed in material as well as imaginative ways. On the marginal cattle stations which are at the centre of this work, black and white peoples' lives were intertwined over the span of 80 years. Illustrations from these lives are used to analyse shifting sentiments and customs surrounding issues of race.

This work is more directly grounded in the specifics of everyday experience and its imaginative understanding than in an examination of the images and representations that circulate on the national stage which others have addressed (cf. Lattas 1997; Marcus 1997; Schaffer 1988). I will trace some patterns of interaction on the 'cultural borderlands' (Rosaldo 1989) to illustrate how anthropologists, pastoralists and government officials squabbled about Aborigines as they intruded into their country, controlled aspects of their lives, and dominated the way they were represented in the public realm. The different relationships pastoralists and anthropologists had with

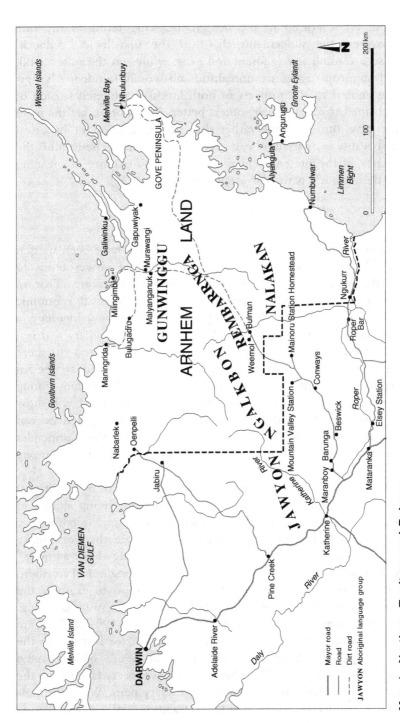

Map 1 Northern Territory and Bulman

Aborigines are captured in the denigrating slang terms of my title which express the judgements that, on the one hand, 'redneck' pastoralists are implicitly ignorant and racist while, on the other hand, 'egghead' anthropologists are unrealistic and woolly minded. Aborigines were central to the projects of both kinds of whitefellas, each of whom claimed to know 'their' others better. The work takes the form of a narrative through time rather than an explanation of historical events, because a narrative can evoke both the genesis and the contingency of the present, and allows readers to explore its meaning beyond the author's particular argument.

Culture

In the many accounts of colonial[3] race relations that have been written since 1970, the emphasis on gross inequalities of power tends to conceal the everyday manifestations of cultural hegemony. That is, European power is commonly seen as manifested in physical, economic and political domination, mediated by a legitimising racist ideology, a racial blot which is treated as separable from a more primary and real settler sociality. Thus, racial assumptions are deplored as mere excrescences, external to the society, rather than analysed as internal to its nature, an intrinsic and active principle in the relationships among white colonisers as well as between them and Aborigines. I will show that an ideology imbued with racial principles and practices was inscribed into the heart of pastoral activities and that these principles and practices were as apparent among 'egghead' academics as among 'redneck' settlers.

Ethnographic analyses of what are considered to be traditional Aborigines have seldom been able to present the living drama of Aboriginal communities cleaving to their own values, faced with a society which demanded an instrumental logic to make the world make sense. There has been much effort put into detailing the 'traditional' beliefs, practices and social organisation among Aborigines of northern Australia, but only recently have there been attempts to examine the experience of interaction between black and white Australians (e.g. Beckett 1988; Carter 1987; Morris 1989; Reynolds 1990). There are only a few ethnographies of developing traditions, for instance in the 'blacks' camps' (cf. Beckett 1964; Collmann 1988; Morris 1989; Sansom 1980; Merlan 1998). The depiction of everyday life in the station homestead has largely been left to literary pens. We anthropologists placed ourselves on the side of tradition, rather than beside contemporary Aborigines; anthropology's role was to interpret Aborigines to colonial society. I am interpreting the relationship between colonial society and Aborigines and will use Rembarrnga reflections on their past to further this interpretation. But I should add that anthropologists were more than fusty scholars participating in a version of Said's Orientalism (1985) by constructing an exotic and primitive otherness out of the Aboriginal culture over which they claimed authority. It was the determined gaze of anthropologists that sometimes partially pierced the distorting mirror with which colonial society surrounded the colonised. Anthropologists tried to bring a sense of legitimacy to the otherness they observed. Today another conception of difference is emerging, one that is not limited to an indigenous tradition.

Two rescuing operations are at work here. 'Culture' needs to be rescued from anthropology and from history—not 'their' culture and not 'our culture', but something in between. Not the high culture of philosophy and art or even of government policy and the bureaucracy, but rather the expressions of particular social forms in everyday places. Also the feminine realm needs to be rescued from the national culture hero, the stockman. Outback mythologies have erased not only the women, but the feminine, the softness, the tears and intimate humour, the warmth and the nurturing. Love between black and white people, for instance, and love of brown children, has had no place in the important tasks of recording men's brave adventures on the frontier or, more recently, in exposing the grim reality behind the myths of the brave pioneers. The ambiguous and ambivalent nature of race relations, the various forms of compromise and their contradictions, will be emphasised in this study.

I bring an anthropological eye to bear on the colonising culture and the domain of race relations. My aim is not to expose further the oppressiveness and the violence of land appropriation which many recent historians have recorded (e.g. Read & Read 1991; Reid 1990; Rose 1991). Nor do I aim to show more of the involvement of the law with race (e.g. Maddock 1983; McCorquodale 1987; Williams 1986). Nor is the economic logic of capitalist exploitation my major concern (Hartwig 1972). Instead I pursue the cultural logic of colonial invasion as it developed into what it is today. My focus is the moral universe of colonial relations which the Rembarrnga people faced in their encounters with their pastoral employers. Rather than examine and explain the genesis of changing government policies towards Aborigines I want to glimpse the everyday forms of race relations in the Territory[4] as articulated by station managers, public servants, anthropologists and Aborigines. Those relations have a complexity that is obscured by the simple denunciation of them as racist. For instance, the monitoring of inter-racial marriages needs to be dealt with in a cultural context which includes passion, anxiety, compromise and ambiguity, rather than being put into a hold-all of horror with frontier violence as another example of a mindless colonial desire to submerge Aboriginality.

The relationships between Aborigines and the whites[5] they came to know so well, and the laws that the whites understood as morality, will be discussed in terms of their mundane, commonsense expressions. Aborigines were not faced with an abstraction called 'colonial relations' but with specific men and women, many of them engaged in the pastoral industry. Others were public servants, protectors of Aborigines, patrol officers and more recently state officials whose presence has increased over the decades. Today the main focus of race relations is at the point of intersection between Aboriginal communities and a massive bureaucratic structure with its concealed and explicit forms of pedagogy.

History

Anthropology is usually a spatial adventure which entails familiarising oneself with the exotic other who is elsewhere. In seeking to understand the dynamics of race relations, I was propelled into a temporal adventure which entailed a long-term engagement with the people at Bulman. The material I have used to mould my interpretation of this fragment of the past came from various sources. My first accounts of Mainoru station came from the Rembarrnga people I met in 1975 when I arrived at a place which was called Bulman by the local whites, Gulperan by the Department of Aboriginal Affairs, and Goinjimbi by the Rembarrnga, though the latter have become adept at using names appropriate to the circumstances. On my first visits I was doing field work, collecting material for a PhD thesis concerning certain traditions and knowledge among Aboriginal women. Even then, and in numerous subsequent visits over 24 years, my interest has been in Rembarrnga interaction with whitefellas. In the country around Bulman and Mainoru there are many Rembarrnga memories attached to events recalled from the past, and I recorded many accounts of the past which were often also comments on the present. The previous owners of the station, as well as neighbours and government officials, provided other kinds of information and different memories.

The government archives in Darwin contain piles of yellowing sheets, files in which are recorded certain aspects of government officials' activities. Those I examined from the Native Affairs Branch (NAB), the Welfare Branch and the Department of Aboriginal Affairs (DAA), showed how state officials monitored pastoralists as well as Aborigines. There were documents about Mainoru which listed the names and pay and commented on the worthiness of Aborigines I was familiar with. Such comments encapsulate messages about how the world was being interpreted and managed. Other documents recorded debates and struggles concerning policies and their implementation, which produced another set of clues to what made the present. Published literature provided another arena for exploration, especially of alternative interpretations, some of which I argue with, or correct, or use as elements in my own account. I have used both academic and fictional works as windows on the created world that made certain things possible and precluded others.

Written sources have to be 'interrogated as actions, not as descriptions' (Todorov 1982:53); that is, as a constitutive part of the reality about which they are also sources of information. It does no service to dead men to take their words literally, or to admire their myth making as if it were their reality. Memo writers, journalists and other recorders of events do not merely tell us 'what really happened', though their words contain important evidence about events. By examining the cultural source of earlier accounts, other elusive meanings can be recovered and used to crack open the surface which hides another, lost past. Documents such as newspaper reports can, like ethnographies (Clifford 1986:98), be seen as allegories, stories with another meaning which can be used for teaching or explaining; that is, for advancing or perpetuating an alternative social reality.

Academic works are judged on different criteria from popular books. But if we flout the categories and look for ethnographic material in travellers' tales, and for the imagination in ethnographies, some common constraints and confusions are revealed, particularly in relation to race and gender. It thus becomes possible to expose the politics of representing the past and the present. That is, those ideas and assumptions shared by erudite texts and popular accounts are a clue to a profound domain of cultural determination. As feminist scholars have demonstrated, silences and omissions in both kinds of writing can tell us what society cannot see as part of the process of constructing what it did see. Further, the implicit moralities evident in many colonial and revisionist histories need to be analysed rather than expunged.

I use these post-modern reading techniques in relation to the problems of evidence to confront the intractable conundrums in the retelling of history and the representing of others. Let me affirm my view that all representations of the world are to some degree partial, flawed, subjective and creative, and that they are in competition. Representations which gain legitimacy do so not simply on the grounds of an objective measurable kind of accuracy; rather they satisfy a query, touch a chord, support a structure or a dissatisfaction, or fulfil some other combination of functions. I am contesting some established representations of the frontier and the outback, of rednecks and eggheads, and of Aborigines. I want to retrieve the confusion, mystery, horror, excitement and humour of a world which well-worn images and explanatory schemata have made dull. Also, I try to suggest meanings in the past that are relevant to the present rather than to an abstract academic debate about race relations. Such debates are not, anyway, separable from popular discourse. I have deliberately smudged the boundaries between academic ideas and the folklore of race which circulates in the public domain because they intermingle in the world, both outside and within this work.[6] Thus, my arguments are intended as contributions to an ongoing debate about race which has always been there in Australian consciousness, sometimes disguised in identity discourse, but often explicit, active and powerful.

The tendency to see the present as if it had been predictable all along, and to look at the past as its cause (Carter 1987), undervalues the struggles that have been conducted among those who could have made a different present for us. Racial structures have been constructed in time through innumerable choices, decisions and conflicts; these are what made up the past as it went along. By emphasising the contingencies associated with individuals who came together in these places and times, the ambiguity in past events, and in their interpretation, can be captured.

Rembarrnga

Until the 1970s when Aboriginal voices began to be heard in Australia, in print and elsewhere, there was little recognition in this country that the colonised have a different version of colonial history. With a few notable exceptions (e.g. Barwick 1972; Beckett 1964; Elkin 1937; Stanner 1979) the vast body of specialised research of anthropologists and linguists until the 1970s was devoted to documenting an Aboriginality which did not speak to the present. Few Aboriginal responses to their contemporary experience of whites were recorded, although the apparently common view among Aborigines that white people were ghosts of their ancestors was alluded to in many a publication. This comforting thought both affirmed the primitive, superstitious nature of Aboriginal belief, and also made the romantic suggestion that we, as colonisers, need not be their enemy but could be accepted as kin. In recent years there have been explicit attempts by white Australians to claim some spiritual affiliation and even kinship with Aborigines (cf. Hamilton 1990; Lattas 1997; Marcus 1997).

The glimpses of Rembarrnga responses in this work are neither complete nor definitive. I am not trying to contrast Rembarrnga accounts with official records to establish a unitary, unambiguous truth about the past. Rather than the history in *their* myths, my primary concern is with the myths in *our* history. Rembarrnga voices are used not to test or contest the facticity of written history, but rather to demonstrate and document the fact that there were other imaginations, other meanings and other lives being lived out in the domain the colonisers always thought of as theirs. These other voices attest to the kind of gulf that exists between different pasts which were created out of 'the same' events. The challenge of these voices is not so much to the factual assertions of conventional accounts but to the silences and absences in those accounts and to the way the past has been received. Occasionally there is an overt challenge or a deliberate re-interpretation of the assumptions made by white land-holders, such as when Ronnie Martin, a Bulman resident, said, 'Blackfella started that place . . . Mainoru is really on blackfella area' (1983). But in general the challenges are immanent rather than explicit, subtle rather than flagrant. It is still the case that the Northern Territory of Australia is not only what white people experience; it remains another country for black people. The paintings of Rembarrnga artist Paddy Wainbarrnga, reproduced in a study of modern Australian art (Smith & Smith 1991:508), are a rich and dramatic example of the other meanings of history, of country, of morality and of race.

Listening to other voices is no simple matter. Black voices challenge the technical, moral and epistemological foundations on which conventional histories are based. The techniques of documenting, dating and naming individual actors as the first step in any narrative of the past are absent from Rembarrnga accounts, concerned as they are with placing people in their social and geographical landscape (cf. Morris 1990).

Rather than aiming for explanation, which is such a salient feature of western epistemology and scholarship, Rembarrnga see all people as having stories. They are tolerant of multiple stories concerning experience and do not necessarily seek the definitive, authoritative account of events such as those contained in written records which are the official memories of English-speaking Australia. Rembarrnga stories of the past expose the particularity and limitations of the written records and interrupt the prevailing sense of what these events were about.

The words of the Rembarrnga people must be read with some understanding not just of the contrasting themes of kinship and place, and the different meaning of racial categories, but of the fact that these are extracts from accounts which were constructed for a different social purpose. They were not produced for history books, and were not intended to convey neutral information. The narration was at once a form of entertainment and an account for contemplation and interpretation, by me as well as others. The stories also affirm, subtly and unconsciously, ways of seeing and being. Some of the intention conveyed in speech itself is lost in transcribing. The feelings expressed through cadence and stress, through fast repetitive chanting, or soft and sweet, low and rhythmic sequences, cannot be put on the page. Indignation which is unmistakably expressed by the body across our cultural divide may be absent from the written words. Sorrow, humour and all kinds of feelings come from the voice and add meaning to, for example, the fact of being a ringer,[7] to the experience of first tasting flour, to the sequence of events and to the meaning of events. These are not merely problems of linguistic or cultural purism, but show the severe and inescapable limitations of writing. But these Rembarrnga voices are not, I believe, calcified (Johnson 1987); a critical edge in the specific meanings and interpretations is retained in the written words. Further, the same loss occurs with the erstwhile Director of Welfare, Harry Giese (Chapter 6), who, when he spoke to me at the advanced age of 83, expressed his sense of authority on Aboriginal questions in every gesture of his white body.

Then there is the issue of language status. If I write what Nelly or Alma says as 'Mifella bin proper myall one. Mifella bin go longa station now', such language might be read as an inferior form of English and may be taken to imply simplicity and cognitive limitation.[8] Rembarrnga people all asked that their stories be rendered in standardised, 'proper' English (Cowlishaw 1995a). Among those who rely heavily on the written word, language itself has a particular meaning and function, different from those in an oral culture (Biddle forthcoming). A related problem is the audience which is neither present nor directly involved (Rhydwen 1996), an audience quite foreign to Nelly Camfoo, for instance. Nelly was happy with the transcription of her words when I read them to her. However, she is not aware of the critical reading audience who will want to do more than simply hear her story and may want to place a different interpretation on her words. I cannot protect Rembarrnga people from a reading of their words which could be wrong or offensive.

Readers should not seek here the depth and richness of a unique Aboriginal domain of meaning in relation to country and kin, or a detailed explication of Rembarrnga cosmology or epistemology. The truth of these matters is the traditional quest of ethnographic work, but such matters are referred to here as context rather than as text. Mine is not an anthropology primarily concerned with documenting the domain of a radical, unique otherness, an agenda which is being ably pursued by other anthropologists (e.g. Povinelli 1993; Tamisari 1998). I believe there are limitations in that enterprise, and I will discuss the indeterminacy and opacity of culture in the conclusion. Rather than presenting a comprehensive understanding of Rembarrnga subjectivity, I document the processes whereby a specific social system—a body of knowledge, philosophy and religion, with characteristic kinship, relations with country, and ceremonial—is being eroded, excluded and overridden by changes in the domains of time, space and social relations. But while conditions of social reproduction within Aboriginal communities are profoundly disrupted, there is a living and changing Rembarrnga world. It is often concealed beneath the business of modernity and hidden by the stigmatised images and popular stereotypes which circulate in the absence of any familiarity among whites with the specificity of this or other Aboriginal social worlds.

Even a map which outlines Rembarrnga country disrupts its meaning. These lines do not indicate the limits of a certain social group's legitimate territory but rather the space where Rembarrnga language belongs (Rumsey 1989). While the country is known intricately, and the particularities of association with clan and lineage are familiar parts of everyday life, the interweaving of the membership of language groups, matrilineal clans, *dawero*[9] and subsections means that there is no equivalent to the borders which mark the boundaries of private property, a state or a designated town. Many Rembarrnga people speak Ngalkbon, Jawoyn and Gunwinggu, and speakers of these languages are members of Rembarrnga clans, interlinked through marriages and descent. Every Aboriginal person has rights in country through genealogical links to mother's land, mother's father's land, father's land and so on. Rather than a set of codifiable, fixed, explicit rights, there is ubiquitous negotiation concerning the activation of rights.

Race

This book asserts the continuing significance of race. It may seem that the concept of race has been worn out, undermined and thus rendered unnecessary. But, while race has indeed been virtually abandoned as a biological concept because it does not make sense as a principle of biological categorisation (Barnett 1988), in the social domain race retains a wealth of meanings, confused and contradictory though they may be. All human groups are biologically hybrid, and it has been a truism in social science since the 1950s that biological characteristics bear an arbitrary relationship to social existence. Social science attempted to replace the concept of race (regressive, fixed and racist) with the concept of culture (progressive, malleable and politically neutral). But these efforts to treat racial and cultural forms of social differentiation as quite distinct, while effective at the level of theory, have had the effect of confusing the interpretation of processes that continued to operate in the world. Notions of race and culture are so intertwined that attempts to separate their functioning were futile. Further, the notion of deep-seated and important differences between human groups has not been erased (Goldberg 1995). It is the rendering of such differences in analysis and in everyday life, rather than their existence, that is at issue. Clearly, those differences commonly seen as racial are not fixed, but do we want them to be erased?

'Scientific racism', which studied bones and bodies in order to construct biological categories of human beings, has declined in importance,[10] leaving a silence around skin colour which, like a racial trace element, marks the presence of anxious denial. The meaning of skin colour is the focus of all kinds of struggles and contested significance, not only between Aborigines and whites, but also within each of these communities. There remains a fear among social scientists that, by examining the use of 'race' and making its dynamic explicit, we are somehow giving succour to racism itself; that is, to racial inequality, to essentialism or to racial hostility. This fear has meant that, rather than racial processes being analysed, the notion of race is outlawed. This fear of biology was evident in the 1960s and 1970s, both in the women's movement and in the anti-racist movement, but there has always been a counter-discourse, expressed cheekily both among feminists who assert the superiority of women's bodies and in the black power movement where black is more beautiful than pink. If prevailing popular judgements deem certain human characteristics unworthy or inferior, they need to be countered with other judgements. I want to replace the pretence that 'skin colour does not matter' with the recognition that of course it does, and to examine the way it matters.

The fear of biology contains an implicit assumption that any recognition of biological difference means complicity with the hierarchical arrangements that were responsible for the domination or extermination of Aboriginal communities. Overwhelming evidence from colonial conquest and white supremacy seemed to support the colonial view that biological inheritance had led inevitably to European domination over others deemed racially inferior. For many activists and intellectuals, the only strategy to reverse this ubiquitous and naturalised inequality seemed to be to deny the importance of biological inheritance rather than examine the specific way that racial theory and bodily characteristics were deployed to justify hierarchy. The cry 'we are all the same under the skin' was asserted by progressives everywhere in the 1950s and 1960s. While today the assertion that we are all different is common, socially celebrated differences are confined to the external symbols of culture. But skin colours, like sex organs, are important, partly because they are implicated in social hierarchy, and also because they are part of social identities. Refusing to recognise bodily specificities implies that they are inevitably burdensome and has led to the privatisation of racism. Racial sentiments are now expressed in private jokes and references, and legitimised as personal opinion (Chapter 9). I am arguing that what are deemed racial categories need not be feared any more than what are defined as cultural categories. But further, I would assert that, like skin colour, cultural characteristics and the meanings they carry are not superficial and malleable, but are deeply internalised and embodied in psychic as well as physical being. To deny the deep significance of cultural specificities is to betray human history. Social differentiation of any kind may sometimes have destructive consequences, but the solution is not to render all human beings the same.

Like Castoriadis I believe that racism is part of 'something much more universal than one usually wants in fact to admit' (Castoriadis 1992:4). It is the nasty side of the process of categorising 'us' and 'other' which takes place at every level of society. Further, to understand the dominant representations of the past requires a focus on race relations. The notion of race was sedimented into Australian society with colonial expansion, and it became a crucial and salient element of the folk taxonomy through which the Territory understood and ordered itself. The hierarchy of race became part of the intimate everyday interactions of white and black people, though the hierarchy meant different things to those differently positioned. Intermingling was outlawed by the state, and attempts were made to control interaction between what were construed as people of different races; thus racial categories were affirmed and perpetuated. I use the term 'the state' here and throughout the text to refer to governments, government instrumentalities, and the whole array of bureaucracies and institutions which officially and unofficially represent the nation's interests. The whole population is involved, though the term 'nation' is used here to refer to the symbolic and affective meanings which are imputed to the notion of Australia.

If we are to understand the world anew, it is not enough to experience those we are unfamiliar with; it is also necessary to recognise the peculiar nature of ourselves and our history. Jackson points out that, for anthropologists, 'Method becomes a question of making a virtue out of what others have historically had to do as a matter of necessity— finding a way across cultural divides and social barriers . . .' (1995:ix). But we must also examine the nature of these divides and barriers rather than reifying them. They are not invariant structures but are experienced differently over time, most importantly on each side of the social schism. They are part of the structured nature of social events, cemented into many institutions and habitual practices, and part indeed of the identities of those who protect them. For some they are no barrier and for others they remain impenetrable. Further, they alter over time as they are variously dismantled and, often unknowingly, reconstructed. They also exist as a consequence of precious difference.

Palimpsest

While the notion of hybridisation is a popular one for post- or neo-colonial studies (Bhabha 1994; Young 1995),[11] the palimpsest may be a more apt metaphor for the cultural processes which have occurred at Bulman as elsewhere in Australia. A palimpsest is the place where a text has been overwritten or erased to make way for another text. Thus we can imagine Rembarrnga country as a place where the existing text, its images and meanings were covered over with other texts, images and meanings. The new design, in this case, was not entirely original but was a copy of what had been created elsewhere, an attempt to replicate forms already in existence and entrenched in those who came and who responded to local conditions only when forced to. The original remains, hidden by new patterns, but still there, and able to re-emerge, perhaps in altered form as the foreign surface fails to congeal or is damaged by the still living original pulsing beneath it. The overlay may be thinned or deliberately removed, giving a new salience to what was covered. These cultural surfaces show traces of unfinished designs and delayed or abandoned intentions.

This palimpsest is not about inanimate paint or printed words, but entails the lives of many disparate people engaged in shaping their own worlds. Those being overwritten find that their images and texts, their relationships with their place, begin to merge with the imported ones and can no longer be expressed unchanged. The new surfaces are moulded to what was already there and one form of meaning can graft itself onto another, using the contours of an earlier text to establish its own shape. If shaken together, they might combine, only to separate again when left alone. In some places the new surface will never 'take'. The Gunabibi ceremony, for instance, does not hybridise with Christian ritual. The struggles to establish forms of autonomy under new conditions can facilitate incorporation in the new structures; or the smothering power of the palimpsest can be repelled by inhospitable surfaces, by separations and defences, establishing spaces for a level of autonomy where 'creative bricolage' (Morris 1989) can flourish.

The state tried to draw two cultural domains of the Territory into one, to erase difference and contradiction and to create a single system of value. But Aborigines were not fully inside the nation because they did not fully understand the state in the terms in which the state wanted to be understood. They could not be fully subjected to its care, and it could not deeply shape their subjectivities because, even with the establishing of solicitous welfare colonialism (Paine 1977; Beckett 1987), they rejected the nature of such care and avoided its meanings. The growing recognition of the purposes of the state has brought modern, conscious and deliberate resistance, but resisting colonial demands had much earlier forms. Even as new possibilities excited interest, Rembarrnga people continued to affirm their established practice and refuse their own demise.

Outline

In the first chapter I introduce myself as an anthropologist engaged in a traditional field-work project whose interest shifted from the cultural specificity of gender in Arnhem Land to a concern with the confused arena of race relations which seemed to necessitate a long journey into the past. Chapter 2 traces the first intrusions into Rembarrnga country by white explorers and pioneers and the emergence there of practices and discourse concerning race and gender around which the new society of the Territory was being constructed. Race and gender categories were normal and universal to the whites; the Rembarrnga people spoke of 'skin' or kin categories, and they were not understood as speaking of family relationships at all. Chapters 3 to 6 trace further the development of a system of racialised human relations as they emerged at Mainoru where Billy Farrar, the McKays and the Dodds made their station and home on Rembarrnga country. The laws and the practices which were intended to keep the races apart, and the ways they came together, are detailed as expressed in interpersonal intimacies and personal as well as impersonal anxieties. In Chapters 7, 8 and 9 I discuss the end of Mainoru and the emergence of 'self-determination' and the era of my own involvement at Bulman from 1975, intermittently until the present. The shifting boundaries of the non-exclusive categories of race and the engagement of brown people in the racialised cultural dynamics of the Territory are discussed in this final chapter.

Perhaps Rembarrnga experiences do not typify race relations in the Territory, much less in Australia generally. But why should the search for typification be used to obliterate particularity and variation? Given the relative autonomy and discretion available to the managers of pastoral stations, as well as those managing missions and government stations, isolated Aboriginal communities experienced varied conditions.[12] However, against the vagaries of individual whites, and local populations and conditions, there were systematic common features such as shared cultural histories and the state's unified policies and practices. Rather than relying on periodisation according to calendar dates, policy changes or major events, I move through various aspects of what can be called a modernising process in the years from the first Aboriginal Ordinances of 1911 and 1918 until the present, seeking to understand the changing domain of race relations from the point of view of those subjected to them. People at Mainoru and Bulman participated in the policy changes both as subjects and objects of the state's project of managing race relations, but were often out of touch and out of phase with those changes.

Finally I should make clear that a major intention in this work is to replace a complacent superiority about racism with a sense of

curiosity about the pervasive and persistent forms of racial differentiation which continue, albeit in a changed form, as an active principle
in modern society. When I evoke the world of pioneering pastoralists,
it is not to judge its deficiencies but to trace the racial intimacy of
both violence and sex, as well as habitual and mundane interaction on
the frontier, and their place in the discourses that developed at the
nation's centre. This racial frontier, I argue, is still present in many
aspects of Australian imagery and experience.

The tension and suspicion between the outback and urban centres
is another significant theme throughout this book, with the state
officials claiming to represent progress against the backwardness of the
outback. But I argue that the pervasive refusal to recognise the
Aboriginal domain in its own terms was shared, if anything being more
pervasive among the progressive state officials than among the outback
stockmen. The era of the policy of self-management has been claimed
by the pastoralists to provide more evidence that it is they who know
the Aborigines, rather than the bureaucrats, the eggheads or 'those
people from down south'.[13] It seems that modernity is only possible
at the price of cultural transformation, which is pursued in the name
of an aesthetics[14] of progress. Thus 'self-determination' is a moment
which, in the nation's history, represents the next step in a colonial
relationship which is to be achieved through the releasing of the state
from its burden of responsibility and the reversal of dependency. This
paradox is explored in the last chapters.

1

oooo

Fields of Enquiry

There is a fact: white men consider themselves superior to black men.
—*F. Fanon*, Black Skin, White Masks, *1986, p. 12*

If I'd learned to read and write I'd be a welfare lady like you.
—*Nelly Camfoo, 1975*

FINDING A FIELD

Aboriginal people do not choose their anthropologist and the
Rembarrnga people did not choose me. It was thus partly by accident
that I came to experience life at Bulman in the Northern Territory
during my first field-work trip in 1975. In this chapter I describe
conditions as I perceived them then, a strategy intended to reveal the
problems inherent in the observation and understanding of cultural
domains deemed 'other'. While the story is set in a remote location,
this cultural frontier provides insights into race relations in all of
Australia.

I arrived in Katherine from the University of Sydney's Anthropology Department seeking a 'field-work site' from which to explore
particular facets of Aboriginal culture. Field work, entailing participant
observation, is the major 'methodology' of anthropology, a way of
intensively participating in an unfamiliar cultural domain in order to
understand, as it were, from the inside. The field is a place where one

encounters otherness and supposedly leaves behind one's familiar social milieu. But the unfamiliarity I encountered in Katherine was that of a profound racial dichotomy. Not only was the population deeply divided, with racial inequality starkly apparent, but there were more embedded and subtle processes, which rendered the strange and distant relations between black and white people normal. Race relations did not comprise a separate arena; 'race', as a social signifier, was immanent in all relations. Moreover, it seemed a disturbing distraction from the intellectual task of understanding Aboriginal culture.

I explored the 'fringe camps' around Katherine. The social life of Aborigines who lived outside, yet as part of, the clean and proudly 'Tidy Town'[1] of Katherine, seemed to have little connection with the anthropological approach to Aboriginal traditions. The traditions of white culture were not then on the anthropological agenda, but these scenes raised questions about the relationship between the white residents who thought it was their town and the fringe campers who lived to another rhythm.

In accordance with anthropological tradition I sought a more remote community where I could avoid local white people and where I hoped to find a more recognisable Aboriginal tradition. A telegram to Bulman, a community living just inside the southern border of Arnhem Land, resulted in a welcoming telegram from Tex Camfoo.

It took seven hours to drive from Katherine to Bulman (map 1) in the dry season of 1975. Forty kilometres down the main road, the turn-off had a signpost for the pastoral property 'Mainoru Station, 170 miles', but no signs for the large Aboriginal settlements[2] of Bamyilli (now Barunga) and Beswick, let alone Bulman. The dirt road became rougher. I was alone in an old green Land Rover supplied by the Institute of Aboriginal Studies. The country was awe inspiring, beautiful, wild and wide. There were streams to be forded, and glimpses of kangaroo, buffalo, bush turkey and parrots. Twice in moments of inattention in the many hours of long straight roads, the deceptive dusty surface, holes and unexpected bends nearly finished my project there and then, when the vehicle flew off the road. This journey established the remoteness, difficulty of travel, danger and exotic, untamed nature of this field site, all significant properties of the authentic field experience. It promised an uncontaminated space where otherness could flourish. I was to be sorely disillusioned.

Eventually there was a fence, then a few tin shacks and some excited black children came running up, showing me where to turn. Then there was a group of people arranged as if to demonstrate that the racial hierarchy of the Territory had invaded the most remote regions. Under a caravan awning, beside a plastic table sat a white man and a brown man, on a gravel area bordered by a line of stones which had been carefully painted white. Outside the border, several black men were seated on upturned flour drums or on the ground. All were drinking the men's daily ration of three cans of beer each. These were Rembarrnga people of central and southern Arnhem Land. They were the workers and the company directors of Gulperan Pastoral Company which had been established with government funding in 1972 at Bulman, inside the Arnhem Land Aboriginal Reserve on the margin of the cattle country. The manager was Peter Hannah, the only white man at Bulman, and the brown man beside him was Tex Camfoo, the Aboriginal supervisor.

I shook the hands of those who proffered them. Tex's wife, Nelly Camfoo (plate 2) appeared and took charge of me. She spoke a mixture of Kriol and English, and showed me to a little shed they called 'the clinic' where I could sleep. As I unpacked my bags and boxes other women and children came and made me feel welcome. But Tex was not welcoming. His view that anthropologists were the enemies of Aborigines was conveyed briefly but without hostility. His few words deflated my initial excitement utterly.

The next day Dolly,[3] Nelly's sister, asked if I wanted to go fishing, and thus began a regular pattern of trips into the bush, establishing a system of exchange of my time and vehicle for sessions of talk, lessons and discussion with several women. Lorna, Nelly, Dolly, old Florry and other younger women and children came and we all fished for turtles, catfish and bream. People disappeared up and down the river, returning later to boil tea and cook some fish. The children, the youngest only three or four years old, caught small fish or turtles, lit tiny fires and cooked and ate their catch. I soon gave up fishing and concentrated on learning kinship and Kriol, and on experiencing and absorbing everyday ways of difference. I was accepted unquestioningly as a participant in daily life.

On returning that first day Nelly made us a campfire and others joined us. She asked who I wanted to be sister to, herself or Lorna (plate 3). Whichever it was, the other would be my *bunji*, a relationship of warmth but entailing different responsibilities.[4] I chose Lorna, believing that a 'cousin' relationship with the powerful Nelly would be easier to manage. Thus I became *Ngaritjan*, (figure 1)[5] which defined my relationship to everyone I should meet among the Rembarrnga,

Fields of Enquiry

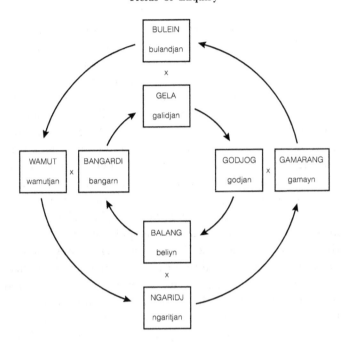

Figure 1   Subsection (skin) diagram
- Males are in capitals; females are in lower case
- Arrows refer to female descent
- 'X' refers to marriage

Source: Adapted from Hiatt, 1965.

Ngalkbon, Jawoyn, Rittarrngu and Gunwinggu, or indeed anyone who interacted with the Bulman mob.[6]

When Tex (plate 4) joined us, another history opened up as he talked of the bitterness he felt about all the years he had been paid as an Aboriginal stock worker when he could, he now believed, have been paid as a white man because his father was Chinese. Some of Tex's interpretations surprised me; he was proud of the mission training which had taught him how to work; mission children had been paid 7 cents a day for weeding, provided the roots came up in one piece (Camfoo, in press). He told of working for a man who cheated him, and of his frustration at having to watch the white stockmen drink cold beer at a rodeo while he and the blackfellas were forbidden grog. He said he had had a very hard life and could tell some stories, but did not want to record anything as 'my words are my own'.

Tex's intense ambivalence about the past and his mistrust of anthropologists were to me rare indications of a political attitude.

Otherwise I perceived no overt protest about the regime of whites among other Rembarrnga people. Nor did I hear explicit assertions of loyalty to an endangered Aboriginal cultural tradition. The Bulman people had grown up and worked on Mainoru station and recalled their lives there with warmth and regret but no blame, even at having been forced to leave a few years previously. But, while I was blind to more subtle expressions of protest, I recognised that there was another form of politics to be uncovered. When one young stockman, Rex Campion, gestured to me with his beer can and said, 'When I stand up and drink a can of beer I'm not like old times. I'm a man', he was clearly articulating the relationship between citizenship and alcohol which existed among Territorians, as elsewhere in Australia. Assertions of manhood and mateship are made in the pub. When Aborigines had been forbidden alcohol, how could they be men among men?

Nelly often echoed, as if testing them out, the edicts she had heard expressed by *mununga*, as whites were known. She concurred with Tex's sentiments about the value of hard work and remarked, 'These people longa camp here, they don't care about keeping clean. Sometimes we clean but sometimes we just relax, do easy way.' Thus the presence of whitefellas' moral judgements in the minds of Rembarrnga did not mean subservience to them. Nelly expressed people's dual allegiances to blackfella and whitefella law by asserting, 'I can live your way or our way, out bush.' Her awareness of cultural differences referred not to ceremonial or kinship matters, or to the technology and institutions of *mununga*, but to contrasting everyday practices and interactions. She was a close observer of whitefellas and able to turn their gaze back onto their own domain. In the face of any perceived criticism, Nelly was passionate in defence of Rembarrnga traditions and blackfella values, but she did not see the presence of white people and their practices as a direct threat to these values. Anyway, whitefellas had become a necessary conduit for the satisfaction of many needs and desires.

Nelly was energetic and curious and, lacking the usual trepidation about speaking with whitefellas, she enthusiastically took on the role of mediator. When some fisheries inspectors arrived one day and demanded to see the boss, Nelly intercepted them and demanded to know their business. One man thrust a paper identifying his department towards me saying, 'Just to satisfy HER,' indicating Nelly, and, 'It's good to see a white face.' Nelly took the first remark as a personal affront.

Straddling the divide between black and white social worlds was excruciatingly uncomfortable for me in the early days and I avoided the manager Peter. But one afternoon Nelly invited the current manager of Mainoru station, his wife and two surveyors working in the area, to a barbecue. She made a stone oven to cook barramundi, the fish that symbolises the authentic outback and which white men travel to remote locations to catch. Tex had steaks for the barbecue. An old door had been raised on empty drums to serve as a table, but it had nothing on it. Rembarrnga men were seated in their usual place with their beer ration, and I was sitting on the ground with Lorna and other women and children, trying to ignore the small group of *mununga* standing with Peter at the end of the 'table'. But I soon felt compelled to help achieve the ordered consumption of the food and consummation of the ritual by finding some plates and bread and serving out the barramundi. Then I had to decide where to be, standing with the whites or sitting with the blacks. After only a few weeks at Bulman I had become used to the way a community of talk flowed around the campfire, in a rich mixture of stories, laughter and remarks directed at no-one in particular (cf. Povinelli 1993:254). The *mununga* seemed strangely aggressive and competitive in their manner of conversation, and routinely crude and insensitive towards Rembarrnga people. The visitors had greeted Nelly and Tex in jovial style, and soon began to speak loudly and confidently to each other about Aborigines and death. 'Old Bulman Paddy, Nelly's father, he died just after she got married,' the wife of the Mainoru manager said. 'He's buried down in the paddock. They won't say the name.' Aborigines were a kind of conversational resource in this context. Knowledge about the natives[7] of the Territory has always functioned as symbolic capital, displayed competitively in certain circles to establish the speaker's authenticity as a true Territorian (cf., Collmann 1988; Rose 1997). Inevitably I was embroiled in such rivalry, and I represented a threat both to the claims of superior knowledge and to the separation of domains of knower and known.[8]

'What are you doing here?'

One day Rex asked me, 'What are you doing here?' I was pleased at the chance to explain and said, 'I want to understand the lives of Aboriginal women.' The enormity and peculiarity of such an abstract and arrogant idea became apparent as I spoke; I blushed and hastily added that I was just writing a book. His question and my answer suddenly seemed to expose my own history, anthropology's history, colonial history and the 'sheer inexplicability' of my presence (Pratt 1986:42). My presence, and even the business of writing, seemed to me vulnerable to ridicule.

But Rex began to apologise, and said, 'We don't understand. Aboriginal people have to ask. Sorry, sorry.' I wanted to encourage his questions and his involvement, but my attempts to explain seemed to increase his worry about offending me. I saw his wife Susan giggling and I could only join in, aware that there was some deep misunderstanding here. My serious wordiness was an alien form of conversation, but I was aware of a more fundamental rupture. Could my project be meaningful to Rembarrnga people? And did it have any importance for them, or was my value here entirely from the pleasure in the relationship and the intermittent access to my vehicle? It seems to me now that the way I was being observed by Rembarrnga, including their perception of my observing them, could be seen as a part of their whole history of such engagement. They were building on years of experience of whitefellas, including anthropologists, as well as an awareness of the state's plans for them.

Another day Tex said that people like me were making trouble. 'Anthropologists will kill the Aborigines,' he added mysteriously.

'What trouble?' I asked but received no reply.

When Tex was drunk one afternoon he became overtly hostile, circling my shed and shouting abuse at me while I cowered inside in tears and fear. After an hour or so, Nelly threw our swags into my vehicle and told me to drive us off to camp in the bush. Our rebellious resolve was somewhat spoilt when we ran out of petrol a few kilometres along the road. I offered Nelly a salami sandwich as emergency food, but she disdained it and instead lit a fire and boiled tea, cooking some beef in the coals. She kept telling me, 'Tex is just drunk; he fights with Peter too, and with me and [son] Warren. But he shouldn't say *that*.' Then she said, 'I told Tex you might think he is lousy father and stop us getting that baby.'

Suddenly the wider meaning Nelly attached to my presence was revealed. The Land Rover I had been allotted had a capital 'W' painted on its side. Nelly cannot read but she knew 'W' stood for the Welfare Branch. She was certain, despite my denial, that I was connected with 'The Welfare'. She was, to my amazement, in the process of officially adopting a baby from Darwin. That I was perceived as part of the state's surveillance was disconcerting but not really surprising. However, I found her acceptance of the legitimacy of this scrutiny deeply disturbing. The Welfare Branch had been replaced in 1972 by the

Commonwealth Department of Aboriginal Affairs (DAA), and this was supposed to be the new era of self-determination.

We walked back to the camp to get petrol. Bruce Murray (plate 5), who was angry with Tex, helped us, then asked if I would drive down the river to Bulman waterhole where, he said, a vehicle was broken down. To me this was a nightmare drive in the pitch dark along a track with huge washed out gullies, fords through deep water, and untold imagined dangers looming in the shadows from the vehicle lights. While we were driving, Bruce's wife Nancy (plate 6) told me that, as *gaman*, she was my 'daughter' and called me *mula*. I felt warmed and reassured by this intimacy. Bruce talked about the early days at Bulman and asked me about anthropology. Between the potholes I tried to explain books, students, the university and the curiosity of the West, but the mystery seemed to increase with the telling. When we arrived at the waterhole there was only one old whitefella called Bert there, who gave Bruce and me two cans of beer each. I hid my annoyance, enjoyed a beer, and speculated whether the reason for this journey was Bruce's recognition of my distress or his desire for the beer. The drive back seemed much easier.

Tex was asleep when we returned. Young Michelle (plate 7), who had been teaching me Kriol, had cried when she was told that I was out in the bush and that I might leave. Despite such reassurances I remained troubled. Should I conform to Tex's wishes when others wanted me to stay? How serious was he? Perhaps Peter was prompting him, or echoing the views of some redneck pastoralists who were notoriously hostile to anthropologists. I was convinced that Tex was simply misguided because surely anthropology had come nearer to respecting and understanding Aboriginal culture than any other segment of settler society. Whatever their failings, anthropologists' desire and effort to support Aboriginal aspirations could not be denied.

We travelled to Malyanganuk (map 1), central Arnhem Land country to which Nelly and her siblings belonged. The journey was an essay in the living relationship Rembarrnga people have with country, uninterrupted by outside scrutiny or comment. Places were intricately affirmed and meanings evoked through constant comments on features of the land and recounting of events that had occurred at specific places: camps, catches of game, bush tucker, accidents, births and ceremony.[9] We had to stop once and cover our heads as a ceremony vehicle went past, taking a wide arc through the bush to avoid us. We met an old song man who had been taking part in a Gunabibi ceremony over the river; the young men were lifting him gently onto the back of their truck, solicitous for his welfare when travelling on rough bush roads. Here flourished the cultural traditions which were the usual objects of the anthropologist's gaze, the specific traditions peculiar to an Aboriginal society and generated in the context of a hunter–gatherer economy over many centuries. But a rude reminder of the other world came when an irritable isolated white storekeeper at Nungalala complained with deliberate ill-will that he had a cold because people coughed in his face. His carelessness about giving change seemed to be in revenge for his discomfort.

Tex and I were driving two vehicles loaded with people and swags. When we stopped and had eaten, Tex offered me a 'coldy' (a can of beer) and said, 'You are in Arnhem Land now' in tones saturated with fearful connotations of wild and mysterious things that would be beyond my control. There was humour in this, but then he started to reiterate the complaints about anthropologists destroying Aborigines. 'You don't understand yet,' he said to me, and warned Nelly and the others that 'it's suicide to put your words on a tape recorder.' Later, at Malyanganuk, Tex expressed two contrasting complaints. Anthropologists had published secret material, a matter which has caused anxiety among senior men in many places (Berndt 1962; Elkin 1972a:3), and they had caused interruptions to station work. The mildness and brevity with which he referred to these things belied the deeper feeling he had revealed when drunk. The following year Tex trusted me sufficiently to invite me to ride his white stock horse, Silver, but it was many years before he asked me to record his life history in detail (Camfoo, in press).

My research topic concerned women's control over reproduction (cf., Cowlishaw 1978), a product of the 1970s intellectual climate of interest in the 'position of women in other cultures'.[10] It retained the arrogant caste of a science which wanted to record the empirical contours of an objectified otherness. Of course I did not see myself as engaged in producing a disempowering Orientalist form of knowledge (Said 1985a), much less complicit in the repressive state apparatus, or part of a Foucaultian panopticon (Foucault 1977). But the discomfort entailed in seeking answers to my questions was linked with my growing discomfort about the oppressive intrusions of the ubiquitous white culture to which, willy-nilly, I belonged. Other anthropologists seem to have solved this problem by temporarily denying their whiteness, repudiating any commonality with the racialised public discourse so unashamedly present in northern Australia.

Evidence mounted that the story I needed to tell was not about a separate Rembarrnga cultural tradition, but rather about the painful drama of race relations in which we anthropologists are actors rather than observers. I felt a distaste for trying to encompass, encapsulate and explain the richness and complexity of Rembarrnga social existence, because the tools to do so were words and phrases of an irredeemably alien quality. As I write today, I see this disquiet as based on the fact that I was forced to participate in the drama of race relations, an unnamed struggle where shifting meanings and painful misunderstandings are rife and where moral and political truths are elusive. My strategy in this book is to attend to this drama as it unfolded over the decades, and to analyse the wealth of misperceptions, difficulties and destructiveness, both for Rembarrnga people and whitefellas. The way particular relationships have been experienced can illuminate the changing cultural meanings of the still living frontier. Before turning to the historical construction of these conditions, I will further explore the field as I experienced it in 1975.

GATHERING DATA?

The limitation of my time in the field[11] was somewhat compensated for by the level of intimacy into which I was thrown. About ten days after I arrived at Bulman a tragic accident occurred. There was shouting and excitement as the big red Beswick truck came into sight, but it suddenly changed to shrieking and wailing, and Nelly was leading a woman with her head covered across the camp. Waves of wailing spread with the news that Dorothy's husband had rolled his vehicle and was dead. He had been employed as one of two stock workers at Mainoru. An intense period of mourning and funerary rites ensued.

Grief

Even in grief Rembarrnga people were not separate from whites, and the death of Dorothy's husband revealed some of the institutional, emotional, economic and discursive dimensions of their interaction. I was there, an anthropologist, initially embarrassed at intruding, though invited to participate with those who had gradually gathered near the camp of old Chuckerduck, wailing, singing and beating sticks. Some individuals restrained others from hitting their heads with knifeblades. The heart-rending wailing continued for the whole day and for several days afterwards, with people joining and leaving the gathering to cook, eat, wash and attend to children. After the first day the stockmen responded to the manager's directions to work during the day. On the second day the dead man's possessions and the house he had once lived in were smoked, a ritual to ensure that the spirit of the deceased has departed (Maddock 1982:153). The intensity of the crying increased and decreased intermittently.

An anthropologist participates, observes and endlessly speculates. While the symbolic meaning of mourning rituals have often been seen as more significant than the expression of emotion (Rosaldo 1989:2), I wondered about the degree of personal grief and pain of loss being expressed in the mourning, especially as wailing could be interrupted and recommenced at will and everyone participated in similar expressive activities. How did this expression of grief represent any particular person's emotional response to the death of a loved one? I compared this with my experience of losing kin. But which kin? The dead man had not only been a husband, son, uncle and brother to individuals. These kin links formed the closely bound, densely interacting body of the community which was in shock and mourning. Further, everyone here had known him all their lives and many had spent virtually every day in his company. Thus the relationship which was being mourned contained intersubjective, community wide meanings with no equivalent in my experience. The communal expression of grief allowed individuals to express their pain in a way that individualised grief could not.

There was no equivalent here of the nuclear family, cut off in everyday life from other related or neighbouring families, with all of its members expecting to live to old age. Rembarrnga people had a much more intimate experience of death because of the wide and close network of kin and because life expectancy was low. Accidents, mortal illnesses and deaths of children were relatively common and they touched everyone. Far from the public recognition of death and grief being embarrassing, it was hidden things which caused anxiety here, and it was whites who hid things. A white man had come upon the accident and called the Katherine police who had removed the body before anyone had seen it or the scene of the death. The absence of the body disturbed the mourning procedures and led to suspicion that something was being kept secret. Dorothy kept saying: 'I don't know. They didn't tell us. They left us by weselves.' She was painted with white clay, a little angular figure under the towel, wearing the wrong clothes for this ceremony. Her skin had to be painted through her dress.

It is common in many Aboriginal communities to expunge reminders of the recently dead, such as their name and possessions, ostensibly to protect kin from a resurgence of pain. Nelly found and tore up Dorothy's photos of her husband. This anxiety about remembering the dead appears to be a complete reversal of the anxiety about forgetting them that is common among whites, as evident in the preservation of memorabilia and the display of photographs of deceased relatives. However, the social conditions in small, closely interacting communities may mean that expunging references to the deceased causes a focus on their absence and, paradoxically, keeps them in mind (Biddle 1996).

The authority of white moral judgements intruded on the expression of grief. The manager expressed annoyance that Rex Campion, the other Mainoru worker, remained at Bulman, saying, 'He can't do things like that, letting his employer down.' Rex's distraught state was interpreted as excessive and a dereliction of duty. The bereaved anticipated police enquiries with resignation and some dread. Dorothy prepared herself to resist expected pressures: 'When that policeman comes I'm going to tell him I'm not going back to Mainoru. Too lonely there, no people. Nikki [the manager's wife] will miss me.'

She repeated this several times, accepting that police and station owners share some authority over Aboriginal lives.[12] The authority of the manager's wife was also expressed in Dorothy's repeating to little Norrie, 'Eat lots of tucker to grow big. Nikki always say that; eat lots of tucker to grow big.' This apparent adoption of the edicts of authoritative whites echoed the dependence on police, medical officials and the morgue, for instance in relation to the body of the deceased and the time and place of the burial. No one at Bulman knew why the morgue had the body or when it would be released for burial. Finally it was the white manager Peter who received the telegram saying that the body was released for burial, and his attempt to arrange the funeral led to a conflict between him and Willy Jailama Martin who was the responsible kinsman.[13]

In this crisis Dorothy was able to camp with me and we formed a 'single women's camp' for unmarried women and young girls who came to eat, sleep and fetch and carry for Dorothy and me. In those first days, as some people's rage at the death led to speculation about some other mob of people having killed her husband 'blackfella way', Dorothy said, 'I can't say nothing. I didn't see the accident. I don't know.' She wept now and again quietly at night alone. I could do

little to comfort her. But as time went by, and when I returned the
following year and later, Dorothy and I had a good time together.

Kinship and ceremony on the cultural borderlands

Despite a certain sense of discomfort and distraction, I did not lose
sight of the anthropological search for the specificities of Aboriginal
knowledge and practice. The diagrams in the anthropology texts had
shown complex lineages and marriage rules, but anthropologists had
wanted to explain the reproduction of the system rather than its
everyday, mundane meanings. Having become *Ngaritjan*, my kin,
kinship terminology and the intricate structure and everyday implications of these relationships began to unfold before me. With some
amazement I recognised that the terms used and the diagrams in the
dust exactly mirrored those drawn by my PhD supervisor, Dr Les
Hiatt, during kinship lectures (figure 1). While the reality of what I
had learned as 'anthropology' became apparent, so did the emotion,
subtlety, colour and style of the messy reality of people's lives.[14] The
arcane and specialised patterns, rules and interpretations taught labori-
ously to anthropology students were a commonplace reality here, even
for children. The relationships I was immersed in were affirmed as
'skin' and family. Some of the rich array of kinship terms, precise
designations for specific relationships, became familiar. I also learned
that Rembarrnga people were shocked that white people did not know
their relationships to other people; how could we avoid marrying those
of the wrong classification? I had no answer.

I soon began to fill pages and books with lines and names, showing
the links which identified dozens of individuals and their genealogical
ties radiating out from Bulman in all directions (figure 2). The essays
we had written at university, naively debating whether affinity or
descent accounted for the significance of kinship, seemed somewhat
at odds with what, in this milieu, were the perfectly ordinary, though
extraordinarily complex, facts of social life.

Many isolated hints of religious belief and ritual practice were
imparted to me during the early weeks, not as secret or arcane
knowledge but as everyday secular information, intertwined with
mundane demands from the manager and visiting officials. Larry told
me he had sent feathers to Elcho Island to ask that mob to bring their
corroboree; 'They will make Murrain ceremony,' he said. Bruce and
Kenneth (plate 5) played the bamboo (didgeridoo) and took part in
ceremonies; as well they wore cowboy boots, played the guitar and

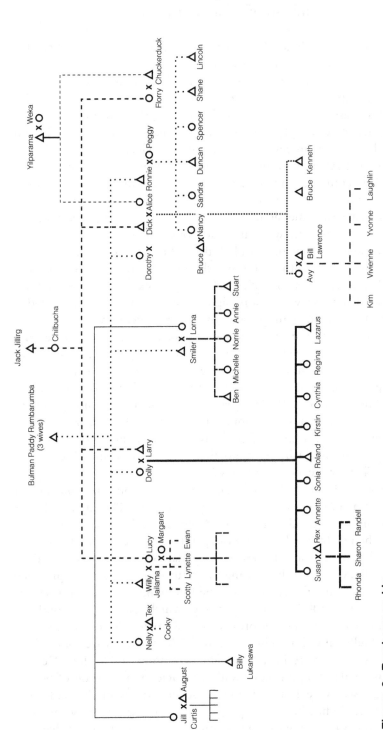

Figure 2 Rembarrnga kin

The main interlinked families who made up 'the Bulman mob' in 1975. Many of the youngest now have children and a few have grandchildren. This is a simplified diagram; other linked families are omitted for the sake of clarity.

sang country music. The children painted their faces with white clay and played 'bush blackfellas' (plate 8).

The Gulperan stockworkers went to do station work each day, creating a pattern of daily activity which sometimes melded and sometimes clashed with the foundations of Rembarrnga life. The Rembarrnga ceremonial rhythms and the power of country pulsed away unheard and unseen by managing whitefellas, except now and again when they erupted and interrupted. They were being revealed to me as the common knowledge and fuel of real life. I scribbled notes about everything; each event and statement could turn out to be an important clue to some significant aspect of Rembarrnga existence.

My interest was in women's traditions, but these were not seen as epitomising what people called the 'old ways' or 'culture'. The women concurred with old men that it was men who held the knowledge of ceremonial cycles, dreaming tracks and totemic affiliations, and that these were more significant than women's knowledge of spirit children, love magic and the Djarada ceremony. Skills such as the gathering of food, the weaving of baskets and matters concerning childbirth were not reified as 'law' or 'culture'. The reluctance of women to claim authority was a clue to an economy of knowledge where specific information is held in trust by individuals representing specific lineages (Rose 1996). That is, women did not hold primary responsibility for major ceremonial information. But their denial of knowledge revealed a further facet of Rembarrnga epistemology. There was no shame in claiming ignorance, even in ordinary everyday matters. There were no 'know alls'.

I wrote and taped, discussed and translated mourning and funeral rites, an initiation ceremony and everyday events. The night before I left after my first period in the field, Nelly and other women took me down to the nearby billabong at dusk, painted themselves and performed songs and dances from the erotic Djarada, promising more when I returned. They were both ensuring my return and making my presence a reason to conduct the ceremony. The following year the promise was fulfilled with a full Djarada ceremony which entailed a month of preparation, a week of performances and many visitors coming to Bulman. Nelly said of it: 'This is our life. We will die if we forget this.'

We also took part in a Gunabibi ceremony at Dortluk. Getting there was an alarming journey. With a vehicle crammed full of people and swags, we were lost and bogged several times in the dark, and camped late, finding the right place next morning. Then we women camped and waited. I wrote an account of the event in my diary:[15]

The boys came down . . . then went off in a group with women ululating and some weeping and sobbing. Billy Lukanawa and another Yirritja man were watching the women's camp . . . An ethno-musicologist who is here, with permission from Bamyilli council, was challenged by two men. One said 'My father used to kill *mununga*. What's that white man doing here?' After a discussion they agreed he could pay a fine of a carton of beer to the two men and return to the ceremony.

The women dance . . . Four old women are singing. After about two hours eight painted and decorated men appear . . . Then the men go to their camps and collect swags and blankets to take 'up the top' where the main ceremony is going on.

The women recommence singing and dancing and continue all night. Children sleep. Some of us sleep for a while . . . About 4 am women gather and [dance; diagram of movements].

Then we wait, and wait, to be taken 'up the top'. Lorna tells me a bit about the ceremony, but is somewhat reticent. A group of *mununga* arrive mid-morning as if for a Sunday concert in the park. German journalists are with them. I manage to avoid them.

Finally, at about 1 pm, a call to get ready. The children and the women line up and we head off over the hill . . . The throng is perhaps a hundred people. Heads are lowered as we go further . . .

Soon we are moved away and we go down, back to camp. The boys soon come down . . . They are fed, sweat is rubbed, and then we all get into the vehicles and go.

Such ceremonies, interwoven and organised through a web of kinship stretching across Arnhem Land and to the south and west, expressed the fundamental form of Rembarrnga philosophical and social being. I felt a sense of amazement and privilege at being able to participate in this ceremony while trying desperately to grasp its meaning. The depth of emotion which this powerful, familiar and awesome event evoked in the Rembarrnga women I was with, made the notion of my trying to understand and explain its meaning to outsiders who had no involvement here seem daunting, if not mis-guided.[16] Dilemmas and tensions surrounded the occasion, due to the encapsulation in a foreign social system and also to the immediate physical presence of whitefellas. Further disputes about the presence of the German photographer and the ethno-musicologist revealed that there was no common, articulated view about how to deal with such people. The Rembarrnga, Ngalkbon and Jawoyn people involved had no knowledge of any legal rights they could exert to exclude outsiders.

But further, the consequences of interaction with whites were unpredictable and intrinsically ambiguous. Who could judge, even in hindsight, which white presences and things had brought benefits and which had not? Technology had interfered with tradition, as illustrated in Chuckerduck's anxiety about his skills as a 'golong', that is, his cleverness or healing knowledge: 'I'm a little bit blocked up now. Too much engine [generator] noise. I can't hear which way it's going to fall down when I chuck the bushes. Too much engine blocked me, sometimes I don't catchim any more.'[17] (plate 9).

Many social forms had been marked by the changed circumstances of recent history. Increased mobility was blamed for an increase in 'wrong' marriages which distorted the kinship system. For instance, women gossiped about one wrong marriage where, they said, a man's wife was in the category he should call *bipi* (mummy). They debated whether the children would go blackfella way, 'to follow mother', or go whitefella way and determine kinship categories in line with the father's subsection. This man was teased in ways that expressed distaste, yet despite the fractured nature of his position, he was part of the social body. In the old days, I was told, he would have been killed. Another circumstance that people had constantly to deal with was English kin terms which failed to make the crucial distinction between matrilineal and patrilineal relatedness, and between parallel cousins and cross cousins, who are quite different kinds of relatives.[18]

I learned that intimate areas of Rembarrnga life, such as marriage and kinship, had been violently and deliberately interfered with when the people lived at Mainoru from the 1920s to the 1960s. Marriages of 'old' men to young 'promise wives' had become illegal and threats of prosecution had been made.[19] Women had been taken into hospital against their will to give birth. Two children had been removed and one adopted by the previous Mainoru land-holders. Close relationships had been formed with people who deemed Rembarrnga wrong in many ways, but who had offered alluring new things and had imposed new patterns of activity from which there was no turning back.

The predicament of culture, not merely as specific practices, but as personal, intimate, everyday ways of feeling and being, became sharply apparent to me as I learned to mimic the cultural practices of Rembarrnga and to fit in with everyday behaviour. But at certain moments I became intensely aware that many of these practices, such as simply sitting on the ground, were signs of inferiority in *mununga* eyes, and evoked a subtle contempt. That contempt pervaded public discourse, yet a psychic distance existed between such judgements and daily life at Bulman. Rembarrnga social life was invisible from outside, except in a distorted and impoverished form. This separate space of being, with its complex dynamics and specific meanings and emotions, seemed a precious and rare thing which was being crushed and reshaped by officials who were unaware of the destructive weight of their progressive policies. I feared at times that I might be seen as a Trojan horse, or as parodying the habits of a problematic minority. I did not want to be one of the *mununga* eyes, fixed on the blackfellas, who in turn watch themselves being watched, and must respond to the images created by these outsiders' perceptions.

While ceremonial life and explicit beliefs are commonly identified as arenas of cultural difference, impulsive and habitual responses, such as physical interaction, sharing of food and style of conversation, are not so readily perceived as cultural. Learning another culture is not just a cognitive exercise but involves deeply embedded responses to these ordinary and intimate matters. Some manners may be easily learned, but other spontaneous and visceral responses resist change. Cultural specificities are thus embedded and embodied in habits and feelings that are, to some extent at least, outside consciousness. Cultural responses are shaped from infancy; the process of socialisation reproduces cultural forms, ensuring their naturalness and normality.

Deeply embedded manners, different from mine, were everywhere. Close bodily contact was normal, with limbs intertwined and stroked, and children and babies constantly cuddled and physically teased. Such physical warmth and acceptance was a joy, but I found it difficult to practice the modern form of hunting, that is, running into a bush turkey on the road, despite being urged excitedly, 'Bumpim Mula, bumpim.' I could not applaud when children flung stones at the head of a blue-tongue lizard, or played cruelly with a cat. 'Killem, killem,' they screamed stamping on a goanna's head in fearful excitement then examining it closely and proudly taking it to be cooked. My different sensibilities were observed with interest. The women showed an acute awareness of 'body language' and the minutiae of social interaction. On the other hand, 'politeness' was absent. I soon got used to peremptory requests such as 'Give me cigarette', and learned to ignore or comply, or to shake my hand saying, '*Waba*; [I've got] nothing.' I learned to demand tea or tucker without a pleading tone and the word 'please' became redundant. But there was a strain engendered by a system of exchange with ever present obligations to kin, a strain known commonly as 'humbug'. Sharing was not as simple as 'to each according to his need', and did not quite reflect the anthropologists' concept of 'generalised'; that is, unaccounted reciprocity (cf. Peterson 1985; Sansom 1988).

The young girls, Norrie and Yvonne, told me that blackfellas don't swear in front of *mununga*, but otherwise they all swear all the time. The word 'fucken' was part of the everyday speech of people of all ages, but for a while I was still considered a 'missus' for certain purposes. For instance Dorothy couldn't stop laughing and apologising for saying 'fucken' in front of me. She said, 'I didn't know there was a missus here, I thought only blackfella. I forget you're a missus.' She assumed I shared the distinction. 'Fucken' had no force as a curse or a taboo word, and when, in the early 1980s, the school teachers campaigned to eradicate this speech habit in children, responsible women sometimes shouted to the little children, 'Don't fucken swear.' Aboriginal practices in relation to obscenity, which Donald Thomson wrote about in 1935, were not visible to those trying to overlay a veneer of propriety.

I did not try to mimic Rembarrnga practices in the sphere of interpersonal violence. When conflicts erupted, often after simmering for days or weeks, there were explicit threats of violence and intense anger was expressed openly. Sometimes physical fights occurred and many people became involved, and it could take hours and even days for the tension to calm down. In view of the depth and complexity of these conflicts I soon suppressed the impulse to mediate or to reason. But the mildness of my own responses to conflict were a disappointment and a puzzle. One day in 1976 I drove up to the manager's new house causing clouds of red dust to cover the wet washing. The newly arrived wife flew out of the house, red faced, shouting angrily at me. I was embarrassed because she seemed to be making such a fool of herself, but Nelly urged me to take a *nulla nulla* (fighting stick) to the woman. My passivity seemed to her to entail humiliation.

I was entranced, intrigued and engaged by a certain style of interaction among Rembarrnga. Sensitivity to the nuances of sociality was accompanied by humour as the common response to the vicissitudes of everyday life. Laughter at small accidents, dilemmas and confusion accompanied most activities. No-one could be self-important when there was such a sharp perception of the social construction of pride and status. The most hilarity was evoked when someone who was absorbed in an activity was surprised or startled by an unexpected event. The shock when someone, with great hunger, bit into a piece of beef and burned her tongue, would be the source of mimicry and laughter for days. But more exquisite humour was contained in the predicament of someone caught between desire and danger. The dilemma of a toddler fearing a stranger but desiring to go past to reach her mother, would delight everyone. This humour entailed a recognition of the ambivalence and uncertainty between fulfilment and fear, and a recognition of the absurd as a facet of ordinary life. The comedy of social pretension was sharply observed, and attempts to dissemble or to impress could seldom succeed in this cultural milieu. A white man bustling importantly across the camp who tripped over would be the ultimate pleasure, but laughter at such an event was neither cruel nor malicious, and its expression was saved for later when it would not cause embarrassment. The white man's loss of control over the presentation of himself, his stumbling and trying to regain a dignified bearing in full view of many pairs of eyes, stood in pleasurable contrast to the controlled reserve and authoritative style of whitefellas, and provided a glimpse of the possibility of social levelling. It was also a moment of power, where the blackfella's unity stemmed not from being the object of the whites' gaze, but from the superior position of observing a white man's rare vulnerability (Sartre 1956:423ff).

Humour seemed to operate often as a strategy to defuse and disempower the judgements of whitefellas, hinting at a subtle and pervasive critique of their power. Humour marked different values in relation to human sociality and to public responsibility. That is, the arenas of independence and interdependence among whitefellas and blackfellas differed remarkably. Many Rembarrnga responsibilities to others were specific and immediate, and the kinship ties through which interpersonal duties and expectations were expressed were activated daily in getting, preparing and exchanging food, assisting in other practical and social ways, and sharing small comforts and talk. These were matters of everyday practice, not requiring the self-conscious, moralistic assumption of a duty to the community or to the wider society. Contrary to the assumptions of white Australians, social responsibility was embedded in daily life, not separate from the interchange entailed in shared experience. For this reason, Rembarrnga understanding of government policy towards the community differed greatly from that of the government officials, and their responses were expressed in a rhetoric which did not meet official expectations.

OUTRAGEOUS FORTUNE

I have illustrated the muting of Rembarrnga cultural patterns under the white gaze in the 1970s. The predicament of the people at Bulman was especially apparent to me in relation to the state. Far from being distant from whitefellas, Bulman was saturated with power from outside, and a silent pedagogy was apparent in almost all interactions with whitefellas. The presence of the white manager, pastoral advisers and government officials had a tutelary, instructive purpose. Rather than enabling Rembarrnga people to come to terms with modernity through their own decisions, there seemed to be increasingly intrusive pressures towards conformity with ideas and practices generated elsewhere. The unique and characteristic practices of Rembarrnga and other Aboriginal communities affirmed an integrated social reality which was part of the landscape, but beneath the line of vision of *mununga* eyes. The affirmation of this underlying, other social reality was a declaration of an outsider status, which denuded blackfellas of power in relation to the whitefellas' world. Far from counting as cultural capital, speaking Rembarrnga and attending ceremonies operated as a handicap in relation to the plans for modernity being offered by the state. This condition was not always apparent to those involved, whether blackfellas or whitefellas.

Nomads

It began to seem to me that specific cultural forms, such as extensive funerals and other ceremonies, and the large number of kin each person was attached to, were the Achilles heel of the Rembarrnga people in their relationships with whitefellas. These practices were part of an established, taken-for-granted moral universe that whites did not share, yet regularly judged. An example is the propensity of Aborigines to 'go walkabout', an attribution which many years ago became a trite stereotype in most parts of Australia. The propensity was usually framed as an accusation, and denial seemed the only defence. Thus it was asserted that Aboriginal workers were no more likely than others to leave a job. The possibility of claiming the moral high ground for nomadism has only emerged recently (Jackson 1996; Muecke 1997).

Some notes I made about people's movements reveal field-work anxieties:

> DIARY 8.8.76: Susan and Rexy have gone and will return God knows when—could have gone to Darwin. Peter Cameron left with them—took Vera to Beswick and left her there; came back to Weemol then back to Katherine. Ronny and Peggy went with Malyanganuk truck back to Maningrida and then flew home to everyone's surprise. Don and Ann

Forbes turned up here and left for Mountain Valley early July. Rosy spent about two weeks here and went back to Bamyilli without planning either trip. Alice and Karl said they were stopping here. Went back. Alice back here now, planning a return to Maningrida again. Avy came for two or three weeks, went back, came again, saying she was staying eight weeks, then returned to Maningrida, saying for weekend, but hasn't come back. Bruce and Nancy are remarkably stable but went away during wet season. Forbes families left for Mountain Valley—but this only third day of departure. Elizabeth and Dennis quietly flit to and fro. Judy comes and goes. Weemol mob shifty. Viv and Yvonne also mobile.

The unpredictability of this mobility aroused both my admiration and irritation. A billy, tea, sugar, fishing line, a bit of beef and a rolled swag, could be thrust into the Toyota at a moment's notice for a 'weekend' up or down the river, or a trip into town. Such expeditions took precedence over planned meetings with the DAA or waiting for the health sisters' visit, and certainly over serious talk to an anthropologist. Even sleeping arrangements were flexible, and when the sun was near setting, young people would decide where to lay the swags, saying, 'You here and me there', affirming in their positioning particular orientations and relationships. Such fluidity of movement conflicts with amassing and husbanding goods. Goods were often left in the wrong place, or abandoned. Nomadic habits also functioned as a strategy to deal with tension and conflict. The response to a fight was to leave, pack up, go.

The fetishisation of goods by whitefellas is displayed in their anxieties concerning supplies in the bush.[20] While Rembarrnga take important things with them, in general there is confidence that the bush will provide. All kinds of improvised tools, comforts and nourishment are available, and if they are not, then one can do without, even food. No-one was anxious if a meal or two were missed. The traditions of a nomadic, subsistence economy did not lend themselves to accumulation of goods or the preservation of food, which partly explains the negative moral implications of conserving wealth and possessions in this social environment. But today these moral codes function to affirm hierarchy and to consolidate the hold state officials have on the purse strings.[21]

The moral worth which managers, pastoralists and bureaucrats attach to being in one place, to forward planning and to the organised management of time, was offended by flexibility of movement and individual autonomy. Conflict about the use of the station vehicle was chronic. Peter wanted to confine its use to the needs of the Gulperan Pastoral Company. The moral force of his judgement was empowered by the historical and cultural underpinning which gave these instrumental values legitimacy. When the Bulman mob expressed excitement about people coming for a ceremony, whites would say, 'But the children will miss school.' If people began to pack up to go to a funeral at Maningrida, Peter's comment was laden with accusation: 'But the travelling Sister is coming on Friday. You wanted to see her.' Spontaneity of movement and apparent lack of forethought led to the Rembarrnga people being seen as capricious and irresponsible.

Rembarrnga people were aware of this disapproval. When people came in to Bulman from a little outstation called Momob, someone laughed, 'Might be no-one there at that little place!' mimicking *mununga* concerns. But whites did not laugh; they spoke with careful neutrality or outright disapproval of this irresponsible propensity to leave Momob after government funding had indulged the extraordinary, almost irrational, desire to live in such a 'remote' place. Such judgements were puzzling to Momob people who wondered why these Europeans were so concerned about things that were not their business.[22] Travelling, far from implying a lack of concern with place, confirmed such concern. There was no sense that a person's life could only be lived in their own country, and no sense of waiting to 'go home'; this country was all home in different ways to segments of the kin network. Moving across the land, and moving among groups of people, moving to take part in ceremonies form the pattern of life which reproduces relationships with the sentient country, with its mythic associations, and with kin. The responsibility to country can only be fulfilled by being in it, and being sensitive to 'the funny tendency of land' (Povinelli 1993:147); that is, its responses to human presence.

But *mununga* lacked any sense of the genesis and responsiveness of country or the pattern of human responsibility towards it, let alone the intimate knowledge that, for instance, allows women to find, in what was to me a vast unmarked wilderness, the specific location of particular rare, small leaves which signal the presence of roots which provide the dye for the pandanus leaves from which baskets are woven. Aboriginal people do not readily go to strange country to which they are not related through kin. All country is identified with either the *Dua* or *Yirritja* moiety[23] first and then as the responsibility of a complex network of clans and lineages. That is, kin of the other moiety have other complementary ties and rights. Degrees of obligation and entitlement are part of the intricately patterned links to country. It is normal to ask permission from the senior custodian of country when one is travelling to or through it.[24]

By contrast, whites see the land as undifferentiated bush. They planned to install the Gulperan Pastoral Company in Rembarrnga country without regard to the meanings and varied responsibilities which this country held for a wide network of people, many of whom were resident in other communities. In 1976 I attended a meeting at Weemol where those who were 'boss for that country' discussed the Gulperan project. This was quite unlike meetings between Rembarrnga people and state officials. Here a series of men spoke at length, reviewing varied aspects of the situation and carefully assenting to others' words while specifying particular priorities and concerns. There was agreement that Tex Camfoo should remain manager of Gulperan, while recognising the authority of senior custodians of each area in the vicinity. Larry Murray, himself a senior custodian, recognised the limited comprehension of officials and warned that at this meeting they were talking about 'country only, not ceremony, because government department doesn't understand'. The meeting demonstrated the presence of an indigenous social organisation based on different principles from those of government agencies. This organisation was not only effectively providing a local forum for debate, but was also responding to problems thrown up by new conditions and seeking to escape humiliating dependencies.

The 'nomadism' of the white school teachers and community advisers, nurses and public servants who staff the remote Aboriginal communities of the Territory for periods of two or three years, is legitimated through notions of career paths and the value of professional and personal experience. There is no sense of illegitimacy in entering and then leaving someone else's country. On the contrary, volunteering to go to what is called an 'isolated' area and serve the needs of the Aboriginal people, takes on the flavour of good works. A martyr's stance is more common than that of a visitor in someone else's homelands, and this brings all the moral authority and debt that martyrs demand and impose.

These trained deliverers of services who visited Bulman mainly came from that place known as 'South' and were stationed at Bamyilli, Katherine or the capital, Darwin. They depended on papers, reports and forms through which Rembarrnga lives and futures were increasingly being funnelled. Many visiting nursing sisters and later the resident teachers became familiar, and some formed warm friendships in 'their' communities. Despite the shallowness of their incorporation into the framework of kinship and country, they were related to not merely as government functionaries but as adopted kin. But they would suddenly depart, often never to be heard of again. 'Must have gone back to 'im own country,' people would say, with a sense of betrayal or disappointment. Some wrote, or promised to, but relations were severed by distance. These encounters were intense experiences and highly valued by both parties, but each side was embroiled in different social institutions which were characterised by different understandings of human relationships. It was the *mununga* view of these encounters that had currency in the world outside Bulman. Rembarrnga understanding was simply a lack of understanding to whites, and Rembarrnga people did not have the power to humiliate whites by pointing out *their* ignorance of other meanings.

Privacy

Can one have a private home without a front gate? Two rows of whitewashed stones leading to a caravan door can suffice to indicate where the manager's private space begins. Community members at Bulman were made to understand that they should not approach Peter's caravan without making their presence known. Children should keep outside the border of stones. This was one way Peter signalled his civilising mission and tried to establish his cultural dominance. Part of that process was trying to reduce the disruptions to his private life by establishing a spatial separation between his private domain and his public, working life, a separation meant to instruct Rembarrnga in how to deal with their manager.

Rembarrnga deferral to the knowledge of whites often meant accepting, and even inviting, intrusions. One evening Kevin was bitten by a snake. There were various cries and advice: 'Take him to the missus.' 'Get razor blade.' 'Where that Peter?' 'Get boiling water.' A fire was built and Kevin was put on a sheet, and the old healer Chuckerduck came forward to conduct a ritual, waving us out of the way. Just then Peter strode into the scene. He pushed forward and examined the leg, gave advice and was listened to. Bruce already had found a razor blade and made several deep cuts in Kevin's leg, but deferred to the white man who soon left to get some medicine. Larry said, 'Let's do it before that *mununga* comes back.' But before they could get ready for Chuckerduck's ritual expulsion of the snake, Peter had returned. Dolly kept asking me, 'What's that *mununga* doing? He might poison him, so I repeated the question, calling out: 'Hey *mununga*, what medicine are you giving him?' Dolly was shocked and impressed by my cheek and Peter said, 'Aspirin.' After Peter left, Chuckerduck did his healing 'the blackfella way', but they said it was too late. Kevin was alright in the morning.

Bodily health and the services that were intended to achieve it regularly caused embarrassment. Visiting nurses and doctors made demands for personal details and spoke out clearly about all kinds of ailments and conditions in order to explain and clarify matters that people would rather not mention in public. The doctor refused to whisper as his patients did. In medical discourse the Aboriginal body is seen both to host disease and to obstruct the eradication measures which are part of the physiological arm of the civilising mission (Foucault 1978:140). The embodiment of inequality meant that force was sometimes necessary if egalitarian ideals were to be achieved.

Moral force usually succeeded, but there were often small crises. When the sisters at Bamyilli wanted to admit Joanne Forbes and her baby Steve to hospital she refused; he had already been in Gove hospital and in Darwin for months.[25] 'First failure we've had,' the nurse said to me loudly and cheerfully. Joanne was crying. Few mothers rejected the sisters' advice as there was reason to fear the medical consequences. Humiliation was sometimes deliberate and public, as when a white-clad nurse descended from the medical plane, approached our dusty little group and took the sick baby from his mother, handling him with obvious distaste as she climbed back into the plane. Shortly she reappeared at the door and, holding out the baby's nappy, she beckoned to me saying, 'Could you see that the mother washes this.' My sense of outrage at such casual, regular insults added to a growing anger at the confusions and reversals of policy concerning the Gulperan Pastoral Company, which was supposedly an Aboriginal cattle station.

The first house built by the Company early in 1976 was raised on stilts, was positioned a kilometre away from the old camp, and was for the white manager. The Bulman mob stayed in their tents and tin shacks with one central tap and electricity intermittently supplied by cords snaking across the camp from the noisy generator (plate 10). The long-term plan, said to have been decided in consultation with the community, and in fact realised in subsequent years, was for everyone to move to the new site. But many expressed a sense of betrayal at the distance as much as at the difference in living conditions between themselves and their supposed employee, the white manager, and the wife who then joined him. The dramas of the Gulperan project will be explored in chapter eight.

Urbanity

Aware of my own body's pale thickness compared with the slim black limbs all about me, and my awkwardness in this environment, I was contemptuous of those powerful whites who felt themselves superior and could not see how alien and ugly they were in the bush. Whites conceived this bush, the outback, as isolated, remote and potentially dangerous, the place for masculine pursuits of fishing and hunting, and also the natural environment for blacks. In the bush the Rembarrnga people were at home, stylishly competent and expressive. It was the town that was alien and dangerous and their demeanour there became awkward, timid and confused, while my confidence increased. In town whites can walk about in public, on show among strangers, an alarming condition for people who have always lived among familiar kin who do not stare.

The language and protocols of urban life seemed so natural that I was not prepared for the helplessness of Lorna and the others on our first trip together to Katherine. Many were unfamiliar with money, lacked shopping skills and sufficient literacy to read identifying labels. People bought hair spray instead of mosquito repellent. They feared and were embarrassed by the people in shops who would help them, and did not know how to tell bank tellers or hospital nurses what they wanted. After I chatted with a shop assistant Michelle asked in awe, 'Is he your cousin?' Lorna assiduously avoided strangers and drunks and waited for me to supply everything. In a shopping mall the children foraged. When a toddler collected a huge block of chocolate from a shelf, the mother praised her and bought it, and who was I to assert that such food is not intended for, or good for, infants? The idea of bad food did not, just then, seem to make much sense; I was resisting the instructive, tutelary role appropriate to my race.

We stayed at a motel in Katherine and when we were in the room with several beds, nine-year-old Norrie looked for swags and said, 'Where we going to camp tonight?'

Michelle asked, 'Whose camp this one?'

Watching TV that night the women enjoyed the news, speculating and laughing about the relationships between the male and female newsreaders and the weatherman. Similar entertaining conjectures were made about the interpersonal relationships of other whitefellas with warmth, curiosity and a sense of the vicissitudes of human emotion. These persistent assessments of intention and desire were an unintentional subversion of the silent tutelary task of the state.

Outrage

Despite the separation of social spaces and the invisibility of the social world of Rembarrnga to whitefellas, the world of *mununga* remained present, foreign, powerful and discomforting. A sense of helplessness when up against whitefella techniques seemed to have been cheerfully internalised, as when Florry (plate 11) chuckled when unable to open the vehicle door and said, 'I'm only a bush blackfella. You're a *mununga*; you do it.' Collmann wrote of the way 'Aborigines are dependent on and typified by whites . . . in ways that deny their persons' (Collmann nd:32). The Bulman community was typified as being in need of guidance, for instance towards better food habits; Peter responsibly ordered wholemeal flour and milk instead of the preferred white flour and soft-drink for the store. There were subdued complaints about this infantilisation and frustrations sometimes erupted in angry revolts, but such outbreaks were dismissed as due to alcohol and the complaints did not survive. The self-image of Rembarrnga as autonomous adults contradicted what was implied by their interaction with whites; that is, that they were apprentices, juniors to those white people who were helping them move into the modern world. The role they had been assigned by the state officials was that of eager participants in the modernity of whitefellas. Rembarrnga people developed techniques of distancing and disowning these roles, but at the cost of being deemed obtuse, passive and backward. They were enmeshed in a double bind and continually had to negotiate an identity for themselves.

Sitting by the fire one day Nelly said, 'You proper blackfella now,' and we laughed. Dorothy groomed my scalp for lice,[26] a common practice and a pretext for the kind of close, affectionate, bodily contact which was part of the everyday sense of a community, where the common interest centred on being together. This sense was affirmed by the minutiae of sharing food and other small pleasures, protecting each other from embarrassment, from men and from snakes, and enjoying common experiences. A little later Nelly said, 'You know, you're the one white lady that sat here on the dirt with us. No other white lady ever did this.' Such comments bolstered my growing feelings of familiarity, warmth and partisanship with the Bulman mob which made field work such a pleasure. But interaction with whites constantly threatened to rupture this cosy sense of belonging and introduce shame, embarrassment and another point of view. In Katherine one day, we were sitting on the grass median strip when a middle-aged, well-dressed English couple approached me saying: 'Excuse me, do you mind if we ask? We are tourists. Is that material of your dress made by these native people?'

It was an Indian cotton print, but it was not their ignorance of design that wrenched my gut but this assumption that all white people can speak together with authority about 'the natives', and in their presence. Here was the familiar common sense of the Territory, that communication about Aborigines can take place among whites at any time. Such an understanding was apparent in the gaze of those who saw me waiting by the main road with a large group of Rembarrnga and Ngalkbon people for the Bamyilli truck. Passing travellers would scan the crowd of black bodies with a kind of knowing, impersonal curiosity; as they caught sight of my white body their faces registered a shocked alertness and embarrassment or anger.

At first the practical and moral anxieties of field work were made worse by speaking with whites. I developed a sense of horror at the seemingly innocent, even concerned, questions which were sometimes broached within the hearing of my black friends: 'Do you think there is a solution to the Aboriginal problem?' A nursing sister suggested, coolly and confidently, 'Their reasoning processes differ, don't you think?' A mechanic, also professing an interest in Aboriginal traditions, offered the opinion that 'The rot has set in now. Look at this camp' as he sat in it, with community members playing cards nearby. These are everyday utterances which render Aborigines and their social world as objects of scrutiny, and my acute embarrassment at being claimed by the cultural world where such scrutiny was normal gradually gave way to a curiosity about its genesis. Where did all this common and taken-for-granted knowledge of how to view and to speak about Aborigines come from? How was what Goldberg (1995:60) called 'the making of racial otherness' achieved?

At Bulman in 1979 I found some people occupying three newly built houses at the new site, but there was no manager, no money, no stores and no knowledge of what could be done. Nelly had appealed for help from the white wife of a buffalo contractor working in the area, who had made urgent public complaints to sundry authorities in Katherine, Darwin and Canberra. Her quixotic attitude caused a flurry of bureaucratic activity and led to the fast-tracking of unemployment benefits. As we shall see below, little else altered.

SINGLE WOMEN'S CAMP

In 1976, early in my second field-work period, I made the following impressionistic record of my experiences which I include here to illustrate some other conditions of this field work:

> I am living under a sheet of calico, on a metal camp bed under which I keep typewriter and papers. Old Judy Farrar protects my interests in the camp by putting some of my possessions (tin opener, Weetbix), under her bed. And I am trying to learn to share! Judy was a ringer in her youth after her uncle brought her out of the bush to live on a cattle station. She left her first husband to her sister, and married a white stockman and has outlived all of them. She led the Djarada ceremony last week and will 'sing' the male anthropologists in Sydney, by getting me to play them the tape we recorded. Since she has been camping with us single girls she has bought black hair dye and asked for an appointment in Katherine to get new false teeth. She confesses to be seeking a husband and her sometimes bawdy humour is the balm of my life. When she heard the University mentioned on the radio she grabbed me and said '*Ngaritjan*, they talking about your place.' She is *Gaman* so she calls me 'Mummy'. She is probably 70 years old.
>
> The others seem by turn amused and embarrassed by Judy's overt concern with material goods and her selfishness. She does not give to the children as others do. My old companion Dorothy is the other more permanent member of our camp. She more often spreads her swag beside the fire outside than under the canvas since Judy moved in, and usually shares it with one or two small girls. We have little protection from the stones and earth, occasional wind and nanny goats, children, cats or the pet cockatoo.
>
> Our camp is a little way out from the main camp because we 'single girls' are afraid of the drinking that frequently enlivens life there. Thus, we have to go some distance for water, which does away with the problem of washing dishes after meals. We eat beef and damper with our fingers, eat food out of tins with forks rinsed in the tea, and drink tea from dusty pannikins. Every day or two someone puts one of the big cut down flour drums on the fire with some water and soap powder, and boils all the dishes. They are immediately used again, often for Weetbix with milk powder and water, a mixture which sets like concrete.

Others have shared the camp with Dorothy, Judy and me. Widow Rosey, about 50, came to stay for some weeks. She is a Christian and softly sings 'Jesus Loves Me' in a Rembarrnga style. She said her husband should have a second, promise wife, and that she would not be jealous because she was a Christian. Judy said succinctly "Im pray; 'im all right', a comment on the sense of salvation that Rosey gains from her religious observances. Another temporarily of our number, Del, has forsworn male company. Others stay in our camp frequently when their husbands go off mustering or to town for a day or a week. Also young girls often share a swag at our fire and are expected to get water and wood, boil tea, and fetch and carry for us 'old people'. The practical advantages of being 'old people' thus far outweigh any possible loss of physical charms, though women seem to consider that we remain desirable at whatever age. The girls, in return for their labour, are given tea and tucker and beef, and also hear the stories told around the fire. Boys are seldom seen here except at meal times. They appear to have no practical duties towards us, though they help us fetch firewood.

When old Judy first turned up on one of the Toyotas that arrived crowded from the middle of Arnhem Land, she was helped off at our camp and for the next three days sat or lay in more or less the same position. She began to move. Said she'd come from Malyanganuk. She set up her little tent and finding a white woman in the camp asking questions, gradually told the story of her life.

As a child old Judy lived 'bush way altogether'. Her salient memories are of walking a very long way and being without food at times and without seeing whitefellas at all. When they did see any they were frightened and hid but felt sorry for them because they seemed to have been cooked. She tells stories of deaths after fights among the blackfellas and about whitefellas chasing and shooting blackfellas. Surprisingly she does not express anger at the latter. She says the blackfellas were taking cattle. Perhaps her experience as a ringer and as the wife of a battling land-holder puts her in sympathy with pastoralists. She lived with her promise husband from before puberty and her younger sister joined her.

She describes how Billy Farrar, the owner of a newly leased property, Mainoru, needed stockmen and rounded up this little group of Rembarrnga people and brought them back to work for him. He trained the men and the women in stock work and Judy and her sister are reputed to have been 'champion ringers'. They in turn taught a group of younger women all about mustering wild country, poddy dodging, tailing, castrating, and all the exciting dangerous work of a stockman. The women camped with the men in the stock camps and seem to have had varied sexual experiences, despite the presence of jealous husbands. Billy Farrar was 'winking at' Judy and eventually she left her old husband to stay with him. Later they went to Katherine after Billy sold the station to the McKays. That was war time. The policeman chased them but they gave him the slip. Then, Judy said, 'they gave me a white dress for married, properly way'.

Judy remained with Billy Farrar until he died. Presumably the policeman's concern was to do with the Welfare Department policy against inter-racial liaisons. Judy says they did not want them to have children who were 'yella-fellas', but she described herself as a 'dry cow'. Judy seems mystified by the idea that such babies would have been a problem, and I failed to enlighten her.

Judy's stories finally sent me to the archives. I wanted more clues to the intimate and ambiguous aspects of the complex history of two different kinds of people whose relationship seemed so tortured. It seemed that Rembarrnga experience of the forces of modernity had changed their relationship with their own traditions. Anthropology required some excavation too; Nelly's account of Professor Elkin's visit to Mainoru put a quite different spin on the solemn expedition made by six experts in 1949 (see Chapter 3). The anthropologist's curiosity about Aboriginal practice no longer seemed an innocent and neutral intellectual inquiry because it harmonised rather too well with the state's purposes. I suspected its complicity in building a body of knowledge about Aborigines which supported rather than contested their objectification. But now the difficulty was that all the words I tried to use to describe experiences at Bulman were already weighted and misleading, and my thoughts fought to escape a web of meaning held by language, which stuck like sweet toffee. How could I write about difference without evoking the same meanings?

2

□○○○

Opening the Country

Before I was born, in this country there were a lot of people here.
People were shooting people.
This lot here, whitefellas used to chase them along and shoot them.
The wild blackfellas. They had no anything, no English, no tucker.
We only knew bush tucker. Bush blackfella speared white man too.
My old Grandpa, 'Old Snowball', he belonged to this country. He was
shot right there and it came out here [points to his two cheeks].
—*George Jaurdaku, 1989*

FINDING THE BULMAN STORY

In the years following my initial field work, I collected many fragments of evidence which collapsed the moral dichotomies of colonial
history as well as the racial dichotomy, Aboriginal and European. The
Bulman past included intimate interweavings of the lives of people
from many categories over the previous 80 years. I found traces
of the emotions and imaginings associated with racial otherness,
and of numerous intelligences at work.[1] The subjects of these events
did not see themselves as merely perpetrators or victims of the
wider set of social relations we call colonialism, but rather had
incorporated the unfamiliar others into their existential reality.
As the Territory's racial hierarchy was established, it became part of

relationships, both imagined and experienced. Through glimpses of some ordinary lives we can excavate the possibilities and potentialities that existed for a different form of race relations, possibilities that remain today.

I found only indirect evidence of how race relations had been experienced in an earlier era. While the idea of race lurked at the margin of every text, neither ethnographic works from the area nor local histories contained explicit information about the social relations between black and white people. Popular reports of wild savages in Arnhem Land illuminated the particular preoccupations of their authors rather than the events themselves. The newspapers in the early part of this century found the natives a valued source of dramatic news. But their printed words have changed colour since they were written; the paper is yellowed and, just as bits crumble off the edge of pages, parts of meanings have been eroded, obscured or have disappeared with the wear of time. For example, the shocking word 'nigger' could be found in early twentieth-century newspapers used in a context of support for Aboriginal advancement, implying meanings other than the active racial contempt it carries today. Among measured comments about colonisers' responsibility lay the image of an ineluctably simple and backward people. Those writing passionately of the terrible injustice of jailing black people who did not understand European law, spoke of them as 'primitive Indians' or 'simple savages' who needed to be treated with paternal care. Though injustices and cruelties were apparent to some whitefellas, many saw 'the blacks' as a nuisance or a fearful threat.

'In order to understand the productivity of colonial power,' argues Homi Bhabha, 'it is crucial to construct its regime of "truth", not to subject its representations to a normalising judgement' (1983:19). That is, the power contained in colonial society's judgements needs to be understood. White settlers were engaged in an ongoing struggle for progress by stamping their own cultural identities onto the country. To the pioneers the existence of wildness was always illegitimate. The natives were not an enemy only because of specific conflict over territory, as in war, but their condition as primitive represented a generic enemy, the enemy of modernity, the enemy of white ontology as it marched progressively through time. In this chapter I will show how the Territory's discourse about itself was constructed in the early days of settlement and how it articulated with the experiences at Mainoru.

Opening the country

The first foreign travellers in Rembarrnga country came from the sea. They were Macassan traders for pearlshell and trepang, and were intermittent visitors to the Arnhem Land coast (Macknight 1976). This interaction is deemed responsible for many words in the local languages, for certain items of material culture and, some believed, for the imagined ferocity of Arnhem Land people. Malay traders are part of Rembarrnga memory. Minnie George, an old woman, spoke in her soft, stylish way of a 'Malaya' from her childhood:

> I bin [was] born Duwingi this way la bush. [H]im bin bush, I been born. I bin longa [in a] paper bark coolamon.
>
> My mother used to cartim up [carry] me la [in] paper bark.
>
> I bin grow-grow la paper bark.
>
> We no more been savvy English.
>
> We no more been savvy *mununga*.
>
> Only one Malaya that's all we been savvy, mine Daddy and mine Mummy. Longa boat they come in, that Malaya, and mine Daddy and mine Mummy sellim stone spear eh? That's all we been savvy (1989).[2]

Later, trade with missionaries in the same area is recalled by Smiler Martin. He expressed a specific sense of time and space as well as nostalgia for events which probably took place in the 1950s:

> We used to go down Goyder River way and follow that river right along to Muruwangi. Me and Willy took them alligator hide. We used to carry them down to Millingimbi, one week walking, and sell them to missionary Mr Wells. He used to give no money but tea, sugar, tobacco. We didn't know money. We used to make bush boat. Motor didn't come through yet. We used to make bush one, paper bark, cut from biggest tree, stringy bark. To get across river to Millingimbi. Used to come past Gatchi, Nungalala, Ramangining, Muruwangi, and back to Goyder River. We were having a good time in the bush (1989).

There is no hint in either account of the anxiety with which the newly established authority in Darwin viewed trade along this coast. For many years, but with little success, immense energy was expended in trying to control the interaction between the natives and the independent hunters for riches, Malayan, Japanese and European.

Further inland, the first foreign intruders, as in the rest of Australia, were English-speaking explorers, surveyors and pastoralists. They saw this land as being there for them and their descendants, and wrote as if the country began to exist when they arrived and renamed it. In a kind of retrospective colonisation, the Place Names Committee in Darwin recently asserted that 'Mainoru Station was first crossed by the explorer Ludwig Leichhardt in 1844' (n.d. Darwin Archives). But there was no Mainoru station then, or when the explorer David Lindsay passed through in 1883 and deposited his name on Lindsay Creek and, I presume, on Chuckerduck Lindsay's uncle. David Lindsay described an exchange of names in which his companion was given the name Jacky and 'the leader Rodunga had also exchanged names with me' (Lindsay 1884:5).

White explorers' purposes were to do with a world which was elsewhere, and to which they would return when they had documented the contours and climate of the land. Their expeditions moved purposively, passed by and disappeared from Rembarrnga view. Later, other *mununga* wanted to graze cattle and wanted natives to help them. They were 'opening up' 'new' land. 'Opening up' the land is an apt metaphor expressing the historical task colonial culture took upon itself. The country was closed, and should be made available to men who would open it for fertilisation. They imagined it awaiting their footsteps and fences, their axes and animals, and their most visually intrusive cultural markers, the buildings. Naming new land and marking it was achievement of the highest order, and an expression of the progressive mission of the Australian nation, though the need to carry guns 'for protection' betrays the recognition that opening up the land might cause wounds. Yet explorers' diaries, settlers' accounts and, in particular, the reports of state officials, regularly expressed a sense of being surprised, offended and righteously angered by Aborigines' hostility and resistance to the civilising process. Having been saved from being lost outside time (Fabian 1983), it was assumed these natives would value the opportunities that settlement offered.

Outback imagery

Early interactions were cloaked by the stereotypical images with which the press, for instance, interpreted the outback to urban dwellers. A series of binary oppositions developed such as that between Aborigines as 'myalls' (wild, bush blackfellas) and as 'boys', between an irreconcilable, barbaric enemy and a domesticated childlike servant. Accusations of 'treachery' by the cultured and civilised Lindsay led to murderous rage when he was attacked by 'myalls' who he believed to be in league with his guides. Having joined the colonisers' enterprise, his 'boys' had betrayed the trust placed in them.

Fear, as well as frustration and anger, may partly account for his rage, but the term 'treachery' was a major tool in the early coloniser's armory. Treachery places the natives in the same moral universe as the colonisers, but as moral failures, not loyal but murderous tricksters. Thus Lindsay is not engaged in the violence of a war of conquest, but is fighting against betrayal, wary of black men who simulate allegiance, and might trap and murder the white man. In fact, Lindsay's relations with 'the myalls' were varied. He befriended and trusted some, shot some, and was amused by the small boy who insisted on joining his expedition (Lindsay 1884:19).

Lindsay's diaries show an ambiguous and contradictory view of the inhabitants which reflects a moral contradiction within colonial ideology. In order to bring a higher form of existence, civilisation, to the country and the people, previous indigenous existence could be effaced by means that were anything but civilised.

Another binarism saw frontier violence as either necessary pacification or natives' savagery. Yet these were interdependent categories because colonial violence was practised in order to subdue and eliminate the greater violence of savages. A calculated, rational use of violence would put an end to the undisciplined violence of the natives. Competing images thus formed the framework for interpreting this frontier, where cattlemen like Billy Farrar, the erstwhile husband of Judy who I had camped with at Bulman, arrived in Rembarrnga country more than 60 years before I did.

While responsible and educated settlers and townspeople turned their eyes away from bloodshed, there were many who thirsted for tales of the bloody frontier which the press tried to satisfy. Paranoid fantasies of unrestrained bloodthirsty natives developed among those urban residents who fed off the settlers' experiences. Morris shows how such paranoid fantasies circulated in an unstable public discourse which was an essential element in the construction of frontier terror. They led, in New South Wales, to savage massacres, often when no threat from Aborigines existed (Morris 1992).[3] The 'hostility of the natives' became a rich mythic theme in the public discourse of the Territory.

The press, which reported on frontier violence with moral indignation and enthralled interest, had its audience in the embryonic urban centres of the Territory and in the south. Bloody violence attracted as well as repulsed. It was not only an organic part of social relations in this era; it was part of the identity being forged in the comfortable houses of Darwin where there was an anxiously ambivalent pride in the frontier. As Taussig says, imaginings and fantasies of violence are 'a potent political force without which the work of conquest . . . could not have been accomplished' (1987:121). Though the period of frontier bloodshed lasted a comparatively short time, the image of the Territory's pioneers' resolute courage in the face of danger became a firmly established source of national pride (Hill 1985, f.p. 1951).

What did the Rembarrnga people see? It is common to speak of the 'mutual lack of understanding of behaviour and motives' (e.g. Merlan, 1978:76) between early settlers and Aboriginal people, but it should be emphasised that this is not merely an absence but rather a presence of other understandings. Blacks' and whites' social worlds were both shaped and meaningful, and new things had to be incorporated into those shapes. While the explorers expected the unexpected, the natives were at home, and probably as often welcomed whitefellas in surprise as they attacked them in hostility. With the meaning of country already known, how could Rembarrnga have imagined what the whites had in mind? How could they share their meanings with people who had no awareness of the nature of the country. As Beluyen people saw it, 'Country must go to extreme lengths to prove its sentient nature to [whitefellas]' (Povinelli 1993:155).

The silence from the other side of the frontier brings, as Morris says, 'its own pained awareness of the thoroughness with which the colonisers implanted their own images of the colonial process' (Morris 1992:73). But Arnhem Land does evoke contrasting images, for instances in the memory of George Jaurdaku. He said, 'This lot here, whitefellas used to chase them along and shoot them. They killed a big mob up here at this spring,' and added, 'Bush blackfella speared white man too.' He speaks of spearing white men as reprisal, though other Rembarrnga sometimes render it a mark of ignorance. There is no agreement about the moral implications of the violence of whitefellas in the past. George continued:

> White man, miners used to come around looking for mine, gold, silver. They [Aborigines] hunt them away. All those people they were angry about white man shooting blackfella, poor bugger. There were a lot of people in this country and they shoot the lot. Big lot I tell you, all round here.
>
> Some people used to go up that hill and used to sing out like 'Come

out here' in language you know, and white man came up with a shot gun. Bang. Shot. And they would hide behind that big rock there and kill them with a shovel spear.

All those first years they were shooting. They want to shoot the whole lot. They shot Tommy with 308 or 303. I heard from Grandpa.

The anger which George attributed to the blackfellas of the past became muted during their involvement in the pastoral industry, although today it is common for the moral illegitimacy of settlers' violence and of white settlement (the land was 'stolen') to be openly asserted with the agreement of whitefellas. Rembarrnga conceptions of violence do not take the form of self-conscious moral fears which conventional histories associate with frontier bloodshed but are related to their historical experience in a stateless society where force has a specific place in social functioning and is recognised as a legitimate human potential. Aboriginal violence can be the source of a certain ambivalent pride in wildness, as when Tex Camfoo said: 'The missionaries were going to get all the Aboriginal people, the Indigenous people, civilised. They were all wild at that time. They could fight like, whoa spear! Well, it was nothing, spearing one another' (1993).

Rembarrnga sense of wrong-doing concerns injustice rather than the fact of violence. Some tried to fight or outwit whites while others avoided them, but over time many accepted their presence and joined their enterprises. The whites' superior weapons and unarguable physical power created a facade of acceptance of white supremacy among Rembarrnga, but their own claims to superior knowledge of country were never abandoned.

In so far as white Territorians developed a characteristic discourse of self-representation, it was about more than the 'horde of savage spearmen' and images of the wild frontier (Hill 1985, f.p. 1951; Pike 1975:50–51). Race and sex, courage, loyalty and suffering also featured in the national imagery which selected and filtered events from pastoral stations and stock camps where close relations between settlers and natives were being established, relationships with far more complexity than was ever imagined nationally.

The state and the outback

In the early years of the century the law was broken regularly and with impunity in the Territory. There was a thin line between mustering abandoned cattle and cattle duffing, and between pioneering necessity and murder. Yet pastoralism promised prosperity to the nation, and these brave pioneers demonstrated Australia's initiative and courage. This is why the early land-owners had their control of huge rectangles of land legitimated by leases, their rents collected by government officials and their right to control and use 'their blacks', albeit in a humane way, recognised. They were heroic figures in the national landscape. It would have been considered improper to subject them to too much scrutiny, and anyway they were too far away.

The white men of the outback called upon the higher authority of the state to assist and protect their interests, but they were at odds with much of the legislation and enforcing institutions which tried to regulate their activities. As they began to have to take account of the state's regulatory powers, they tried to retain control of their domain by asserting that the administration was out of touch with practical realities. Their maverick position has become definitive of the outback Aussie, and his relationship with the modern, progressive Australian state. It was played out most clearly in relation to the series of regulations concerning Aborigines in the Territory.

'City bred men' such as journalists and government officials accepted the superior authority which accrued to bushmen who had experience of the primordial land and of the natives. These urban scribes and 'pen-pushers'[4] assisted in the powerful mythologising of the outback, according an awe to 'the frontier' and 'being there' which mediated the contradiction between the civilised values that were being officially asserted, and frontier conditions where these values might have to be temporarily held in abeyance. Journalists in the little town of Darwin took pleasure in imaginatively celebrating the dangerous historic enterprise being mounted just out of sight in the vast 'outback'. Readers were thrilled by their vicarious participation in frontier violence, and the privation of living far from the major centres of civilisation was made significant by being close to the enterprise of settlement.

There were those who challenged the attempts to inspire dread of the fearful and unpredictable savages, for instance by reporting atrocities committed against Aborigines. These heretical observations challenged not just the settlers' morals but the legitimacy of the nation's sense of ownership of Aborigines, of having the right to know and speak about them. Aborigines were a feature of the pioneer's identity, fiercely cared about; they could not be represented as independent beings with their own critical eye on the brave pioneers. A counter discourse which surfaced intermittently, consisting of evidence of whites' violence and cruelty and assertions about the motives behind Aborigines' actions, aroused disproportionate fury.[5] The anger unleashed by any contesting of the popular images, and any attempt to alter the relationship between the races, underlines the significance of racial identity for the Territory. Aborigines were to remain objects on the margins of humanity and of the nation. Consideration of their subjectivities had to be limited to a series of deficiencies and abnormalities, differences on which the racial hierarchy was founded and which were, it was believed, destined to gradually fade from sight as the space of otherness was covered over with civilisation.

The state never legitimised brutality or supported an ideology of violent subjugation. This is not a judgement quantified in terms of deaths or physical cruelty, but is based on the limited duration and contested nature of such practices. The state has always aimed at other irresistible means of control. Yet the stories of the wild frontier flourished and, as Fanon observed, 'when a story flourishes in the heart of a folklore, it is because in one way or another it expresses an aspect of "the spirit of the group"' (1986:64). Fanon is discussing a black man's story, but there was a genre of 'nigger yarns' and stories of 'white women held captive by cannibals' which express an important element of the spirit of whitefellas in the Territory (Cowlishaw 1996; Schaffer 1988).

The government officials who produced Aboriginal ordinances, regulations and amendments in rational and measured tones occupied the same social world in which the creative, fictional endeavours of the journalists and other contemporary writers expressed the racial passions which saturated the public rhetoric of the Territory in its formative period. Thus the legal structures which sought to manage the race relations of the Territory were generated within a racialised cultural space inhabited by the sinister fantasies described above.

BOUNDARIES

The harshness and isolation of the outback was gradually invaded by the state's attempts to manage things, to curb the excesses, dampen the violence, reduce the distances, and to impose rationality both on the pastoralists' lawlessness and the natives' untamed waywardness. Managing the natives' role in the pastoral industry became a central focus of the Territory administrators' modernisation discourse, which was directed towards bringing the backward country and people into the present. The high moral worth of civilisation was the faith on which the national conscience rested, and the inevitability of progress gave it a firm foundation. The settlers were on the side of history and their efforts in developing the country acquired the virtue which clung to the notion of progress. This assumption of virtue added to the state's difficulties of ensuring that the outback was properly managed. For, despite the common purpose of the state and the settlers, there were conflicts both over the regulation of relations with Aborigines and over everyday practices and understandings.

Everything outside Darwin, where the Administrator and the Chief Protector of Aborigines resided,[6] was the 'outback', though 'down the track' included the small settlements which waxed and waned, such as Pine Creek, Katherine, Maranboy, Mataranka and Alice Springs. The techniques of daily life in the towns, even in little depots like Katherine, were quite different from those on the land. The distances meant that stations had to be largely self-sufficient in their everyday practices while relying on food and equipment from outside. But the major social difference between town and country concerned the native presence on the stations, as a responsibility, as a resource and as part of the world of social, interpersonal relations. The urban bureaucrats were distant from these relations, yet it was they who developed the laws and policies which were intended to re/form the relationship between the races.

Spaces for races

The country was marked out in squares on a map ready for leasing (Bauer 1964), and one of the squares became Mainoru. Marking boundaries with straight lines was a major technology of invasion. Naming spaces is a way of claiming them (Carter 1987:327ff). Exploring, surveying, drawing maps, marking their scale and contours, establishing borders, measuring distances, forming roads, constructing fences, naming places: all these activities undertaken by state officials impressed a certain set of intentions on the country. Land was parcelled out to private owners, town sites were marked and areas for natives and areas prohibited to them were specified. This enabled the policing of space and more insidiously came to mark the contours of a social reality which was antithetical to that already in the country. The indigenous meanings of country remained only for Aboriginal people. Few if any white people seem to have noticed, let alone understood, the particular and local meanings of country for Aborigines and no anthropologists then explored the significance of Aboriginal identifications with, and attachment to, specific country, or the mutual responsibilities in the interaction between the country and its clanspeople. While Aborigines were seen as belonging in the outback, an organic part of the land, their manner of being was rendered illegitimate by the new markings on the earth's surface. The struggle to make the land produce in the new economy was paralleled by the need to make its inhabitants cooperate in this productive process which resulted in denying their separate social reality.

The 1911 Aboriginals Ordinance replaced the Aborigines Act 1910 (SA), and extended the state's power by establishing the Administrator's right to declare prohibited areas and to grant licences to employ Aborigines (McCorquodale 1985:26; Rowley 1972a:232). The law began to define spaces for races, using a technique of declaring town areas from which Aborigines were prohibited, and declaring (and revoking) camping areas and reserves for Aborigines only. The Government Gazette, published as part of the Northern Territory Times (NTTG), listed these decisions each week along with the statutes and ordinances which governed the Territory. The other business of the Territory, the sale of land, also took place through the pages of the Government Gazette. It is important to recognise what was involved in granting these land-holders grazing licences and pastoral leases with innocent little numbers like GL 87 or PL 2397. It meant that, over a few years, vast areas of the country were occupied by pastoralists and overrun by cattle. For instance, in 1919 the NTTG offered 11 000 square miles north and south of Roper in leases of 600 square miles each for 21 or 42 years (NTTG 26 April 1919).[7]

The Darwin newspapers reported the consequences of these administrative actions almost entirely in the simple stereotypical images and processes discussed earlier. For instance, '[P]eriodically the bucks sally forth on a cattle slaying expedition. The squatter puts up with a certain amount of this as a necessary evil, but when the attacks become too frequent it is trooper Hall's job to administer justice' (NTTG 1929, 26 Feb.). 'Justice' here refers to punishment for interference with the noble squatter's enterprise. The notion of 'sallying forth' implies that these 'bucks' (Aboriginal men) lived elsewhere and were attacking the innocent squatter's property, rather than hunting on their own land.

The local constable stationed at the Maranboy depot and tin mine, where Nelly Camfoo's father and other Rembarrnga people visited and worked, illustrated the importance of the technique of defining spaces for races when he wrote:

I have the honour to apply for an area of ground to be declared a camping place for Aboriginals on this field. The unemployed natives camp pretty well where they like . . . At times the bush blacks come in in big mobs and loaf about these camps and there does not seem to be any way of preventing them (FI 23/294 Jan. 1923).

The prompt reply from the Director of Native Affairs (DNA) says: 'send a sketch of place as well as area required so that may be shown on map and position defined in gazette' (ibid.).

This move was not sufficiently effective and a year later 'a prohibited area for Aboriginals to make the supervision of the natives easier to carry out' was requested. The problem was that they 'camp all over the field', and when miners are away 'the blacks sneak into their camps and steal . . . it is very difficult to catch them' (ibid. June 1924).

During World War Two, the system of control of space and the mustering of people were justified in terms of military necessity and of protection.[8] 'Natives who come within the contact area of the Army camps along the overland route in the north have been placed in the native compounds' (F1 42/461, 1944). Metaphors of herding and domestication abound in the memos concerning the establishment of 'settlements' which were modelled on the Christian missions, that is, areas set aside for Aborigines and staffed with managers who had an explicit tutelary role. The geographical containment of the population had a moral and racial intention. A settlement too near a township was 'easily accessible to those persons who desire to make contact with Natives; likewise, opportunities exist for the native to make contact if he is so inclined' (F1 49/113). Because natives 'roamed' about, 'no hardship would be imposed on them if they are removed to a Control Depot in the Maranboy District' (ibid.). 'Absorption' into settlements was supposedly to protect Aboriginal people from contact with 'undesirable Europeans', opium and methylated spirits as had been occurring before World War Two: 'With the return of civilisation to Katherine and Pine Creek evidence is already to hand that the incidence of these vices has been re-born, thus supporting the contention that natives should be excluded from these areas' (ibid.).

The irony of 'civilisation' precipitating such uncivil vice and disorder among the natives was lost on the worried officials who attributed the problem to Aborigines' inability to properly control their impulses in the face of civilisation's temptations. These are people construed as victims of their desires, rather than in command of their actions. They are said to 'drift' and 'wander' as if such movements were natural and instinctive to a population without purpose. This movement had to be controlled, if necessary by harsh measures. A spatialisation of race was being implemented, with settlements such as Maningrida formed explicitly to provide for Aborigines within Arnhem Land and to keep them out of Darwin. No recognition or legitimacy was accorded to Aborigines' purposes. There is nothing instinctive or natural in the description Willy Jailama Martin gave of his experiences during the war:

> Later on when the bombing in Darwin, World War Two, the government went all around to the coast right through the middle of Arnhem Land . . . All the government, the welfare people went all around, Bathurst Island, Melville Island, Croker Island, Millingimbi, Lake Avella, all the middle area. The Army want to get as much as 10 000 Aboriginal people at Mataranka homestead. That was the biggest settlement. Maybe seven or eight thousand people they got to work there. Just feeding people. Work all day, never stop. We went there, the Mainoru mob went there. We stop at Mataranka about five, or maybe three or four years. But I know some stayed longer . . .
>
> First the welfare men got many old people, young people get that job, work in the Army . . .
>
> Myself I was initiated at Mataranka. My father make my ring place there after I'm maybe sixteen or seventeen. Army bloke fixing me up to work. But we went back to Mainoru again because my father didn't want to work on the Army. Because too much job. Lifting the bomb up, push him up.
>
> We went back again to Mainoru all the time foot walking. No truck that time. After that, after we walk, they say: 'All right you're going to have to bring them back.' That's because we don't want to be shot because Japan was at Milingimbi. Japanese all around. The stories come right up to Maningrida now, they had submarine come under the water, all around the sea. So we went back to Mataranka again. After that, maybe one and a half years time, the war finished. It's gone. And the government say, 'Righto, everyone back to Arnhem Land.' And by that time we lost our father and mother (1989).

Willy accepts that the fear of Japan meant they were not allowed to remain at Mainoru after his father had taken them back there on foot. The particular circumstances meant that initiations had to take place in inappropriate places and that people were kept working at jobs they did not want to do and living where they did not want to live. Despite the fact that there is only a general abstract appreciation of the circumstances which determined these events, Willy expressed no blame or resentment towards the authorities. They are assumed to have legitimate purposes and benign intentions towards blackfellas.

Protective legislation emanated from the nation's centre in order to extend civilisation to the periphery and to protect Aborigines from exposure to elements of white society such as liquor, sex and money, which were presumed to be both irresistible and dangerous. Intimate involvement with whites was made illegal. Thus the exclusion from town and confinement to reserves, missions and government stations were a cornerstone in the administration's policy and a clue to its principles. More than simply a technique of control and governance, the racialised designation of space expressed and reproduced social and ontological categories on which colonial society was founded. It was understood that the social existence of the natives and the settlers were separable, and ideally separate, because of the different natures of black and white peoples, a difference construed as natural and inscribed in each individual. The logic underlying a human universe structured as a racial hierarchy was never fully articulated, and in fact some aspects of policy contradicted it. However, the urge to categorise and position bodies, whether as male or female, mature or childish, normal or abnormal, white or black, was a general and fundamental characteristic of western epistemology, and of colonial culture and social practice.

Wives and lubras

The spatialisation of race had important links with the proper placing of men and women. Like the natives, women seldom appear as subjects in the texts of the Territory. However, white women were essential adjuncts to civilisation, defining the domestic sphere, a feminine realm which ensured a private space for the establishment of the family, the protection and socialising of children and the expression of emotional intimacy. Aborigines' public sociality was construed as a realm of disorder and untrammelled desire, so that the 'blacks' camp' represented a threat to the establishment of households as the proper form of family life. Against the imagined threats of dirt, disorder and animal passions, white men were positively encouraged to marry their own kind and create a home. Wives who joined their husbands in the outback received encouraging and admiring comments. The remote stations were a source of fascination in the burgeoning centres of civilisation and details of the visits to Darwin by the owners of stations were reported in the NTTG. Billy Farrar's mother, Mrs John Farrar, was heaped with praise: 'She ranked absolutely first of the women who nobly pioneered the Northern Territory . . . the Farrars' infrequent visits to Darwin were very much appreciated by their many friends' (NTTG 5 Jan. 1918).

Other women who featured in the social pages of the NTTG were Mrs J. W. Rogers and Billy Farrar's sister-in-law and niece, each of whom spent some time in Rembarrnga country. When Andy Ray, who later became Billy Farrar's partner at Mainoru, brought his bride to the Maranboy tin field and 'made a comfortable home for her', he was held up as a model: 'If every single man on Maranboy would follow his excellent example this would be a place worth dwelling in' (NTTG 11 May 1918). Men were assumed to be naturally reluctant to take a wife, and the scarcity of white women seemed normal in this masculine realm. But these naturalisms were linked to the presence of black people and, in the discourse of the bush, relations with Aboriginal women were seen variously as a necessary sexual outlet and a barrier to the establishment of civilisation. To urban authorities, such sexual relations were decried as allowing white men to avoid the responsibilities which should have been associated with their sexual needs. This contradictory and unstable discourse about Aboriginal women is present in many representations of the outback (McGrath 1984).

In other ways black women were becoming part of the civilising mission. As domestic workers they could help to make 'The Home' more desirable, and in town most middle-class households had at least one Aboriginal servant. On the stations, besides pastoral work, they were taught domestic skills and gardening as well as performing many of the chores. Minnie George recalled how she gradually learned:

> But we got used to it. We learned that tucker. We savvy work. Garden. Picking up manure for garden. I was big girl. We started learning washing up. Plate. After that we learned cooking longa [with] some girls. We learn right through. We know work, properly now (1989).

Alma Gibbs' memories are of harsh conditions:

> Me, I really learned at Roper Valley. I was really stupid one. Myall one. But they taught me to cart water. That water had no pump or engine. Only just the well there. And we had to put the bucket down and take the water and lift it up. Haul 'im up. Well there, I tell you, fill up water and two girl, they cart him up from that well, up the hill, up the hill

I tell you, right up to the top. And fill up that tank, or tub. Big square one, long one. We gotta fill up that one might be seven times. From that high bank, down and up we got to walk. With that yoke and two bucket. That's what we learned there. Hard work I tell you.

We came more strong. Two bucket we can carry, next time four bucket together longa that yoke. Two kerosene tins of water this side and two this side. Up the hill. We were strong enough then, properly strong. And some for the bathroom, manager's bathroom. I tell you that place was more hard than any place (1983).

When black women's bodies were introduced into the heart of the nation's domestic sphere, they were shorn of the dangerous properties attributed to them in other contexts. They could increase the status of the home in town, and on the stations they could provide comfort and ease. The newspapers reported that they assisted the pioneering women who 'stood by their husbands' going into wild country 'when communication with the outside world was by pack-horse, and food supplies came to hand once a year [and] . . . the only female company was the domestic lubra on the station' (NTTG 23 May 1922). 'The domestic lubra on the station' gained appreciation as narrated in the famously patronising account in *We of the Never Never* (Gunn 1963), set at Elsey Station near Katherine. 'Little Black Princesses' could relieve the isolation, loneliness and strain which were seen as part of the white women's lot on the stations. The relationships which developed between individuals in innumerable remote places were represented as between charming infantilised 'lubras' and the mature whites who carried the burden of civilising them. The 'domestic lubra' was thus the female equivalent of the station 'boy' and any intimacy, warmth or respect could only be conveyed as part of a hierarchical order. Some novelists (e.g. Herbert 1977, f.p. 1959; Pritchard 1975) and diarists (e.g. Durack 1974) have depicted the way relationships on outback stations were marked by the emotional valencies of racial practice. That is, interdependence gave rise to resentment and suspicion as well as affection and loyalty, and interactions within as well as between the races were compromised by racial markers. There was no space outside the racial hierarchy for relationships to develop.

Alma Gibbs' description of her experience of learning stock work for a white boss who she later married conveys another kind of intimacy in the bush, where the racial and gender hierarchy complemented each other, and where a rare and partial melding of cultural spaces took place:

Jimmy Gibbs was boss. I was only working for him. And all the stock boy, Aboriginal one, was there at Limmen River. Stingy one grass, heavy sand too, all the stone there too. But we had a good time in that country.

We got a big mob of cattle, bullocky. Then we had Christmas there in the bush. We kept on living on sugar bag, no matter we were riding horses. Plenty of bush tucker there. We didn't starve (1983).

Alma conveys the physical harshness as well as the satisfactions experienced in this life. Her voice conveyed more strongly than her written words the incongruity she perceived in combining the practice of riding horses, which belongs to the domain of whitefellas, with the practice of eating sugarbag, that is wild honey, which belongs to the domain of blackfellas. She is commenting on a moment when the two social domains came together, a hybridity which was not to last. The notion of 'bush tucker' as a separate and strange form of nourishment is a whitefella construct. Most bush tucker has been eschewed by whites, and few whites have shared things from the domestic domain of Aborigines. In those early pastoral days, especially in the stock camps during the long mustering journeys, there was a coming together of white and black subsistence practices and an experience of substantial equality in the living conditions of black and white people. This situation changed, and bush living and bush tucker, and the sharing that took place during mustering, were for decades relegated to the past and to an earlier state of being, one concerning which there is both longing and embarrassment among black people and nostalgia and fantasies among whites. Today bush tucker has moved into the realm of a fashionable commodity, and is marketed as both food and style, but primitivity had to change its meaning before that could occur.

PASTORALISTS

While Aborigines represented powerful images of otherness and became a repository of imaginary fears and thrills, they were also everyday companions or intimates to many whites of the Territory. The legislation being formulated to order these relations, as well as the dominant images of the outback, were at odds with the daily existence of individuals who were participating in the construction of the nation as they were mustering cattle at Mainoru. There, a narrative unfolded which illustrates the material, experiential dimension of racial sentiment and which confounds the competing interpretations of frontier violence as part of either a heroic or a demonic era. Lives such as those of Billy Farrar who established Mainoru station, and George Conway who owned and lost a series of stations along the Roper River, illustrate the ambiguous nature of these relationships.

Billy Farrar

In 1917 an enterprise began which gradually drew in many Rembarrnga people over the next 50 years. Some of the country that had been intricately named and lived in by Rembarrnga, Ngalkbon and Jawoyn became Grazing Licence 87 and then, in 1920, Pastoral Licence 2397, and white men claimed it and named it Mainoru (map 1). The relationship that consequently formed between the black and white people cannot be understood simply in terms of superior white power or a unitary process of colonialism. Within the colonising process, the station community nurtured changing forms of desire and possibility, as well as a series of adjustments to the otherness of each other. The ambiguity at the centre of Billy Farrar's role among Rembarrnga people illustrates some formative elements of the traditions and relations of production which came to characterise the pastoral industry.

Billy Farrar's father, Mr J. S. Farrar senior, was one of the early pioneers.[9] When Farrar senior died, a fulsome obituary said he had had:

> Not so much trouble with the savage blacks as some other settlers but had two narrow escapes from death. He was speared twice . . . On one occasion the weapon pierced his shoulder and on the second occasion he was wounded in the chest. But generally speaking he was well liked by the aboriginals whom he had the knack of treating in the right way (NTTG 14 Dec. 1918).

This only makes sense in terms of the binary opposition between 'myall' and 'boy'. The 'savage blacks' who speared him are different from 'the aboriginals' who liked him well. His skill in inveigling them is one of taming and controlling wildness and creating the 'boys' and the 'lubras'[10] who accompanied the explorers and surveyors and helped work the cattle from the very early days. From the most aggressive to the most gentle accounts of life in the pioneering era, this division between 'myalls' and 'boys' is crucial. The latter have 'come in', apparently accepting the legitimacy of white power.[11]

The first lessee in the Bulman area was John Warrington Rogers.

He soon abandoned his holding, leaving traces of his presence only in the memories of some old Bulman people who showed me where his house had been. In 1917 Billy Farrar, then aged 25, took up a grazing licence for an annual rent of six pence an acre over the area then known as Maneroo Spring and three years later converted it to a pastoral lease (NTAS Land Branch Files quoted in Forrest 1989; van der Heide 1985:93). On various expeditions in the late 1920s and 1930s, Farrar mustered cattle and horses from the abandoned Arafura station in Rembarrnga country to the north. It is at this time that he is reputed to have shot many Rembarrnga people near Muruwangi. His friend Bert Nixon asserted that, as punishment for a thwarted insurrection and threat of murder, and with the help of George Conway, Billy Farrar had belted several Rembarrnga men and branded one of them (van der Heide 1985:95; see also NTTG xli, Oct. 12, 1918). He is said to have 'married a half-caste girl in 1919' who had at least one son (NTAS 1043 F630). While today's historians would assume that if Billy Farrar shot 'myalls' he was an enemy of the blacks, this is not the view of his Rembarrnga kin. The ambiguity is starkly indicated by Tex: 'An Aboriginal walking in to Mainoru met [Billy Farrer] on the road and asked him for a smoke and Farrar shot him right between his eyes. A young fella. But he got on good with the Aboriginal people' (1996).

I first heard of Billy Farrar as 'Uncle Billy', deceased husband of Judy, whose subsection was *Wamut*. When 'Aunty Judy' (or *Mula*, or *Gaengana*, or *Biangduyu*)[12] and I camped together in 1975–76, she talked of her husband as 'that old man' with pride in the toughness he had shown to 'myalls' who killed cattle. Someone else said, 'No-one could creep up on Billy Farrar.' Judy told me that Billy Farrar took her away from her family and taught her and her sister Fanny to read. They worked for him at Mainoru, and Judy lived with Billy. Their relationship was confirmed later when they married in a Christian ceremony on the verandah of Bert Nixon's house on his property near Katherine. Far from being typified as a white man, let alone the representative of a dominant or oppressive order, he is claimed by many Rembarrnga people as a classificatory uncle, brother or cousin, as a teacher, and as a man always ready for trouble. While this last characterisation hints at his violence, the integral place of Rembarrnga in the pastoral industry is affirmed through their kinship with Billy Farrar.

Judy's marriage to Farrar did not threaten her other relationships but led to his incorporation as her husband into the social system, at least in retrospect. Aboriginal women and men could play on the sexual desires and emotional needs of white men. For instance McGrath shows how some white settlers became dependent on 'the elders' for wives, and 'bonds of mutual affection and dependency' developed (McGrath 1987:82; see also Elkin 1972:365). Such Aboriginal people incorporated white men into kinship networks as a way of embracing and entangling them with obligations which the white men had to respect if they were to retain their workforce and ensure their security in the country. How common this process was in the social dynamics on pastoral stations is unclear, but the effectiveness of such a strategy was limited. It is unlikely that many white men understood such obligations or took them seriously. Whether Billy Farrar complied with the obligations entailed in his kinship classification is a mystery which it did not occur to me to enquire into when Judy was alive.[13] But Judy had adopted the principle of private and exclusive ownership of property, at least in relation to cigarettes and Weetbix. That is, it appears that she adopted some of Billy Farrar's economic practices, rather than he hers. Further, while relations with white stockmen often included an exchange of practical techniques in the bush, it was rare indeed that whitefellas participated in Rembarrnga law. However, as we shall see below, some agreed patterns of exchange and reciprocity became established which gave a degree of balance and stability to ongoing relationships at the station.

Billy and Judy's marriage has further significance as it entailed not only the complexities of an intimate relationship between people from contrasting cultures, but also public confirmation of a relationship across hierarchically positioned groups which were, in a sense, at war. The equality this implied was affirmed by Peter Lee who told me:

> I grew up gotta [with] my old grandpa old Billy Farrar. He was married to my sister-in-law Mrs Farrar, Judy.
>
> Billy Farrar used to have pistol revolver. He's Queensland man. He was riding along. Well he was tracking another lot of blackfella you see. They chased those cattle. Then bush blackfella way, [the others] come along behind and BANG with shovel spear. Bang at that man. They got shot two or three men might be, or six or seven. That's why we shifted out there [from Arafura] to Mainoru. We've been there for ever now (1989).

This account recognises that a state of enmity existed and entailed the pursuit of different interests. The superiority of firearms did not mean that Peter Lee recognised the ontological superiority of whites, which is implied in colonial representations and is often unintentionally reinforced by post-colonial revisionist histories.

As Billy became more strongly entangled with his black kin in his later years, his contact with his natal family seems to have diminished,[14] due more likely to having married rather than having shot Rembarrnga. As an established pioneering Territory family the four sons of J. S. Farrar senior were often mentioned in the press. 'Wm. Farrar of Mainoru Station is in town. He reports a good season and has a number of fats on hand' (NTTG 27 Aug. 1929). After the 1930s this particular son was not mentioned in the social pages, though the others flourished in public view.

More well known than Billy Farrar's violence was that of his friend George Conway, an 'old hand' who claimed to have taken part in raids to clear the country in north-central Arnhem Land for the African and Eastern Cold Storage Co. (Powell 1988:129; Bauer 1964:157; Lockwood 1964:156–58; Willey 1964:103). Another local cattleman said that Conway 'used to boast about the number of blacks he had shot in the early days. I don't know if he was telling the truth, but he was one of the old hands along the Roper. He was a likeable old character but had a weakness: he couldn't stop "poddy-dodging" '[15] (Teece 1978:81). But George Jaurdaku had a somewhat different view of Conway's role:

> One man, George Conway, he came from Queensland and he came to this country and he told them, 'Don't shoot blackfella, blackfellas are all right.' He went all round this country, George Conway. He died at Mataranka station. He's in the cemetery there.

This black man's view does not derive from any textual representation but from the oral legacy of his kin. Who can know which represents best the relationship of this particular whitefella to blackfellas, or how many violent events he engaged in as opposed to the peaceable opinions he expressed? Conway lived for many years with an Aboriginal woman and Teece tells of the day when he had to 'dress for the occasion' of visiting another stockman:

> George lay on his bed and called for his lubra.
> 'Will you get my Indianas?' They were his black socks. He put one foot up in the air and she put a grey sock on it.
> 'Take that off,' he demanded. 'That is not an Indiana.'
> He did not feel properly dressed without his Indianas (1978:83).

The rather feeble humour of Teece's account gives a rare glimpse of the domain where 'lubras' were an intrinsic part of the intimate, everyday lives of stockmen. We know little of how race relations were played out in the minutiae of domestic life, but this scene hints at how gender mixed with race to create its own rituals of intimacy, subordination and love. Alongside signs of interdependence are other examples of commonplace cruelty and even malice. Teece detailed the practices of Hugh Byers, a pastoralist in the district who took pleasure in deceiving, mocking and humiliating his Aboriginal workers. This man's actions were spoken of as humorous and even courageous by some, and were widely known in the district in the 1920s and 1930s (1978:78–81; see also Costello 1930).

Both Conway and Farrar lived and worked with people whose relatives they killed. They were also part of a cultural realm of cattle workers where black and white people enjoyed an intimacy and experienced a rough equivalence of the physical conditions of life, at least when mustering cattle. Behind this day to day equivalence there was a vast gulf in the implications of what they were doing for their respective races. A bifurcated social realm was being established which reified and reinforced cultural differences between white and black society. In this social realm, the productive, economic activities of the invading whites directed the labour and sexual power of the blacks. These activities and the meanings they carried blanketed the indigenous domain which was imprinted on the land and lived in the minds of the people. An incontrovertible power over the future was wielded in the name of the civilisation to which these marginal white men belonged. They were equipped not only with guns, but with knowledge of horses, houses and markets, of writing and radio, and connections with an ever growing armory of techniques of documentation which would saturate the world with accounts of their experiences.

Whether Billy Farrar killed one or several 'myalls', domination through killings and other kinds of violence was part of the inter-racial world he and his wife Judy inhabited. Rembarrnga people had learned about the mortal danger wielded by whites, as is apparent from their fear when whites appeared (van der Heide 1985:16). Further, such sexual relationships as those of Farrar and Conway were laden with meanings from the scientific discourse of evolutionism to which all whites were party. Even the most gentle pioneers were armed with a belief in their own superior position on the tree of human evolution.

Cowboys and Aborigines

The Mainoru settlers brought more than Queensland cattle with them to the Northern Territory. They nurtured among themselves that burgeoning Australian hero, the outback stockman with his struggles against nature, his privations and resourcefulness in danger, and his exotic adventures with blacks in the bush. The glamour was absent from the actual stockmen who became familiar to Aborigines during weeks of mustering and droving, pursuing the economic purposes of whites. No accounts of the boredom and deprivation that many stockmen experienced mar the romantic outback images, due perhaps to the fact that many of these stockmen were semi-literate at best. While the fondly imagined laconic, sun-bronzed outback stockman might be embarrassed by his redneck ocker mate, the national imagery managed to incorporate both figures within the idea of a rational, progressive, modern Australian nation.

The white men who drove the cattle and managed the stations in this area were poor 'battlers' for whom substantial rewards seldom materialised. Few who ventured out from urban centres stayed (Bauer 1964:157) and those that did established their lives in isolated, often uncomfortable and sometimes dangerous conditions. They often stayed in this region for many years, intimately involved with Rembarrnga, though to Rembarrnga they remained immigrants and their departure after 30 or 40 years back to Queensland or elsewhere was assumed to be back to 'his own country'. Many of them were uneducated and most remained poor.

What do interpersonal relations mean to men who leave their families and familiars to be isolated in the outback, who live in discomfort and privation, who pride themselves on being able to defeat their own desires and overcome their own pain in order to achieve a reward that seldom took any material form? Mateship and the masculinity of the bush are common themes here. Perhaps men who distance themselves from friends and family find communication with cultural others less burdensome than those more dependent on everyday affirmation of their cultural practices. Some men may have 'gone bush' to get away from intimacy and sex, particularly the social expression of urban sexuality. A dogger's[16] wife I knew was certainly escaping femininity. V. S. Hall's account of the standard 'plant' for bush travel provides a picture of the self-denial which was an intrinsic part of the asceticism of bush life. The rejection of domestic comforts is apparent in the meagre basics of flour, tea, sugar and salt beef, sometimes reluctantly supplemented with luxuries. Hall says:

> There are bushmen who consider it 'sissy' to carry even jam in addition
> to the four staples. Potatoes and onions are carried by such men as

consider that their reputations for robust manhood will stand the possible implications . . . the list of necessities is extended by soap . . . for those who like to wash (1955:15–17).

The cowboy's craft was taught to Aborigines and with it, poddy-dodging. The words of Bandicoot Robinson illustrate the way Aboriginal children were socialised into a stockman's identity and skills:

> When I was ten, or eight or nine, somewhere, and they put me on a horse then. Billy Farrar used to tie me with a tie strap on the saddle . . .
>
> We used to chase up one bull, draft it out from the mob, throw it. Make a fire, cut the horn. Make another fire, brand him . . .
>
> That's the time I was a really smart young fella. Nothing knocked me up. I used to work very fast. I worked at Mainoru then, and they knew I was a really good man. And Mountain Valley manager used to come over there and whisper to me, you know. Whisper whisper to take me away from there. So I pulled out from Mainoru. I worked at Mountain Valley then (1989).

Bandicoot recognised the competition for labour and his own worth to the whites as a particularly good worker. Peter Lee explained his association with another 'old hand' and his experience of the law according to whitefellas:

> Joe Dowling, that's the really good man. That's the man who was teaching me, stealing bullocky, poddy-dodging. I used to go with my little swag, my tucker longa saddle bag, I went to a different station. I had to steal cattle from another country.
>
> That policeman was chasing me, but we put shoes back to front. Horse shoe. I'm travelling up this way to another station. Those shoes going back this way (1989).

Peter Lee found this tricking of the policeman a matter of hilarity. The native had out-manipulated the white policeman who treated natives as people without reason and intelligence. However, poddy-dodging was also spoken of with a certain bemusement about the nature of the white man's law. On the one hand, some white men enthusiastically stole and found it humorous while policemen tried to stop them breaking the law. On the other, Aboriginal people knew that savage punishment followed even the suspicion that they killed cattle for beef. And it was not only policemen that made poddy-dodging dangerous, as George Jaurdaku made clear:

I was shot by one boss. Alec McDonald shot me for poddy-dodging. We used to break into the yard in the night and take away cattle to make a lot of cattle for Roper Valley. They were at the top of the hill with a telescope, red handkerchief and cowboy shirt. They shot one old man, Dicky, they made him bleed. They shot me and missed me three or four times. And they chased me . . .

Alec McDonald came along the road. I didn't see him. I took my hat to get water and drink. Then I walked along swinging my hat. Then I heard pscheww [gun shot], blow my leg up. I galloped along that hill and I got off. I said, 'Alec come over here. Come and help because you break my leg.'

I said, 'You can shoot me if you want to.' I stood up there but no bullet came. He must have had a bullet but he couldn't shoot me any more.

'I said come over here and lift me up,' I said. 'You break my leg.'

I said, 'Just put me on the horse. You can go home,' so I just went back to camp.

One boy jumped on the horse and he went and told Mr Chisholm [his employer]. He caught him before daylight, half past five. Soon as everyone had breakfast Mr Chisholm was there.

'Where's Alec? He shot my boy.' He was going to shoot Alec McDonald, but he ran away. He went to Alice Springs. That policeman wouldn't let him come around this territory.

I stayed out in the bush for two years. Then I went to hospital. I got the lead here, under the skin (1991).

George experienced the violent justice meted out in the bush, where the blackfellas belonged to their employers. White men were not shot for poddy-dodging, but if observed they were taken to court. If a 'boy' was shot for stealing cattle it was a matter between white men; their cattle and their 'boys' were protected by their owners. George sees the issue as having been resolved in the white domain of land-holders and the police who 'wouldn't let him come around this territory'. Thus the order of race relations was expressed within the specific form of law breaking known as poddy-dodging, with the body of the black man bearing the scars of the violence perpetrated among white men as a necessary form of control and order.

A moral contrast between white cowboys and Aborigines is exhibited in the realm of desire. It is not merely that desire and its objects were differently structured, but, as we have seen, the white stockmen took pride in denying the value of desire itself, particularly for comfort, company and consumer goods. They gained gratification from being able to do without, a view of the self which was not shared by their black companions. Rembarrnga show no shame in having been seduced by their desire for the goods offered by whitefellas. As Smiler said: 'Soon as people been tasting smoke, we say we'll have to walk this way [Mainoru] now. So everyone came to this place then' (1985).

And Ronnie Buck explained:

The first thing people see was that black tobacco, what it tasted like. He found something that is very, you know, good.

'Who from that special thing nikki nikki come?'

Not only that but sugar, first time people taste different thing from any bush tucker. Different from sugarbag [wild honey]. Different from yam. A lot of the people keep telling one another.

'Where you get this from.' They used to say, 'Well we got this from a place called Mainoru' (1991).

The explicit logic of seeking to satisfy one's desires forms a radical contrast with the stockmen's pride in self-denial. But Minnie George resisted the blandishments of the police and school teachers at Roper. She did not want their sweets or schools, refusing the clothes and punishment of an alien discipline, desiring 'we [our] own tucker':

We used to play hiding, and run away from school in the bush. We'd drop down dress, put on cockarag [cloth] and go. My Mummy and my Daddy follow us, right up to Arnhem Land, pick us up and take us back. The missionary was going to belt us all. So we run away again.

And that policeman now, he came with his missus. She brought a tin of lollies. We were looking at her, from the hill. She was following us with that lolly. She took out that lolly, and showed it to us, waved the tin at us. We shook our heads.

'Hey come back,' she said like that, that missus. 'You mob come back.' We just shook our heads. 'No. No more been wantim' . . .

We wanted bush. They wanted us to wear clothes but we chucked them out, and wore cockarag. That teacher was too cheeky [rough, aggressive], belting us . . .

And we were starting to get English now, a little bit . . .

But that tea we didn't know. He used to make tea for us, that policeman, and we took it and we tipped it out. We lived on water.

We told him, 'Whatabout givim alabout we own tucker?' [Why don't you give us our own food?] That sugarbag [wild honey] now, and lilly root, lilly seed. That's how we lived (1989).

The old colonial notion of cheeky natives is reversed in the Kriol term 'cheeky' which is here applied to the teacher. Minnie George describes the combination of enticement and punishment used to draw her family into the embrace of the police and missionaries. She presents a form of resistance natural to children who did not want the food they were offered, yet it is a response of dislike and disdain apparently shared by her parents. In the midst of acknowledging the process of learning, she takes pleasure in the stories of subversion and rejection. Access to the space of Arnhem Land was a necessary element in this assertion of another identity which the policeman, the school teacher and the missionary were trying to negate. This illustrates the need for social identities to be located in specific places. That is, identification with territory, even an imagined territory, is crucial to the establishment and re-establishment of social identities. Rembarrnga were at home in Arnhem Land as they had ceased to be at the mission. The spatiality which is a characteristic of all social relations and social identities (Bachelard 1969) is also recognisable in the struggles of the colonial order to establish control over the territory of culture. With this in mind, we will follow the settlers as they established on others' country, not just their own lives, but a wider cultural hegemony which allowed many white people to identify this outback as a crucial dimension of the most personal and precious aspects of themselves.

3

OOOO

Civilising the Country

All the *mununga* come down to blackfella country. We don't go out to
whitefella country where you people stay. We can't go as far as Sydney
or Adelaide or whatever, or to London or wherever people live. We
can't even go to Hong Kong . . . Us mob of blackfella look silly when
whitefella come over and take all the country from us. For instance
especially Mainoru and Mountain Valley. Why is that, will you tell me?
Why?

—*Nelly Camfoo, 1991*

ESTABLISHING CIVILITY

We white people may think we know the answer to Nelly's question,
that we know the identity and intentions of our forebears. But I want
to use her question to unsettle the past rather than reproduce a 'history
where the past has been settled even more effectively than the country'
(Carter 1987). The moral binarism between remote, racist rednecks
and educated, civilised officials needs to be unravelled. It is true that
there was entrenched and horrific cruelty and violence on many
pastoral stations, and that the state made efforts to control it. But the
concerns of the state officials were largely with physical well-being,
and while their humane intentions are significant, they often entailed
no greater recognition of 'the natives' as fully human than that

displayed by pastoralists. The state was always preoccupied with rep-
licating in the outback the social relations of its own subjects. Thus,
Nandy's comment that 'Colonialism minus a civilisational mission is
no colonialism at all' (1983:11), is as true in Australia as it was in
India. This chapter will trace some of the techniques of governance
and the themes of civility which they expressed, as they were
re/formed and adapted for local conditions in the Territory. There
were constant struggles to define what was happening, to assert a stable
identity, a settled future, a predictable order made up out of the
imagined past and the experienced present. What was made was a
distinctive, complex cultural domain we think of as 'the Territory'.

Establishing Mainoru

After the explorers had passed and before the pastoralists came to stay,
there were intermittent brief intrusions of miners into Rembarrnga
country. The idea of hidden riches is part of the romance of the
Territory and the 'Boolman Boom' was headlined in the press for
three months in 1910 when a Melbourne prospecting company was
formed on the basis of a report from two travellers in the area. Before
the company's expert could reach the field and assess its worth, the
£10 shares reached £190. Two other companies were formed and
local syndicates sent out fully equipped parties. In May the *Times*
reported that 'There are now 6 different parties on the way to Boolman
or Mount Maroomba, probably the native name for Mt. Catt' (NTTG
May 1910). In June 'an imposing cavalcade left Pine Creek for
Boolman' with 'a long string of packhorses' (NTTG 1 July 1910).
Before a pick was put in the ground the expert's report arrived saying
that the 'field is of no practical value' and the shares tumbled to £20
(NTTG 22 July 1910). This was the first of several mining ventures
at Bulman each of which started with a flourish and ended with the
miners giving up and departing, leaving some huts or tools and some
memories. George Jaurdaku told me that when miners 'used to come
around looking for mine, gold, silver', his uncles would hunt them
away. Jackie Ryan recalled that in his youth: 'Tiger Brennan mine
was at Goinjimbi [at Bulman]. Tin mine. They used long pick axe
and get tin from under ground, like coal. Get a lot of money. I been
there too, working. I'd get killer [a bullock] for them you know. That
time I was working for old Jimmy Gibb' (1987).

Rembarrnga people learned something from these encounters with white men's form of foraging. As Nellie said, 'We didn't know rocks got money in them.'

The elision between civilisation and business (Taussig 1987:134) is clear in the news reports from the Maranboy mine which flourished in 1918 with boom prices of tin and 'openings for men of a wiry type with plenty of punch' (NTTG 11 May 1918). Andy Ray was one such man: 'Andy Ray and Ernie Marshall are men of whom any field in Australia, or the world, would be proud. They are young and experienced and have plenty of punch in them and their hard work at Maranboy had rewarded them handsomely' (NTTG 2 June 1918).

When Andy Ray invested his few thousand pounds in the Mainoru pastoral lease he was applauded: 'The miner who makes good has a seeming weakness for the land and Andy Ray . . . is now a full partner in the station on the Roper known as 'Myneroo' (NTTG 18 Jan. 1924).

Andy Ray and his wife did not join Billy Farrar at Mainoru, but appear to have remained resident at Maranboy where their role in establishing civilisation was greatly valued. Civilisation here refers to that which 'Western society seeks to describe, what constitutes its special character and what it is proud of' (Elias 1984:3). Thus 'Mr & Mrs Ray gave an epicurean dinner to 20 old residents' (*Northern Star* 15 Jan. 1929). They were reported to be a successful and popular couple, taking 'a well earned holiday' (NTTG 1927; Dec. 1929). Not only were these markers of a particular cultural tradition recorded and applauded, but readers were assisted to identify their, as yet precarious, social existence with a recognisable set of stable social practices. They were participating in the world where people gave dinner parties and took well-earned holidays. Such codes of propriety were developing in the towns, far from the dramas, anxieties and new experiences that were part of domestic racial interaction on the stations.

The establishment of new stations was reported with great satisfaction. While there had been two stations in the Roper River patrol district until 1918, 'now J.W. Rogers was established, and Paddy's Lagoon and Mataranka [part of Elsey] were taken up' (NTTG 19 Jan. 1918). Then followed J. Gibbs and G. Stevens on St Vigeons followed by T. Sayle and George Conway on Roper Valley station (map 1):

> The last addition to the district is the Farrar Brothers who have taken up country along the valley of the Wilton north of the Roper. All the parties named are practical stockmen and all appear well satisfied with

their prospects . . . in early months of the wet season the grasses of this coastal country could fatten the cattle of all Australia (ibid.).

Fat cattle by the thousands filled everyone's heart with satisfaction, as they represented both virtue and prosperity for all in the Territory.

The images of the settlers in these written records differed sharply from the 'Mister Rogers' and 'Uncle Billy' Farrar in Rembarrnga accounts. In these, such men appeared and introduced cattle and 'work' and new experiences of life and new sources of death, and eventually they died or left, many going back to their 'own country'. In retrospect they are seen to have changed Rembarrnga people's lives radically. Memories are vivid and particular, and include detailed accounts of experiences and relationships with individuals. George Jaurdaku recalled Mr Rogers: 'This country belong to my father. Mr Roger was there too. He had a station there at Bagetthi. He had a little house there. Before I was born in this country there were a lot of people here. People [whites] were shooting people . . .' (1989).

And Minnie George recalled: 'Mr Roger, we started work longa[for] him now. Mr Roger and Willy Moko two brother-in-law. Mr Roger had the sister bla [of] Willy Mocko. We learn work there now. And I know English, more properly (1989).

Here Mr Rogers is a man like other men, with his own kin and concerns, living in Rembarrnga country and teaching Rembarrnga things which have since become part of everyday life. J. Warrington Rogers was a respected man of substance with considerable influence. He, and his son 'Mr Rogers jr', were often mentioned in the news columns in the 1920s as bringing cattle in from his 'fine station property, Roper Valley' to the railhead at Katherine, to be shipped to Manila. By 1930 Katherine had developed into 'a decent little town', with a brick Post Office, railway station, and two pubs (NTTG 1930).

The long distances, the sparse European population and the personal nature of business are all illustrated in Billy Farrar's application for a pastoral lease on the country where he already held a grazing licence at what was called Myneroo Spring. His letter to his solicitor in Darwin requested that he: '[F]ix up Number eleven block country with 500 square miles for me. And obliged, hope this short note finds you OK. Yours Truly W Farrar. P.S. If you havent sent the kerosene stove don't send it. Send me a Baroba Dover stove instead by next boat' (NTAS 1043 F630 Aug. 1919).

In 1920 Pastoral Licences 2397 and 2423 were granted to William and Robert Farrar for 42 years with seven-year reappraisals of rental.

There were three requests for the same block and the Farrars' success over rival applicants was explained in the following terms: 'Mr Farrar (sen) was engaged in pastoral pursuits south of Roper River for very many years and W. Farrar, his son, has lived on Grazing licence 215 for the past two years and effected certain improvements . . . he is married to a half-caste girl'[1] (ibid. Dec. 1919).

The references to his father and to his 'half-caste' wife affirm Billy Farrar's insider status in the Territory community. His commitment to the industry and the locality were judged to be sound. In this developing social domain, the line between marginal battler and man of substance and status in the Territory could be crossed with the help of time, industry and a little luck. A valuation of the lease at this time indicates how quickly the invasion of foreign fauna and other paraphernalia had taken place. There were 500 cattle, 400 horses, some mules and 400 goats, tailing and branding yards and a shed. The house, valued at £150, was 55 feet by 50 feet, had a paperbark roof and a verandah on three sides and was subdivided into three rooms. Andy Ray paid £1000 for a half share in this property in 1924 (F1 52/759).

While the rent of £75 per annum remained the same from 1920 until at least 1941, the ease of paying it varied greatly. During the 1930s there was a series of rent demands and requests for postponement, pleading: 'Unable to sell bullocks—had to return them after droving them to Mataranka. Some horses were sold but not paid for' (NTAS Lands & Survey Dept 1930). Under threat of forfeiture of the lease, Andy Ray composed an elaborate plea that he and Farrar's 'long occupation' of twelve years, the £975 rent that had been paid and the construction of roads, merited the deferral of payment. The official response was, 'postponed to July 1931' (NTAS Lands & Survey Dept 1930). Sympathy and support for these men on isolated properties was apparent in the administration's response to Andy Ray's untimely death in 1935. With the note that 'Few cattle sold. Mrs. Ray is in Darwin doing domestic work and Mr. Farrar is down on station' (NTAS 1043 F630 1937), the Interior Minister approved the forgiving of outstanding rent of £385.15.0.

Billy Farrar's vicissitudes after Andy Ray died included two years serious illness necessitating his absence from Mainoru, during which time a partner, one Tom Boddington, mismanaged the property, lost cattle, horses and saddles, allowed outstanding rent to accumulate and then wanted to be bought out. Bandicoot Robinson's account of Boddington's crimes has a different emphasis from the archival records which explain that it took a Supreme Court action to dissolve the partnership (NTAS 1043 F 630). Bandicoot (plate 13) was one of the long-term Mainoru stockmen and a brilliant raconteur. His dramatic account of Boddington's activities made the most of the deliberate lies, attempted poisoning, theft and the eventual arrest and court appearances at which Bandicoot was pleased to give evidence. This is an edited extract from his story:

> Another bloke took over Mainoru. Tom Boddington, and I work, work, work there. He was a bad bloke too. He used to shoot, frighten the hell out of all of those people . . .
>
> Billy Farrar was half sick too. He went to Sydney hospital, that time for his leg and foot, that went crooked you know. Just some sort of sickness and Tom Boddington ran that place.
>
> That Tom Boddington had everybody all cleared out. He was hunting everyone out. Blackfellas, and old Billy Farrar too. He didn't hit me, but he just hate anybody.
>
> Then we went to Katherine, me and Tom Boddington. Before we left he put all that arsenic, poison. He poisoned the salt, he poisoned the sugar, he poisoned that box full of tea leaf.
>
> [Billy Farrar arrived back at Mainoru after Boddington left.]
>
> That old Billy Farrar mob got a killer [bullock], shot it and salted it up. Next morning they were going to start to eat now. They boiled up the tea. And when they drank the tea everyone started vomiting. Vomiting, everyone vomiting.
>
> 'Hey what wrong, everyone vomiting?' All that thing, tucker, all had poison. Sugar, tea-leaf and salt . . .
>
> When we got to Katherine Tom Boddington told me, 'You know that Mainoru mob. Billy Farrar went back there. I sang them that song. They're all here at hospital. Or might be they all dead now,' he reckon.
>
> 'Yeah,' I reckon. 'Is that true?'
>
> 'Yeah. I sang them all, that song,' him reckon.
>
> 'Alright.'
>
> But nothing. He reckoned he sang them blackfella way.[2] I believed him too. And I was silly myself, to believe that . . .
>
> [Later the police set a trap for Boddington.]
>
> We waited for Tom Boddington at that low level bridge. Coming up, one horse with rider. I was by myself, and when he was getting close, he got off his horse and started walking up.
>
> 'Hey,' he reckon, 'what are you doing?' As soon as he said that, a policeman came up from another corner. He held him up with a gun.
>
> 'Don't move Mr. Boddington. You're in bad trouble.' . . .

I went to Katherine court. Then we went to Darwin. War was still on. I told Darwin Court just straight out what we were doing. He told me this and that, and I told them about everything, that judge in Darwin. And he shot my uncle too, that Tom Boddington . . .

We went to Alice Springs. I met the Supreme Court there too. And I told them straight. They put Tom Boddington straight in the army. He went to New Guinea, fighting. That old Tom Boddington just disappeared there now, finish. Might be he got shot now! (Bulman Oral History Series No. 4 1996.)

Boddington's murderous attempt at poisoning was directed at Billy Farrar and the police as well as at the Aborigines, and Bandicoot positions himself as assisting in the establishment of the rule of law by bringing the man to book. Bandicoot presents his participation in these events and in the station generally as autonomous and significant, in marked contrast with archival records of the period which erase any significance of Aborigines' active participation in local events.

It was after the departure of Boddington that Andy Ray's nephew, Jack McKay (plate 14), joined Billy Farrar at Mainoru and began to take over the station. This was the start of an era of increased bureaucratic control activated by the Native Affairs Branch (NAB).[3] A government file, begun in the early 1940s, on the 'Employment Of Aboriginals—Country Districts' contains Mainoru station's first six monthly return of employees for the second half of 1944. The employers are J. McKay and C. Peterson[4] and ten male employees are listed by the names bestowed on them: Chuckerduck, Bandicoot, Larry, Left Hand, Slippery, Diver, George, Jack-in-Box, Lame Jack, Dick. Their tribe is 'Bulman', the work 'stockwork'. Six wives are named, two of whom are co-wives and two children are mentioned. Under the list Jack McKay has written 'The above aboriginals are paid 5/- weekly and supplied with food, tobacco, clothes, blankets etc. J. McK' (F1 52/759 June 1944).

The men and women who became 'aboriginal employees' had not previously used personal names as markers of identity. Use of personal names was avoided in favour of kin and 'skin' terms. Familiar, often childish nicknames were bestowed on these workers, such as 'Old Left Hand', 'Jack-in-Box', 'Smiler' and 'Coffin'. Some of the names seem to represent Aborigines as caricatures of ordinary humanity, but they may not have been conferred with malicious intent. Hitler Wood said, 'Joe Dowling, he was overseer good stockman, bushman. He couldn't read or write. He gave me the name "Hitler".' This Hitler was no doubt named after another whose straight hair also fell across his forehead. Nicknames which may appear contemptuous to outsiders are a feature of outback communities in Australia, where joking references to an individual's weaknesses or oddities can become a familiar and affectionate designation. But the Rembarrnga named were not party to the jokes, and, while time may have eroded the negative meanings, in recent years such names are often rejected as the contemptuous connotations come to be understood. The names they had replaced are re-emerging, with renewed meanings and different usages. Aboriginal names which were once a secreted clue to a protected personal identity are now openly used in official discussion and documents.

When Ronnie Martin, son of Bulman Paddy, one of the first workers at Mainoru, tells of the early Mainoru days, he implicitly questions the legitimacy of European ownership. 'Andy Ray started that place. Just bush house. He used to have a lot of blackfella. Blackfella started that place. Blackfella area. It's really on the end of Arnhem Land. Mainoru is really on blackfella area (1987)'.

Ronnie is asserting not only that the land was owned before but also that the state has affirmed Arnhem Land as Aboriginal country, and further, that the labour which originally made the station was Aboriginal labour. Such claims have only been articulated in the recent past, partly because, in Rembarrnga conceptions, the land always remained 'blackfella land'. Whitefellas, insofar as they knew of such beliefs, denied that they were anything more than quaint naivete. Willy Jailama Martin also recalled the work as giving rights to the station:

> A lot of Aboriginal people make that station. Well, what happened in the early days was that me and my sister [Nelly] were born at Mainoru and my father was building the yards for the first white man after Billy Farrar, before Jack McKay. I was told by my father, not only himself but a lot of people came from Goyder River, Arnhem Land group of people.
>
> They never used to speak English, only finger talk telling them to work. Just hand talk, telling them, you chop wood, you get water. My father used to work, everybody used to work, building house, butcher shop. Only one European could not do all that building that's been done. He must have help. All the stations had a lot Aboriginal people making those stations.
>
> No money. Only free rations, sugar, tea, flour, tobacco, or something like two bob, one shilling, five shilling (1989).

Race relations were also labour relations, and the dispassionate ordering of labour was one concern of the state's administrative policies and practices which were increasingly inserted into the relationship between Aborigines and pastoralists.

THE PRIMITIVE PAST AND PROLETARIAN FUTURE

The protectors, the police and later the patrol officers had the responsibility of enforcing the rule of humanitarian law and bureaucratic order in the pastoral industry. The archives contain records of policy debates, of disputing administrators and of the everyday problems of enforcing the will of legislators on their officers and on the populace. Here the constructions and confusions of the workings of state power are exposed. The first protector's instructions in 1864 were: 'To win the confidence and respect of Aborigines and make them aware of their legal rights as British subjects, as well as to prevent sexual intercourse with them or the sale of liquor to them; and to use the law against settlers who ill treated them' (SA Parliamentary Papers cited in Rowley 1972a:211).[5]

'Better Black Men'

The state wanted Aborigines to be recognised for their potential. They were to be wooed initially in order that they could understand their place in civil society and be protected from the dangers they might encounter from settlers.

Ordinances set out the legal basis for ruling the natives. The Aboriginal Ordinance of 1911 was replaced by the 1918 Ordinance which remained in force through a series of amendments until repealed by the Welfare Ordinance of 1953. A series of regulations enhanced their effects. The Ordinances were directed first to defining Aborigines, usually as 'aboriginal natives' (McCorquodale 1985:25), but the purpose of this definition was to draw a line between those inside and outside the category: in other words, to specify whether only 'full bloods' were 'aboriginal natives' or whether 'half-castes' and other fractions, and 'civilised Aborigines' would be included (McCorquodale 1985; Rowley 1972a:341ff). This task proved to be an ever more complicated one of deciding what various degrees and types of hybridity meant, and there were challenges and changes over the years.[6] The other aim of the Ordinances was to regulate interaction with whites. To this end they allowed for the mapping of areas for Aborigines and areas forbidden to them. They made sexual contact between Aborigines and non-Aborigines illegal. They provided for the licensing of persons to employ Aborigines. They named the person in charge of implementing these laws the Chief Protector of Aborigines and specified his responsibilities. The term 'Protector' was intended to refer to the protection of Aborigines, but the notion of protection is deeply ambiguous. Both informally and in law it was recognised that white miners and cattlemen were to be protected from black 'depredations', in the early years at least. Further there was a covert recognition that it was the savagery of 'civilised' white men from whom Aborigines had to be protected. Finally, it is apparent, though unstated, that Aborigines were to be protected, not just from white men but also from themselves. It is this latter form of protection which saw the gradual development of a whole array of practices and programs which were to re/order Aborigines' bodies, subjectivities and relationships.

The recognition that some white men represented a threat to Aborigines may seem to destabilise the positioning of all white people as having legitimate authority over all black people. The threat was averted by defining certain white men as low or immoral; that is, civilisation's failures. These men were to be controlled through the techniques of protection; they were to be refused licences to employ Aborigines. Such discourse and techniques of protection did not emanate from the whitefellas in the bush, and, of course, were not generated from the black victims' complaints. The discourse and the authority to act on it came from the centres of state power and were part of a wider program of domestication and normalisation (Foucault 1977; Morris 1989:129). It was exercised most directly by the police and by the protectors, who were replaced by patrol officers in the 1940s.

Aborigines' position as 'natives' within nature and close to the land could be easily transposed to an association with pastoralism. Their labour became naturalised as an organic part of the cattle industry, and stockwork was thus more natural than mining for Aborigines. One protector said: '[T]he blacks working on the wolfram field . . . are not in a natural state and I do not think that the environment is good enough for them . . . they are much better off in the stock work' (F1 49/532 May 1944).

But the state did not envisage Aborigines' position as static. The link between Aborigines and the land was to be maintained as a stage between the primordial past and the proletarian future. From the 1920s politicians and bureaucrats repeated endless assertions about the linear progression that was believed to be taking place: 'The natives need continued protection meantime until they can emerge from the primitive state to enter the ordinary Australian community' (F1 52/1118). This emergence from one state of being and entering into another was to be managed so as to facilitate the inevitable evolutionary progress towards modernity. Thus, in one form or another, the eventual assimilation of the Aboriginal people into the culture and structure of the nation was always the policy of the state. There were other images and theories such as 'smoothing the dying pillow' of the 'full-bloods' and 'breeding out the colour' from the 'half-castes', but while these provide important insights into the racial forms of Australian society of the early and mid-twentieth century, they did not, at least in the Territory, form the basis of any ongoing policies. Thus I would argue that while the state supported neither violence nor physical genocide, it did deny the legitimacy of an Aboriginal community with a different social system. A separate social body with some other cultural form inside the nation but outside the sphere called 'civilisation' was never imagined.

Exactly how the process of changing Aborigines was to proceed remained vague, though the rhetoric of 'training' began to emerge. The 'natural' relationship with stockwork was to be enhanced. 'Better Black Men' was the heading for a report on a scheme for the 'betterment of Australia's aboriginals', and in it the Interior Minister is reported to have said, 'I do not propose to educate them as bachelors of arts and barristers but as good stockmen and men of the land as they are meant by Nature' (NTTG 1929). Beswick Creek Native Settlement was eventually established for this purpose by the Native Affairs Branch in 1947, but it did not produce a body of native stockmen, partly because most stations trained their own stockmen in the way Farrar did Bandicoot, by putting them in the saddle as children.[7] Nor was Beswick ever profitable, a fact the administration blamed variously on the workers, the weather and the managers. However it served other functions, such as providing a place of exile for 'troublesome natives' from Darwin, and as a site where the Darwin Administration could develop its techniques of re-ordering Aborigines' lives, particularly around housing and provisioning of the residents.

Beswick also played its part in mediating Aborigines' service to anthropology, with Bill Harney arranging for the anthropologist Elkin to break his journey there on his 1948 visit to Mainoru. The manager reported a later visit with satisfaction: 'Professor Elkin and his party of scientists were camped to the east of the settlement. They were moving to Mainoru with [patrol officer] Mr. Ryan on 31st May. Mr. Ryan is co-operating well with the party' (F1 52/775 June 1952). Elkin worked with Rembarrnga people in the 1940s and '50s, and in the 1960s some Rembarrnga residents of Beswick worked with Ken Maddock (Maddock 1977; Maddock 1982).

Poor pastoralists

Pastoralism was a brave, dangerous and new adventure for many of the Europeans involved and they were remaking themselves as well as remaking the world about them. In the early decades of this century, pastoralists were largely able to determine their relations with Aborigines, while governments protested at violence and inhumanity when it came to their notice. There was great variation between particular stations and in the extent to which the policing function of the state was brought to bear on them. Many managers of pastoral properties built their power around a mixture of gifts and the law of the gun. In this cultural mystique of power these men could claim superior authority stemming from their experiential knowledge which, many said, had convinced them of the need for more coercive race relations than government policy allowed. The pragmatic local techniques for managing Aborigines were seen by the state as arbitrary and despotic, and in need of replacing by a bureaucratic order which would control race relations through formal rules and obligations.

It is now well known that there was coercion, persecution and exploitation of Aboriginal people on many pastoral stations, conditions which have often been understood simply in terms of economic rationality or economic necessity. Such explanations do no justice to the lived reality of station life or to the dreams of the owners. There were of course immediate financial reasons for local managers coercing Aborigines into work, underpaying and undersupplying them with rations, and exaggerating the numbers once the NAB started funding the upkeep of station communities. This was a custom commonly known as 'nigger farming', one owner saying that Aboriginal pensioners 'were better than cattle' (Peterson 1985:88; Stevens 1974:90, 180). But such economic rationality fails to account for either the kindness and solicitude we will explore below, or for the gratuitous cruelty that has been revealed in historical research of recent years (Berndt & Berndt 1987; May 1994; Millis 1992; Read & Read 1991; Reid 1990; Reynolds 1981; Rose 1991).[8] At one station in the 1950s, Aborigines who prepared the household food were not allowed to use the tap water that supplied the homestead, so were forced to use the horses' trough for washing and drinking water (Berndt & Berndt 1987:79). Financial advantage can hardly explain this carelessness concerning the hygiene of house servants or the starving of Aboriginal workers, let alone the murderous savagery often meted out ostensibly to protect the cattle. There is no indication of the prevailing pedagogic humanitarianism in these harsh regimes. They made no attempt to reform the people. A narrow notion of 'economic interests' has never been sufficient to explain the movements of capital and is certainly not able alone to account for the violence of colonial repression (Morris 1989; Taussig 1980).

Rather than evidence of the profit motive or some other form of self-interest or moral depravity, such inhumanity may be grounded in a deeper awareness that Aborigines' existence was in symbolic opposition to the system that was being established. Perhaps such pastoralists recognised and feared an integrity among Aborigines, an alternative state of moral being that was the negation of their own. The basis of Aborigines' life in this country was the antithesis of one based on the private ownership of country, on individualism and the nuclear family, and on hierarchical human relations. An example is the fear engendered in pastoralists by reciprocity, and the state's recognition that a system of reciprocity was dangerous because it seemed to have no limits (Rowse 1998:28–31). Violence then could be seen as stemming from the invader's conception of the other's alterity as inseparable from their very existence and as a threat that had to be removed.[9] Those who practised violence wanted to use, but not to change, the Aborigines, who they denied were susceptible to a pedagogic regime. In contrast, the benign humanitarians, including state officials, denied others the right to exist as *other*; they preserved life in order to transform it.

Pastoral conditions were not preordained by the colonial order, and station communities resulted from a series of contingent and disputed events composed of the desire and striving, hope and disappointment of particular individuals, new and old owners. When Andy Ray used his mining profits to buy a half-share of Mainoru from Billy Farrar in 1924, he founded a dynasty. Perhaps 'dynasty' is too grand a term for a tin prospector who struck it lucky, and his young nephew Jack McKay who was in turn joined by most of his natal family, and a niece who eventually inherited and sold the property in 1969 (figure 3). But the importance of this particular family to the local people was immense, as they came to possess and then sell this land, transforming the lives of all involved. Over a period of 50 years a

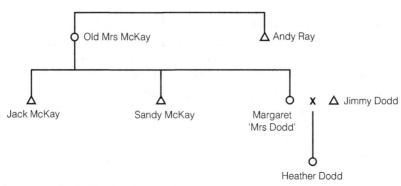

Figure 3　Andy Ray's 'dynasty'

kinship-linked group of Rembarrnga and Ngalkbon people of all ages had the margins of their land invaded, and some were enticed to join the enterprise of a family of white people, with consequences for their future that they could not have imagined. Though Jack McKay's family was limited in size, they brought guns, writing and laws, and an absolute conviction that, in the human race, they were ahead of the natives. Rembarrnga people may in general have conceded the superiority of the invaders' knowledge, but they certainly did not conceive of a hierarchy of human groups engaged in a race through time.

Far from a wealthy pastoral property, Mainoru, like many stations in the Territory, was a marginal concern run by marginal men. The tin prospector's cash infusion was used to pay arrears of rental (Forrest 1989:16). Jack McKay was only sixteen when he first left the Maranboy tin mine with his uncle Andy Ray to join Billy Farrar at Mainoru (H. Dodd pers. com.). In the 1930s Jack became a partner. He was the boss by 1943 and the sole owner in 1947. When there was profit there were demands for investment in yards, fences, vehicles and equipment. Jack's house still had dirt floors when Elkin visited in the 1940s. Cement floors were eventually put in by his brother-in-law. Jack McKay indulged in frequent tots of rum, but there seem to have been few other material rewards, either in terms of consumption or capital accumulation. In the 1950s Jack's niece Heather Dodd was clad in clothes made from flour bags. Heather told me that 'by the time our grandmother made my shirts and our sheets out of the flour bags there was nothing left for the Aboriginal kids' (interview 1988). The strong cotton fabric was often put to such use in rural areas. The station was in debt when sold in 1969 after Jack McKay's death.

Professor Elkin, who held the Chair of Anthropology at the University of Sydney from 1933 to 1956, visited the Northern Territory each year from 1946 to 1949 and again in 1952. With Jack McKay's cooperation, and the assistance of Patrol Officers Bill Harney, Raymond Evans and Ron Ryan, Mainoru was one of Elkin's research sites and his visits culminated in a five-week expedition to record 'chants' and ceremonies at Mainoru and Beswick in 1949 (Elkin 1961). Elkin's diary contains comments on Jack McKay, emphasising his historic role in relation to Aborigines:

> At night there is radio, electric light and kerosene refrigerator. Thus the modern world comes to the heart of Arnhem Land. A quarter mile away the sticks tap, the Bungal is sung and feet stamp as the primitive meets the meta-modern. The settler is between . . . gone primitive, no sheets, enamel mugs and plate and a few cracked china cups and plates but plenty to eat (Elkin papers, box 16, transcript:119).

Here Elkin reproduces the popular, reified dichotomy between the primitive and the modern. He affirms the universal historical trajectory from one to the other, with its minor interruptions. This poor pastoralist was in danger of abandoning his civilising mission by 'going native', like the 'feral pastoralists' (Rowse 1998:121) who were the focus of administrative disapproval and public scorn. The paraphernalia of sheets and proper china are the material markers of the direction of evolutionary change. Without them the settler is 'in between' or 'gone primitive'. 'Civilisation' is nothing without its physical accoutrements, and it was only when Jack was joined by his female kin in the following years that Mainoru began to fully take up its proper historical function of introducing civilised practices, both by example and tutelage, to the Aboriginal population. Mainoru then fulfilled that task so well that administrators in Darwin considered it a model for others to emulate, the ideal owner–manager relationship with the 'natives'. The difference is noted in Elkin's comment on his third visit that 'the men cannot just walk into the house as in Jack's day when goats and all walked in' (Elkin's papers, box 16:120).

Elkin's work had the scholarly purpose of recording and analysing the ceremonial life of a people who he defined as remote in time and space from the taken-for-granted arena of modernity. His article 'Maraian at Mainoru, 1949' (1960–61), parts 1 and 2, detailed careful observations, information, interpretation and speculation about elusive meanings of the Maraian ceremony. He recorded the different versions of the myths given by the oldest men, Bulman Paddy, Old Jack, Kundamara and Milirbom. He carefully spelled out the terms and places of greatest significance and identified the major themes and the relationships between kin, clan, myth, country, species and ritual. He admitted to baffling, contradictory and unresolved aspects of what he observed or was told, and offered tentative interpretations of some aspects of the ritual and its meaning. He relished the future possibilities of tape recording which would allow informants to give 'free' statements in their own language, overcoming the problems of accurately writing down what was said. Elkin's account of the Maraian demonstrates a commitment to ethnography, and also shows the complexity, mundanity and difficulty of anthropological field work. He tried to focus directly on this quite other domain of meaning and to explain what the Rembarrnga men were doing and how they wanted it to be understood. But the contrast between this article and Elkin's more public pronouncements make it clear that understanding and respect for the Aboriginal classical realm was expected to remain the provenance of a few specialists.

The scientific work of collecting exotic knowledge was accomplished through the cooperation of patrol officers, pastoralists and anthropologists with their common interest in Aborigines. Elkin's working relationship with Jack McKay illustrates the unity of the 'civilised' in their dealings with 'primitive man'. Elkin saw himself and his task as representing the 'meta-modern'. But Jack's task and techniques were also modern. Even the poorest pastoralists were introducing a complex and specialised technology, not just in the form of electricity generators and kerosene refrigerators but fences and spades, houses and saddles, paper and money, to mention only material technologies. And it was not only the anthropologist who wrote the Aborigines down. The humble pen allowed a most powerful form of knowledge to expand, that is the recording of peoples' 'particulars'. Though only very specific and perhaps superficial details such as bestowed name, immediate relatives, presumed age and place of residence were recorded by state officials, this work was enclosing Aborigines' lives in a net of knowledge owned by others. Rembarrnga people remained largely unaware of its existence, though they became aware of its effects.

One of the first patrol officer's reports recorded the isolation of Mainoru: 'there are only two men on the station and one of them is a half-caste' (F1 52/759 1946). The comment that 'only' two 'men' were at the station established civilisation's vulnerability in the face of the many 'natives' who are thus placed outside the category 'men'. The half-caste was Billy Moore who was 'declared exempt' from the Ordinance and who is said to have owned Mountain Valley station and lost it in a poker game.[10] The outback, the home and security of Aborigines, was perceived by the state officials as a place of isolation and danger for civilised whites, who nonetheless were creating enclaves for the establishment of an inevitable modernity. Their contemporary forms of social life would enable Aborigines to begin the mimetic process necessary for their future. A group of Rembarrnga formed a 'blacks' camp' on the station and, as they put it, 'learned' tobacco and tea, English and work, and supplied their visiting kin with those things they began to need. Many of these relatives remained quite free of station life, continuing to come and go from their country to the north, which was designated as the Arnhem Land Reserve in 1931. The protection from commercial exploitation that this reservation gave has been of immense significance to the people of this area.

Ronnie Buck's account of the seductive nature of tobacco and other 'good things' was quoted above. He continued:

Not only that but sugar, first time people taste different thing from any bush tucker . . .

'Where you get this from?' . . .

'Well we got this from a place called Mainoru . . .'

So one or many people, tribe—get a taste of that thing tucker, or damper, all travel . . . Even though they was told there was white bloke, different from us and a lot of the people was still frightened. They could tell the difference because of strange language, wearing clothes, even though there was a lot of [Rembarrnga] family there, working there (1989).

Ronnie Buck's view that people overcame the fear of *mununga* to satisfy the attraction of 'different thing' could be seen as confirming the image of Aborigines as victims of their desires, an image perpetrated by colonial discourse. But in this self-representation, desire is not to be repressed and reproved, but recognised and affirmed as both a source of vulnerability and of humorous comment on the vicissitudes of life. He further explained the strategies for gaining access to these things without becoming subject to whitefellas:

What usually happened was, if people want to get some more tobacco, they used to wait around till late in the night. During the day they used to stay out where they thought no white going in that direction or mainly just roaming around where there's a lot of scrub. If ever they want anything they used to sneak up, say one family sneak up. Tell other family. Count the day.

'Give me four days, and I'll come back sometime in the night and get some more.'

Some of this Kriol talk you know. Next time if white man catch 'im, all the *mununga* come up . . . We been between Mainoru and Mountain Valley, just hiding, you know going round from place to place until I was say one and half year old.

This is what used to happen (1989).

When Ronnie Buck comments that when they 'get a taste of that thing . . . all travel', he is on the one hand proffering an explanation of the predicament his parents found themselves in. But he is also recounting, as a source of entertainment and enlightenment, the story of the weakness for sugar, damper or tobacco, and their resulting plight. Stories which entail frights and plights experienced by members of the community are a major form of conversation and entertainment. Rembarrnga understand the dilemmas of individuals caught between desire and danger as fundamental themes in human experience.

Native depredations

There was a flurry of concern in 1947 when Jack McKay wrote to the Director of Native Affairs to complain about the 'losses in cattle . . . through the depredations of natives. Last year I counted 27 head of fat bullocks which had been speared. In addition they dammed the main channel of Mainoru spring which runs through my bullock paddock, thereby causing me a loss of between 700 and 800 head by bogging' (52/759 1947).

Jack McKay had been at Mainoru for twenty years and had just become sole owner. His complaints have an air of exasperation, yet also an acceptance that 'the natives' are there and are a normal part of the environment. He went on: 'The natives are entitled to one dog a head but they have many more. An average of 50 aged and infirm natives are living on my property, and I am keeping them. At times there are up to 300 natives on the station' (ibid.).

His exasperation resulted from the inability to keep the 'boys' separate from the 'myalls'. The core residential group supplied the essential labour of stockmen and house workers, and were an organic part of the station's existence. But its members had 'myall' relations, who, as Ronnie Buck showed, visited and sometimes stayed. The station's struggle to establish this dichotomy continued for years.

Patrol Officer Evans investigated what was called 'cattle-killing by myall natives infiltrating into [McKay's] property from the Arnhem Land Reserve' and 'interference by natives with the water-channels feeding the Mainoru River' (F1 42/367 1947). The patrol did not manage to contact the 'nomads', but found that '[t]he barrier erected by the natives was very elaborate', with long stakes holding paperbark in place. The patrol officer's lack of any recognition of the social domain of the Rembarrnga is clear in his report:

> The only reason I can suggest that prompted the natives to go to so much trouble was to facilitate the catching of fish . . . they had ample time to operate, as Mr. McKay and his head stockman were both away for a period of nine weeks on a fencing job on the far boundaries of the property. Intensive questioning of the natives working on the station elicited no information as to the likely culprits, although I feel that the natives concerned are known to the station hands . . . Mr. McKay is of the definite opinion that the natives responsible for the cattle-killing and channel blocking are nomads living in the escarpment, Bulman waterhole and Wilton River areas.

He concluded:

> I feel certain that the visit and patrol will have a salutary moral effect insomuch as those responsible for the offence will doubtless learn, if they do not already know, of our presence and interest in their misdeeds . . . I made it very clear to the station natives, their dependants and other walkabout natives at present on the station, that the trouble has got to stop and that drastic steps would have to be taken if further bad reports are received from Mr. McKay. These natives promised to tell any nomadic tribes who they might meet on walkabout (ibid.).

I have no doubt (but no direct evidence) that the patrol officer's speech evoked both fear and hilarity among 'the station natives', who probably mimicked his solemn instructions in the camp. They would have recognised his view of themselves as more malleable than their cunning and recalcitrant relations. As with the explorer Lindsay's report 50 years earlier, this report shows no recognition that it is the colonisers who are intruding on a society for whom 'channel blocking' is an ordinary means of subsistence. The indigenous population is construed as intruding, with their disruptive and illegal practices, into the pastoralist's space. They are discursively placed in the civil, moral realm of whites, but as wilfully ignoring its rules. The desires and practices of 'the culprits' are frustrating, interfering with their own and our future. Unlike the explorer, the patrol officer speaks with openly tutelary intent, placing the whole of the 'nomadic tribes' and 'walkabout natives' in a position of naughty children who will be constrained by his superior authority.

Evans recommended a further patrol in the Bulman area to 'pin-point the camps of nomadic tribes to a few remaining waterholes'. Further 'contact with these little known tribes is of interest also from an anthropological point of view, and a peaceful excursion into their country may meet with greater success than one in which the police are interested' (F1 42/367 1947).

The interest of 'little known tribes' to anthropologists alludes to Aborigines as a curiosity for the academic discipline of anthropology to record and explain to the nation. Jack McKay, who mustered cattle with Rembarrnga men and women, could not know them as 'nomadic tribes', that is anthropologically, but only as individuals with certain problematic racial characteristics such as the habit of 'intruding' onto his property. These intrusions, McKay complained, created an economic burden for him. His Darwin solicitor Mr Coop wrote to the Director of Native Affairs (DNA) concerning:

> The natives who are camped near his homestead in fairly large numbers and for whom no provision is made for supplies of flour, tea, sugar tobacco or beef. They are camped in a separate area from the natives who are employed by Mr. McKay and they are entirely dependent on him . . . there are about 100 males, females and children, the number having increased since the visit of your Mr. Evans . . . a few months ago. This increase appears to have been brought about by a number of natives having left the Maranboy Settlements . . . a fair proportion of the males are aged and sick and quite unable to perform any work (F1 52/759 Sept. 1947).

The Director, Mr Moy, immediately apologised and acceded to McKay's implied requests that some provision be made for the 'congregating natives'. A note ordered that 1000 pounds of flour, 140 pounds of tea and three bags of sugar be dispatched. The rations were to assist Mr McKay in 'feeding the people who have congregated around his homestead'. Further, Moy wrote, 'As all my patrol officers are absent on duty I am unable to take steps to disperse the gathering but will do so immediately an officer is available.' 'Dispersal' did not here have the brutal connotations it did elsewhere (Reid 1990). In January 1948 the NAB issued 31 ration cards to named Mainoru residents who were defined as the dependants of workers in a vain and soon abandoned attempt to distinguish them from the 'myalls'.

This wholehearted acceptance of the duty to provide sustenance for Aborigines was more than a humanitarian response to need. It also heralded the beginning of the era of government rationing. Jack McKay found the requests of many people who were apparently hungry[11] difficult to ignore, and the government was beginning to accept the responsibility of provisioning the dispossessed throughout the Territory by funding the regular supply of rations (Rowse 1998). But the Rembarrnga people had not been dispossessed of land, though part of their country had been invaded. In public and official government discourse there was no recognition that Aboriginal people had been living independent of flour, tea and sugar for centuries. Nor was Arnhem Land conceived as an economically and socially autonomous domain despite its designation as an Aboriginal reserve. Nomadic hunter–gatherers' lives were not viewed as a valid form of existence in the contemporary world. This was so, not only due to the spectre of dispersed, unsupervised natives hunting cattle instead of kangaroos. A more profound judgement deemed all Aborigines in their nomadic state as indigent, unable to care for themselves.

Dorothy Murray recalled the 'myalls' as creating a dilemma for the Mainoru residents. She spoke of Jack's brother Sandy McKay:

> That man was a really rough one you know. When they used to make trouble he used to fire shot. Fire over head to frighten people. For anything. Sometimes they [myalls] used to go along and kill his bullocky, Sandy McKay used to reckon. That's why he used to go mad to all them people. Poor bugger, they been making me sorry too. Everybody couldn't say nothing. We can't stop them and that man used to say, 'I know when they get hungry they'll killem.' Jack used to blame them people too (1983).

Dorothy believes that even though Jack and Sandy McKay understood that 'people' (relatives who were not usually resident at the station) would kill bullocks when they were hungry, they still blamed them and fired shots to frighten them. She and other station people couldn't say anything because it was true; still, he should not have shot at them.

Four years later, another cattle spearing story emerged which illustrates the bizarre and humorous qualities that denizens of the outback love to emphasise. A dramatic headline in the Melbourne *Herald* in September 1952 announced: 'STARVING ARNHEM LAND NATIVES SPEAR 200 HEAD OF CATTLE ON MAINORU STATION'. Anxious telegrams flew backwards and forwards between Darwin and the Minister for

Territories in Canberra. Jack McKay was in Katherine and was astonished to hear the story on the morning radio. No-one seemed to know where the news had come from. Finally the patrol officer concluded: 'It is common knowledge that Mr McKay is very garrulous when in town. He is a popular man and his friends don't take much notice of some of his conversation: however, it appears that a reporter must have taken his words literally' (F1 52/759).

The 'reporter' was the Magistrate's Clerk who had been at the pub with Jack and had sent the story to Melbourne from the Katherine post office. Jack had forgotten the stories he had recounted in the pub. The power of the newspaper account drew on the stereotypes circulating in the public domain, distorting the reality of Mainoru.

Jack McKay was well known as a rum drinker, and on his trips into Katherine his story telling entertained many. One of his old Rembarrnga employees Peter Lee recalled, 'Oh old Jack McKay drink any kind, rum, anything. Poor fella.' Paddy Cavanagh, a white stockman who once worked at Mainoru, told me:

> Old Jack was a wonderful little fellow. He certainly wasn't what I'd call a wonderful stockman. He was comical, had a split lip. Cleft palate. Unfortunately when he'd go into the pub and get drunk he'd start to sing. A great spray would come out, everybody would duck. But he was a pretty good old worker, you know (1989).

A popular song by singer–songwriter and outback identity Ted Egan about the 'bloody good drinkers in the Northern Territory' has a verse describing Jack McKay's travelling habits:

> Jack McKay used to measure the bogs on the road to Mainoru,
> By the number of bottles of OP rum it'd take him to drink his
>   way through,
> His best was a twenty-seven bottler in a wet when you'd bog a duck,
> But it didn't worry Jack on the Mainoru track, he kept bellowin' out
>   'Good luck'.

Tex Camfoo took part in Jack McKay's adventures on the Mainoru track where the wet season renders dirt roads impassable for several weeks every summer:

> Old Jack McKay used to say, 'I'll go into town and get us Christmas supplies.' We never used to have Christmas at the right time. We always had it about two weeks after because he was bogged out of sight. He'd

go and get a few beers and O.P. rum, State Express. Then Jimmy Dodd would ring up the Cox' shop [in Katherine].

'Jack left yet?'

'Oh, he left about, oh, four days ago!'

'Oh, he'll be halfway home now. Right oh, pack your gear up and get tucker and we'll go and look for him.' And it took us about couple of days before we'd get to Jack. He knew that we would come looking. There he is, bogged down, laying down, with a bottle of rum at his side there. He told us, 'Have a nip.'

Then me and Jimmy Dodd, we end up getting drunk with all this Christmas supplies on board! They were waiting for us for Christmas!

Anyway, it took us about three days to get home from there. It was only about sixty miles out he was bogged. Oh, water all over the place. Some places, we used to have half a day putting timber across the bog-hole so they can get across. Luckily we had two vehicles: the old International and he had a Connel three tonner.

I used to love it you know, in my young days. When we got there, 'He's all in one piece. Half of the beer's gone!' (1993).

The humorous acceptance of Jack's foibles makes an interesting contrast to the lessons about responsibility towards money, goods and alcohol that have for decades been so patiently and impatiently conveyed to Rembarrnga people by whitefellas, and which have been the basis of endless judgements of the moral worth of Aborigines (Langton 1997).

Despite Jack's casual management practices, the comings and goings of his workers' relatives between Arnhem Land and the station were a continuing source of annoyance to him as well as to the patrol officers and the NAB in Darwin. Rembarrnga people refused to recognise the crucial distinction between those who belonged to the station and those who did not. In 1950 Patrol Officer Ryan saw 'over ninety strangers' in the 'blacks' camp'. But in 1951 a corroboree took place somewhere between Mainoru and Roper Valley station and both 'strangers' and 'station natives' were gone. The only people Ryan found in the camp were 'the aged and infirm and four employees' (F1 52/759 Sept. 1951). These nomadic habits were seen as hangovers from a past which was in the process of fading away, disappearing under the mantle of modernity. The anthropologist's work could perhaps have discouraged this fading process. Elkin sometimes used informants' English names (Paddy Bulman, Lame Jack), and sometimes Rembarrnga names (Milirbom, Kundamara), thus blurring the distinction between 'boys' and 'myalls'. His interest in the classical Aboriginal tradition could have been seen as reviving what was dying, and reversing the historical movement being promoted by the state and the industry. Perhaps the notorious hostility of pastoralists to anthropologists (Berndt & Berndt 1987) stems from this threat. But far from any complaint being made about Elkin's party, assistance was offered by the NAB, and the Mainoru owners welcomed him. Here, the scientific study being pursued by anthropologists rose above the pragmatic needs of the pastoral industry because it contributed to the higher purpose of civilisation's authoritative knowledge of the primitive.

To enhance their control, the NAB considered establishing a government station in the Bulman area to serve southern Arnhem Land. 'Their country' became 'our Reserve north of Mainoru [which] has undoubted possibilities for exploitation' (F1 42/367 May 1947). Patrol Officer Ryan suggested that 'the McKay brothers are quite capable of administering properly an Aged and Infirm Depot' (F1 52/579 1948), at which those not working would be designated as aged or infirm and be fed government rations. But no depot was established, and two years later Jack McKay offered to sell Mainoru for £20,000 to the NAB. The Branch spoke of the station's 'strategic position to control one of the major drift lines from the Arnhem Land Reserve'. Further: 'The Government ownership of [Mainoru] Station would complete the encirclement of the Reserve by control, protective and welfare agencies for the aboriginal inhabitants, prevent the present serious drift from the Reserve and permit the extension of developmental activities into the Reserve' (F1 52/579 June & Aug. 1951).

But when McKay put the price up to £25,000 the Branch changed its mind and instead suggested a pastoral holding at Bulman waterhole in the interests of the natives, as Patrol Officer Ryan had suggested:

> It is a natural and traditional area for aborigines . . . *a stricter control of their movements would be more beneficial to the breeding of cattle.* [The country to the north] was equally as good as Mainoru station and I could not help but feel that it is being *wasted* by being included in an aboriginal reserve . . . It is possible that the *development of the NT* may be retarded by the retention of the Arnhem Land Reserve in its present size and further, it is also possible that the *development of the aborigines* themselves is, at least, not expedited by the isolation associated with such a vast block of country (F1 52/579 Sept. 1951, emphasis added).

The language of the patrol officer here reproduces the opposition between the natural and traditional on the one hand, and control and development on the other. The former is associated with waste and with leaving both the country and the Aborigines 'isolated' and stagnating in the past. There is an explicit link between the development of a modern pastoral industry and the modernisation of Aboriginal people. A further step towards this future came with the entrenchment of the system of regular provision of rations to 'tribal dependants', a practice which advanced the persistent attempts to have Aborigines congregate at missions and stations. If they could be induced to stay still, their difference could be masked by the enforcing of 'normal' habits and practices in everyday life.

An insight into the daily life of Mainoru is provided by the diary that Jack McKay's brother Sandy kept in the early 1950s (NTAS). He made a detailed record of mundane work and comings and goings, in which visitors appear with surprising frequency. These include state officials, surveyors, people from other stations, travellers to the Bulman minesite, and contractors or stockmen working on the station. Most visitors were named as 'Mr', occasionally with a 'Mrs', while the handful of household members are identified by first name. The work is recorded as 'Tex and boys left for the stock camp. Jack on truck.' Bandy and Larry are named once, but otherwise 'boys' are virtually absent. One could read the entries in this diary for 1952 and remain unaware that there were at least 50 and sometimes 150 Aboriginal people living and working on the station. The significance of their presence is only apparent in all the fencing, yard building and mustering that was recorded. The relationship with these black pastoral and domestic workers and fellow residents in this isolated place was taken for granted, at once intimate and distant.

Nelly Camfoo says that about this time she ran away from her job at Beswick where she had worked for Mr Frazer-Allen of the Native Affairs Branch. She took her young sister Dorothy and walked back to Mainoru. When she arrived Sandy McKay said 'that young girl's a good sort' and told her to come up to the house to work. The policeman and Frazer-Allen came from Beswick looking for her:

> They found me right there in the house.
>
> 'We want you back. The manager wants to take you to Adelaide.'
>
> He liked me. If I'd have gone I'd have to go *mununga* way altogether. I wouldn't know blackfellas today. I'd be wearing high heels, socks and boots, everything. But we didn't want to. They asked Jack McKay and he said, 'You can't take that girl. She's already working. You can't take her off the job.' Good job too. I had good *binji* [literally stomach; a

good feeling]. I was really pleased when he said that. Well I told that policeman, 'I'm sorry. I can't go back with you,' and I told that manager too (1976).

Like Bandicoot Robinson, Nelly took pride in knowing herself to be a good worker, appreciated and protected by the whites she worked for. Here is a changing sense of self in response to affirmation from whites whose powerful judgements constituted an irresistible force in reforming subjectivities, one all the more effective because of the more usual negative judgements about the Aboriginal realm and the lack of appreciation of any independent Aboriginal agency. That is, individuals could gain appreciation from whitefellas by fulfilling their expectations, supplying their needs or furthering their enterprises.[12]

EXPERTS

There was a more serious level of public debate about 'our' responsibilities and 'their' racial characteristics which appealed to the nation's experts. In the 1920s typical comments were: 'higher authorities predict [Aborigines] dying out'; 'nothing can save those who have run their course . . . we may be able to treat our natives a little more kindly since they won't trouble us long'; 'Our first duty is to protect them from degradation brutalisation and abuse'; 'learned brains must now protect [natives] and fit them for their coming struggle with fierce civilisation'; 'You cannot convert a primitive race into a civilised race. It is against nature . . . if it were not for hypocrisy, that would be faced . . . and the dying pillow smoothed' (NTTG). The form of knowledge appealed to in this debate did not come from experience but from abstract formulations.[13]

Two realms where systematic knowledge of Aborigines was being constructed were in the academy and the bureaucracy. Like cattlemen, anthropologists relied on 'being there', but their manner of interacting with Aborigines was based on quite different principles. They would study Aboriginal social organisation by enlisting Aborigines' cooperation as informants. Elkin typified this task with the publication of his academic article 'Maraian at Mainoru' in the journal *Oceania* (1961). While based on careful observation and information from Rembarrnga people, the only hint of the contemporary conditions of the event was provided by the names of two informants, 'Paddy Bulman' and 'Old Lame Jack'.

On the other hand, the administrators' knowledge of the natives they were re/forming into workers was not based on direct interaction. They took for granted the generally accepted principles of social evolution, and occasionally and selectively conferred with anthropologists about specific characteristics of Aboriginal belief or practice. The general form of the state's understanding of its task came from the long history of British colonial administration. It was governed by principles such as that enunciated by Cromer who said that the British administration should 'in the light of western knowledge and experience, tempered by local considerations' do what we think is best for the subject race without consideration of British advantage (Said 1985b:37). A 'collective imperial knowledge' was shared among colonising powers (Stoler & Cooper 1997:13). The Native Affairs Branch even showed an interest in community development in Zanzibar (F1 59/3141 1955). Thus the general task of administering native peoples in the Territory of Papua and the Northern Territory for years came under the same Department of Territories (Rowley 1972a:223).[14] The administrators, unlike the rapacious, conquering first generation of colonisers, were 'well-meaning, hard-working middle-class missionaries, liberals, modernists, and believers in science, equality and progress' (Nandy 1983:xi).

The humanitarianism of colonial administrators was apparent in their alacrity in feeding the 'myalls' at Mainoru. But it was tempered by anxiety about the real nature of this particular 'subject race' because of the extreme primitivity ascribed to Aborigines. Although the complexity of their religion and social organisation was being documented by anthropologists, Aborigines were identified as the lowest race on the evolutionary scale. Stanner confessed to a rueful awareness 'of the extent to which the literature fastened on the Aborigines a reputation of extraordinary primitivity' (1979:224).[15] This perception of generic and extreme primitivity did not change for many decades and is still prevalent in some discursive domains. This may explain why little effort was made here, unlike in other colonial states, to consult the elders and promote indigenous leaders or to establish a system of indirect rule as had been the practice in India, Africa, and more recently in Papua New Guinea (cf. Lattas 1996).[16]

The administration's only direct source of knowledge of Aborigines came from the experience of the officials themselves in towns, and from the patrol officers who travelled in the bush. As we shall see below, the patrol officers' reports display a lack of attention to the specificity of Aboriginal social life, and seldom attempt to explain its particular characteristics to their superior officers. This suggests that the administration did not claim or aim to know the Aborigines as they were; what they knew was what they were to become.

Experts were often appealed to, but experts disagree. Administrators and missionaries shared a sense of responsibility for their colonial subjects, and they debated theories about social evolution, racial hierarchies and Aborigines' future. The common argument was that those at the bottom of the evolutionary scale required more effective tuition. 'The native race had all the mental equipment necessary for complete assimilation to civilisation, provided it received the necessary training' (NTTG 16 May 1924); 'While aboriginals were lowest on the scale and could not develop while nomadic, they needed to BE developed' (NTTG 1928). These statements illustrate a discursive moral realm where the white man has a responsibility to manage, not only the lives of Aborigines in the present, but the survival or the demise of their whole race, a grand and tragic scenario either way. The discourse of 'wild savages' was gradually being replaced by a popular paternalism, in which expert white men had the responsibility of knowing Aborigines and of managing them.

Despite much anthropological work being confined to arcane journals and consumed only within an academic environment, certain anthropological formulations gained a wide currency. Social evolutionary theory was virtually universally accepted, but anthropologists contributed to local understanding, for instance of why it was often unnecessary to coerce Aborigines to 'come in'. Aborigines congregating at the stations was interpreted as 'intelligent parasitism' (Elkin 1951) or 'the super waterhole' (Hamilton 1972). These concepts allowed Aborigines to be seen as simply responding naturally as hunter–gatherers to a permanent food source, with no awareness of other consequences of their actions.

Aborigines' apparent unawareness of the destructiveness which contact with whites represented was read as confirming their helplessness. Only we whites who are further on in time could perceive the dangers of a too sudden meeting with modernity. Concepts of adaptive responses, cultural fragility and linear progress are elements in the enacting of a particular pattern of race relations and concretising it in government policy. Rather than allowing for reciprocal curiosity and exchange between the newcomers and the incumbents, Aborigines were being presented with two possible roles in a 'modern' society. Those who could not be useful as labourers in the pastoral industry were encouraged to make claims on the state as a people in need. This choice is clear in relation to Mainoru, because its location on

the border of an unsettled Aboriginal domain could have been construed as an opportunity for reciprocity between equivalent human
realms. Rather it became a problem of the Aborigines' disharmony
with the industry of the pastoralist, and therefore with the state, and
this was to be resolved by enticing the Aborigines out of their
autonomous arena to become workers or dependants within the
enveloping embrace of the nation.

Popular discourse did not trouble itself with legalities but public
servants, on behalf of the state, pondered legal problems, such as those
raised by the definitions of 'married', 'native custom' and 'wife' in the
Aboriginal Ordinances. Under English common law, wives could not
be compelled to give evidence against their husbands, and courts
needed to know whether this rule applied to Aborigines. Were 'lubras'
wives? Perhaps it was not just in relation to land that Aborigines strayed
from the natural order of things but also in the realm of gender
relations? On the basis of advice gained for the purpose from Professor
Elkin, it was concluded in the 1930s that 'The legal meaning of the
word "wife" is quite foreign to the mind of an ordinary aboriginal'
(F1 38/536 1936). Not surprising perhaps, but the ease with which
such assessments of marriage and other 'customs' were proclaimed
indicates the extent to which Aborigines were becoming the property
of the state, both in the sense of state officials being responsible for
their disposal in space and also in the sense of the Aboriginal problem
being owned by governments (Cowlishaw 1994; Sansom 1985).

State officials were taking charge of this racial frontier and deciding
how the standard legal and cultural categories were to be applied to
Aborigines. They gave consideration to their capacity to be susceptible
to western legal and ethical precepts in the light of their racial and
cultural characteristics. The symbolic place of 'wild natives' as the
repository of imaginary fears and thrills, as well as their place in the
redemptive mission, was built on an understanding of their capacity
to understand. Aborigines increasingly represented a difficult otherness
to be altered as the civilising mission advanced. Taking this otherness
seriously did not involve speaking to its carriers or representatives, but
rather meant that the expert anthropologist had occasionally to be
consulted, not about the future but about what was there already. The
elite discourse of senior state officials and law makers, informed by an
international rather than a local framework, came to understand that
primitive otherness was a reality towards which the modern, internationally engaged state had to show responsibility by encouraging
specialised study by anthropologists.[17] Their own pragmatic task could

be pursued separately. A more direct connection developed later when training programs for patrol officers were conducted in the Anthropology Department at the University of Sydney through cooperation between the Department of Territories and Professor Elkin.

4

Reforming the People

I been come down, learn tucker. This flour here. New tucker. 'I'll have
to stay la this place now. You mob got a good tucker.' That's why, we
have to learn tucker, tobacco. And soft drink, them lolly water too we
drink. And tea too, we been learn that tea now.

—*Jacky Ryan, 1989*

LABOUR RELATIONS

Re-ordering the outback was a gradual, uneven and contradictory
process, and one that met with complex responses. While pastoralists
sometimes ignored and obstructed particular regulations, and often
despised the townsmen who promulgated them, they wanted the
assistance of governments and they prided themselves on their historic
role and national identity, and especially on knowing the natives. They
did know the Aborigines they worked with, sometimes as friends or
lovers, sometimes as enemies or problems, and in a multitude
of everyday interactions, but always as blackfellas, people subject to
different laws, moral, social and legal. In the first section of this chapter
I will draw attention to some features of the changing administrative
policy and practice in the first half of the twentieth century, especially
the attempt to regulate labour relations which were also race relations,

before focussing on the way these were played out at Mainoru station in 'Jack McKay time'.

Through the seemingly innocent, but culturally specific art of writing, the administration disseminated instructions to managers of pastoral stations where the Aboriginal residents were in a somewhat similar condition of encapsulation as on missions and government stations. The Native Affairs Branch (NAB) was established in Darwin in 1934, but it was not until after World War Two that the regime for monitoring interaction between the races became more explicit and more vigilant. The Director of Native Affairs (DNA), like the Chief Protector before him, often found himself awkwardly placed between the demands from the national capital in Canberra for humane modernisation, and the more urgent and confusing demands from the outback settlers for either swift justice or freedom from the law; that is, for both protection and autonomy. Licences and permits, records and accounting, rules and instructions, were promulgated in increasing detail over the next three decades, and specialist intermediaries were employed to oversee practices on the stations. For these patrol officers, the everyday objects, pen, ink and paper were the central tools of their trade.[1]

Patrol officers' reports, memos, letters and policy documents from the archives provide glimpses of the anxieties, confusions and under-lying certainties shared by men in Darwin offices, men on distant stations, as well as patrol officers who oscillated between them. The documents encoded a specific kind of power, first in the form of instructions going out and information coming in, but more funda-mentally in the language through which the outback and its people were defined. The official forms that were created to record and monitor people and events constructed a view of the outback which was employed both at the apex of the administrative structure in Darwin and at its base, on dozens of missions, government stations and pastoral stations like Mainoru. The scaffolding consisted of a set of terms, columns and categories in which people were racially either white or black, and thus managers or managed. There were columns for tribes, ages and wages, and men, women and children were arranged in families consisting of a mother, a father and their children. The categories seem natural, but they express particular beliefs about race, gender and normality, about progress through time and the development of space, beliefs which were the shared common sense of whitefellas. But Rembarrnga spoke of 'skin' and called their parallel cousins their sisters and brothers. Moreover, they camped in what appeared to be undifferentiated groups, so that they appeared to lack real families. Thus, in terms of the most primary human relations, they were construed as wanting. Furthermore, to whitefellas, they had no history.

The categories enacted by officials constructed a facade of control and a systematic relationship where what was written became what was real. Only certain things were recorded, things which the administration could make sense of and make use of, and this documentation linked the stations to the state in a mutually empowering relationship. At Mainoru, after Jack McKay was joined by his family in 1948 and 1950, the correspondence expanded far beyond the official forms, instructions and reports. Jack's brother Sandy and his sister Mrs Dodd were both trained school teachers, and the tutelary techniques of the state flourished with their support.

Permitting labour

Human labour had been dehumanised and cruelly exploited at many moments in history before pastoralists arrived in the Northern Territory, but modern, free, egalitarian and unionised Australia long kept secret the fact that, until the middle of the twentieth century, Aboriginal labour was often unpaid and sometimes brutalised as well. In the pastoral regions in the north it was recognised that Aborigines were not a barrier to pastoralism, as they had been publicly construed by earlier settlers in the south, but were a useful, indeed a crucial, source of labour for the industry.

Labour relations were first regulated through a system of permits to employ natives in the 1911 Ordinance which, with amendments, remained in place until 1968. Permits were to be granted only to 'persons of fit and proper character'. Not only was the racial hierarchy concretised, but a moral hierarchy was registered among whitefellas. The law recognised that pastoralists had different labour needs from town employers, and specific conditions were developed for miners, drovers and pastoralists. Licences specified whether 'male aboriginals only', 'female aboriginals only', or 'male and female aboriginals' could be employed. 'Native worker' was a distinct legal category and 'native workers' were excluded from the industrial awards from at least 1923 until 1968 (F1 49/574; McCorquodale 1987:28, 29; Rowley 1972a:338). The employer was responsible for them, and the employer was answerable only to the Director of Native Affairs. The impeccable logic of the labour hierarchy is evident in the rates specified in the

Pastoral Workers Award of 1919: 'Stockmen with not more than 1 working aboriginal to each white, £3.10.0. Stockmen with not more than 3 working aboriginals to each white, £3.18.0' (NTTG 25 Jan. 1919). Here the labour power of a 'working aboriginal' provides an addition to the value of a white stockman's labour as he assumes responsibility for black stockmen.

As the government extended the regulation and modernisation of racialised labour relations after World War Two, the Northern Territory Pastoral Lessees Association (NTPLA) became active in opposition, a role they continued to play for decades.[2] The NTPLA asserted that 'native labour' was inefficient, but nonetheless valuable so long as it was cheap. It recognised that the more 'native labour' was brought into the realm of efficient, regulated labour, the more expensive it would become. The NTPLA based its arguments and authority on its members' personal familiarity with and therefore superior knowledge of 'the natives' and 'the native problem'. In these circumstances, it seemed, the employer was the only one who could judge the worth of his labour. While paying lip service to progress and development, the NTPLA depicted the administrators as incompetent because, while lacking experience of Aborigines, they interfered with normal and natural relationships. Another strategy was to greet any suggestion of the need for regulating its members with a sense of offended pride at the implied slur on the pastoralists' integrity. Even when the NTPLA accepted the need for regulation its members tried to insist that they write the rules themselves.

Pastoralists would not provide houses until Aborigines had been moved along the path of social and moral development, which in turn was measured by the poor state of their housing. The NTPLA said that 'housing and messing needs to be related to the degree of development of the natives' (F1 54/991 1954). The 'blacks' camp' would be the evidence about the 'degree of development' rather than a clue to a history of exploitation and discordant visions of how to live. Thus a situation was created in which the poor state of Aboriginal housing was taken to be a measure of their moral and intellectual inadequacies. In the 1950s, home ownership with all its associated images was becoming an attainable ideal for suburban and rural Australians, and in this context, the fact that Aborigines could not reproduce the prevailing images of order, discipline and hygiene in their own homes was a heavy moral indictment. The alienation of Aborigines from the white population, and from the white working-class poor, was mediated by visions of the tranquillity of the suburban home, beside which images of 'blacks' camps' appeared the negation of the domestic ideal.

The administration engaged in endless debate with the NTPLA, and accused these vociferous spokesmen for the pastoral industry of causing continual conflict and of not representing the small owner–managers who 'are vitally concerned with any policy affecting native welfare and employment as they are directly concerned personally and economically' (F1 54/984 Oct. 1954). In fact the owner–managers were not represented either by the NTPLA or in the national imagination. The interdependence, intimacy and ambiguity of relationships between 'boys' and 'bosses' on these smaller, poorer stations were seldom represented at all.

At one time the possibility of moving Aboriginal people was considered as a means of adjusting the labour supply to need in specific areas. Jack McKay had too many natives while some areas had too few. What was to be done? The answer contained a rare recognition of Aboriginal people's priorities and traditions; the administration rejected the idea of moving the 'surplus employable natives' to areas where there was 'difficulty of meeting the demand', because of 'the problem of moving natives from their tribal area into strange country'. Rather, it was said, an attempt should be made to 'create employment within their own tribal areas in order to absorb this waste labour' (F1 54/111 1954). But the recognition that 'natives' were attached to 'tribal areas' did not include any legitimation of their tribal existence there. They should not be left 'idle' on undeveloped land and their labour 'wasted'.

Despite their conflicts about the regulation of native labour, the pastoralists accepted the legitimacy of the state and its functionaries, and the state was as firmly wedded to the fetishised notion of economic development as any redneck. Thus it is as misleading to juxtapose cruel, exploitative pastoralists with progressive, humanist state officials as it is to see the officials merely in league with the exploiters. The state's practices, and the attention and intentions of state officials, were generated from governing both Aborigines and pastoralists, and legislators understood their own task as balancing different interests within a complex nation. Forms of control, including taxation and rental, were directly related to the intelligent management of pastoralism and of Aborigines. In so far as the bureaucracy developed an autonomous realm of action through its own techniques and forms of knowledge, these activities remained partly parasitic on others' domains, and its own interests were disavowed. The cultural priorities and proclivities embedded in the state's activities were rendered invisible, and conflict was interpreted as due to particular pastoralists' backwardness or to Aboriginal primitiveness, rather than to administrators' attempts to interpose regulations and practices into the often harsh but complex relationship between blackfellas and whitefellas in the outback.

Surface conflicts concealed a fundamental understanding and accord between the interests of pastoral capital and the regulatory intentions of governments. But as untrained police and protectors were replaced from the late 1940s by more specialised patrol officers, they enforced the existing laws and labour regulations more assiduously and tensions were exacerbated. There were even attempts to enforce native rights on leased land, either through excisions from new leases or explicit covenants, and by reminding lessees of their legal obligations (45/150, 1945).[3]

The legitimacy of the laws and their enforcers in the outback was certainly established by 1951 when 'Billy Farrar of Mainoru' lost his licence to employ Aborigines after being convicted and jailed for one month, for supplying liquor to them. 'As a result of their performance following supply' three natives were also convicted and sent to Fannie Bay prison (F1 52/512). He again lost his licence for the same offence in 1952 when he was chronically ill and living at Bert Nixon's farm near Katherine. The conflict of loyalty inherent in the state official's position is exemplified in Patrol Officer Ryan's sympathy with Billy Farrar. Ryan reported: 'He is married to a full-blood', and the decision was appealed on the grounds that Farrar was 60 years old and not physically able to do stock work, and finally because 'Farrar has his counterparts in the NT. They are a dying race from a previous era of native welfare.' The appeal was refused (F1 52/512). The pastoralists, at least when in town, now had to adopt proper practices and obey the law.

Farrar was convicted for supplying liquor because it occurred in Katherine, but rum was an occasional treat out at the station. Jacky Ryan recalled the strange ritual:

> We didn't drink grog yet. When we work, around Christmas, we'd drink rum. Have a glass each. Got to put it in glass, all around [indicates circle of men each having a drink poured]. Christmas party.
>
> First we brand the bullocks. After we brand them, we have Christmas holiday. We were all drinking beer, not beer, I mean hot stuff. Rum, like that, got a glass all round. Serve it to all the working boys. Right up. Finish it up.

Jack McKay was there. He's the boss one. We drink, finish. Satisfied I am. Make us happy (1989).

The force of government regulations did not always penetrate to the stock camps on outback stations. But while racial conditions depended on geographical position and local personalities, the policy directives and changing standards affected everyone.

Tribal dependants

A principle of 'not disturbing the tribal life of the natives' was agreed to by the Territory administration and the NTPLA at a conference in 1947 in Alice Springs. The 'tribal life' in this case was that of the Aboriginal communities on stations, and it was to be protected through the government's maintenance of 'tribal dependants' on pastoral properties, as laid out in the Aboriginals (Pastoral Industry) Regulations (1949). The government began to fund the rations of those in the 'blacks' camps' who were not employed. Although the NTPLA resisted as usual, this legislation was a coup for the pastoralists because the stations gained a regular source of income from the public purse. Large groups of people for whom the pastoralists had been responsible in the past were now funded from government coffers. As a result, patrol officers were sometimes asked to supply land-holders with some 'pensioners', and a common jest in the pub was the invitation to 'have a drink on the pensioners'.[4] The new regulations also saw Aboriginal wages quadrupled from the previous five shillings a week,[5] but this was still one quarter the wages of white stockmen. One wife and child of an Aboriginal worker were to be maintained by the employer. Further, provisions were also made for proper accounting. Forms were supplied for keeping records of workers and wages, of clothing issued, of illnesses and so on (F1 52/759 1946; 49/574 1949). The stations had to complete claims every six months, and a set amount was reimbursed for each individual who was accepted as being a government dependant. They were listed with their age, their offspring and their status (wife, unemployable, etc). These accounting techniques were put in place to control the level of exploitation of Aboriginal labour, but the effect was far wider.

The legislation does not, of course, tell us about the subsequent labour conditions of Aboriginal pastoral workers, not least because so many employers ignored it. But the intention and effects can be gleaned from the plethora of regulations specifying exactly how white bosses were to provide for black workers and 'tribal dependants'; that is, how Aborigines should eat, dress and be housed. A native camp area was to be set aside and only natives were to be allowed in it. The precise amount of dry or cooked rations and the clothing to be supplied to each worker, wife and child were set down. Pastoral stations were to provide accommodation measuring twelve by twelve foot if married and six by twelve foot if single. The unlined tin sheds which sprang up all over the Territory as a result of this policy illustrate the fetishisation of the house as a foundational element in civilised society. Life could not be lived without being encased in a building. The 'transition houses' with their walls, floor and roof, were defined as a stage in development which would allow adjustment to modern family life. They comprised one lesson in the education of the black body. But everywhere Aborigines ignored the instruction to turn the shed into a private 'home' and used the 'accommodation' in other ways. Ironically, these sheds, which were to be the first step in creating conditions of order and hygiene, themselves often attracted vermin and disease.

These regulations were not simply, or even mainly, about labour relations, but about re/forming the people. Characteristic of the process is the individualising theme, encapsulated in the transitional term 'native worker'. 'Native' refers to an undifferentiated population, whereas 'worker' refers to a single named person who is to be employed and paid as an individual. The former was supposed to dissolve into the latter. To this end each worker's particulars and pay had to be entered onto forms which included, after 1952, a column for the worker's 'European name' and another for his 'native name', and further columns for dependants; that is, wife and child or children. The family connections had to be precisely specified in ways that conflicted with and delegitimised the practices and meanings of the Rembarrnga kinship system, which is based on multi-stranded, complex and flexible relationships. Rembarrnga neither organised themselves nor thought of themselves in terms of these categories of 'worker, wife and child', or as 'tribal dependants' (meaning those deemed old and sick), much less as 'myalls' who were not supposed to be on the station.

Defining workers as merely individuals with a severely limited number of dependants, specified in terms of one genealogical link, did violence to the way all Rembarrnga people were interlinked into a community of ever active reciprocal relationships. Dolly was not merely Larry's wife and the mother of Susan and seven other children, but she was Nelly's *yabok*, Tex's *bunji*, Judy's *gaengana*, Yvonne's *mula*, Michelle's *murmbine*, Smiler's *biangduyu*; that is, like everyone else she had specific, reciprocal and multi-stranded relationships across a community of a hundred or so, and further afield into other places. These relationships are rendered trivial in an edict which makes Dolly financially dependent on Larry and makes him responsible solely to her and their children. Everyday practices contradicted the categories. For instance co-wives and their children formed a social unit among Rembarrnga, but a worker with two wives had to occupy the twelve by twelve foot accommodation with one wife and her children while the second wife and her children resided elsewhere. The cooperative domestic life of women was not reflected in the state's categories, or in the housing and economic arrangements. The violence done to these forms of social organisation by the imposition of the notion of husband as breadwinner was effectively documented by Hamilton (1975). She showed the way the wage system, the shop and the school at Maningrida interfered with women's subsistance and educational roles, and destabilised family relationships, prevailing responsibilities and moral assumptions. Morris has detailed forms of resistance which emerged among the Dhan-Gadi Aborigines in New South Wales in response to the states' attempts to reshape domestic and community life (1989).

The provisioning of those not employed was directed at breaking down precisely that characteristic of Aboriginal sociality which most challenged the reshaping process; that is, the sharing of goods, especially food, among a wide social group in certain systematic ways. Such sharing, and the social interdependence of a wide network of people which it entailed, interfered with two crucial elements of the economic logic being established. One was individualised paid labour and the other was the family structure of the breadwinner and his dependants. When the 'able bodied' were seen to take food from 'workers', it was interpreted by the Native Affairs officials as 'bludging'. Jack McKay agreed, complaining that 'These outside people who have taken residence here are definitely bludging on my working boys and girls' (F1 56/2209 Jan. 1957).

Rationing, it was argued, would ensure that the labourer's reward was for himself and his immediate family. However, rationing breached another principle of the logic of labour by providing unearned sustenance for 'able bodied natives' who were, for some reason, 'unemployable'. The administrators were in a dilemma, for if rations to the non-workers were cut off, the consequence would be that 'the rightful recipients of rations and employees of the station would be deprived of a big part of their sustenance by these unemployable able-bodied natives' (F1 54/111 1954). But this process also meant removing responsibility from kin and forcing dependence on the state. State officials were assuming legitimate control over 'tribal dependants' who became 'state dependants'. In fact the wage and rationing system continued to operate without achieving the aim of establishing the nuclear family as a circumscribed economic unit in Aboriginal communities. Sharing remained and became a chronic problem of disorder for the administration.

Besides attempting to dissolve Rembarrnga social relations, the legislation illustrates the racialisation of labour relations. These labourers were to be protected not only from employers but from too much cash, from their own impulses, and thus from the conditions which white workers experienced. The contours of their sociality were being specified by the state. Over time the family structure of these workers was to replicate those of the station owners and they would become 'normal' employees. The anomalous position of their relations was encoded in their status as 'tribal dependants' whose future remained unclear. Before examining what these conditions meant for the Mainoru mob, the patrol officer and for Jack McKay, some of the contradictions within these developments require attention.

Bureaucratic anxieties

Despite the assertion that nothing should disturb tribal life, the administration did not examine what 'tribal life' meant. There is an air of perplexity in many documents, not directly due to recalcitrant pastoralists or Aborigines, but more fundamentally to do with the contradictions within the edicts which were driving the discussion of Aborigines' future. If 'nothing was to disturb the tribal life', how were Aborigines to become autonomous workers? The notion of 'pastoral worker' was antithetical to that of 'tribal life'. The use of the vernacular term 'mob' evaded the necessity to decide whether the 'blacks' camp' was an extended family or a community. The way family organisation among Aboriginal people differed from that of white workers was not examined or discussed. The regulation of wage labour was a site of tutelage directed towards an unexamined and unknown social body. But state officials achieved access to 'tribal dependants' through the practice of providing for them, and tutelary techniques could thus be extended to the whole population on the stations.

The NAB was constantly worried about the division of financial responsibility between pastoralists and the government, and a mountain of documents was produced in regulating pastoralists' claims for maintenance of dependants. Much energy was put into ensuring adherence to the rules of reimbursement from public funds as well as into refining the rules. For example, one worried official in Darwin noted that: 'One working wife of an employee is to be supplied with 2 ounces of tobacco and a wife if not employed is to be supplied with 2 sticks of tobacco. Is that intended?' (F1 49/135, 1947).

Such meticulous and petty accounting is in stark contrast to the casual nature of decisions about the personal lives of 'myalls' and 'nomads', who were subjected to sudden changes in town boundaries and camping areas and often trucked from one place to another without warning. Cattlemen poured scorn on bureaucratic controls. They were hostile to the forms which required supplying details of employees and dependants and were confused by the requirement for different kinds of licences for droving and for mustering. But their pecuniary interest in these matters forced them to conform to the accounting procedures or forgo reimbursement.

Nowhere was there serious consideration of why the Aboriginal people were not simply fitting in. The way such rules might appear to Aborigines or how they were responding, let alone what they might want, was not mooted in the vast body of written evidence left by those who administered Aborigines in the 1950s and 1960s. Such myopia may partly be explained as due to a continuing paranoia about the dangers of recognising the humanity, and interacting with the subjectivity, of 'the natives'. Any active objection to the administration's control was put down to 'sophisticated natives' and 'malcontents'; that is, aberrant Aborigines in the towns.[6] The silent outback natives were the authentic ones, and the ones who could be spoken for without fear of contradiction. They were in fact segregated. Station residents could only complain to their patrol officer, who would explain to them how the government's policy would secure their future and was in their best interests.

The question of whether the Aboriginal future was to be proletarian or tribal was never resolved. When Mainoru was sold in 1969 it was apparent that they were neither. The community was forced to leave Mainoru, and some returned to the Bulman area in Arnhem Land after a period of being made less and less welcome by the new owners. Only two married couples, who would work for equal wages, were allowed to remain (Cowlishaw 1983). The Bulman mob became indigent, and since then have had to deal with a quite different kind of whitefella, one who insists on meetings, on self-determination, and on a whole array of new techniques and social practices, which are often more mystifying in their intent than were the earlier ones.

But this was a long way off in 1952 when it was reported that Tiger Brennan had discovered silver lead at Waimuna (Bulman), the site of the Boolman Boom of 1910. Brennan was a well-known identity in Darwin and had called upon personal friendships to gain a conditional permit to enter a small area in southern Arnhem Land to prospect a known copper deposit. He wrote from Bulman to the Director, Mr Moy, for a permit to employ Dick, Henry and Bill underground, 'as discussed in Darwin during July'. He would pay them '£5 per week no explosives' (49/532 Sept. 1952). Moy sent permission at once, noting the requirement for 'supervision of a competent miner' (F1 49/532 Sept. 1952). Dick, Henry and Bill were Rembarrnga and Ngalpon men from Mainoru. Three years later the new Director of Welfare, Harry Giese, was far more assiduous in applying the rules and wrote to Tiger Brennan at Bulman noting that: 'Mr Jim Dodd [Jack McKay's brother-in-law] will be engaged in the supervision of Aboriginal labour. I would appreciate your advice indicating the number of natives you are employing in the Bulman project together with the nature of their duties and the rates of pay in each case' (53/290 October 1955).

No reply appears in the files and the venture was probably about to peter out quietly. These events illustrate the persistent attempts by miners to gain access to Arnhem Land and other reserves which were usually resisted by the NAB on the grounds that, while the natives were progressing from their primitive state, they needed some protection from aggressive, exploitative forces of settlement (F1 52/1118). As was characteristic of the Territory, Tiger Brennan could use personal connections to bypass the policy intent. He left behind some tools, timber and a tin shed to be used again after the Rembarrnga exodus from Mainoru in 1969. Another legacy is the belief of many Rembarrnga people that Tiger Brennan and other mining companies gained great wealth from mineral deposits on their land. Rembarrnga responses to contemporary requests for exploration licences from large companies have been partly shaped by these early experiences of secret wealth hidden in their country. As Nelly Camfoo said:

> We used to walk over pretty stones, with lead or diamond . . . The
> snake made that stone, and big kangaroo, and goanna made them. We

say it is goanna *guna*, kangaroo *guna*, snake *guna*, and that was made out of our own body, our own culture. We didn't know money can come out of those rocks. *Mununga* call it lead or diamond or silver-lead and they know there's money there. Mining people want to come up and dig all that up, so we might lose our life (1993).

PEOPLE IN THEIR PLACES

As go-betweens, patrol officers undertook much of the paperwork associated with managing Native Affairs (Macleod 1997). They were educated men and confident in their knowledge of the black and the white people, the country and the government's will.

The go-between

Ronald Ryan, an ex-serviceman in his thirties, became a cadet in the NAB in 1946 and a patrol officer based in Katherine in 1948. The following year he was sent to do the six months' course in Anthropology with Professor Elkin at the University of Sydney (Long 1992:77). He was the local guide and manager for several of Professor Elkin's visits to Beswick and Mainoru. The close and mutually reinforcing relationship between the administration and the academic specialist was an important but unacknowledged element in the production of a good deal of ethnographic knowledge.

The wider role of patrol officers is exemplified in the 'principles regarding dress' which said: 'The appearance of a patrol officer in the field is vital to the respect in which he is held by employers and employees alike and can materially affect the efficiency of his job' (cited in Long 1992:148). In the bush they were to wear khaki, but there was a series of warnings against unacceptable dress such as T-shirts, desert boots and 'shirts that needed ironing' (ibid.: 149). The proper apparel for this all-male calling contained lessons about the necessary proprieties of civilisation. The fear of slipping standards, of losing civilisation's edge over outback disorder and over primitivity, was ever present and had to be especially guarded against by the emissaries of the state.

Patrol Officer Ryan was the government official who was responsible for Mainoru from 1948 until the 1960s. His reports reveal the aims and anxieties associated with managing race relations in the outback. He was the one who took the half-caste children away to school in Darwin (Chapter 5) and took messages about them back to their parents. His job entailed checking the station's accounts, and he was diligent in relation to wages, especially, as he said, 'now that pastoralists are being substantially rewarded for maintenance of aboriginal dependants'. He approved nothing less than the minimum weekly payment of £1, even when the payment was for 'odd jobs'. He explained to his superiors that Mainoru station was different in that:

> The employees have more freedom (possibly too much for the efficient running of the property) and they are treated conscientiously [however] the manager of Mainoru station must be informed that the Pastoral regulations must be conformed to and that the next NAB Officer . . . would check what the 'odd jobs' entailed. My interpretation is that 'part-time employment' may have been meant (F1 52/759 Feb. 1952).

A hand-written note on this report says:

> Mainoru is in the unfortunate position of having large numbers of semi-nomadic natives wandering on their block. In an endeavour to control their movements the Manager engages some of them in employment, which is actually in excess of their requirements. However any rate of pay for experienced boys at less than £1 per week should be covered by an authorisation . . . I will advise the Manager of Mainoru (F1 52/759 Feb. 1952).

The Director warned that McKay should be treated tactfully 'because I believe Mr McKay is really a good employer & has the proper outlook towards the aborigine' (ibid.). Jack McKay was sent a letter which very politely suggested he discuss the matter with the patrol officer. Thus, with insistent and tactful advice to the pastoralist, a meticulous scrutiny of elements of race relations practices was established. The systematic documentation produced a kind of order and predictability. The freedom at Mainoru had to be balanced with obedience to regulations which ensured that the state officials had a sense of control. The NAB's major concern was usually with curtailing the excessive exploitation of Aboriginal labour, but Mainoru evoked a different kind of anxiety. Too much freedom could interfere with Aborigines' proper development. Ryan explained Jack McKay's unusual methods:

> [T]he Mainoru native employees still work when and if they feel like it. Mr McKay's somewhat lackadaisical and easy-going administration of his property is principally responsible for this attitude of the employees.

He complains about them but I don't think he would refuse them anything within his power to give. I am sure also that, although the employees seem to do as they like, they would be behind Mr. McKay to a man if he ever wanted them to do anything in particular . . . his view seems to be that if a job isn't done today there is always a tomorrow . . . Mainoru station is certainly unique in regard to the employment of blacks (F1 52/759).

Despite the incredulity at Jack McKay's relations with his Aboriginal workers, Mainoru was held up as a model for others. The regime here seemed to fit the progressive vision for a gradual placing of Aborigines into a secure niche as useful labour in the pastoral industry.

The conception of human labour as a commodity to be put to rational, that is, productive use, is commonplace in capitalist society, but an additional assumption emerged in the NAB files. The actual experience of disciplined, paid labour was to be a valuable, instructive stage in Aborigines' evolutionary road towards becoming part of civil society. This was one of the shared conceptions which enabled patrol officers and pastoralists to cooperate in reshaping Aborigines. The process contrasts with the physically brutal and oppressive treatment of Aborigines on some cattle stations discussed above, but both were founded on a negation of the specificities of Aboriginal life. That is, the forms of sociality which characterised Aboriginal life were to disappear, in this case by being overlaid by another, apparently superior, set of behaviours. The management of pastoral workers occupied a separate discursive arena from notions of 'tribal life' and Aboriginal culture where philosophical and anthropological theories about the human condition, evolution and other abstract questions were relevant.

While pastoralists claimed to be 'not disturbing the tribal life of the natives', 'tribal life' was certainly not to be allowed to disturb the pastoralists. The Rembarrnga 'nomads', as they were increasingly called, continued to come and go from Mainoru, either ignorant of, or wilfully ignoring, the administrative directions. For instance, Mrs Dodd wrote of the Forbes that 'This family has been coming back to the station from the bush over a period of years but has not left this year. At present I am also caring for the mother' (F1 55/1126 Oct. 1957). Others were said to 'periodically return'. Ryan complained that: 'Medicine is an able bodied man with three wives and seven children. He does not work. I moved him off Mainoru in September this year. I have instructed Mainoru that if they continue to feed aged and infirm natives such is a further encouragement for aboriginals to congregate there' (F1 52/759 Dec. 1952).

The patrol officer said that the trouble was that Jack McKay would rather feed them than have them disturb his cattle and that his sister Mrs Dodd 'could not see them without food'. While the provision of food is seen as the major attraction of Mainoru, Patrol Officer Ryan emphasised that they were not in need of subsistence as there was:

> Ample natural food for aborigines and if they want tea and tobacco they can go to the Beswick Creek Native Settlement . . . Mrs Dodd has been instructed that Mainoru is not a 'dumping place' for wives and children whilst the husband or father goes walkabout. She has also been notified that I will not certify any more claims for such people, nor for the families of Medicine and Bandisporie (ibid.).

Ryan accepted that new desires had arisen, but they should be satisfied by going to the native settlement. The provision of 'maintenance' gave the government officials the authority to demand to know the whereabouts of people. When the management at Beswick station was found to be 'sending aboriginals to Mainoru . . . with written authority to holiday or walkabout' the practice was stopped with a sharp note from the DNA saying, 'No natives are to be sent to Mainoru Station for holiday without the permission of the owner Mr. J. McKay and an understanding as to responsibility for maintenance' (F1 52/759 Dec. 1952). The challenge for the Rembarrnga was to gain access to the goods without the administration gaining total control of their lives, and without having to walk 160 kilometres to the west and walk back again to their country. Many of them did not want to 'come in' to a station. They were, as Minnie George and Ronnie Buck indicated, avoiding tutelage. They knew that the administration disapproved of their presence and took to disappearing when Ryan appeared. He complained: 'I noticed some crossing the river soon after I arrived . . . because they thought I would remove them from the area. I estimated about twenty ran off when I arrived' (F1 52/759 Nov. 1953).

Money matters

In Rembarrnga accounts of the past, learning about food and English is more salient than learning about money. But the documentary trail left by patrol officers' activities indicates that accounting for government expenditure generated the most work, and of course money has a pervasive significance in the modernising process. Among his other tasks, Ryan was a money manager for Rembarrnga people, and was executor of Billy Farrar's will in 1953 in which £46 was left to his widow Judy. Because she was a 'native', an officer of the DNA directed Ryan to ask Judy what she wanted done: 'It has been suggested that Mrs. Farrar arrange with you for any advance that she may require. On application, please advise this office the amount required and a cheque will be forwarded immediately.'

Ryan replied: 'Please forward to me a cheque for £6 for Mrs Judy Farrar and £5 there-after on the first of each month unless otherwise advised' (F1 54/821 1954).

Here Judy was benefiting from the state laws concerning wills, and she was being taught to manage money by having it gradually disbursed. The wages policy shows similar protective and gradualist themes. Rather than letting the workers gain experience of earning and spending their money, trust accounts were set up for the purpose of collecting and distributing a portion of money withheld from wages. The simultaneous protection from exploitation and from money illustrates further the contradictions of a gradualist tutelary regime. The intent was also undermined because, in many cases, regulations were evaded. Wage payments could not be easily policed; the management could determine prices at the store; few Aborigines had knowledge of their rights or any redress when the accounting procedures failed them.

The 1949 Aboriginal (Pastoral Industry) Regulations, which stipulated wages of £1 per week for experienced cattle workers, provided for the money to be paid to the protector, as the five shillings had been previously (F1 49/574 reg (5) (d)). Under this system the pastoralist wrote down the amount of the wage and provided the native with goods from the station store. At the end of a stipulated period the balance owing to the worker would be paid to the protector who would bank the money in a trust account.[7] The individual workers could then ask the protector, later the patrol officer, for their money. However, stations were encouraged since the 1940s to pay the workers at least a portion of their wage in cash, which they spent themselves at the store (F1 49/574 May 1949, 1954). In either case, the fact that the pay and expenditure of each worker was accounted for separately reinforced the individualising process.

When pastoralists complained about the complexity of the system, especially the difficulty of explaining deductions to the workers, the administration expressed sympathy for their difficulties and suggested that: 'It would be a reasonable way of overcoming this difficulty if wages were increased' (F1 53/307 Jan. 1954). Given the long, intense resistance to increasing wages, perhaps this was a rare touch of ironic humour. But when there were public protests that pastoralists were not paying Aboriginal workers properly, the NAB defended them, saying 'employers will not pay award rates to Aborigines unless they are sufficiently advanced in intelligence, experience and responsibility to earn award rates . . . Three Aborigines are now receiving award rates in the NT' (F1 52/778 Jan. 1954). The criterion of 'responsibility' set up a tension between loyalty to kin and duty to the boss. The individual worker's worth would be judged on the basis of how far he or she had rejected forms of sociality and interdependence stemming from the kinship network. The administration and the patrol officers supported the employers' right to judge whether their workers were worthy of a full wage. Here the administration protected the pastoralists from public criticism and displayed their responsibility to the industry. Their complicity in supporting the pastoralists in this exercise of power was also dependent on shared racial typifications. That is, behind the employers' specific judgements of individual workers lay notions of race and of a natural tendency to idleness, irresponsibility and low intelligence. These stereotypes were thus instrumental in maintaining low wages and maintaining the pastoral industry's profitability.

The injustice of these racial practices seems obvious to today's white audience, as does the self-interest of the pastoralists and the contradictions in the policy. Rembarrnga people also discovered this injustice when they learned that whitefellas place a great deal of importance on the principle that work should always be paid for, and at a standard rate. The fact that theirs was poorly paid, if at all, has, for some individuals, required a re-assessment of their past relationship with Jack McKay and others. People recall Jack only giving them money when they went to the Katherine show, and then they were grateful. However, the common exclamation 'We been work, NO MONEY!' is not related to the moral fault of a particular boss. Feelings of resentment and anger are muted by a general sense of having been foolish and ignorant. Minnie George has now discovered how hard the past was:

> They never paid. I didn't get paid yet, when we were working every-where. Me and my husband should get paid eh, when we two were working?
>
> We helped every station. Early days, we used to get up at four o'clock. Six o'clock breakfast. Mustering, no spell. Proper hard eh? Easy time now. Sometimes we had Christmas in the bush. Still mustering.

Still getting bullock from there, bring them here to the station. Early days it was properly rough.

We were only working for tucker line, no money, just for ration. We had to work through the wet. But we didn't have a holiday, nothing (1989).

Alma Gibbs said:

I was stock girl then. I liked it, used to ride horse, tailing bullock. Get up might be four o'clock, make tea, five o'clock have breakfast, six o'clock we go. Like that. They were really hard-work times then. We've got easy one now we can get up when we like. Before it was no good, rough. We used to work no money, no wages. Only rations, blanket, boot, hat, towel, you know. Jimmy Gibbs came out and said: 'There you are—40 cents.' No, not 40 cents, 50 cents.

That was the wages. All the time 50 cents. Then dollar came out. One dollar. I don't know what they used to call them. Ten shillings. That's the one, ten shillings. Then pound came out. All the way that one. It grew and grew and we waited and then ten pounds came out. Ten pound all the way now. Then one time, citizen was coming up. More than little bit wages we got then. Oh before, really rubbish time that time we worked, hard work too, no money.

During the 1970s Alma worked as a cook for full wages at Mountain Valley and designates the granting of equal pay as 'citizen coming up'. While she was aware of increasing pay and increasing amounts of money circulating, her reversal of the change to decimal currency attests to a lack of experience with money. Alma and other women only recognised later that they should have been paid for the hard work they did. Thus, while money crept into many different relationships, the tutelary aims of the administration did not necessarily result in the right lessons being learned. The transformation from native to worker through the rewarding of labour on an individual basis could hardly be achieved when the administration protected the workers from too much exposure to money and to commodities until the late 1960s. In many cases, the employers failed to pay them at all. Thus resistance to the values associated with individualised wages was compounded by the lack of rewards usually associated with money.

Tuition

The little community of whitefellas at Mainoru consisted, after 1950, of Jack, his old mother Mrs McKay, his sister and brother-in-law

Margaret and Jimmy Dodd, and their daughter Heather, as well as Sandy McKay on occasions when he was not working as a school teacher in one of the remote Aboriginal schools (figure 3). Heather told me that her grandmother, old Mrs McKay, came to Mainoru when she was 78 to see her two boys before she died, but lived there well into her eighties. Led by the diminutive Mrs Margaret Dodd, the whole family became increasingly involved in the task of teaching 'the native children'. Their desire to improve their charges was in harmony with the NAB policies. Patrol Officer Ryan mentioned in 1953 that Mrs Dodd was giving some of the children elementary lessons and commented that a school could achieve the aim of management:

> Undoubtedly the natives need more control in this area and a government officer in the form of a school teacher could be advantageous both to the management and to the aboriginals. It could also be a means of a check on the nomads and visitors . . . The natives cannot be blamed for desiring to visit Mainoru as apart from its traditional importance to them it has unsurpassed natural advantages (F1 52/759, Nov. 1953 report).

Ryan's recognition of the 'traditional importance' of the area is an example of the kind of knowledge claims which pepper such texts. The 'traditional importance' of particular country appears to this official as a quaint, ephemeral thing, with no lasting significance.

The policy of establishing schools on pastoral stations for Aboriginal children was being implemented in the Territory, but the authorities warned that 'the remove from camp urchin to pupil in a fully equipped school should be done by stages' (F1 53/659 1954). The widely espoused theory of gradual social development in this case meant a gradual supply of material resources. New schools were encouraged to start without furniture to prepare the children for the 'next stage' when equipment would be provided. It was three years later that an education officer visited Mainoru with Ryan and gave official encouragement to the school. His report said that the 'Rembarrnga and Ngalkbun tribes . . . rarely move out of their areas, are strong virile tribes and large families are prevalent' (F1 56/2209 Oct. 1956). Mrs Dodd was to allot the south and western sides of the verandah as a classroom and Mr McKay had commenced to glass in the two sides. School equipment was sent out for the beginning of the 1957 school year. Mrs Dodd's report at the end of that year, as well as recognising the children's unique eagerness, makes the wider function of the school clear: 'So far our problem has been not how to get the children to attend but how to get rid of them . . . a nice bunch of intelligent youngsters well worth anything Welfare will do for them . . . Chalk, pencils readers etc. would be appreciated but clothes are an absolute necessity' (F1 56/2209 Dec. 1957).

Professor Elkin was a fierce proponent of Aboriginal education, and Heather Dodd attributed the government's support of the Mainoru school to his intervention. She claimed:

> Things improved a lot after Peter Elkin had been there . . . he was very impressed with the kids. This was 1958 and he said to Mum if you can't get any help from the government my university will supply you with all you need. So the government immediately sent out a bolt of cloth and half a dozen grade six arithmetic texts, which meant all the kids had clothes at least (1988).

Ronnie Martin recalled his transformation from 'camp urchin' to 'pupil' as well as his other lessons:

> 1958, I start school. I went to school for three years. Then after that I went mustering with Tex Camfoo. Every year during the school break we used to go out to the stock camp, help old Tex, for a couple of months. I was at school three years, 1958 to 1960 or '61.
>
> We used to write with ashes [charcoal] first and writing on tea chest. No paper or pencil. For one year anyway. Then we got all our gear. Then after, we got uniform (1987).

To all involved, this school represented the best and most progressive aspect of European relations with Aborigines. It would enable Aborigines to 'advance'. As Heather Dodd reflected, 'we won some really wild kids when the school opened' (1988), indicating the sense of a struggle against primitivity. Even today's critics of the assimilationist implications of schooling, with its inevitable privileging of textuality over orality, and western over indigenous values and practices, do not deny that an illiterate population is rendered helpless in the modern world. The fact that, as Mrs Dodd said, 'Some of the older ones were asking about learning to read and write at night' (F1 57/981 Dec. 1957), indicates Rembarrnga were aware of the disadvantage of illiteracy.[8] The empowering aspect of schooling is combined with its role in re-ordering the self (Foucault 1977; Srivastava 1996), and we shall explore this schooling further below. But it is important to recognise that tuition had begun many years previously through participation in pastoral practices.

Much had been learned already. The interaction with material technology was a compelling element in pastoralists' relationships with their untutored workers. The necessity to teach the primitive was shaped by the need for stockmen to know not only about cattle, but also about bridles, boots and rations; that is, about the paraphernalia and pattern of everyday life on a station. Hall's fond account of the bushman's equipment quoted above, shows that these material things represent far more than mundane technologies; they also represent normality and virtue. Implements often entail forms of social relations which are transparent and thus invisible to those socialised into their use. They are, for instance, owned.

Western, modern, civilised life is marked by a vast array of things from which emanate specific and general meanings (Dening 1988:8–9). The common knowledge of the ordinary technology of daily life, of guns and butter, books and flour, horses and houses, is taken for granted. The objects seem to create their own discipline in that they have to be looked after, oiled or cooked, kept from the children or from the sun. This knowledge is a necessary part of the techniques for living which we acquire in childhood. Its value, in relation to ourselves and our desires, is part of our being and, consciously, of our common sense. When these new things appeared, Aboriginal things and techniques were overlaid with different meanings and shifted under their weight. Spears became inferior, in most circumstances, to knives and guns. 'Foot walking' became more difficult. Some skills in the bush flowed across the racial boundary in the other direction. Certain techniques, some modest ways of achieving a greater measure of comfort in the bush, such as cooking on open fires, placing a stick to stop sand from creeping into the swag (Poignant & Poignant 1996), were taken up by whitefellas. Many practices went underground, held in memory, imbued with conflicting emotion.

Practical knowledge is especially dear to whitefellas who produce from the land, and their desire to instruct is also part of the colonisers' common response to those who lack this sense of what is what. Pride in knowing how things work, and frustration when we don't, is a crucial feature of the experience of modern technology. The meaning of supposedly inert, secular objects must be imparted. For instance, saddles and axes encapsulate the power of the pastoral industry over nature, and thus the reason for white people entering Rembarrnga country. The use of these things, and the forms of discipline associated with them, were imparted to Rembarrnga people before Mrs Dodd's school began, and their adoption of the tools caught them up in the purposes for which the tools were made.

Foucault has discussed 'technologies of human training', a concept which is apt for the tutelary regime at Mainoru because of the wide effects of this program, or regime, on its subjects (1977; Morris 1989). The principles of pedagogy, involving discipline through surveillance and reward and a reshaping of subjectivities, diffused into the arena of race relations and reverberated across the Territory's cattle stations, missions and government stations through official and unofficial practices. The moral order being expressed in these forms included the principles of hierarchy in human relations and of ownership in relation to objects. The notion of ownership embraces morality, order and knowledge. Taking care of possessions is rational and virtuous for whites, and is linked with habits of denoting who is responsible for an object and the need for others to defer to that possessor. This is another field where blackfella practice came into direct conflict with that of whitefellas. In the social arena of Rembarrnga life, possessiveness about objects is irrational if it means refusing others. Moreover it is a fault. Someone who hoards and does not share is said to be deaf, a characteristic which evokes contempt. Such generalisations as this could do with a good deal of exegesis, as they are liable to be read simplistically. Just as whitefellas' characteristic possessiveness shows a wide variation and has all kinds of particular expressions, so Rembarrnga practices of sharing and lack of emphasis on personal ownership is nuanced and uneven. Where there is a form of ownership it is seldom exclusive, individual or lasting. Rather than learning possessiveness from the McKay family, Rembarrnga speak critically of its manifestations. This alternative order of moralising was submerged, but a subcultural domain existed within which Aborigines subverted the moral authority of whites and claimed a higher ethical status for themselves. Far from adopting individualistic possessiveness, they donned a facade of respect for the bosses' practices while continuing to share their things.

In speaking to me of the past, Rembarrnga people repeatedly remarked, sometimes evincing embarrassment, anger or derision, on the way little bits of rations were measured out for the old people from the big stock that was obviously there. The parsimony of this practice indicated a shameful calculation in the face of others' desires. The historical circumstances and material conditions which produce judgements of parsimony, profligacy and meanness could be examined in detail. Suffice it to say here that the subsistence technology of

Rembarrnga before the arrival of whites did not lend itself to the accumulation of goods or food preservation, and that the moral worth attached to the conserving of wealth and possessions in a capitalist economic system has negative implications for Rembarrnga interpersonal relations.

This extract from Willy Jailama Martin's (plate 16) account of life at Mainoru indicates how the rationing arrangements affected those subjected to them:

> Old Jack McKay was there after Billy Farrar . . . Welfare used to come along. And every Sunday they used to say, 'Come on King and Queen.[9] This is you mob's ration day.' That's the white man's way. And we could see that old people, say like old Florry now, old people used to be ready waiting for that time.
>
> 'Today is Saturday' see. They used to go up then wait around, like a big mob of duck-duck or mob of goose. They used to get a bag for putting the flour in, for the people to fill it up with their own cup. About ten cup each, and treacle, brown sugar. Only about ten cup. We had a lot of old people then, must be ten or twelve people.
>
> We still had bush tucker every time. And ceremony (1989).

At the same time as Willy comments on the humiliating effect of rationing practice, he expresses pride in that independent source of sustenance—bush tucker—which was always available, ensuring at least a symbolic independence. Minnie George's tone expressed disdain for the meagreness of rations when she said, 'My Mummy and Daddy, they used to get pension tucker. No more big one, little one like that. Pension, ration, they used to get.' Alma Gibbs contrasted today's 'buying business' with the ration system:

> We go walkabout, might be Christmas time, we take rations. None of this buying business. That's only this time [now] . . . Old people got ration too. Not really drum of flour. Only that big you know. [She shows small size.] Enough for, might be, few days. Saturday they got it. Not enough to last to Saturday, ration day again. Not enough for them. They had to help themselves with bush tucker.

A more ambivalent view of rationing was expressed by Annette Murray (plate 17):

> Our mother would go up each week for the rations, waiting in turns to get her little share. Mrs Dodd would spoon out with a teaspoon, and she would chant, *'One for Larry, one for Dolly, one for Susan, one for*

Annette, one for Sonia, one for Roland, one for Kirstin, one for Cynthia' and we kids would copy her when we were playing, chanting like that, *'One for Larry . . .'.* That's why we had to go hunting for bush tucker every time. But they were teaching us to be careful, to save food. My family learned that. We always are careful with food (pers. com. 1995).

The precise measurement, which was displayed as a virtue and as a pedagogic device, as well as the ordered, individualising system of distribution, has left its virtuous mark on Rembarrnga consciousness. The authority of Mrs Dodd commanded attention and attraction, even while her practices were offensive. Blackfellas became aware that to the whitefellas, bush food was the mark of a previous, inferior life, yet the rations were never enough to do away with the need for bush tucker. Because accounting and conserving were superior among whitefellas and in the powerful world outside Bulman, bush food became imbued with a moral and aesthetic ambiguity, and uncoordinated sharing was tainted with the mark of backwardness. The presence of the whitefella's gaze destabilised the meanings of things. There was both attraction and repulsion towards the new values which disturbed and threatened to smother the foundational categories of everyday life which bound the community in a moral order.

'Where things cross a cultural boundary we reinvent their meanings', says Dening (1988:8–9), and Rembarrnga spontaneously re-invented the meanings associated with many things. Nelly Camfoo was conscious of changing the meaning of Rinso soap powder when she said, 'You don't use this for hair, eh? Us blackfellows change it. We take it from you, then we use it different way.' More often the intended meanings and 'correct' usage were merely absent or refused. Houses did not become the sites of domestic activity. The shacks supplied for Rembarrnga at Mainoru were used for storage rather than sleeping. But attempts to avoid the authority and discipline of material things by placing a different order on them could only succeed to a limited extent (cf. Morris 1989:74ff). A change of meaning was interpreted by the whites not as an expression of other cultural priorities or a rejection of foreign values, but as a lack.

Refusal to respect the goods sufficiently, to oil the leather, shut the gate, pump the tyres, own the clothing, husband the food, monitor the children, that is, to adopt European values, were interpreted simply as indications of laziness, ignorance or backwardness. The clever ones learned, but some adjustments of these judgements were made when the clever ones were insubordinate. For instance Willy Jailama Martin was seen as 'intelligent but lazy' and a 'trouble maker' (Heather Dodd pers. com.). In subsequent years he became an active political figure in the National Aboriginal Congress and later in the Northern Land Council. Those Rembarrnga who were obedient as well as clever were a continuing source of pride to the Mainoru owners who believed they created them. The seductive pleasures of pleasing the whitefellas, and of gaining competence in the use of their things, led Rembarrnga to some measure of acceptance, not only of white teachings, but also of white authority. Smiler Martin's cooperative attitude and sense of responsibility was rewarded when he was entrusted with the station truck to drive people to ceremonial sites:

> I did a bit of riding first and then, after that, I had that motor car job then. Every ceremony I used to take the people with the big truck and leave them at Bulman waterhole and go back to station on the old road. When that ceremony finished I used to go back and get them then. And on the weekend, when they all finished, load up everybody and go home.
>
> We used to have tea and sugar, flour, for a couple of weeks and then run out, and all the way just have bush tucker, bush beef. Really good then. All the little kids taste that bush tucker and they like it (1985).

The availability of a truck entailed a vast change in Rembarrnga relationship with the country. That relationship was formerly expressed through 'foot walking', sleeping on the journey, awaiting others, producing subsistence supplies from the land. Relationships of time, distance and subsistence were all sharply changed when Smiler was allowed to drive people to the ceremony ground at Bulman waterhole. The administration's model of a gradual process of instruction and shaping of responses to a new rhythm was not in fact what occurred. When a truck was supplied, a whole set of practices lurched into a different gear. When rations were supplied, a brake was applied to the relationship between people and country. There was nothing gradual about the presence of whitefellas.

RACE RELATIONS

The exercise of power is neither a self-evident motive nor an explanation of social relations. Power is exercised through everyday cultural practice, through the logic associated with evolutionary progress, with capitalist production, and with gender relations and domesticity. In the control of movement, in recording names and numbers, in assessing the quality of the workforce, providing food and buildings and so on, specific practices developed which were culturally informed, pragmatic responses to particular and changing circumstances which were themselves neither predicted nor understood. This was a program in Foucault's sense, the logic of which was generated less by a coherent set of ideas than by the practices which grew out of local responses to particular conditions (Foucault 1991:80–81). The gaps and contradictions in the program of race relations in the Territory are obscured by an enfolding faith in progress. The policies for Aboriginal advancement lacked any explicit overall plan, justification or methodology. Nonetheless, specific forms of discipline were apparent in 'the generalised interconnection of different techniques themselves designed in response to localised requirements' (ibid.).

It is also important to recognise that these programs had limited success in individualising the Rembarrnga social body, and that this failure was also due to 'local' conditions. Conditions at Mainoru were one part of this, because proximity to Arnhem Land and Jack McKay's flexibility allowed Rembarrnga people to enhance their freedom from the discipline of the regime. But more generally the mark made by these disciplinary programs was limited by the particular characteristics of this racialised cultural domain. Contrary to what was implied by official policy, there was no empty social space for the new practices to fill. The social lives of Rembarrnga were already occupied with other, different, and often antithetical ways. Thus Rembarrnga subjects deflected the teachings. The straight rows demanded at school were conformed to for fun or out of fear, or perhaps with the desire to please, but the worth of such a practice was not internalised, or generalised to other situations. Geometric, mechanical or military forms of ordering people are not evident among the Bulman mob today.

Also present was an imagined savagery built out of the tenacious images of the primitive and of its necessary conquest. This savagery remained as an imaginative space with Heather Dodd who took pleasure in telling me the shocking story of a Maranboy policeman who, she claimed, in about 1960, punished Aboriginal men for killing a buffalo shooter and eating some of his flesh. They were made to eat putrid flesh, but, because one was a good tracker, he was let go and employed instead (pers. com. 1989). Whatever events gave rise to this tale, it was used to keep a fearful otherness alive and present. This element of the grotesque secreted under modern bureaucratic relationships is apt to emerge at unexpected moments. Thus race relations is not a unitary phenomenon. The cruelty and terror which were common in some places, combined with insistent forces of modernisation, progressive development and paternalistic repression in an unstable and volatile social cauldron, never quite under official control.

At Mainoru there remained physically separate spaces for white and black residents' more intimate sociality, with the camp some distance from the house. This meant that the new forms of discipline, such as rationing and housing, paying and teaching, could be accepted at the surface level of obedience and in relation to specific whitefellas. Some of the physical habits of Rembarrnga people changed. The wearing of clothing became normal for adults, and damper and johnny cakes became staple foods. However, these changes do not indicate anything general or predictable about the relationship with the domain of whitefellas, and specific practices require further investigation if the nature of the relationship is to be understood. For instance, while the black workers showed deference to the boss, I would argue that this was a form of mimicry specific to particular circumstances rather than an acceptance of the need for hierarchical labour relations. It was easy for Rembarrnga to outwardly conform, or at least not disrupt whitefella practices, without adopting the meanings which the whites took for granted. Yet experience of these relationships opened the possibility of new forms of consciousness and new emotions. The stock workers' relationships took place in the context of mustering and branding cattle where the boss's authority had an obvious purpose in relation to the task at hand. However the more intimate relationships entailed a much more ambiguous form of authority. Before examining these, this chapter will explore further the way the administration and the McKays combined to exercise authority over Aborigines.

Too easy with the natives

Patrol Officer Ryan's first detailed report on Mainoru was made after his one-day visit with Professor Elkin in August 1948:

> The McKay brothers showed me around the native quarters which were very clean and tidy. I was pleasantly impressed by the native huts. These have been constructed under supervision and apart from being waterproof have ample standing room. The natives were pleasant, contented, clean and appeared to be well cared for . . . [though] they needed treatment

for their eyes . . . I saw evidence of a soap issue . . . A neat record is kept of all native employees indicating their dependants and itemising all issues and wages . . . A beast is killed periodically and an arrangement has been made with the natives that when the wood is cut it is collected in a truck, half of which goes to the homestead and the other half delivered to the native quarters (F1 52/759 Aug. 1948).

Such an ordered and benign station was a rare delight to the officials. Cleanliness and soap, tidiness both in people and in the records, and a program of distributing things, such as wood and food, in an orderly and apparently equitable fashion,[10] indicated progress and contentment. The neat records were not so much to enhance the station's management as to allow an outsider to easily assess and understand the station's functioning. Or seem to. The officers in Darwin felt they were able to exercise control by reading the reports, checking the names and adding up the figures. At Mainoru: 'All employees are paid regularly in cash . . . The store sells at cost price such items as playing cards, scented soap, extra clothing, hair-oil, pipes etc. and items such as bobby-pins and tommy-axes. Fine cut and ready rubbed good quality tobacco is also sold' (F1 52/759 Sept. 1951).

Ryan's satisfaction is again evident two years later, despite the non-conformity with the work ethic which seemed so crucial to the administration's plans:

In spite of the owner's lack of conformity in many respects with the Pastoral Regulations the natives have compensating benefits. They have a life of comparative freedom, they have an ideal country in which to hunt and often they seem to please themselves when they work. On the other hand the owner had to contend with the disadvantages of having too many aboriginal visitors to his property (Ryan, F1 52/759 Nov. 1953).

The categories and calculations in the six-monthly returns for reimbursement for dependants were carefully scrutinised. The 1952 claim was large, and in approving it Ryan said he was 'satisfied that the natives in question were on Mainoru station'. But Ryan had to satisfy the Darwin office and he went through the next return 'twice with Mr Jack McKay' to be sure that 'all the claimants are legitimately qualified government dependants'. While he accepted, for instance, that Florry's and her son Ronny's maintenance was for the period when husband Chuckerduck was not working, he deleted a claim for Maudie because her husband Bandicoot was employed. McKay humbly accepted corrections to the claim as he accepted the authority and the rules of the NAB. Mrs Dodd also reassured the Branch that she was maintaining the scrutiny of worth when she wrote to the Director in 1954 saying: 'I also understand that it was only necessary to pay the woodboy twelve shillings and sixpence (12/6)—the matter was rectified but I would appreciate an award book. Our woodboy wasn't even worth feeding [He was Dick] the father of Alice's kids [who] passes through occasionally' (52/759 1954).

The careful accounting to protect government coffers became an end in itself. While one claim was adjusted down from £623.4.11 to £595.8.9 another was adjusted upwards from £468.8.4 to £489.12.3. Calculations of times were altered and amounts adjusted in ways that appear ludicrous in the light of the weeks of mustering with no break or accounting for time, and other casual station practices. But more serious discontinuity is expressed in the reason for one correction: 'The aborigine Mary LYEENA, second wife of Larry has been claimed as an adult, however as this native is 15 years of age, she must be classed as a child dependant, until such time as the marriage is consummated or she attains the age of 16 years' (52/759 1953).

This coy reference to polygyny and to Dolly's[11] promise marriage indicates a silence in the face of practices which were not only somewhat abhorrent to the officials, but which would, if legitimated, have the potential to upset the categories the state relied on. Rembarrnga social categories were not allowed to intrude. At best they were respectfully left alone; it was taken for granted by both station management and officials of the state that better, normal practices would eventually take their place.

Despite Ryan's admiration of the Mainoru management he retained the official language and approach of the vigilant public servant:

> I am sometimes suspicious that Mainoru might be making money out of the maintenance claims but these ideas are dispelled when visiting the station on which occasions the dependants are particularly well catered for. Most of them seem to get cooked meals from the kitchen and these include eggs and custards for those needing them. It is difficult to tell Mrs. Dodd not to give food to a pregnant woman, to children or to infirm . . .
>
> It is apparent that either there is a large percentage of ailing blacks on Mainoru Station or else other stations do not care for them to the same degree as does Mainoru (F1 52/759 Aug. 1954).

Jack McKay and Mrs Dodd assumed a common purpose with the administration but their vision of the future revolved around particular, familiar individuals. The NAB could not deny that Mainoru, and Mrs Dodd in particular, were fulfilling their modernising task in relation to Aboriginal development. Their sense of that responsibility was observed by Ryan: 'I was amused to hear Mr. McKay criticising his sister for being too easy with the natives. She had previously told me that Mr. McKay was too compliant with them' (F1 52/759 Sept. 1951).

The issue here is implicit in a great deal of the NAB practices. What is the correct level of authority and control which should be exercised over individuals? The answer emerges in specific practices such as responses to disease. After listing 'legitimate government dependants', Ryan says of Medicine and his three wives and seven children: 'They are not employed, nor are they classed as dependants although they are fed by the station. They disappeared the day after my arrival as one of the wives may be a leper suspect' (ibid.).

The NAB forcibly removed people who were thought to have leprosy, a practice surrounded by secretiveness at the time and since.[12] Clearly Medicine was aware of the danger. Such removals formed the state's ultimate sanction. Like Mrs Dodd's care for those who appeared in need, removals of leper suspects were made to protect people who were seen as incapable of caring for themselves. Their actions were taken as proof of the fact; requests for food were interpreted, not as affirming a relationship of mutuality and attachment, but as indicating a childlike state of need, and as an invitation for Mrs Dodd to take responsibility for the supplicant.

In the forms to claim reimbursement for those being fed by the station there was no space for 'nomads', 'myalls' or 'Arnhem Land natives' who were not in the category of 'tribal dependants'. The unpredictable propensity of such people to appear intermittently at Mainoru and stay a while meant that the administration was repeatedly faced with making decisions about their status. When four dependants' names appeared which were not on Mainoru's previous list of claims for reimbursement, and had not been mentioned by Mrs Dodd on the last inspection, a clerk in Darwin expressed suspicion saying, 'Mrs Dodd is inclined to talk too much of the work she does for the natives' (F1 52/759 Aug. 1954). The claim was returned to Ryan for checking, with the comment that, if these were 'infirm natives', either a doctor or the natives themselves should be asked to confirm the illnesses. The patrol officer often mediated in this way between the Darwin office and the station and smoothed the relationship. A few years later Ryan said that people were being drawn in to 'sit down at Mainoru because of the school'. While it was undesirable that the station should have the expense of supporting them, it was equally undesirable that they should move back to the bush taking school children with them, 'since the children are now showing the benefit of regular feeding'. It was finally agreed that families with children at school would be supported as 'dependants' (F156/2209, 1958).

This situation at Mainoru does not conform to the popular images of race relations in the outback. There is not the blatant contempt expressed by the Chief Protector Cook when there were plans for native constables: 'We shall be dealing with natives without a background and the slovenly dirty habits which are their present characteristics will not be eradicated without some difficulty' (F1 40/203 1936). Nor is there evident the paranoia of one pastoralist who, during the war, advised that: 'I have worked with blacks all my working life . . . and I know they are not to be relied on. They will come amongst us, find out the position, then go back at night and enlighten the enemy. [They should be] kept in camps . . . one stick of tobacco a week would hold them' (F1 43/24 1943). Nor was there the kind of cruelty which the Berndts found at many of the stations they visited during the 1940s (Berndt & Berndt 1987).

But Mainoru was part of the era that produced each of the above, and typifies one crucial aspect of the deployment of colonial power. It illustrates the way the varied threads of race relations were spun from a fleece of convictions about the nature of social life, and woven into a seamless regime of governance strengthened by a body of legislation and, intermittently, by the use of force. While the everyday aspects of this regime were expressed in a variety of apparently contradictory and uneven practices, from extreme racial violence to a sentimental form of solicitude, they shared the hierarchical, racial structure which, I believe, is still apparent in the rural present.

On paternalism

When I try to explain something of what happened at Mainoru, people like to say, knowingly, 'Oh yes, paternalism.' This popular notion implies a kindly but deceptive exercise of power. It is a concept called upon to describe regimes where authority is exerted within a relationship of solicitude and even affection, and ongoing and stable trust. Perhaps such a relationship was the best that could be hoped for in the Territory. This may have been the view of Charles Rowley (1972a, b and c) when he researched and wrote his encyclopaedic, groundbreaking account of colonial relations in Australia, detailing the vast dimensions of the previously well-concealed history of racial laws and practices directed at the indigenous population of Australia. Rather than having to explain why it was that many pastoralists saw human decency towards their Aboriginal workers as antithetical to their self-interest, Rowley, and many others, had to argue that essential labour should be treated humanely, though this argument might seem to have been settled in the nineteenth century.

Like the Darwin administration, Rowley admired the management at Mainoru because they were 'able to reconcile humanity with their own long-term self interest' (Rowley 1972a:217). There were nightly ceremonies (ibid.:209) and 'the homestead seemed to operate as a place of resort for those with troubles in the camp, as well as the school for the children' (ibid.:218). Rowley went on to argue that these observations verified what Mrs Gunn had said decades earlier in the acclaimed account of Territory life, *We of the Never Never* (1963); that is, that 'some autonomy could be maintained' (Rowley 1972a:217). In other words, the suppression of Aboriginal practices through violence and cruelty was not a necessary part of race relations on pastoral stations. Rowley saw Mainoru as evidence that a degree of cultural freedom, as well as respect and care between black and white residents, was compatible with pastoralism and was an ideal to be striven for.

Rowley's commendation of Mainoru for its humanity does not recognise the extent to which this 'humanity' was directed to controlling and re-directing Rembarrnga lives. Nor does it take account of the tenuous nature of such a regime. While Rembarrnga residents at Mainoru did enjoy considerable 'cultural freedom', that freedom was not secure. Not only did it depend on these particular owners, but on a concealment or erasure of those elements of culture which were deemed reprehensible. Rather than positive respect for the specificities of Aboriginal social life, we have seen revealing hints of contempt towards this domain. Solicitude for the welfare of specific Rembarrnga people was linked to a necessary tutelage to overcome their lack of culture. The lack had to be rectified by instilling in them the same disciplines which the invaders took to be the mark of human competence. The identity of whites was affirmed by forcing a particular order onto the natives in the name of a universal humanism.

Conferring on such a relationship the benign term 'paternalism' relies on a metaphoric reference to a traditional ideal of western parent–child relations, which ensure that authoritarian structures are accepted as entailing trust and mutual affection within an ideology of individual autonomy which is realised as the child grows to adulthood. Such a pattern differs markedly from parent–child relations characteristic among Rembarrnga, which display what appears to whitefellas as extreme indulgence of children, with no equivalent of a single adult male who is the authoritarian father on whom the family depends (Cowlishaw 1982; Hamilton 1981). The concept of paternalism is thus itself an example of a specific cultural practice embedded as metaphor in language which is taken to be neutral. While the beliefs about human relations generally, and Aborigines in particular, which prevailed among the Mainoru whites could well be described as paternalistic, such a description implies a reciprocal understanding. But the management's emotional investment in their Aborigines over the relatively short period of 50 years that the regime was in place should not be confused with any complicity of Aborigines. That is, unlike the circumstance in the slave society described by Genovese (1974:661), this paternalism did not become so well established that it was systematically understood and adhered to by both master and servant.[13]

Elements of paternalism did complement the state's more formal regime of power. The personnel on small stations such as Mainoru, and some long-serving patrol officers, expressed affection and solicitude towards Aboriginal individuals and families, identifying both with those being cared for and with the process of instruction and reshaping of their persons. Such interracial attachments as formed with government officials were increasingly vitiated by changes in policy and the turnover of staff. But it was through a multitude of everyday techniques in the context of these relationships that white people managed their interactions with black people and re-ordered the outback. These activities deposited an overlay of colonial culture on the country, beneath which Aborigines continued to pursue their own meanings.[14]

Despite the white people's ascendancy, and perhaps because of the savage power they wielded, not only with guns but also through the police removals of suspected criminals and lepers and through the moral judgements they spread over everything, the form of human relations based on a categorical inequality remained for the Rembarrnga a foreign surface masking another social life. Outside the context of Mainoru station, Rembarrnga, not whitefellas, remained knowledgeable, and their knowledge remained part of an ontology which was inaccessible to whites. However, as noted above, there developed an ambivalence about the earlier state of being when the knowledge of flour and tea, work and English, was absent. The status of Aboriginal knowledge of country was implicitly challenged by fences and cattle (Williams 1986). Rembarrnga today do not see what was learned as directly at odds with, or dangerous for, Aboriginal law. But for those who grew up on Mainoru, the inferior knowledge and power of Rembarrnga in relation to the increasingly intrusive domain of whites was a foundational experience to which we will return.

Thus control was exercised by Europeans over a social domain which was denied any positive meaning in the modern world and could be painted out without shame or regret. As the Welfare Branch Annual Report of 1960–61 stated, 'We must concern ourselves with individuals at all stages of social development towards assimilation, that is, from groups of nomads to individual Aborigines with full citizenship rights' (WBAR 1960–61:3). We saw above that anthropologists continued to articulate their theories of social evolution which were the popular common sense of science about racial histories, about progress from the primitive condition through colonisation. These theories made any idea of a dialogue between whitefellas and blackfellas appear impossible, and no compelling alternative concepts or interpretations of social change emerged. The laws and policies in this arena depended on a series of myths and mysteries which were systematised and scientised into the progress of a racial hierarchy and the supremacy of the charms of civilisation, that is, 'our way of life'. Stanner, in a passage discussing the 'wrong *emphasis* of much of native policy' asserted in 1938 that 'scientists have noted for years a serious undercurrent of unrest among these [northern Australian] tribes' and observed that they were dissolving into 'small floating segments' and becoming 'parasitic', attributing the transition to 'drift' driven by 'craving' for goods which were available from Europeans (1979:12). He implies 'movement devoid of agency' and 'desire not checked by reason' (Rowse 1998:33). It was such theories purporting to describe the confusion and aimlessness of Aborigines in the modern world which underpinned protective and tutelary programs as well as the wider public sympathy for the tragedy of Aborigines who really were seen to have no future. Yet on pastoral stations there were patterns of interaction and intimacy which demonstrated a more complex and changing order of race relations hinting at a potential for some quite different future.

5

Racial Intimacies

Jack McKay said, 'She's half-caste and you are full black Aboriginal.' I told him, 'Your sister can't claim my kid. If you claim, you should claim your own colour. This my colour.' I told him like that.

—*George Jarngawarnga, 1993*

Mrs Dodd was very proud of her flock, of their capacities and so on.

—*Robert Smith, 1989*

BUREAUCRATIC SAVAGERY

The previous chapters have discussed the way land was parcelled up and categorised for certain purposes and for certain people, and how, within the spaces for Aborigines—the 'blacks' camp' or 'native quarters' on cattle stations—people were categorised as workers, the dependants of workers, or 'tribal dependants'. All these 'natives' and their employers were administered by the NAB, which instituted specific forms of surveillance, recording and accounting in cooperation with the emerging station communities. There was an unusual degree of harmony between the state officials and the land-holders at Mainoru, especially after the women arrived and the station enthusiastically took up its civilising task. The humane and solicitous practices for which the station became justly famous had an ambiguous racial core, composed of love, fear and hierarchy.

While violence and physical brutality on the racial frontier were deliberate though officially condemned, cultural violence was unrecognised but was officially encouraged. I use the term 'cultural violence' to refer to the whole gamut of conditions that made the maintenance and reproduction of Aboriginal social life difficult or impossible. Alienation from the land was one such condition, though for Rembarrnga the alienation was, to some extent, voluntary.[1] Other conditions were whitefella laws and practices which, in attempting to remodel social relations within Aboriginal communities, rendered such relations irrational and inferior. Another condition was the regulating of social relations between the races in ways that made many interactions illegal. The illegality of relationships which in other circumstances are the ordinary stuff of social life, is a clue to the passionate investment in categories of race which persisted despite the interweaving of the social lives of many black and white people.

In public discourse and in administrative circles massive importance was attached to the boundaries between the racial bodies, both as social groups and as individuals. There was no explicit colonial intention to destroy a domain of social order and meaning. Rather, the colonial officials seem to have seen the space they were intruding into as one of lack, absence, meaninglessness. Their actions appear myopic, but they could more accurately be described as self-absorbed and narcissistic, obsessed with their own role as saviours, and filled with a love of the self, in fact of the white body. The facade of rationality gave way to incoherence and hysteria in the establishing and enforcing of the racial boundaries, and they produced chaotic and unpredictable results. This chapter will explore the way that, while busily applying a civilised facade onto the outback and over Aboriginal social forms, whitefellas were secretly preoccupied with the sexuality of the racialised black body and other anxieties generated by fantasies of racial grotesquerie. Forms of intimacy emerged that were chronic threats to the racial dichotomy, subverting and reordering racial boundaries, destabilising racial categories and forcing rewritings of the racial rules. While the colonising eyes were riveted on sexual relations between the races, officials blindly trampled over Aboriginal marriages and family forms. The cultural obsession with colour fired a lurid imaginative space where actions of considerable savagery took on the appearance of mundane necessity.

Aborigines fulfilled a series of imaginative and symbolic functions in the nation's social and psychological dynamics, and these are evident in the various solutions to the problems that Aborigines seemed to pose. One well-recognised feature of colonial discourse is the conception of different cultures as contradictory, sealed into their own meanings, in danger of contaminating one another, and losing their integrity and strength if the seals are breached. The symbolic meaning of being white was to be not-black; to be modern was to be not-primitive; to rule was to negate the will of the ruled (cf., Fanon 1967; Nandy 1983; Young 1995). This dynamic explains why the state's endeavours did not involve any intersubjective engagement with the primitive domain. Were that domain simply another, equivalent human space, the structure of colonial culture and colonial authority would be threatened. Disengagement was further assisted by the idea of the extreme primitivity associated with Aboriginality. The colonisers, as the antithesis of primitivity, could retain their integrity by rendering the primitive domain subordinate. Having no authority over its own meanings, the Aboriginal social realm was made to appear meaningless.

But rendering the primitive domain meaningless was not effective where white and black people lived cheek by jowl. Administrators of the Territory devoted much energy and attention to the control of inter-racial sexual activity, but the living out of social intimacies was a valued feature of daily life at Mainoru. One aim in this chapter is to understand how the colonisers, while forming relationships with Aborigines, and attempting to re/form them, were also re/forming themselves. Besides exploring the inter-racial relationship at Mainoru, the effect of terror on the terrorisers, of violence on the violent and silence on the silencers will be attended to. As Nandy says: 'As a state of mind, colonialism is an indigenous process released by external forces. Its sources lie deep in the minds of the rulers and the ruled' (1983:3).

Primitive practices

Elkin's visits legitimised Rembarrnga culture as anthropology, but the culture which remained at Mainoru when the experts left attracted ambiguous responses. The habits of these familiar inferiorised people were ignored, patronised or condemned, though small signs of strangeness seem to have enhanced Mrs Dodd's fondness for 'her flock'. A few kin terms and other vernacular expressions were transferred, in a distorted, impoverished form, into the sphere of whitefellas' everyday knowledge, and served to affirm white authority. Otherwise Rembarrnga language was virtually ignored and Rembarrnga practice was subjected to the confident colonial official's gaze with its authoritative sense of what was normal. Dorothy laughed, somewhat nonplussed, about the patrol officers' misunderstanding:

> One old man, Charlie, he had six wives, and all these government men, when they used to come down there and count how many kids, they used to ask him,
>
> 'How many kids that old man got? That girl married [to him] got all this many kids?' he said. [Dorothy's voice conveyed the man's astonished disbelief.] And we used to say, 'No, those kids are from another wife.'
>
> 'Which one? How many wives has that one man got?'
>
> 'Oh, four or five wife. Sometime six you know. Sometime seven. And they got big bunch of kids.' Those kids had one father, different mother (1987).

Officials named the relationships they defined as mother and father, son and daughter, and made moral and organisational judgements based on the expectations that flowed from these definitions. But some habits disturbed and even repelled these whitefellas. The marriages of men in their middle years to young girls were surely not one of the exotic practices that the anthropologists or the dancer Beth Dean were interested in when they visited Mainoru together in 1949 (Dean & Carrel 1956). Rather, the practice was assumed to be sexually motivated and was interpreted as an embarrassing moral failing.

Systematic disorienting interactions with whitefellas were underpinned by dramatic and destructive legal weapons. The Australian law which forbids the marriage of young girls conforms to the popular morality and common sense of a society where marriage means legitimate sexual intercourse. This law conflicts with a cornerstone of many Aboriginal marriage systems. Among Rembarrnga, a baby girl was normally promised as a wife to a man who cared for and protected her and 'grew her up'. She might join his camp while still a child, and mature or old men might have several wives 'bestowed' in this way (Burbank 1988; Hiatt 1965).[2] When Gsell, 'The Bishop with 150 wives' (Gsell 1955), stopped girls from joining their promise husbands' camps by putting them in dormitories, the girls' male relatives expressed alarm that they were let run free without husbands to protect them and grow them up. To them, immorality consisted in leaving young girls unattached and unprotected.[3]

Marrying young girls was both immoral and illegal to Europeans. Polygamy did not provoke the same moral outrage, but it was illegal. Rembarrnga were forcibly made aware of whitefella's sexual morality.

Rex Campion was threatened with arrest for 'carnal knowledge' when marrying Susan Murray in 1968. Susan's father, Larry Murray, tried to protect him by saying that 'it is Aboriginal law' and that 'it was alright', but this defence meant that Larry 'nearly went to jail' himself (Annette Murray pers. com.). Smiler Martin told me that Mrs Dodd had threatened that, if he married his promise wife Lorna, the police would arrest him because it was against white law. That was probably in 1958 and Smiler's understanding is that blackfella law triumphed:

> They tried whitefella law but blackfella law beat it. Mrs Dodd hated that marriage law, but Mr Giese came up to Mainoru and asked the girls, 'You got a promise husband?' and the girls said, 'Yes we got 'im.' 'Well alright then.'
>
> Mrs Dodd didn't like young girls to be promised, but Mr Giese came up and then it was alright. Some girls had babies and they were still in school (1985).

Apparently Harry Giese decided that Rembarrnga practice should be recognised in this case. But the law did not change and nor did the moral judgements of the owners of Mainoru. Heather Dodd told me that Lorna's first baby was born when she was only twelve years old, taking this to be confirmation that they had been fully justified in trying to stop this marriage practice.

More humiliating recollections concern 'brother–sister avoidance', a term anthropologists use for a set of everyday practices in Rembarrnga social life which at first appear to whites to be bizarre, ridiculous and even nasty.[4] Larry was chided when, in response to the patrol officer asking for his sister's name, he called her 'rubbish'. Had he used a Rembarrnga word *jarnga* or *biangduyu*, the whites would not have understood, but as it was, Jack McKay, who undoubtedly found the term 'rubbish' an unacceptable appellation for a sister, insisted that Larry should say Florry's name. This was a shocking suggestion, implying an incestuous intent. On another occasion, a photographer wanted brothers and sisters to stand side by side, Larry beside Florry, Willy beside Nelly, and so on. This was a man who had spent some time at Mainoru and was regarded as a friend. Annette, then ten years old, tried to explain to him that these individuals could not stand next to each other, but the photographer would not understand. Annette told me, 'When that bloke said come close to Florry, my father just bolted like he got electric shock. He never had anything to do with white people after that. If *mununga* came he'd be gone' (1993).

Here, a highly emotional and intimate arena of interpersonal relations was intruded on and censured by outsiders to whom avoidance practices are, at best, meaningless and at worst, indicative of ill manners. In ignorance, but with the supreme confidence of the 'civilised', these whites thus exposed Rembarrnga people to acts bordering on the heretical or obscene. Of course cruelty was not intended. While such particularly painful experiences may not have been common, they show that the nescience of whitefellas was not an innocent, careless lack of information, but an active erasure of the subjectivities and sensibilities of the blackfellas they lived beside, and who they made use of. This wilful blindness seeped into the capillaries of daily race relations.

But not all the blackfellas at Mainoru wanted to preserve the tradition of brother–sister avoidance. Susan and Dolly told me with satisfaction about the policeman who came to Mainoru and broke all the men's spears. These women considered that a good thing because, Susan said, 'Brothers can't spear sisters now. They are not allowed to hit them with hands because the main thing is they can't touch their skin.' But these women continued to respect men's wish to avoid direct interaction with their sisters. They were still shocked by the flouting of such rules and their daughters were expected to be careful not to offend their brothers.

Willy Jailama Martin, commenting on the problems Rembarrnga people experience with whites said, 'Our law is not written down. Before we had no bosses; we had ceremony.' The inchoate and disembodied authority which is expressed in ceremonial life was invisible to whitefellas. The state's attempt to acknowledge 'tribal custom' resulted in a double movement of erasure and affirmation. 'The elders' and 'tribal law' were recognised and reified at certain moments, but while they were spoken of with formal respect, they were not, in fact, consulted.[5] In principle, elders were taken to be the source of what little order might exist in the domain of the primitive, but in reality the practices over which these elders exerted authority, such as marriages and initiation,[6] as well as relations with country, belonged ineluctably to the past and were being rendered illegitimate in other ways. Further, even if the elders could be useful in the present, they were destined to be superseded by the authority of the state. Aborigines lacked suitable leadership directed at the future, and this gap was to be filled with the authority and the teachings of people like Mrs Dodd.

The gestures towards the recognition of Aboriginal law represent a denial of the authority of that law by circumscribing its arena of legitimacy. In the 1930s the administration attempted to separate the policing of 'criminal' from 'tribal matters' even in cases of homicide. The Chief Protector concluded that an arrest should be quashed on the basis that there was 'No evidence that the offence was anything but a tribal custom' (F1 36/592 1936). Patrol officers were advised to conduct careful enquiries to differentiate 'tribal customs' from 'criminal' acts. Some customs were not to be 'meddled with', others were to be 'suppressed' (ibid.). Patrol officers' reports often refer to 'tribal names' and the 'tribal significance' of various matters. Such references to another cultural domain within the state's jurisdiction at once assert an ability to know 'tribal custom', and at the same time render it anomalous, a primitive arena over which colonial authority is legitimately exercised. The category of 'tribal custom', which allows the bracketing off of things specifically Aboriginal from the colonial obsession with progress and rationality, has echoed down the decades since. The preservation of custom was part of the ethical discourse of being a good coloniser. There was little evidence of its effects among Territory officials apart from the provision of reserves, which implied, without explicitly affirming, a legitimate domain for tradition and custom.

If the recognition of 'tribal' matters was limited and impoverished, there was virtually no recognition at all of mundane differences in everyday habits, except as inferiority or ignorance. Because Aboriginal people did not live in houses they were not seen as having a domestic sphere, and the provision of houses, food and clothing for them meant simply extending a humane helping hand to their deficiencies. The teaching of 'normal' domestic practices was not seen to be replacing an established sociality but rather to be filling a void. Also, the teaching of English was not seen as replacing anything of importance. When people learned English they would not need Rembarrnga any more.

Smudging boundaries

The future trajectory for Aborigines relied on the desire to help the natives 'rise culturally—if only we knew how' (Elkin 1974 preface to 1st edition 1938:xiiv). The means was not to include intimate contact with white individuals. The familiar narrative of evolutionary progress, with its metaphors of 'steps' and 'stages' of development, and the 'gradual process of change', was the basis of the progressive policy of assimilation.[7] This benign public discourse co-existed with more anxious and confused debates about inter-racial interaction and with the changes that were occurring in the racial categories. 'Half-caste' people were a conspicuous challenge which demonstrated that the categories were not, in reality, antithetical but could be synthesised. In law, hybridity was a non-condition—one was either subject to the Aboriginal Ordinance or not.

Anthropologists in the 1950s avoided the growing controversies concerning who should be exempted from the Ordinances.[8] Elkin, from his early writings in the 1930s had passionately expounded progressive racial policies, and berated both governments and the racially prejudiced for their limited understanding, saying, 'it should be the desire, as it is the duty, of non-Aboriginal Australians to understand the Aborigines' (1974:362). But his wisdom was based on the same vision as that of the state officials, with a hierarchical racial structure and a historical movement upwards. Elkin saw the 'mixed bloods' as experiencing a 'cultural hiatus' [ibid.:379], but did not mount a critique of the policies which created this hiatus. Further, he bought his considerable influence to bear against those whose views differed, such as Piddington and Thomson (Cowlishaw 1990a; Gray 1994; Wise 1985).

Intense public debate surrounded 'the half-caste problem'. If European identity was the antithesis of the primitive black, social and sexual relations across the racial boundary constituted a major challenge to that identity. Because the whole social order was prefaced on the logic of discrete racial categories, their breaching seemed to presage disorder. The smudging of the boundaries was therefore of greater concern than anything the natives themselves represented.

It is now well recognised that there was extreme and vicious cruelty systematically meted out to Aboriginal women in the outback, and that in many places they were forced to suffer sexual degradation without remedy (Berndt & Berndt 1987; McGrath 1987; Reid 1990). In these accounts, white men have been demonised and Aboriginal women rendered passive victims, and thus the possibility of loving relationships between people of different races has been denied. Such a denial pathologises the sexual relationship, rather than identifying the patho-logical social context that destroyed the inherent possibilities in human attraction. Young asserts that: 'Anxiety about hybridity reflected the desire to keep the races separate, which meant that attention was immediately focussed on the mixed race offspring that resulted from inter-racial sexual intercourse, the proliferating, embodied, living lega-cies that abrupt, casual, often coerced, unions had left behind' (1995:25).

There is abundant evidence of the anxiety he discusses. However, to imply that 'inter-racial sexual intercourse' was *necessarily* a matter of 'abrupt, casual, often coerced unions' is to reproduce stereotypical image of sexual relations at the colonial frontier. The fact that some intimate relationships did manage to flower in frontier conditions indicates that colonial pathology did not infect the whole social body. In the Mainoru story, white men such as Billy Farrar and Jimmy Gibbs defied the social stigma involved and married their Aboriginal women companions, though their continuing relationships did not depend on their doing so. Further, some Aboriginal women took a great interest in the sexuality of white men and were active in seeking relations with them. They studied white men as intimate companions and saw no barriers to forming emotional ties with them.

The blanket denial of the possibility of mutually desired intimacy between individual whitefellas and blackfellas reinforced the purely masculine image of the outback. Other feminine elements managed to survive. Tex Camfoo's account of mustering emphasises women's presence:

> When Billy Moore was mustering, he used to take out three women. Slippery's wife, old Fanny, she's died now, and old Lucy and Florry. They used to go out, maybe one cooking and two tailing cattle. Some of them used to be marvellous ringers too.
>
> When Billy Moore finished [died], Jimmy Gibb was head-stockman, and he used to take Alma. They used to live together. I think they married after. She was a good cook. She used to go out with her old boyfriend, old Jimmy and tail coaches [quiet cattle] for a day or two, while we went out and chased wild ones in to them.
>
> After a while when I took over, I used to take Nelly out, because we were married then. Well, we weren't really, just roosting marriage. When I found Nelly first she was only about nine years old. I think must have sung me with Djarada. I sweated for her for about five or six years (1991).

These women were an organic part of the camp as ringers, cooks and sexual partners. Racial boundaries were muted in these places distant from official scrutiny, and could be breached and subverted with relative ease.

Half-castes themselves represented quite a different administrative problem from the control of inter-racial sex. What was sometimes called 'the half-caste menace' menaced the racial binarism, and the solution was to replace the binary opposites with a racial hierarchy.

An upward historical movement was instituted with half-castes representing a stage between the primitive and the modern. The removal
of half-caste children from the camps enabled them to be repositioned
in space and time. Schooling could equip them to be placed in charge
of black workers under the direction of whites, for instance as head
stockmen and foremen; what Beckett called 'an intermediate stratum'
(1988:198). Such a vision became a logical part of an assimilation
program, with tribal blacks occupying smaller and smaller spaces as
they were transformed into workers. While passionate debates about
the quality of half-castes raged in the press and in the bureaucracy,
this hierarchy was instituted at Mainoru with half-castes running the
stock camps and Mrs Dodd protecting or adopting the paler babies
born to Rembarrnga women.

Consorting

The separation of racial bodies was conceived as the protection of
natural categories, and the desire for sex across the boundaries was
deemed sinful though ever present. The concerns expressed by officials
and experts, and the laws which they formulated not only failed to
control the more exploitative and violent sexual relations but forced
peculiar and painful meanings onto racial interaction. Informal sanctions contributed to these tortuous conditions. All interpersonal
relations were shadowed by the fears, fantasies and theories which
circulated around that imagined racial frontier. There were many kinds
of relationships between individual white and black people in the
outback. Some survived and even flourished for a while, but they have
tended to disappear from consciousness and from historical records. As
we have begun to see, several lives at Mainoru illustrate these other
possible forms of race relations which have been denied expression in
our history.

An emotionally charged vocabulary developed around the notion
of 'consorting' with Aborigines, and any consorting was seen as tainted,
mired in sexual immorality. The relevant legislation began with the
1918 amendment to the Ordinance which said it was an offence to
'*unlawfully*' have carnal knowledge of a female Aboriginal or half-caste
(Markus 1990:14, emphasis added). The wording had left a legal
loophole which was plugged in 1936 by making it an offence for a
white male 'to live or cohabit or have sexual intercourse with any
aboriginal or half-caste not his lawful wife (100 pounds or six months
or both)' (F1 39/408 Sept. 1938). This law rendered Aboriginal

women as passive victims, having no responsibility for sexual intercourse with white men. They were coerced, they had no will, they
knew no better. While women were in this way infantilised, Aboriginal
men were rendered passive, not involved in these relationships. The
public rhetoric was one of concern for Aboriginal women, but the
white man was prosecuted for not controlling himself, rather than for
any harm he did to the woman, let alone to her relations.[9] The real
target of these laws was the blurring of the racial boundaries, both by
intimate contact and by the production of half-caste children.[10]

The official obsession with consorting, evident in the often bizarre
and hypocritical attempts to police such relations,[11] today seems as
irrational as it was implacable, but those who lived out their lives
subjected to contempt and suspicion, had either to try to hide the
association, to avoid contact with others, or to build a separate social
domain among 'combos'. 'Combo' was one of a plethora of lurid
vernacular expressions surrounding these associations; other common
denigrating terms were 'black velvet' and 'gin shepherd'. A burnt cork
given to a man who had fathered a child by an Aboriginal woman
was a recognised symbolic insult (McGrath 1984:238–39). The haven
afforded by isolated stations like Mainoru did not entirely protect its
residents from emotions of defiance, defensiveness or internalised
shame created by these laws, official and unofficial.

It was a practice among drovers to avoid the law against cohabiting
by dressing their Aboriginal women companions as boys. The romantic
rendering of the song 'The Drover's Boy',[12] as a relationship of secret
love and loyalty of the drover for his 'boy', is a refreshing counter to
the usual understanding of inter-racial sex as always coercive and
exploitative. The song emphasises the poignancy in such relations. The
law responded to this practice in 1934 (McCorquodale 1987:71) with
a regulation stating: 'If any female Aboriginal or female half-caste is
found dressed in male attire and in the company of any male person
other than an Aboriginal or half-caste, she and the person in whose
company she is found shall each be guilty of an offence against this
Act' (quoted in McGrath 1984:267–68).

It was a declared concern for moral standards, concern for the
protection of Aboriginal women, and concern about the problem of
half-caste children, which fuelled the sexualised racial discourse that
emerged from Canberra, Darwin and other urban centres. Inter-racial
relations were visible in the towns of the Territory, but were not part
of the lives of the respectable populace. But on pastoral properties
interaction was a constant and ordinary part of everyday life. On many

stations there was systematic exploitation of Aboriginal women for sex, and for some workers 'black velvet' was accepted as a necessary perquisite to working on outback stations (Berndt & Berndt 1987; Cole 1988; McGrath 1984:256–57). On other stations, Aboriginal people were active in drawing white people into the kin networks of the local Aboriginal clans through marriage or other associations (McGrath 1987). Billy Farrar's putative kin through his marriage to Judy claimed him as uncle, grandfather or brother. The extent of Jack McKay's sexual relations with Aboriginal women is shrouded in the secrecy of the times; women deemed both him and his brother 'rough'.[13] He was, as a matter of course, given a 'skin' designation. Perhaps the arrival of Jack's mother, sister and brother-in-law obstructed any further development of hybridity.

The white family at Mainoru was, as we saw above, very limited. Neither Jack nor Sandy married or had children of their own, and Heather, the Dodds' only child, was often away at boarding school. For men such as Jack and Sandy McKay, the appeal of the bush may have been its asexuality rather than its masculinity. Indeed it may have been an escape from urban masculinity, sexuality and domestic demands.

Of course mateship is not 'consorting', and there was no shame in the affection and solicitude Jack showed towards his old friend 'Yellow Bob' as expressed in a long letter to the NAB. Jack told how he had met this Rembarrnga man tin-mining and had later heard that Yellow Bob was 'sitting in the blacks' camp at Roper Valley' where he was 'having a lean time of it'. Jack had brought him back to live at Mainoru and made him comfortable until forced to take him in to the East Arm leprosarium. Jack concluded his letter: 'I don't suppose [he] will ever come back and I would like to send him a pound now and then to buy a few things for himself but would like to be sure that he would get it' (F1 52/759 Feb. 1949).

Jack was assured in an anonymous letter from the NAB that if he 'pays money to Trust [Aboriginal Benefits Trust Fund] we will see it is given' (ibid.). The mythic mateship of the bush seems to be realised in this moving glimpse of the affection and care Jack showed towards his ill, incarcerated 'half-caste' mate.

Like most cattle stations, Mainoru was separated by long, rough and dusty roads from the legal and social strictures of the towns. Thus it was not fear of police which led the Mainoru regime to eschew exploitative, casual sex between white men and Aboriginal women. Rather it was internalised edicts in obedience to a moral order that deemed such relations immoral. On the other hand, lasting sexual relationships across the racial divide were accepted; they had been instituted by the founder of the station Billy Farrar with his marriage to Judy. Mainoru was also a haven from persecution for Alma Gibbs who had developed a relationship with the white stockman Jimmy Gibbs (plate 18): 'We stopped there at Mainoru, for a while. It was alright then, nobody talked about us two. We lived together one house. We lived in that big shed, where Jack McKay lived. Me and Jimmy Gibbs and Jack McKay, we lived together there. We didn't camp.' (Alma Gibbs 1989)

Nelly and Tex were also part of Jack McKay's household for a time. Despite the disapproval of casual sexual relations, a few light-skinned children appeared, not to Judy or Alma or others in known relationships with white men, but to Rembarrnga women who had Rembarrnga husbands. One reason for this was explained by Dorothy:

> When Avy had that half-caste baby, old Bill sent her away. Bill said, 'The government might blame me and think I sold my wife.' They did that at Mainoru. Florry, Lucy, Alice and Abie had half-caste kids. We never used to get much smoke, nickynicky we used to call it, so they'd go along [to a white man] for smoke for husband, and for tucker. Now, this time, they can keep the yella-fella kids. [At] that time they took them away (1987).

Here is evidence that shame, or at least fear of the consequences, had been successfully inculcated concerning what was called 'selling' one's wife, a shame that seems absent from the women's pragmatic way of gaining access to tobacco and tucker. Like many other women Dorothy was puzzled and saddened by the policy of taking the 'yella-fella kids' away.

Heather Dodd's description of the same situation is quite different: 'Both Florrie and Lucy presented Chuck with coloured [half-caste] children. He wasn't really pleased. My Uncle Sandy McKay took care of the kids as they were getting a poor deal in camp. No [they were] not his. Anyhow the Welfare Department removed the girl, Florrie's daughter, who is a trained Kindergarten teacher, married, three children, lives in Darwin' (letter 1981).

Heather's brusque manner was accompanied by a considerable sense of satisfaction about the education and social status of Florrie's daughter Eileen. Even more satisfaction was expressed about Alice's light-skinned daughter Pixie who was adopted by Mrs Dodd (plate 19). Pixie, Heather asserted, 'refuses to take any money for being

Aboriginal'. Heather was candid about her view that a great deal of harm has been done to Aborigines by misconceived policies in recent years, formulated by people who know nothing about them.

When Mrs Dodd needed an assistant teacher for the school, she explained to the Director of Education why a young man would not do ('I shudder when one comes on the place . . . it's a trap—too many girls with still different outlook to ours'), and she asked for a man 'set in his ways and in charge' (F1 56/2209 1961). When Eileen was born 50 years ago the sanctions against inter-racial sex were substantial enough to command Florry's silence and she refused ever to name Eileen's father in a desire to protect him. For her part, Eileen refuses any interest in the question of her biological paternity, thus making a deliberate statement of her rejection of the importance of her white heritage and, by implication, a rejection of the significance of this sexual liaison. She firmly asserted that Chuckerduck was her social, and thus her real, father.

CLOSE RELATIONS

The law echoed the fear among the ordinary white populace that there was something unnatural and wrong about inter-racial relationships, and the pseudo-scientific term 'miscegenation' (Bloch 1958; Cowlishaw 1988:4), used in the elite academic discourse, did nothing to dispel it. As well as the permits for employers of native labour, a system of permits to marry or associate with natives was also established, allowing the borders of the racial domains to be closely monitored. Public interaction between white and black people was made discomforting and awkward unless it was firmly hierarchical. In the towns, those classified as racially different could request permission to associate. A formal response might say 'X can associate with Y after sunset on Fridays' (F1 39/408 1940).

Asking for a hand

Mr Moy, as Director of Native Affairs, was authorised 'to grant permission for the marriage of any *female* aboriginal with any person other than an aboriginal' (F315 49/189 1944, my emphasis). That is, such permits were only ever envisaged as applying to white men marrying black women. In such marriages, the gender hierarchy and the racial hierarchy reinforced one another. Marriage of a black man to a white woman was unthinkable because the gender power which a black man would attain by becoming the husband of a white woman would subvert the racial hierarchy. The inter-racial marriages which the administration did allow[14] were an attempt to control and regularise relationships, many of which were already established in remote places and could not be eliminated. The system of monitoring ensured that they did not become commonplace. In these intimate relationships, the gender hierarchy merged with the racial hierarchy to reinforce but also partly to subvert racial inequality through forms of collaboration and complicity which love itself helps to sustain.

The officials of the state are not automatons but individuals whose task, in this case, was permitting and refusing particular marriages. The marrying couple, who were the targets of the laws, can be seen as the clients of those persons who devised and executed the official functions required by the Ordinance. The white man had to write a letter, or have one written by the local protector, police officer or missionary, and a series of officials had to make judgements and decisions. Neither the requests nor the responses reveal any questioning of the meaning of the racial categories, though a few were angered by the refusal of permission. Transgressive individuals who did not request permission to marry were sometimes hounded through the bush by police and patrol officers for years.

Requests for permission to marry were usually humble and deferential; the replies were sharp and to the point. The applicants took a supplicant position, exposing their personal lives as a matter of course, and setting out a defence of their integrity, honesty and good intentions toward the intended brides. There were no notions of 'civil rights' among these people, but rather a sense of shame, especially among those applicants who were called half-castes but who had been exempted from the provisions of the Ordinance.[15] The DNA often addressed a terse request for more information to the policeman or protector who would assess the man's relationship with the woman, his circumstances and his probity. If these were deemed satisfactory a permit was eventually forwarded giving the date on which the permission would expire. Seldom was anyone refused if the reports were satisfactory, though the time limit on the permit sometimes expired before the roads were open after the wet season to allow the preacher in to perform the marriage ceremony (F 315 49/265).

One such request was received from Mainoru station in 1950. It was forwarded from Protector Johnson of the Maranboy police station to the Director of Native Affairs saying:

Attached please find an application by James E. Gibbs of Mainoru Station, to marry an aboriginal woman, namely, Alma (Knutchimboo). The applicant is well known to the Police of the Northern Territory, having been a resident of the country for about 35 years. He at one time held country on the Roper River at St. Vidgeons and later Urapunga Stations. As far as is known he is a man of good character and has no convictions recorded against him judicially. I have no objections (F1 52/519).

However, Director Moy replied that: 'Mr Ryan is to investigate this matter. I think Mr Gibbs should reconsider his application.' He told Patrol Officer Ryan that he was 'strongly of the opinion that Mr Gibbs should reconsider'. Ryan was unable to contact Mr Gibbs and told the Director, 'I don't think Alma would lose anything by the marriage; financially Mr Gibbs is sound. I believe he has associated with Alma for over four years according to information obtained recently.'

But it was the interests of Jimmy Gibbs rather than those of Alma that Director Moy was protecting, and the patrol officer's concern for Alma shows a discontinuity between the priorities of senior administrators and those in the field. In February 1951 Moy sent a memo to the manager of Beswick station asking him to discuss the matter further with Mr Gibbs and ascertain if he wished to proceed; 'Personally I am of the opinion that Mr Gibbs would be rather foolish to do so.' Finally on 18 April 1951, permission was given via the Beswick manager (F1 52/519) and the marriage service took place.

Alma and Jimmy; Nelly and Tex

These events were first described to me by Alma Gibbs in quite different terms. Alma was not literate and the law was known to her only through the police, the protectors and the patrol officers. Her account reveals significant details, not recorded in the archives, about the lengths to which the officials went to separate her from Jimmy:

> Jimmy Gibbs and me were staying at Beswick. He was mending saddles. I was cooking in the stock camps. That's the time we got caught. Native Affairs came out because somebody reported us two. They reckon, 'That old man Jimmy Gibbs, he's got a black girl there. He's living with her.'
>
> They came to Beswick at night time, all that lot. We were having breakfast, morning time, and this old man[16] [Jimmy Gibbs] said, 'Hey, all the welfare are here. They've come after you and me.'
>
> 'Alright, they can come,' I said to everyone. They came up: 'We

know you, old man. You've got a girl here. You can't marry her. You're not allowed,' they said.

'Not me,' Jimmy Gibbs said. 'That girl works for me, cooking in the stock camp.' Well, they carted up all the books. And they brought up two or three boys [Aboriginal men] too, to give me a black one.

'Well,' they said, 'we can't let you marry that man. You pick which boy you want.'

'I won't pick anybody,' I told them like that. 'I'll stop with this old man.'

'No, you not allowed. He's not a young man. He's a bit old for you.'

'No matter he's an old man, I'll stay with him. I work for him. I can't help myself. I've got to look after his clothes, everything for him. You can't make me feel different.'

'No, you're not allowed. You've got to marry your own colour,' they said.

'I don't care about my own colour. I'm married to this white man. You can't make the law all the time,' I said to them. Then they said, 'Alright, do you want to leave this old man?'

'No, I can't leave him. I'll stay with him. No-one can force me,' I said. So they had to believe me.

'Alright, well do you want to be married?'

'No, not married to him, I want to live with him, that's all.' After that they said, 'That's alright, you two can walk about free now.' We went to Bamyilli, Barunga now, and had a party for us. That tall welfare man and his missus made that party. I was drinking too that day. I wasn't really drunk, but old man was drunk, Jimmy Gibbs (1989).

Alma recalled the happiness everyone expressed that day and her only taste of alcohol. She presented her story to me with considerable puzzlement at Moy's prevarication, and bemusement and even embarrassment at the ludicrous efforts of the Beswick manager and the policeman in bringing three 'boys' to the camp for her to choose from. She was triumphant about forcing them to accept her assertions that Jimmy Gibbs was neither too old nor too white, and believes that her assurance that she did not want to 'marry' him, but just wanted to 'live' (live together) had something to do with it. Jimmy did not believe their liaison could gain official recognition, and Alma is sure that her own persistence led to their success. She did not have to test the system any further; like Judy Farrar, she never had children.[17]

Rough riding was said to be responsible, though more sinister reasons have been suggested:

> I never had a kid. Once I lost one riding, I think. Too much galloping. I was not very pregnant. It just started. Hot day, we'd been travelling and I got sick and had to go to Springvale Army hospital. They said, 'You've killed that kid. I don't think you'll make one again.' Anyway they'd have taken it away. They were really silly then, taking away all the half-caste kids from their mothers (1989).

The archival record reveals a series of solemn letters, in which the missionaries at Roper and Harry Giese competed for the high moral ground concerning the legal and moral dimensions of Tex Camfoo's wish to marry Nelly (plate 20). Their evidence about the views and character of the parties was slim but nonetheless they debated the proper outcome at length. Tex told me: 'I had to go through Native Affairs in those days. Jack McKay wouldn't help. Jimmy Dodd wouldn't help. They didn't want to be mixed up in it. So we pulled out and went to Mountain Valley. Ray Hood helped us fill out all the forms.'

It appears that Mainoru was not so liberal when it came to marriages. Along with three other men who wanted to marry Aboriginal women, Tex had to wait years for a response. He said: 'They gave us three years of trouble. They wanted to be sure. I don't know why they didn't like white man mucking around with dark girls. They could get a fine, or six months in jail.' Nelly said:

> Welfare wouldn't let us marry half-caste men or whitefella men. Tex had really big trouble, because those days we weren't citizens yet. Policeman and all they came out [to Mainoru] and question me: 'Did you muck around with that boy?' I said, 'Yes.' I didn't tell lie. I wasn't frightened . . . They called me to the table and I said, 'Well you can't stop my love. If you going to take Tex to jail you might as well put me in too' . . . I thought we'd get a letter and get summonsed, go in jail because you muck around with one another. But we got an engagement paper. It said, 'You're entitled to go with your girlfriend in town'.

Eventually, when Nelly was working at Katherine hospital and Tex had driven stock to Mataranka, he was told to come quickly, that Reverend Lang was in Katherine and was going to marry them. Tex continues:

We went up there, just a private place. The doctor was our best man. Mrs Ryan, that's Ron Ryan the patrol officer's wife. She had the wedding ring. I didn't have any money to get a ring. We put it on and that's it. They took my photos and everything like that. We signed the paper and Ron Ryan said, 'You'll never run away now!' I was hobbled.

This use of the white stockman's rhetoric of marriage as a 'hobble' sits strangely with the lengths to which Tex had to go to gain permission to marry. The layering of Tex's identity is evident in these varied moral assertions, in his social relations with whites and his legal status as European, which conceal the domain of Aboriginal ceremonial life he inhabits. Nelly describes how white ritual was used to adorn their relationship: 'The welfare lady dress me over there. Tex went one way, I went another—you know how you do it. A few Aboriginal people were at our wedding but nearly all whitefellas. Mr Ryan this welfare man was saying, "I'm handing Nelly to Tex Camfoo."'. And Mrs Ryan gave me the biggest ring. I couldn't fit it. They got another one for me from Darwin.'

This wedding was a welfare production. No one from Mainoru was present. These events affirm Nelly's sense of being able to manipulate whites, for which she was rewarded by their admiration for her smartness. She believed they said, 'I suppose we can't stop her because that girl's too smart' and echoed words she had heard in this context: 'I was really spoiled girl in one way, but one way I made a lot of trouble for Mr. Giese. He won't forget me, that Mr Giese. He always said, "By golly Nelly and Tex, you can get me in a lot of trouble."'

In both these cases the Aboriginal women are convinced, with good reason, that it was their determination and their assertion of love which won against official disapproval. In monitoring the racial boundary, the state made magnanimous gestures and clothed them in official celebrations of formal wedding ceremonies, and thus retained their sense of control over the racial boundary.

Taking the children

The idea of motherhood carries a far weightier moral burden of social morality in the Australian nation and the west in general, than does the metaphor of paternalism discussed above. Yet for 60 years, from 1911 to 1970, certain Australian children were systematically taken from their mothers and other kin by the state and put into communal homes to be looked after and taught in ways believed suitable to their racial designation.[18] In the Territory this tragic drama was played out around the colour of the children's skin. Unlike the southern states, the difference in colour between the children and their parents was the major sign that led to Aboriginal children being removed from their families.[19]

In exploring how the removal of Aboriginal children from isolated communities took place, I am contesting the popular view that this was an example of an irrational racism which emerged at specific moments in the past, an aberration in the major trajectory of Australia's history. Rather, it was a logical development of two wider social programs which encompassed the whole population. One was the increasing state intervention into poor families in the name of a scientifically informed effort to create social and physical health, which occurred from the 1930s onwards (Reiger 1985). But it was also another step in the logic of racial categorisation which further separated the colour categories and created an in-between category in the racial hierarchy.

The policy and practice of taking Aboriginal children has been discussed in recent years by some of the officials involved (Hasluck 1988; Long 1992:81–84; Macleod 1997:166ff) as well as by many of the 'stolen children' who gave evidence to an enquiry in 1997.[20] Taking the children entailed the personal involvement of colonial officials. They responded to systematic protests in the 1950s by setting out an elaborate justification, beginning with the emphasis on re-education:

> [I]t has always been the policy of the NAB . . . to remove part aboriginal children from their native environment into institutions where they may receive education, vocational guidance and in general fit them for their absorption into the community on attaining adult age . . . Patrol Officers . . . prepare the mothers of these children for the eventual separation . . . If, at the first visit, the parents are loath to part with the child the matter is left until the next visit when another attempt is made and the process of 'educating' the parents is continued. Eventually (and a period of two years may elapse between the first attempt and final success) the child is willingly handed to the custody of the Patrol Officer. Under these circumstances there is no distress—in fact it strengthens the confidence of the native people in the work of the Patrol Officer . . . Some patrol officers take photographs of the children and forward prints to the mothers as a keepsake. This is always appreciated . . . field staff must

maintain harmonious relations with the full-blood aborigines in their districts . . . and they accordingly do nothing that would upset that harmony (F1 52/250 Oct. 1951).

The patrol officers' role is here described as one of enticing and bullying parents and indeed the whole Aboriginal community into relinquishing their children to the state's care. Because the 'full-blood aborigines' also relied on 'harmonious relations' with the patrol officers, the latter's insistent admonishments could not be resisted forever. A further memo followed with further justifications which rely on the stereotypes of moral unworthiness. For instance, half-castes have an 'innate tendency' to break from native environments at adolescence and become 'misfits'; the males, if they stay, are a 'constant source of trouble' in tribal group; females are apt to be attracted to 'low white men'; these children are more readily assimilable if early educated (F1 52/250 Dec. 1951). New instructions told patrol officers: 'With . . . new procedures, distress minimised . . . in difficult cases await mother's permission or allow her to accompany child and visit it; no use of aircraft . . . no children to be removed under four years' (F1 52/250 19 Dec. 1951).

The following year the instruction about the age at which children should be taken was reversed. They were now to be removed as young as possible, always *before* four years of age. This change was based on new scientific evidence that younger children would suffer less, and the mother likewise. The science of psychology was here used to authorise a sudden change of practice from one form of savage intervention to another, a practice which was deliberately intended to sever the most intimate and intense emotional bond. The patrol officers who were policing the margins of civilisation, bolstered by their faith in science, did not argue with the experts from powerful institutions. The awkward strategies to relieve distress are attempts to mute the agony caused by such social surgery.

The legal basis of these actions was again the Aboriginal Ordinance which, from 1911, had made the Chief Protector the legal guardian of all Aboriginal and half-caste children to the exclusion of parents or relatives, and had passed that responsibility to the Director of Native Affairs, and then to the Director of Welfare in 1953. While the law was a crucial element, its enforcement was an extension of the logic and emotional force of racial ideology. Public protests were directed at the cruelty of the specific act of removing children from their mothers, not at the associated beliefs that the races should occupy separate domains, or that the government should take responsibility for Aborigines' social existence. The official response was to reassure the public that the mother's suffering would be minimised. The patrol officers were engaged in a painful but necessary task. Their personal responses to a policy that entailed them inflicting the grief and pain of separation on parents and young children were subordinated to the insistent demands of history as Macleod, a patrol officer involved in these events, recognised (Macleod 1997:166ff).

Ryan was the patrol officer who took the half-caste children away from Mainoru, and when Jack McKay enquired about these children on behalf of their parents, Ryan took the messages to and from Darwin. Florry's daughter Eileen remembers being taken away at about three-and-a-half years of age with her cousin from Beswick. She kept some contact with her mother through the cooperation between Patrol Officer Ryan and Jack McKay and she renewed contact with her mother in the 1980s. She said:

> I asked Mum how she felt when we were taken. She said, 'Well it broke in here', but she said old Jack was good. He always checked to see what was happening. He told her what I was doing and who I was staying with in Darwin and when I went to Brisbane. Jack was a good old man but a tough old fella they reckon.

Heather Dodd explained that there were conflicts concerning such events:

> Leslie Moore lived with us up at the house. He is Ronnie [Lindsay's] cousin. His father was head stockman part white. [Leslie is] a quarter white . . . Coloured children were fairly badly treated, and Sandy eventually took them into the house. Then the government swooped and took away the girl Eileen and we could never get her back. This was before we arrived—Mum tried for years. They said we were not suitable people to handle the rearing of a child. Leslie stayed with us until he was sent to Reta Dixon to school and they never allowed him to return (interview 1988).

The explanations and justifications for removing these children relied on two 'facts', the meaning of which was taken to be obvious. These were the colour of the children and the nature of the 'native camps'. The hysteria caused by the image of white women among the black tribes (Cowlishaw 1996) is echoed in the consternation caused by pale children's bodies among the black ones. The very sight convinced the authorities that something was wrong. The meaning of the colour of the body here becomes crucial and is clear in the statement of Paul Hasluck, Minister for Territories in the 1950s, when he was asked about the policies in 1988. He said:

> To give the protectors their due, if you saw pale skinned children in the camps among the dirt they were going to be brought up with all the others. It seemed to give them a better chance to lift them out of the camps . . . there was the same separation of white children from unsuitable homes, especially single mothers.
>
> I'm primarily an historian not a moralist. Try to understand what happened and why ('Science Book Shop', ABC Radio, 21 May 1988).

Hasluck did not want to justify the practice in the contemporary climate, but would not condemn it because he saw it as having been self-evident then that removing 'pale skinned children' from 'the dirt' among 'the others' would 'give them a better chance'. Yet he denied the moralising inherent in these policy decisions. The evoking of an undifferentiated mass of black bodies in the dirt, with the pale child inappropriately placed among them seemed to Hasluck a rational rather than a flagrantly moralistic reason for removing them to a half-caste home or a mission, institutions that would teach them how to live in ways appropriate to their skin colour. A pale skin meant that the child had a different destiny. Hasluck further equated these removals with those from 'unsuitable homes', thus consigning the social domain of Aborigines to a generalised unworthiness as a source of culture and socialisation.[21] Invoking fears of 'dirt' is especially ironic given that the government officials, who were not able to fulfil their legal obligations to ensure decent conditions in the 'blacks' camps', nonetheless were able to systematically remove light-skinned children from their families. In this task they usually seem to have had the cooperation of the pastoralist, though not in the case of Mainoru.

Dirt is a powerful element of much racial discourse. When Patrol Officer Ryan took three children from Beswick, he reported that 'there will be no necessity for coercion . . . mothers are not clean in themselves and do not keep the children clean . . . They look like full-bloods they are so dirty . . . In my opinion these three children have no further prospects while they remain with their mothers' (Ryan Beswick, F1 55/414). This judgement of hygiene was based on superficial appearances, but Elias (1984) and Foucault (1978) have shown that Europe's civilising mission came to be mediated by medical notions of hygiene and by a rising threshold of disgust against dirt and the body's secretions. Racism is fuelled by such disgust over the polluted nature of other bodies. White people are unable to accept differing corporeal regimes and habits, and imagine that proximity to the earth is itself polluting. This explains the emphasis on redisciplining the half-caste children in hygiene and personal cleanliness. However, a major hypocrisy is revealed in the fact that the emphasis on hygiene often remained rhetorical. Simply being in urban white spaces, away from 'the blacks' camp' was assumed to achieve cleanliness. In fact half-caste homes may sometimes have been unhealthy both physically and psychologically, staffed as they were by charity workers or missionaries. The half-caste compound in Darwin was said to represent a serious danger to the health of the inmates (Cummings 1990; HREOC 1997:134).

Missionary dedication is exemplified in the words of Miss Cross who ran the Groote Eylandt mission home for half-castes. She claimed that the children were removed 'from among the black children at Roper River mission station . . . so that young half-castes might be brought up under ideal conditions away from undesirable influences' (NTTG 7 Aug. 1931). She said, 'it is a beautiful home for the children', but the aesthetics were less apparent to Tex Camfoo when he was taken there at about eight years of age. He was baptised Jimmy because 'There were just too many Harrys there.' The missionary said:

> 'I'll change your name and call you Jimmy. Oh, you'll like that name. You're still wearing your father's name.' So he baptised me there, then, Jimmy Camfoo. After about four years the missionaries decided, 'We've got to send all the mainland mob back to see their parents.' Well no use following our parents after all this time, especially me! I was taught Ngalakan [Ngalkbon] but after three or four years we forgot, even our parents. Anyhow, they shipped us back to Roper River.
>
> My mother and my stepfather were at Numbulwar. They knew we were coming back, and they were waving, waving to us. And we went alongside the bank, just not far away. And we couldn't know them! We all sat looking at them and they looked at us! They didn't know: 'Maybe my son's there somewhere? My daughter there somewhere?'
>
> My mother knew I was there. I didn't know my mother. I ran away from her, you know! After a while they talked to me: 'That's your mother, that's your mother! You don't want to run away! That's your proper mother! Old Florida!' After a while I knew then. I met up with my mother.

In his reference to the suffering of his mother and to the parents and children who did not recognise each other after years of enforced separation, and to his own confusion, Tex was conscious of the peculiarity of the situation in the eyes of the very whites who created it. Subsequently Tex was placed in the dormitory at the Roper mission for many years where worse things happened (Camfoo: in press). He lived under the authority of white missionaries, but, except for the four years on Groote Eylandt, he was in the country of his mother and step-father and was intermittently socialised by them into the law. Thus, Tex's experience was of a bifurcated racial identity.

One of the popular ways of justifying the removal of these children is that they were not wanted by their parents. Heather Dodd said: 'People make such a fuss about this but I fail to see what else the government could have done. Leaving them there didn't seem a viable option because they weren't wanted' (1988).

Her other stories seem to contradict this view, though no doubt there were husbands and other kin who resented a white man fathering a child.[22] As mentioned above, several light-skinned children were taken from Mainoru, and one was adopted by the Dodds to avoid her removal. Heather would not have imagined that one source of anxiety for Rembarrnga was that the removed children would not know their kin and might inadvertently marry 'wrong side' relations. Those taken were often mentioned in Rembarrnga oral autobiographies, with stories and speculation about their whereabouts. By contrast, I present in full George Jangawanga's successful struggle to keep his child:

From Mainoru I went away to Mountain Valley, working as a bullock tailer. And that's the time, behind, at Mainoru, that *Mununga* claimed my daughter, Elaine Jangawanga. Heather Dodd, Mrs Dodd, Mr McKay from Mainoru, said they were not allowed to give me back that kid:

'No, you won't get that piccaninny back. We've got to take that kid,' they were telling me.

'No, that's my colour, that's not your colour,' I told them.

'We can't give you,' Jack McKay said, 'because she's half-caste and you are full black Aboriginal.'

'Your sister can't claim my kid. If you claim, you should claim your own colour. This is my colour,' I told him like that. Well I went to Mountain Valley and I came back with a spear. I thought, I don't want to let my kid go. I'll have to go and get her back. I said my opinion. I was upset about my kid. When I went back to Mainoru my sister, Dorothy and Nelly and Susan Murray's mother, and my brothers, all these, they come and said: 'Hey, Mrs Dodd wants you to go up there for that little girl. She wants you mob to go up, to say something to you.' I said, 'No, I can't go up there. Let them come down to the camp.' I thought about it in another way, they might beat me there in the court. I sat down and by and by I got a woomera and bundle of spears. I waited. Sandy McKay came down with a little revolver. He called me like, to come here. Then he shot that drum and tried to frighten me. He shot low, bang that drum. I didn't move, I stood up to him. After that I grabbed that man and hit him, and chucked that revolver away. After that he got up and said: 'Oh. Leave it alone now.' And my uncle was there, two of my uncles. And my brother and all of my sisters and brothers. Smiler was there, and Ronny. All my uncles and fathers, they came in and stopped me there. He started to walk up then to his place, to the house. That Bedford truck that's where I grabbed him now, and thumped him at that Bedford truck. I picked up the axe and tried to cut him. Old Chuckerduck and his wife grabbed me.

'Leave him, young fella. Don't kill him poor fella. We sorry for him.'

They stopped me. And after that the Welfare they came and got a policeman, Mr Mulligan and Mr Morrison and Mr Lovegrove and John Gordon. That was Mr Ryan's time, you know. A lot of people came, Alan Pitt and Tom Farrell. They were talking about sending me to Alice Springs. They said: 'That's not his fault. We can't send him away. That's not his problem. He'll have to work, prisoner.' They had my girl Elaine up there at their house and I got her out from there and brought her back. They gave me a welfare job, for punishment. For one year I worked at the airstrip and other places (1993).

This account reveals elements of the system of social relations among black people at Mainoru. Preparing himself with spear and woomera, sitting awaiting his adversary in his own space, the display of courage in the face of threat, and the participation of his relations as supporters, witnesses and as moderators of the fight, brought to bear Aboriginal rules of engagement with white power. Sandy's attempt to bully and frighten George brought into play a form of white power largely concealed in the expressions of affection and care. George was vindicated when a large number of white authorities accepted his right to keep his child, though they still punished him for attacking Sandy McKay. This case is especially ironic because the child had two black parents. She was not 'half-caste' at all but happened to be somewhat lighter skinned than other babies.

INTIMATES AND ENEMIES

While an invariant primitivity clung to the official conception of Aborigines, they could be induced to give up this condition of their being. The psychological and social mechanisms of this transformation process remained vague in official discourse, but there was faith that it was occurring, and indeed something *was* occurring. The relationships between white and black people at Mainoru were lived by the whites in terms of an imagined evolutionary process, but the theories of evolution were being sublimated and played out in bonds of affection and nurturance. Entwined with domestic practices and patterns, these personal attachments became the means of asserting and clarifying, but also of subverting and rendering ambiguous the codes of the racial hierarchy. A commonsense acceptance of racial inequality as a basis of daily interaction was apparent on all visible surfaces of station life. The one taught and cared for the other, and knowledge and nurturance did not flow the other way. Yet there was ambiguity created by the affection and intimacy which everyday contact made inevitable. Thus the meaning of the racial hierarchy was not even or predictable, and the pattern of human relations affected by it was also unstable.

Intimacy and hierarchy

In the white cultural space at Mainoru there was a rich mixture of loving kindness and punishment, affection for working 'boys' and 'piccaninnies', as well as imaginings of monstrous habits. In the stock camps the 'men' and 'boys' would travel for days, or often weeks, of cooperative mustering and droving, eating together and sleeping at night in their swags under the stars.[23] There was usually only one white or 'half-caste' head stockman, and often a 'stockboy', that is a Rembarrnga man, would be in charge of a small mustering team. This racial hierarchy was never seriously challenged.

Before the arrival of other members of his family, Jack McKay's social interaction was mainly with men such as Billy Farrar, Jimmy Gibbs, Billy Moore and Tex Camfoo who were all racially marginal, either married to Aboriginal women or designated as 'half-caste'. While the remote location insulated these relationships from official scrutiny, the state was not absent. Ryan applauded Jack and Sandy for caring 'most competently' for Leslie, the 'three-quarter-caste' son of Billy Moore. Though care and affection crossed the racial barriers, it did not protect Leslie Moore from removal. The patrol officer noted that Jack was 'willing to assist financially in his education' though 'his financial circumstances at present [are] not very sound' (Ryan F1 53/184 July 1952). Jack showed solicitude also in writing other letters asking that money or messages from their mothers be passed on to children who were at one of the half-caste establishments.

Personal warmth and concern could ameliorate the racial hierarchy but the spatial structuring of lives at Mainoru confirmed it. Domestic interaction between the races took place in the white space of the station house, or in the stock camps, but not in the 'blacks' camp' where the Rembarrnga community cooked, ate and often slept in the open. The camp was visible from the station homestead which was about 200 metres away on a low hill. This positioning affirmed the right of whites to scrutinise the lives of their black subjects who seemed not to value privacy or individuality, but were willing to present themselves as 'the mob' to the white gaze.

A vision of domesticating the wild was quite explicit in the mind of Mrs Dodd, but domestication required firm authority. The official approval to conduct a school on the verandah of the rough station house from 1957 meant that she was paid as a regular teacher. She lavished affection on the children and adults she tamed, but the taming process entailed elements of a harsher discipline. Besides the usual instruction in reading, writing and arithmetic, her pedagogic role involved the inculcation of a whole range of personal habits and techniques: wearing of clothing, washing with soap, manners of speech, regulating food intake, and measuring time according to the calendar and the clock. She made clothing and provided nutritious food. The patrol officer Ryan said: 'At no station in my district are the natives better fed . . . Eggs, milk and custards are on the regular diet . . . A book is kept showing the issues of clothing and other items to the females who are entitled to free issues. Mrs Dodd and her mother make the clothes for the children. Under-clothing is issued.'

But he also sounded a note of warning: 'If she can be criticised it would be on the point as to whether she might be spoiling some of them. There is always a large number of girls and children in the house and although some of the domestics are capable it is possible that on many occasions Mrs Dodd does the work while they look on' (F1 52/579 Nov. 1953).

The anxiety here is because the hierarchies of race and labour may not be reinforcing each other. Mrs Dodd must not be doing the work for the girls. In fact these girls came into the house to learn, and their

Rembarrnga identity was smothered under other meanings. They became an extension of the social world of the whites, with limited opportunity to appropriate the things of whites. While they helped shape the life on the station, any challenge they were making to its form or its practices was ephemeral and disappeared when they left Mainoru.

Mrs Dodd delighted in her task. She washed and uniformly reclothed the Rembarrnga children. She seated them in chairs, at desks, in rows (plates 21, 22) and expected them to be silent and receptive: their impulses and habits of moving, feeling and thinking were being re/formed. She told the education authorities that: 'A school for natives at the present time should start with the two year olds—get them out of the camp away from the environment and lingo every day. I have all the threes up, but haven't time to do much with them only keep them out of the camp as I have thirty-four on formal work, all stages from nil to 6th grade' (F1 56/2209 1961).

The 'environment' and 'the lingo' are the enemies of proper teaching, and echo Hasluck's reason for taking children from 'the camps'. The discipline which was necessary for these children could be shocking to Rembarrnga. Though only aged about twelve or thirteen, Lorna had her baby at the breast when she was at school. At first she told me that Mrs Dodd was 'the best teacher, really good', but later angrily recounted the corporal punishment for untidy writing which Mrs Dodd inflicted with a ruler. Lorna still has a sense of resentment; hitting people, unless one is angry, is savagery indeed.

Harsher forms of discipline were practised in many stock camps. Rembarrnga told of physically rough treatment and being hauled out of swags before dawn, sometimes with a flick of the whip, and made to work all day and every day for many weeks. Complaints about such hard work are expressed in ambivalent terms which include appreciation of the discipline and the learning of stock work. By contrast, the cold, deliberate inflicting of pain on children at school for trivial misdemeanours implied what was manifestly untrue, that is, that the children were deliberately disobedient or unwilling. Indeed it seemed to imply intentional cruelty or dislike.

I doubt that Mrs Dodd smacked children often, as their lively autonomy was clearly a source of pleasure to her, at least outside the classroom. She would have revelled in the children's eagerness to cooperate, learn and to enjoy the experience. The lack of diligence that lead to punishment, I suspect, also led those punished to absent themselves. But the very existence of corporal punishment could be seen as both a physical and a symbolic form of violence, the latter because deliberate reprimand and rational, unemotional punishments entail specific theories of human discipline, authority and learning which are quite foreign to Rembarrnga. Such theories are also reflected in a multitude of alien practices and pedagogic techniques, such as the correcting of spelling and sums, which are based on an epistemology at odds with that of Rembarrnga where knowledge is always partial and embodied; that is, living individuals carry segments of a body of knowledge which circulates according to specific principles and is safeguarded by certain practices (Michaels 1990; Rose 1996). Such profound differences meant limited absorption of the lessons, as discussed above.

A broader form of discipline was exercised over what Rembarrnga call 'women's business'. When babies were born at Mainoru, Mrs Dodd took an instructive role. Lorna complained that Mrs Dodd would not let her tie the cord when her first child, Ben, was born in the camp. Mrs Dodd also attempted to have Rembarrnga women taken to hospital in Katherine to give birth. Some women resisted by running away and staying in the bush until the baby was born. Mrs Dodd sent them to hospital earlier, so they ran away earlier. Larry 'wouldn't let Dolly come to the house' wrote old Mrs McKay to her grand daughter, Heather Dodd at her boarding school, 'I wonder who Larry thinks he is. When he knew the doctor was due he went bush and took Dolly . . . Larry would have died years ago if it hadn't been for Jim's attention' (NTAS 291).[24] Mrs McKay was accusing Larry of ingratitude, disobedience and arrogance for protecting his wife from the goodwill and interference of what were, to him, foreigners. Such struggles became part of the relationship between the camp and the homestead, and appeared in everyday Rembarrnga strategies for deflecting the desires of those who would control their lives.

The NAB was at one with these station owners concerning the proper age of marriage, the importance of hospitalisation for births, and the moral and even physical force they applied to make Aborigines learn their lessons. Mrs Dodd could appeal to the Board for help when faced with problems of control. This letter to the Director belies her usual affection and possessiveness, with quite other sentiments, evincing suspicion and mistrust when her authority is questioned: 'Tommy Dodd—native—is a menace and I consider drastic action should be taken. He is forever creating trouble here . . . a spear fight . . . Last night he took off with Clara, an eight year old school girl. The others vow they could not catch him but that is of course a lie' (F1 55/1126 Feb. 1959).

The NAB's less intimate technologies slowly and subtly impinged on the relationships between black and white people. For instance, there were consequences that flowed from naming and written records. Once names, ages and relationships were written down they became commonly used referents, even from strangers. Thus a new state official armed with a list of names could identify people and ask for those who were not present. The use of English names in this way made it more difficult for Rembarrnga to adhere to their practice of discarding and adjusting names to a changed social landscape when someone died (Biddle 1996). However, these new names were less heavily loaded with Rembarrnga meanings, and at times could be used to bridge the awkward gaps between a domain where a range of identities was available for particular circumstances (A's niece; B's mother; of C subsection, of D clan, etc.), and a world where strangers could confer a specific name on a specific individual which could be used in any circumstance. Whitefellas wanted to use names as public instruments, to call them out, to say them to relatives, to make them represent one unique individual, rather than to shade one person's identity into the space of her sister as happened with designations by subsection or kin terms. English names had a different kind of power, and became a way of both breaking up the power of old practices and of cushioning the blows of new ones. The fact that new names could be, to an extent, absolved from the old strictures had both a conserving and destructive effect.

Rembarrnga could only retain intimate habits to do with food and babies and domestic life while there was physical and moral distancing from the whites. But the white land-holders at Mainoru felt close to the black people and tried to narrow the distance between their lives, ostensibly with love and care. They drew black people into the white world, refusing ever to step in the other direction for fear of interfering with history's trajectory.

'I would like to keep the pics'

This interaction created its own mythology and mores, such as the warm and humorous way Mrs Dodd spoke of her tasks when writing to the NAB in Darwin, pretending that she was helpless in the face of the importunate native children. The children came to school every day, she said, even on Saturday and Sunday and during the holidays.

Mrs Dodd wrote to enquire about the holiday dates, and when she was told the dates she tried to make the children stay at home. 'When my daughter returned to [boarding] school several took it as a sign that school was starting for them. No amount of explaining turned them away and they have been up daily' (F1 56/2209 1957).

The children came up for school every day because they wanted to, and, far from disapproving, the NAB expressed admiration and support:

> Mainoru station is unique and outstanding for the attention paid to the school children and pre-school children . . . From 7am until 8pm on seven days a week the bulk of the children are in or adjacent to the station homestead. Not only do they receive excellent academic training but the attention paid to their general well being is most creditable (Ryan F1 63/3200 June 1960).

However, they were gradually taught that, in contrast with the social environment of the camp where personal autonomy was enhanced, the ordering of time was independent of their own desires. Some other authority, one received from Darwin via Mrs Dodd, would say when school was in. The school inspector's report expressed complete approval of Mrs Dodd, commending her on the remarkable achievement of the children as a result of her 'intelligent and selective use of all methods', adding that 'her interest and love for the children has contributed' (F1 56/2209, 1958).

Mrs Dodd's letters to the administration in Darwin were conspiratorial in style, emphasising the mutuality of their efforts. But when she asked Ryan whether the NAB could supply a new sewing machine 'for the girl's use. I cut their frocks and they do the sewing' (June 1952), he refused, saying that the granting of her request would establish an unwarranted precedent in view of the reimbursement pastoralists get for the maintenance of dependants. The Director said: 'The request cannot be entertained—clothing issues are laid down for the first wife and child of an employee. Other unemployed women should learn to sew by hand' (F1 52/759 Moy, Aug. 1952).

Mrs Dodd saw herself as waging a wider campaign, one which was orchestrated by the state but was the duty of all whites. Clothing the black bodies was a crucial task: 'I have made twelve frocks and thirty pairs of pantees but have not issued any of these but wish permission to do so . . . most of the pantees await elastic' (F1 52/759 March 1957).

Respect for the authority of the state and the unity of purpose between the state and the pastoralists in their civilising mission is made explicit in this letter. The white sense of ownership of the Aboriginal domain is expressed in another letter in which Mrs Dodd asked whether she could include Alice and her child on the claim for station dependants. She has to care for them because:

> The father Dick Billingwonga has a young lubra and frequently goes— taking the young lubra and leaving Alice and the children . . . Dick does not like work . . . I suppose it is natural for the older ones to still prefer walkabout . . . I know they could all go to the compound and be well treated, but to use their own expression, this is their country and I would like to keep the pics (F1 52/759 Dec. 1953).

Here 'their own expression' of ownership of land is turned into a quaint cultural practice, denuded of any challenge to the cultural hegemony of the white residents. The desire to 'keep the pics' refers to piccaninnies in an innocent, even a virtuous request to fulfil the duties that the natives leave undone. Mrs Dodd is not disapproving of Dick; she understands his cultural preference for 'the young lubra' and for 'walkabout'. In fact his preference conveniently allows her to fulfil her desire to 'keep the pics'.

The McKays eschewed sexual relationships with Aborigines, but there were other ways of making families, or perhaps remaking them (plate 23). One was the nurturing approach to Rembarrnga people by which the whole camp was infantilised and owned. The community thus became a surrogate extended family with Mrs Dodd as the nurturant mother. Another means of creating a family was by taking responsibility for those children who were born at Mainoru, particularly those that were 'part-coloured'. Mrs Dodd formally adopted Alice's 'half-caste' daughter Pixie to stop her being taken away. Heather Dodd told me: 'My sister is a half-caste, Pixie. She was born on the station and her mother and mine were terrified this [removal] might happen. She came into the house when she was four and then Mum adopted her legally later on' (1988).

Mrs Dodd wrote to the Director about Alice's oldest daughter Abie:

> I have had [Abie] round the house daily for the last 2 years . . . She is too intelligent to be allowed to go wild altogether. The other little girl is just 3 yrs—also intelligent . . . I have two other piccaninnies I hold onto—also kept round the place. They are very intelligent too.

She has to support these others because:

They belong to Willie who is even now away at some corroboree. He does work at times but just about retiring. Has a terrific cough and is not so young so it is only a short time when he will become an all time dependant not only when he ails (F1 52/759 Dec. 1953).

Mrs Dodd projected her own subjectivity onto her black tribal people and took the standard western view that the intelligence of the children made them worth redeeming. With intelligence they would be able to learn to be other than their parents.

This privileging of intelligence denotes the rise of the significance of psychology as a means of understanding society, and the incorporation of that science into the values and judgements of ordinary citizens, and in this case into the affirmation of racial ideology. A new form of ranking was being scientised in psychology, and Aborigines became a testing ground (Elkin 1932; Gould 1981). Deploring the squandering of intelligence is a popular way of deploring some specific consequences of marginality at the same time as refusing to problematise the general social conditions that give rise to it. Thus the emphasis is on the potential of the *intelligent* child if educated and enabled to participate in the benefits and freedoms which education brings. The communities and relations of the intelligent child can be left to wilt in the wilderness as the less gifted will not suffer from being deprived. This conception sees 'intelligent' individuals as having potential qualities which can only flower when severed from their social context. This image is not balanced by any recognition of the destruction that can accompany being plucked from the weft and warp of relations and enticed into the impersonal and kinless space of whitefellas. When recognised, the pain of bereft parents was, as we saw above, ameliorated by the reassurances of patrol officers.

Mrs Dodd did not express shock or disappointment when Abie, at twelve years old, produced a baby son, Kim. He was one of three babies she reared in the house, because, she told the administration, their mothers were working. She confided in the Director about her duties in relation to the children: 'August was born on Mainoru and returns periodically with his parents. This time however someone else brought him and left him here on his own. I put him in charge of Dorothy a tribal relative and enrolled him. I will hold him until his parents claim him' (F1 56/2209 1958).

This is a distorted representation of life in 'the camp' because it only recognises immediate parents as responsible for children. The child is 'on his own' rather than among close kin and the 'tribal relative', Dorothy is put 'in charge' by Mrs Dodd. Thus the authority which these whitefellas assumed was over the *relationship between* the charming 'piccaninnies' and their parents, and was premised on the whole Rembarrnga people remaining passive in relation to the desires and programs of the white owners.

Mrs Dodd's own daughter, Heather Dodd, was subject to a quite different form of tutelage than the black children though she lived in intimacy with them. She explained to me:

> I was the only white child for hundreds of miles in three directions and ninety miles in the other direction and I didn't see those kids at Beswick except once every two years. So there were no children at all—of the white variety. As far as I could see the Aboriginal kids had all the fun. I had to do school work. Mum didn't start the school until she got shifted of me and sent me off to boarding school (1988).

Earlier Heather had to do correspondence lessons while the black children played and swam outside, and later they had all her mother's attention while she was away at boarding school in Brisbane. Her intimacy with Rembarrnga was a source of great pride: 'I saw a lot of the Aboriginal kids: not the girls so much because girls being in promises and shoved into marriages at the age of nine or ten they weren't much value as playmates. I played with the boys a lot and worked with them all out on horses' (1988).

In the course of telling me of what she saw as the disastrous effects of recent government policy since the station was sold, and in case I thought she was criticising Rembarrnga people, she said, 'Bear in mind that my earliest and closest friends are among these people . . . You realise five of their generations had lived and worked with three of mine.' Heather's claim to intimacy often took the form of correcting conventional views about Aborigines. She explained that 'Smiler liked to learn to cook and I was the one that was out scrambling around in the scrub hunting for his tucker.' Once when a policeman wanted a tracker, Smiler said, 'You'd better ask my friend here,' meaning Heather, but the officer had insisted on having a *black* tracker. Heather's expertise was due to the instruction she had had from Chuckerduck: 'I think the lucky thing for me was that Ronny got leprosy. Having his only child taken away [Chuckerduck] rather concentrated on me. He gave me [knowledge of] all the hunting, tracking and fishing—Aboriginal food that otherwise he would have exerted on Ronny. We didn't get Ronny back until he was seventeen or eighteen' (1988).

Heather's own sense of identity was formed among her small family of adults and among the Rembarrnga people. She was both an intimate companion of the black children, and a jealous rival for her mother's affection. This situation generated intense conflict which I believe remained unresolved. When away at school in Brisbane, her father Jimmy Dodd would write to her with stories of the household, including details such as her mother reading stories to Pixie (NTAS 291). Her life was intimately engaged with her mother's noble task. After they left Mainoru, Heather had to nurse her bedridden old mother, and I glimpsed there, in 1979, the conflicting emotions these circumstances had produced. Old resentments were being played out, with the honoured nurturer now helpless and requiring nurturance, from her daughter whose services will not be honoured and whose sense of being wronged cannot be admitted. Heather had identified with her mother's heroic task and felt herself a privileged insider in her familiarity with, and authority in relation to, Aborigines, yet her own sense of deprivation stemmed from these very sources of pride. Thus the hidden injuries of race can wound those who wield racial power.

This chapter has set out the way racial categories were both affirmed and subverted by the intimacy which developed at Mainoru. There was close proximity, care and tutelage. Yet there was also a form of social savagery, hardly ever expressed as hatred, anger or even contempt but appearing in the guise of solicitude and love. The mundane necessity of history was also being played out, located in the practices attendant on the responsible administration of people who were seen as needing to learn to be more human, more manageable, more able to participate in a world dedicated to specific forms of productivity and progress. Racial hatred was not recognised as having any part in these progressive efforts. The attempts to cloak the realm of Rembarrnga in modern garb and spread the semblance of civilisation, modernity and industry across the places they settled was itself clothed in noble sentiments. Nelly, who herself would have participated with enthusiasm in modern spaces had she learned to read and write, expressed her appreciation of the McKay family in a way that epitomises these ambiguities: 'That McKay family was really good. Mrs Dodd knew about the delivery of babies, about doctor. Mrs Dodd adopted only Pixie . . . Pixie is a flash one, another one who was taken from her home. She's my cousin's baby but she don't look at [my cousin] like a mother' (1987).

The child who was adopted into the Dodd's home became 'flash';

that is, she adopted the manners of urban whitefellas and has had few contacts with her natal family. This is the woman that Heather Dodd proudly stated, 'refuses to take any money for being Aboriginal', seeing the refusal to take advantage of Aboriginal welfare measures as proof of the worth of her family's efforts at Mainoru. Be that as it may, the social experiment of these years did not represent a coherent policy or set of coordinated practices, but was a disjointed and ad hoc series of responses to the anxieties roused by racial difference in the conditions of the pastoral enterprise.

6

A New Modernism

And after that, in your time, we are all quiet now. We smoke and work.
—*George Jaurdaku 1989*

HASLUCK'S FINAL SOLUTION

In the mid 1950s, a legislative move of breathtaking simplicity was made which eradicated 'Aborigines' from legislation, replacing them with 'wards' by a definitional sleight of hand. The Aboriginal Ordinance would become the Welfare Ordinance, no longer applying to a race but to those who were unable to look after themselves. This brainchild of Paul Hasluck, Minister of Territories, passed into legislation in 1953.

Creating wards

The public concern and confusion in many quarters about the laws concerning 'half-castes' had become excruciatingly embarrassing for the Commonwealth Government. Internationally, racial terminology was being abandoned and the United Nations had made its second statement on race in 1951, affirming the fundamental unity of the human species and undermining the use of race as a form of biological categorisation for social purposes (Montagu 1972). Locally there had been court challenges to racial identifications, and interminable arguments about the correct definition and category for half-castes and others whose legal status depended on the fraction of 'Aboriginal blood' they were believed to carry. With some 'full-bloods' exempted, the logic of the Ordinance was becoming harder to defend (F1 57/145; Rowse 1998:194). Hasluck reasoned that the social problem was not one of race but of people who were incapable of looking after themselves. Why not simply name them wards, rename the Ordinances and the Native Affairs Branch, and go on as before?

With a stroke of the ministerial pen, the increasing problems of deciding who was Aboriginal disappeared, complaints about racial injustice were silenced, and the numerous legal challenges to the Ordinance and regulations were ended. Now instead of defining and naming who could be exempted from the Ordinance, those who were subject to it would be named. It was imagined that this category of people, to be listed in a Register of Wards, would gradually contract as the assimilative process inexorably continued and one by one names would be dropped from the list. It was individuals who would cease to be wards, independent of their biological heritage; the degree of need would be the only criteria for being 'declared'. The general assumption that virtually all 'full-bloods' were in need of care by the state was thought so obvious that it was not explicitly stated. Whether a particular 'half-caste' was a ward would be decided by the patrol officers, police or other local authorities. When someone's behaviour demonstrated that he or she was ready, that individual would cease to be a ward. The adoption of this new system of naming those in need meant that the state now generated its own categories and clients.

This was part of what Hasluck called the 'new and vigorous approach to the problem of Aboriginal advancement' (F1 56/1331).[1] These laws were not so much directed to reforming the relationship between Aborigines and the state as at rationalising and streamlining the discourses and laws, and replacing the smudged racial boundaries with a dynamic of movement from one category to another. It was another step towards replacing the dichotomous, antithetical races with a moving racial boundary that would gradually obliterate the category 'Aboriginal' altogether as wards ceased to need care. In other words, the logic of assimilation was made plain, and perhaps it could be argued that this provoked a reaction of distaste which led to more serious attempts to abandon the policy in the late 1960s.

Hasluck's intention in rejecting racial categories was, as he said in a parliamentary speech, to avoid 'a two caste society in which a lot of low caste people live their own lives and another lot of high caste people live their lives. That is an evil for society' (F1 54/1013 1955). In this formulation it was the fixity of racial categories over time that was the problem, and this fixity was not the consequence of skin colour or other racial markers, but of the use of racial categories. It was also assumed that difference equalled hierarchy. To recognise and legitimise what we now call cultural differences, to allow different cultures to live side by side, would be to entrench an unacceptable inequality and threaten the unity of Australia. Hasluck's assessment did not consider the social processes involved in the maintenance of social inequality, or in separation and togetherness, but was premised on there being one form of sociality inscribed in the notion of 'the opportunity to live a happy and useful life' (ibid.). In fact Hasluck erased the social arena from consideration; there are only dark and fair individuals: 'Our ideals about life in Australia are to give the opportunity to all. That applies to those who may be a bit dusky in their skins as much as to residents of the poorer parts of our cities, or to any other under-privileged persons in any section of our community' (1988).

The establishment of a naming system which allowed for movement between the categories was a way of establishing egalitarian principles and erasing injustice, because every individual would, over time, be given the opportunity to be removed from the category of 'ward'. Failure would be due to their own condition of need, not a consequence of their race. This is an example of the way egalitarian ideas can contribute to the entrenchment of inequality (Kapferer 1988; Morris 1997).

Darwin officials were alarmed at Hasluck's solution, predicting that it would lead to major legal problems and social difficulties. For instance, the legal force of the new Ordinance depended on being able to identify the wards. The Administrator pointed out: 'As soon as it comes into operation it must be possible to declare all Aborigines who in their own interests must come under control as wards of the Director of Welfare . . . some means of clear identification of individuals will involve . . . the adoption of a system of naming' (F1 52/ 1160 (2) June 1953).

This was a task of immense and unforseen difficulty. The limited extent of the state's scrutiny in the past was revealed when patrol officers and police found they had incomplete knowledge of many Aboriginal groups and were quite unprepared for the task of sending in exhaustive lists of the names of people in their districts. Even among communities they were familiar with, only some individuals were known, and the majority of names, family relationships, language groups and clan identities were not known. These and other legal difficulties meant that the Welfare Ordinance, though passed in 1953, did not come into operation until May 1957 (McCorquodale 1985:122). The complementary Wards Employment Ordinance, which was also passed in 1953, did not come into force until late in 1959. By that time Harry Giese, the new Director of Welfare, appointed to replace Moy and bring the new progressive policy into effect, was well entrenched. He complained:

> With the single exception of Mr. Lovegrove, field staff, missionaries and police are too busy and other informants too unconcerned to furnish information of a satisfactory quality at a reasonable rate. Advices come in too slowly, spelling is generally faulty and group and tribal names are nearly always omitted . . . (F1 57/145 (2) Aug. 1958).

A systematic way of recording names, transcribing Aboriginal sounds or defining groupings had to be devised. What were their *real* names and how were they to be spelled? Which was the surname? Should 'clan' or 'tribe' be identified? How were double listings to be avoided when people did not stay in one place? In the first list compiled from the varied police and patrol officers' reports, many names were missing and many people were listed twice.[2] The register became known derisively as 'The Stud Book' of which Stanner said, 'it shows no understanding of the Aboriginal name-systems, of the facts of local organisation, of the structural divisions of groups and of the language differences' (1979:43). The legal position remained troublesome, as the Minister was forced to recognise after being subjected to a barrage of anxious memos: 'Any doubtful cases, such as that of Namitjira,[3] must be considered and dealt with before and not after the declaration is made . . . to do otherwise would put the aboriginals in exactly the same position as they are at present' (F1 57/145 1957).

In fact it is clear that 'full-bloods' outside the towns were 'in exactly the same situation' as before, automatically listed as wards and subject to the Ordinance. Judgements about whether or not to list a number of 'full-blood' Aborigines were based on their 'social habits', degree of dissociation from 'tribal life', and the ability to 'operate as an individual in the European domain'. Thus, these judgements about individuals were judgements of their degree of individuation. That is, the disassociation from family, clan and tribe was the crucial measure for not being declared a ward.

Field officers were continually to review the list of wards with the object of 'getting these people on their own feet the moment they are ready for this' (ibid.). 'Getting people on their feet' is an evocative metaphor for lifting them out of the status of ward, where they are presumably on their knees, supine among a community in like condition. The term 'ward' carries a particular sense of institutionalisation, a custodial condition characterised by a lack of responsibility, autonomy or judgement. Thus, Aborigines in the Northern Territory progressed, in the 1950s, to the condition of explicitly living in the custody of the state.

The Welfare Ordinance could not be deemed a success on any criterion. It took four years to come into operation and only four years later, in 1961, it was substantially revised. Three years after that, in 1964, the more limited Social Welfare Ordinance came into effect under the Director of Social Welfare. Though much shorter, and omitting the punitive aspects of the earlier Ordinance, the duty 'to inculcate proper habits of hygiene and sanitation and to improve their standards of nutrition' (McCorquodale 1985:124) indicates that the state's tutelary task was still paramount. The public servants who had administered the old policies were retained to implement the new ones (Long 1992:169). And when the Social Welfare Ordinance was replaced by policies of self-determination in the early 1970s, many of the staff remained to help administer the new policies in the newly formed Department of Aboriginal Affairs (DAA).[4] Convinced that these later changes heralded disaster, Harry Giese resisted them and was removed from office.

Wards at Mainoru

Mainoru, like other isolated stations, was insulated from the direct effects of these laws. The change to wards and then to welfare status did not alter the relationships within station communities where Mrs Dodd's efforts continued on the same path through the 1950s and 1960s, as did the attempts to separate the 'myalls' from the station community. The changing Ordinances did mean that Tex Camfoo, with Aboriginal and Chinese parentage, found his legal status somewhat confusing. His racial designation not only affected what he was allowed to do, but interfered with his legal relationship with his own family, both natal and marital. Tex told the policeman at Roper that he did not know he had an exemption and had never applied for one, and in fact he wanted to return the exemption card. This was because he was in trouble for having intercourse with 'lubras'. The policeman complained about his conduct to the DNA and said, 'I consider it is a case of taking it from him—not him giving it back.'

Tex is reasonably literate but had no access to information about the relevant laws. In his own account he was bemused to find himself a European and not needing the exemption certificate which Patrol Officer Ryan had obtained for him. These events must have occurred in the mid 1950s early in the era of the Register of Wards, as 'the big book' was competing with the exemption card and the 'big board in the bar' as determinants of racial status:

A lot of part-coloured people are Aboriginals straight away, you know, and they were all in the big book. But my name was classed as a European. Ron Ryan brought me an exemption card. You used to carry the little card in your pocket. So, when you go in the bar, you just show that, so you can drink. And they got a big board up there in the bar where all the names are of people who've got a licence to go in the bar to have a drink . . .

When we went to Mataranka, I was sitting back and Ron Ryan went straight into the bar there. Same old pub. And I'm sitting there and old George Conway seen me: 'Oh there's old Tex Camfoo eh?'

'Yeah.'

'Can he come and have a drink?'

'Course he can!' So Ron Ryan come over.

'Here's your exemption card! I was going to give it to you! But now everybody should know, you're not an Aboriginal, you're a European!' So I grabbed that thing and tore it up and threw it away in the bin! And then I went and had couple of beers and oh, everybody was looking. Then I went to Katherine and I went straight in the bar there. I wasn't drunk. I never used to drink much. I was young then, somewhere about 26, or 23. And then they asked, 'Do you have an exemption card?'

'No, I'm already European, like I can come and have a drink in the bar.'

'Go look his name up!' He looked in the book and said, 'Yeah, yeah, you're all right.' I went in there and crossed the name off [the exemption list] because I'm automatically a European. But all the Europeans knew I was a ceremony man also. Even at Mainoru I could sneak around. I could go mustering and all that and I could sneak around and go in the *Yappaduruwa*, that ceremony with Larry and Dick. My brothers were all one, same mother but different fathers (1991).

In their conspiracy to break Tex's ceremonial identity, the Christian school he attended as a boy and the law had been spectacularly unsuccessful, but they had placed a pall of illegitimacy over it. He spoke of 'sneaking around' to the ceremony, indicating his sense, even now, that ceremonial activity was a forbidden domain for people 'classed as European'. Tex's sources of identity in his Aboriginal, Chinese and European heritage have coexisted all his life in ways that, to some extent, he takes for granted. He is aware of the racial judgements with which he is surrounded, yet in the world of stockmen, the space between the races was always well occupied. In the outback the familiarity of those 'in-between', as well as the slippage of practices across the boundaries, meant that racial domains were not distinct or evocative of the same fears as in towns. 'Pollution', 'cross-fertilisation' and 'hybridity', though discomforting at times, were all familiar and commonplace.

> To tell you the truth, I feel both European and blackfella. I can't help it, because I've got a bit of mixed blood in me. Chinaman and blackfella. Sometimes they call me a black bastard. I just laugh at it, I just say, 'I'm proud of it.' I say, 'You're a white bastard too. What's the difference?' Sometimes it sort of makes me shame . . .
>
> I always say, 'You're to blame for it. You've been knocking around with my mother, that's why I come out a bloody yella-fella. That's your blame'. And he just shut up like a book then (1995).

Tex displays humour and charm, as well as toughness when required. Thus he has managed to ride out the occasions of shame concerning his racial designation, the sense of having to 'sneak around' to ceremonies, the competing loyalties of his identity among whites as a stockman, and his pride in being a ceremony man. There were many others who had to deal in some way with the complications and contradictions given by the racialised circumstances of their lives. Many opted to live in towns in communities of brown people which gave some protection from the changing racial laws, most notably by challenging them in the courts.

The expanding Welfare Branch was appointing assiduous new patrol officers in the 1960s. More elaborate maintenance claims were instituted, which included the reasons for individual Aborigines being eligible for maintenance, using categories which obscured kinship and social relations with comments such as 'father is a pensioner' or 'father single and unemployed' (F1 71/1922 Nov. 1966). The practice of listing and categorising natives had been established in an earlier era of racial differentiation by long standing and familiar patrol officers in cooperation with the pastoralist. Now it was being transformed to serve an extended bureaucratic machine which required and provided more detailed information. This was not to do with an explicit change in racial consciousness but with a set of specific knowledge practices, the collection of certain kinds of information about a population, which had become racialised in the process of managing colonial relations. These practices, directed to the production of modernity, development and progress, continued to produce racial inequalities but in more systematic and impersonal ways.

The new programs of the Welfare Branch meant more intense scrutiny, enumeration, assessment and inscription. The class of wards at Mainoru now included parents whose children were at the school, and a ration depot was again being debated in 1958. Numbers increased from seventeen children in 1957 to 31 a year later. The redemptive project was imagined to be evident in the children's bodies, though Giese must have relied on Mrs Dodd's evidence when he made the comparison: 'The children who have come in from the bush . . . have been transformed from undernourished and almost deformed little creatures to healthy attractive-looking youngsters (Giese, F1 66/3583 Oct. 1958).'

More government staff allowed for more patrols, and more intrusion into the camp. More staff were needed also because, if the school was to be expanded:

> It will be necessary for them not merely to make a thorough census of the people who are in the area but to chart their affiliations and movements accurately. They will have to decide what the degree of contact had been for the people who are in the area but who are not employed regularly at Mainoru Station, and what could be done with the adults if the children were moved into the school at Mainoru. Presumably all the people in the area will be of the same tribal groups . . . The patrol will have to test out the feelings of the people in the area on the matter of moving . . . This question of finding employment, it is realised, will depend not only on whether there are vacancies for employees at these stations, but also whether the adults themselves would be competent to fill these vacancies (F1 66/3583 July 1960).

The administration was here developing more specific kinds of knowledge about the local situation, which included the need to 'chart their affiliations and movements' and to 'test out the feelings of the people'. Yet their distance from the people is also evident in the instructions that are contrived not to suit their desires but to improve them. When the wards said they had come from Bulman, it was to be interpreted to mean that Bulman was 'a welcome staging camp with good facilities for resting up after long journeys from the coastal areas'. Therefore the Welfare Branch should not set up a ration depot there because it would make the task of 'inculcating proper work habits of a stable nature' more difficult because wards could 'spell up' comfortably on prolonged walkabouts (F1 66/3583 Aug. 1960).

Giese required much information to pursue his aims, and his instructions constructed more categories into which to slot people. He required 'a complete census of natives at present resident at Mainoru' including the number 'regularly employed, and dependants', the number 'able bodied but not employed and their dependants', the number of 'pensioners and dependants', and the number who have 'migrated solely for the purpose of having their children educated' (F1 66/809 Aug. 1961). The implication is that these are stable, discrete categories and that their enumeration would provide the basis of a rational decision about a ration depot.

When the detailed census was conducted in 1962, the patrol officer combined the task with conducting a shoot of dogs. Dogs are companions, are given 'skin' and have a kinship-like status: the deliberate killings of such companions is brutal and murderous. The patrol officer reported:

> At the conclusion of the census the wards were grouped together and told of the necessity to reduce the number of dogs in their camp. After being told to chain up their good canines, a shoot of other dogs was conducted resulting in 22 kills and 2 or 3 possibles. The manager was extremely pleased with this result (F1 66/635, 1962).

No mention is made of the resulting grief, let alone any anger from 'the wards'. Patrol Officer Evans reiterated the view that 'There is no doubt that the Mainoru natives are among the best cared for of any on a station property in the NT' (F1 66/3583 Jan. 1961). But that care, and the regime of which it was a part, was to be radically altered within a few years.

LEAVING MAINORU

The Aboriginal people left Mainoru in stages between 1968 and 1971. Florry Lindsay, one of the last to leave, says they left of their own free will, though her story reveals it was not by choice. That is, they left when conditions became intolerable. Those Rembarrnga people who had identified themselves as the Mainoru mob had assumed that the McKay–Dodd family was there to stay, and that they themselves would remain part of the whites' endeavours. Some said, 'We wanted Heather to marry' as if such a marriage would have assured continuity. Mainoru had created a certain stability for its residents with an interweaving of Rembarrnga people with the McKay family, but its bifurcated nature was revealed with dramatic clarity at the end of what Bulman people call 'Jack McKay time'.

Death, debt and equal pay

The end of this regime came in the late 1960s and some of the reasons can be traced to events at the nation's centre. The race relations system had lurched forward again, deciding that otherness should not exist in the form of unequal wages. The decision of the Commonwealth Conciliation and Arbitration Commission (CCAC) was the result of a case taken by the Australian Workers Union (AWU) to delete the clause which exempted Aborigines from the provisions of the NT Pastoral Workers Award. The case was heard and decided in 1966 with the ruling to be enforced by 1969. To the pastoralists the reversal of the principles of care and protection seemed a betrayal, but among those who governed it was merely the next step in a natural development towards racial equality. The exodus from Mainoru was a direct result of the 'equal wages case', which thus warrants further exploration.

It seems there was little doubt that the case would be decided in the AWU's favour, despite the union members' undoubted ambivalence.[5] A shift had occurred in race relations which made the inequity of paying Aborigines one-fifth of the rate payable to whites unacceptable (Stevens 1984:23), and the union, the Cattle Producers' Association and the Commonwealth appeared before the Commission, each presenting themselves, in a sense, as the Aborigines' 'best friend' (Stanner 1979:255). The union called no witnesses and produced no evidence but relied on arguments of necessity and justice (ibid.:256) to counter the detailed submissions of the pastoralists concerning the lesser worth of Aboriginal labour.[6] The Commission thus accepted the pastoralists' evidence that Aborigines' labour was not worth as much as that of white workers' 'supported as it was by what we ourselves saw and by the anthropological and other material' (CCAC 1966:661), but nonetheless found against them. That is, the principle of equality, boosted by incidental evidence that Aborigines were changing rapidly, over-rode the major finding of fact. The recognition that Aborigines had different capacities or skills was interpreted as a lack, even though some pastoralists admitted what a survey party had observed; that is, that Aboriginal cattle workers were more productive than whites (CCAC 1966:667; McCorquodale 1985:214).

The equal wages case was more than simply the commercial interests and old-fashioned views of employers pitted against the morally progressive force of the modern state. The consequences of equal wages for the Aboriginal population was one concern of the pastoralists, and they predicted that whole Aboriginal communities would be turned off stations (Stanner 1979:260).[7] Although accepted, such concerns could not dampen the desire to overcome the national and international embarrassment caused by unequal wages based on a racial classification. The decision again threw into sharp relief the contradictory way the Aborigines' future was being imagined. The Commission observed: 'If the employers' application were to succeed and if the aborigines were to remain living on stations it seems to us likely that their assimilation or integration into our white economic society would be delayed' (CCAC 1966:668).

'Assimilation or integration' was taken to be the desirable condition which would flow naturally from the granting of equal wages. Present conditions were recognised when the Commission agreed to delay the order for nearly three years to minimise the disruption that it would cause. The judgement included the admonition: 'The aborigines will need guidance to understand and appreciate the implications of moving from a semi-protected situation to an exposed industrial situation whereby they have to care for themselves and their families out of their wages' (CCAC 1966:669).

The reality of the actual communities, consisting of groups of inter-related kin, with webs of interdependence and ceremonial responsibility to country, was absent from consideration. Instead there were imaginary male breadwinners, each of whom cared for his own wife and children. If such breadwinners did not yet exist, it was implied that 'the exposed industrial situation' would soon bring them into being. The Commission's concern with what it called 'disemployment' referred to 'males over 16 years' rather than to the whole of the station communities, or the 'tribal dependants', whose modest keep had been funded by the government.[8] They seemed set to become homeless refugees, but the Commission reassured itself that the Aboriginal population in pastoral and agricultural areas was diminishing, implying that the problem, if not dying out, was moving out. It was further asserted that those affected by the decision would 'move from stations to settlements or missions' and that the Commonwealth Government 'will accept responsibility for any displacement that will occur' (ibid.:666).

The pastoralists convinced the Commission that they wanted to help their Aboriginal employees, and that 'they did not wish to have the Aborigines removed from their tribal lands' (CCAC 1966:669). But whatever level of affection or loyalty had developed between the white owners and black residents on pastoral stations (Doolan 1977:109–10), the inherent conflict between their economic interests was an implacable force which, in broad terms, determined the consequences. That is, masses of Aboriginal residents, including the Mainoru mob, were ejected from pastoral stations in the Territory. But by historical chance, the memory of the McKay–Dodd family was enhanced rather than damaged by the sequence of events which led to Rembarrnga people departing from Mainoru.

To the participants, the salient reason for their departure was not the equal wages judgement.[9] It was the sudden death of Jack McKay in 1966 which sealed the fate of this regime. Sandy McKay had died earlier, and Mrs Dodd was now old and frail, and unable to teach. Other teachers were appointed, one of whom had Florry Lindsay coming to the school 'to instruct and sing for the girls in the dances'. As well, two old men 'came to tell stories in the vernacular' (E 242/5 K1/1/7 1967). These are signs of the new place 'culture' was to assume in race relations.

When Heather Dodd inherited the station she found that: 'Jack left the place in a mess and with huge debts—I had to sell. For me it was a major calamity but for the aborigines it was a tragedy. Nobody stayed more than a year or so after my leaving' (letter 1976).

Heather was young and energetic and would have liked to stay on. After she inherited the station she was given assistance and advice by new Welfare staff about slow worker provisions, age pensions and 'how to assist any Aboriginal stood down to apply for unemployment benefits' (F941/0 64/256 1967). She hoped to continue with the established community of about 70 people. The 1968 'Inspection Report', as patrol officer's reports were now called, contained ominous implications: 'Miss Dodd is a "sympathetic" employer of her group of Aborigines. However she may soon be moving from Mainoru . . . and we may see a change to a business like attitude in the employment of Aborigines. The controlling interests are American' (E 242/5 K1/1/7).

The burden of debt and the requirement to pay equal wages, as well as her mother's increasing frailty, led Heather to sell her share of the lease and buy a house in Darwin. She was caring for her mother there when I met her first in 1976.

Rembarrnga people have described leaving Mainoru not in terms of economic compulsion, but rather as a consequence of human vicissitudes, especially the new owner's dislike of blackfellas. The fact that Heather was not married was a major factor. Nelly expressed a common view:

> They liked blackfellas that McKay family. Pity we lost that girl Heather. She'd be still running that place. We wanted her to get married but she didn't want to marry . . . The Foster family, they're the ones go hard. They just didn't like blackfellas. They don't want blackfella round Mainoru. Yanks took over, otherwise we could stop at Mainoru (1985).

And Tex said: 'We tried hard for Heather to get married and don't sell it, for Aborigine people, so they can live there. They were born there. We tried hard, but when Jack McKay died, it was a heavy, heavy debt' (1991).

Willy Martin expressed his sense of the illegitimacy of this buying of country, and was told that, like the change to decimal currency, 'that was the law for everyone'. He knew that 'white man's politics' was involved:

> Then all of a sudden, I don't know what happened, but a millionaire just came along and bought that country, just straight out. That Yankee from overseas. That time the money changed. The dollar thing from pound. And they said that was the law for everyone.
>
> Anyway as soon as that thing happened, that Yankee came out and said, 'We don't want anymore blackfellas here. Get out. Finish.'
>
> And we took off. And I'm the one bloke that said what sort of white man politics is going on, and what it meant. He came and said, 'We want to get a lot of whitefellas to build this up, build the house build the yard. We don't want any more blackfellas.'
>
> We said, 'Alright, we can go back.' We took off (1989).

The nature and culture of the pastoral industry was changing under pressure from various forces, including shifts in the market and technological developments such as the use of helicopters for mustering, which meant a reduction in the use of labour. Increased urbanisation and modern transport and telecommunications helped undermine the old pastoral traditions. New owners amalgamated stations and in some cases cattle were harvested once a year.[10] Overseas companies, often investing in the land rather than the industry, added to the rupturing of established practices. The decreasing profitability of cattle breeding exacerbated the effects of the granting of equal wages to Aboriginal workers, so that few pastoralists wanted Aboriginal labour, let alone an Aboriginal community residing on their station.

The end of an era

The 'millionaire Yankee from overseas' that Willy spoke of was Max Foster of Fosters' Fried Chicken, who employed a series of local managers to run Mainoru. Foster stayed at Mainoru for a few weeks on several occasions, but it fell to the local managers to exercise the new direction of colonial power; that is, to put pressure on the community to leave. The new owner knew that the logic of capitalist production could not accommodate 'unnecessary' people; that is, unproductive dependants. He wanted to retain only a few full-time Aboriginal workers and their wives and children. Over the next few years successive managers, whose liking for Aboriginal people seems to have varied considerably, tried to achieve a small, stable labour force from among the previous residents, with varying success. Heather Dodd said of this process:

> I can completely understand it because this coincided with equal wages. There was no way you could employ all those people and you certainly don't want a hundred unemployed people sitting right there. I mean what do you do with them? It's even worse having them all there and only employing two (1988).

The patrol officers' reports after the new owners acquired Mainoru were fewer and briefer, and they reveal a shift in the style of station management as well as in government practice. No longer was Patrol Officer Ryan, the familiar state's emissary, inspecting the work of established and trusted owners and reporting on their progress in the task of managing and developing their familiar Aboriginal community. The new patrol officers were suspicious of the new managers who were unfamiliar with official requirements. The first report written after the change of ownership found much to criticise: the camp was run down; the kitchen had no fly wire; no books were being kept; the manager had claimed maintenance and also deducted money for keep from employees' wages and from pensioners' cheques; insufficient rations were supplied; the teacher was unhappy about being 'denied free contact with the Aboriginals' by the manager (F1 83/441 April 1969). These negative reports revived plans for a government presence in the Bulman area, which was to include a new school, ancillary buildings with accommodation for the patrol officers and even a small police station.

However, by the time of the next patrol report there was another manager whose desire to employ many Aborigines was favourably reported: 'He would like camp of 200' (F941/0 64/256 Sept. 1969). New managers and new patrol officers were adjusting to the demands of the social welfare and equal wages era. The disorder attendant on these changes is apparent in the report of a break-in at the newly installed school which led to a school inspector's report stating, 'it would take two 4″ side bolts, 6 heavy duty padlocks and 3 lengths of stout wire to make the van and blue shed secure' (E 242/5 K1/1/7, 1971). The familiar group of cooperative Aborigines had again become a threat against which civilisation must defend its resources.

An incident appears in the archives from this time which illustrates the way information which circulated among whites who were unfamiliar with specific individuals and circumstances could reinforce the backwardness of Rembarrnga even as they were obediently trying to go forward. Susan Murray was one of the Mainoru teenagers attending the residential Kormilda College in Darwin for secondary schooling in 1969. The patrol officer recorded his disappointment when she refused to return for the second term. He reported that Nelly Camfoo (her mother's sister) was 'most upset' and would persuade Susan to return to school, but that her parents, Larry and Dolly, supported her refusal and said they would look after her. The patrol officer concluded, on information supplied by the newly installed manager's wife, that it was 'because of pressure from the group and her parents' desire to "marry her off" that Susan will not return' (F 941/0 64/256 June 1969).

But in 1991 Susan explained to me that she had left school because a senior male teacher had begun to molest her. After staring at her and keeping her in when her work was finished, he came into her room one night and tried to kiss her. She escaped by climbing over the partition into the next room and subsequently ran away from school with two others. Neither she nor her parents accused the teacher or told the patrol officer, being both embarrassed and afraid. Besides the power of gender, there are two other mutually enhancing forms of power operating here: the power and desire of an opportunistic staff member to sexually exploit a socially isolated and vulnerable young school girl, and the power of white discourse to interpret what is occurring; that is, to decide that it was a backward set of social relations which was responsible for obstructing the chance of this promising pupil to transcend her background. In such a set of asymmetrical power relations the white interpretation assumes the order of truth and the Aboriginal discourse is rendered silent, silenced by the weight of years of such interpretations and the truths they have constructed.

A replica of the past surfaced in a report in 1969 complaining that 'Aboriginals were congregating at Mainoru'. The patrol officer did not recall Jack McKay's story of 'starving natives spearing cattle' (Chapter 3), but responded in a way reminiscent of his predecessors, sympathising with the manager Mr Brodie, who, he said, 'could not keep supplying food to these people as station stores were limited and it was difficult to obtain sufficient beef . . . some 50–60 people were contained in this group' (79/11922 Dec. 1969).

The patrol officer concluded that 'Mr Brodie appears to have a genuine case. He is employing 8 male Aboriginals and 3 females and providing for 31 dependants plus 5 pensioners' (79/11922 Dec. 1969). Because the station herd had run down there was even a shortage of beef. This patrol included a nurse who found 'only two' malnourished children, 'whose mother is known as an extremely poor manager'. These officials offered the station manager assistance to process unemployment benefits 'for those people stood down'.[11] The language of care ('malnourished children'), the surveillance ('mother is known') and the control of labour relations ('stood down') are part of a program where the state officials remained oblivious of the historical experience, cultural proclivities and particular characteristics of the people they were managing. They were able to judge what they observed by overlaying it with a set of universal, modern and therefore unarguable criteria of health and well-being. Where the standards were found wanting it was increasingly the state which proffered services directly, for instance by including a nurse in this patrol.

In the past it was the commonsense of Mrs Dodd which would minister to such requirements, but now the previous policy was interpreted as racist neglect. The fact that these Rembarrnga people considered Mainoru a permanent home and had, many years before, thrown in their lot with Jack McKay and had complied with the whitefellas' demand that they become sedentary, was not something the bureaucrats knew about or responded to. The state seemed to have forgotten the interest it had previously taken in these people.

In the absence of the long-standing familiarity among the station community, the sharper logic of economic viability became salient. The state officials accepted the station manager's definition of his problem as one of unwanted people:

> There remained 30 persons whom Mr. Brodie says are definitely not wanted on the Station . . . [examples are] Larry Murray . . . [seven dependants are named]. Larry is an unsophisticated Aboriginal who is not employable having never acquired any reasonable work habits.
>
> William Moore [eight dependants] . . . William is unemployable by choice and was regarded as such by Miss Dodd some years ago.
>
> William Martin [eight dependants] . . . has a history of agitation both with the Dodds and with the present management. He is intelligent but unemployable.
>
> Ronny Lindsay unemployable by choice.
>
> Singleton . . . refuses to adopt reasonable work habits (79/11922 Dec. 1969).

These judgements feign a disinterested, objective stance but rely on personal, moral evaluations of work and obedience which were directed to solving the problem of managing a population that was awkwardly placed in history. Mainoru was 'being developed' and could not supply the resources to distribute rations and 'look after' these people. The judgements of worth sever individuals from their place among their kin or their place as leaders or representatives of the community. Willy Martin's 'history of agitation' presumably refers to his practice of questioning of whitefellas, something which he seems to have always taken to be his responsibility. Yet the same report indicates his willingness to cooperate, for while he and Larry refused to go to the larger settlements at Roper or Bamyilli, they agreed to 'move out to the Bulman Waterhole' (79/11922 Dec. 1969). They also both asserted that they were willing to work at Mainoru. However, the patrol officer agreed with Mr Brodie who 'insisted that they were unemployable'.

Thus the voices of Aborigines were over-ridden or made to comply with the manager's judgement, as when a statement from Ronnie Martin is quoted, in which he agreed that he 'was having trouble at present' after he was assessed as a 'slow worker' (F941/0 64/256). The familiar complaint that the managers were 'unable to prevent Aboriginal employees and their dependants from sharing out food to non-working relatives' emerged, but the manager had a two-stage solution. The patrol officer reported in neutral terms that when the new kitchen was built 'he intends to police the provision of food and hopes to literally starve out those persons who will not work and who refuse to move' (79/11922 Dec. 1969). The next strategy would be when he 'asked the Police to remove them and their families from the station homestead site' (ibid.).[12] Here the gloves are off. The pastoralist assumed that the police would assist him in getting rid of people who had become nuisances. The state had long experience of uprooting and transplanting Aboriginal people according to the specific and temporary requirements of one or another program of development.

We are dealing here with a reassertion of the logic of capitalist labour relations in conditions where the racial division had interrupted them for a time. While the state had assisted station owners to maintain a pool of cheap labour, now, with the reformulation of race and labour relations, it provided support for their removal. This was a form of capital cleansing where unproductive people, those deemed incapable of contributing to capital development and accumulation, were removed. In the name of racial equality, managers and state officials acted in collusion to turn Aborigines into displaced populations dependent on the state for succour.

The walk-off

Florry and Chuckerduck Lindsay were not the target of the manager's complaint about unwanted people, probably because they were more cooperative than others. However, they were caught up in the conflict that stemmed from the tension between the logic of the station economy and the inherited conditions of racialised labour. There is both anger and pride in Florry's description of the exodus from Mainoru. She explained the tension that led to the trek to Bulman waterhole, situated in her and her brother Larry Murray's country, near a major site for the Yappaduruwa ceremony.

> My husband [Chuckerduck] and that manager had an argument. We didn't like that manager. He was too cheeky. Those two had the biggest row. He took a rifle, and my husband got a rifle too. That old man [Chuckerduck] said, 'I'll shoot your tyre.' That manager said, 'No more. Not you, not you. All the boys, the young people, we don't like,' that *mununga* said, 'you two fellas are alright.'

'Might be we can't stop here. We'd better go away with the nanny goats,' we said (1989).

Florry noted the manager's attempt to separate herself and Chuckerduck off from 'the boys', grown men such as Willy and others, who he defined as 'cheeky' trouble makers. This differentiated the old people, who could receive the old-age pension, from young men who were 'workers', and whose presence constituted a problem. Florry continued:

'Well we've got to go Bulman waterhole now, to our country,' we said like that. Willy Martin was there too and [his children] Scotty, Lynette, Ewan. They were little little one when we went away from that place. I said, 'Alright you fellas got to wait yet. I've got to go back and get my nanny goats.' Me and my husband rounded up the nanny goats. I counted them all and took them down now, to the crossing. We rolled up swag and went to Gum Creek with the nanny goats. All the little boys looked after them and milked them. We camped there one night. That white man was following us to Gum Creek. We heard that motor car. 'You gotta come back,' he said. I got my swag. I got my dog. I got my nanny goat. We kept going, shifting to another creek.
    'Well here now we'll camp.' We camped there two days. We were tired from carrying swag. We waited to see when that man was going to come, but he didn't come (1989).

Florry's emphasis on the manager's concern for their welfare reflects the sense of human interdependence in Rembarrnga social relations. Interdependence had characterised the relationship with the previous owners and even the recently installed managers were understood not simply as bossy newcomers, but as humans with their own reasons and mysterious practices with whom a relationship should be established. But the station's identity had changed. While the Rembarrnga/ Ngalkbon/Nalakan community had been an organic part of this station in the McKays' time, the new owners had stripped down the meaning of Mainoru so that its economic dimension was dominant. As an enterprise of the 1970s, Mainoru could survive without the blackfellas.

Ronnie Martin was one of two men Foster continued to employ intermittently, perhaps partly because he took more account of the motives of economic rationality than many others, or perhaps because he was a good mechanic. Ronnie said:

Max Foster bought that place from McKay. We had this bloke Jim Barrett then another supervisor Len Brodie. He's the one that pushed them off and then the Mainoru mob left for Bulman . . . Max Foster owned the place for eleven years. He was there some of the time every three or four months. I was with him at Mainoru all the time, nobody else was there with him. That's why I left Mainoru. Everyone went away (1987).

It was bare economic logic which led to the manager's view that 'the problem' at Mainoru would be solved when 'a few unsatisfactory workers have been sacked and moved on' (79/11922 Dec. 1969). The presence of 'unsatisfactory workers' is not considered part of the general condition of Aborigines and their historical and cultural connections with this place. Brodie was sympathetic to the immediate plight of the people. For instance, he was concerned that some workers' pay was a mere pittance after deductions were made for their dependants' keep. This was because the station's practice was to feed the children and other people who were designated dependants, and then deduct the worth of the food from the wages of the person they were assumed to depend on. The men who were 'workers' were forced to 'support' people deemed their 'dependants', on the basis of calculations done by the station's bookkeeper. The dependent kin became a burden to those who had attained the status of 'worker'. The worker had little control over identifying these 'dependants' and none at all over determining the extent of his responsibility for them or what they were fed, let alone the monetary value of the labour or the food. The manager construed the problem as one of understanding and said sympathetically: 'No matter how often the situation is explained to the workers and how often they agreed they understood, each pay day they saw some men receiving twenty and thirty dollars to their ten or less' (E242/5 K14/3/32 Aug. 1970).

The idea that the problem would be solved by explanation illustrates the way the exercise of power, when manifest as reason, is invisible to the agent of domination because the power relations embedded within rationalities are so taken for granted. It is assumed that once the master's/parent's reasoning is clarified, the servant/child will accept the system and cooperate. Any contesting of the explanation is construed as either flawed understanding or deliberate defiance, indicating a lack of either intellectual capacity or moral worth. These men may well have understood the manager's explanation, but this manner of defining and ordering their family and social relations through the provision of food, goods and money did not thereby become reasonable in their eyes. Rembarrnga had contrasting interpretations of interpersonal responsibility, of work and its rewards, of the meaning of food and its supply and consumption. It was the categories themselves, as well as their consequences, that they did not accept.

The walk-off in 1970 was not predicted by the patrol officers, though they perceived some tension. The manager warned that a 'sit down strike' or a 'walk-off' might occur in protest against the latest government's proposal for the area; that is, a cattle project in the Bulman area with cattle from Maningrida. The patrol officer reported this, saying: 'It seems that the locals claim this area as their country' (E242/5 K14/3/32 Aug. 1970), but he failed to recognise the level of discontent that was being signalled and suggested other reasons for Mainoru's depleted population. Thus it was that when Florry and Chuckerduck and others took their goats and swags and children and walked off the station, there was virtually no official response. The anger and disillusionment of the Mainoru mob at being increasingly made unwelcome and then forced into virtual refugee status, hardly caused a ripple in the official version of the smooth transition to what was beginning to be called 'self-management'.

The Commonwealth Government was not oblivious to the consequences of the equal wages decision. In 1970 it commissioned a report into the conditions of Aborigines on pastoral properties. This 'Gibb report' foreshadowed a crucial shift in the state's approach to managing Aborigines. It recommended that communities be encouraged to 'maintain and take pride in their identity, traditions and culture' (Gibb 1971:2). While 'the relationship between the Aborigines and the pastoral industry is appropriate and appealing', with changed conditions Aborigines would be encouraged 'increasingly to manage their own affairs, as individuals, as groups and as communities (at the local level)' (Gibb 1971:3). This bracketed qualification seems to preclude their managing themselves as a political constituency and the 'local level' implies that there is no relationship between these station Aborigines and the fringe dwelling and urban Aboriginal populations.[13]

However, this report did signal a profound change in government discourse about how Aborigines were to be managed. Not only was there an emerging recognition of the legitimacy of 'culture' as a social reality, but the state began dealing with Aboriginal *communities* as if they were autonomous entities. The 'encouragement' of pride in 'identity, traditions and culture' was an element in a widespread realignment of race relations and a changing governance of Aborigines. Thus amid broad social and economic changes, a reified notion of culture emerged which was deployed to legitimise a progressive discursive framework of self-determination. Culture was the familiar unchanging essence of an earlier anthropology, something thought of as separate from Rembarrnga people's lived experience of the previous 50 years.

Recognition that communities could proclaim an Aboriginal cultural identity was quite new. What was meant by culture in the Gibb report was 'language, tradition and arts', a set of specific practices which were defined as separate from economic and geographical conditions and from everyday mundane practices. Such a culture could be incorporated within the nation. However, there were limits to this new found tolerance. The report continued: 'The Government recognises the rights of individual Aborigines to effective choice about the degree and pace at which they came to identify with [Australian] society and believes that they will do so the more readily and happily when they are attracted to it voluntarily . . .' (1971:2).

There is a concealed duplicity here. The intention to encourage Aborigines to 'maintain and take pride in their identity, traditions and culture' is combined with the firm assumption that they would 'identify with . . . society'; that is, non-Aboriginal Australia. It was only the timing and degree of that identification over which they had a choice. 'Choice' is imagined as something that does not require any specific space, yet the most fundamental cultural choice of the Mainoru community was to do with a geographical space; their first choice was to remain in the place they were being removed from. Further, there is no perception of a conflict between their 'identity, traditions and culture' and that of 'society'. Had culture been seen as involving internalised identity, morality and manners, forms of attachment and authority, humour and emotions which inform every aspect of daily life, then Aboriginal culture might have been recognised as more seriously at odds with other elements of Australian society. No cultural conflicts were envisaged in the new era of multicultural tolerance, where the difference of Aborigines was to be recognised as part of the Australian nation.

Rembarrnga had been living among *mununga* for 50 years when this invitation to express their culture arrived. What had the power of *mununga* done to them? In Foucault's terms, power 'reaches into the grain of individuals, touches their bodies, inserts itself into their actions and attitudes, their discourses, learning processes and everyday lives . . . a regime of its exercise *within* the social body, rather than *from above* it' (1980:39). However, in this case there had been many barriers to this ongoing process of insertion of power. While the power/knowledge of the invading whites' regime was ever present and interfered with and shaped everyday lives, placing a different level of meaning on every action, it sometimes seemed to flow past like water off a duck's back. Although the consequences of whites' judgements, practices and knowledge are apparent in the silences and demeanour of black bodies in the *mununga* domain, these consequences remained in some ways external, a surface shading over the community's internal dynamics, distractions rather than destructive of the established psychic and social relations which pre-existed *mununga* interests. The meanings inherent in the land and evoked in the ceremonies have remained the foundation of life. Yet the external conditions acted as irritants in the Rembarrnga social body, and over time they had not only physically changed the quality of life, but offered new languages which altered the value of the old ones, imperceptibly and gradually, but inevitably. Thus the cultural tolerance of the multicultural era did not, as many officials believed, answer a longing for cultural legitimacy felt by Rembarrnga people. Rather, it brought demands for new and even more alien forms of social interaction to enable new forms of governing.

7

Betrayals

I put the first pair of trousers on those blackfellas. It's not them that asked for land. It's the Land Council that's told them to ask.

—*Bert Nixon, Katherine, 1987*

It used to belong to Billy Farrar but it belong to me. It's my land, from my father.

—*George Jaurdaku, Weemol, 1987*

FORGETTING THE PAST

Radical changes were made in Aboriginal policy after the referendum of 1967 which saw the constitution altered: the national census would now count Aborigines and the Federal Government would have the power to legislate concerning them (Attwood & Marcus 1997).[1] The changes were wide ranging, beginning with the establishment of a Council for Aboriginal Affairs in Canberra and culminating in the funding of hundreds of Aboriginal organisations throughout Australia by the new Labor government in 1972. One consequence in the Northern Territory was the disruption of some of the established meanings of race. Attempts to equalise Aborigines shattered the cultural domain of pastoral life with its characteristic racial hierarchy. Racial tensions arose as the population separated into the two racial domains which I encountered in 1975 and discussed in Chapter 1. The immediate consequence of the state's insistence that Aboriginal employees have the same conditions as other workers was that many Aboriginal communities not only lost their access to paid work, but lost their homes as well. Rembarrnga people at least had somewhere else to go.

Governments have selective memories and no loyalty to past policies, and in the 1970s the Commonwealth Government showed no compunction about betraying the pastoral culture it had protected and the Aborigines whose assimilation it had nurtured, as well as its own officials who had been convinced of the progressive nature of the Welfare Branch's assimilation policies. By divesting itself of its powers *in loco parentis* over the Aboriginal population, the state reversed its tutelary and protective role, delivering a radical blow to entrenched practices. Suddenly the discursive climate changed. What had seemed normal race relations were now deemed unspeakably racist, including the affectionate tolerance towards the racial attitudes of men deemed 'old timers'. There was a shift in the way Aborigines were spoken about, especially as they were sometimes present and had to be spoken *to*. The particular separations and inequalities which had become established in the Territory were officially replaced with discourses and consultations about land claims and Aboriginal enterprises. A new kind of progressive public servant derided the pastoral industry's protests as redneck reactions, while the betrayal of previous promises to Aboriginal people was not recognised at all. Resistance from old Welfare Branch employees continued in the form of quiet subversions and obstruction of the new policies. Before examining how Rembarrnga country was invaded anew, the precise nature of the 'betrayal' needs to be understood.

Pastoral culture

Bert Nixon told me, 'I rode over from Western Australia with nothing. I made this station.' Sitting in his dilapidated little house he described his 40-odd years of harsh and absorbing work on a small holding near Katherine. Bert's experiences of working in stock camps, sleeping on the ground with what he called his 'black boys' for company, typifies a central feature of pastoral culture. Such small holders are the so-called cockies (farmers) or rednecks, much maligned and devalued in the national imagination, except when they gain sympathy as the proverbial battlers. Bert Nixon, Jack McKay and Jimmy Gibbs could hardly have imagined donning the trappings of a cattle king's lifestyle. Unlike those heroic figures, they are accorded little moral authority outside their limited social and cultural domain. Encased in the trajectory of European history, such men were participants in the enterprise of establishing a rural industry, creating the nation's values through which they also created themselves. They shared a faith that betterment and progress would occur cumulatively with hard work, frugality and practical knowledge. Such faith is as mysterious as any, based as it is on a particular theory of causality, particular forms of desire, and a mythic vision of prosperous land. Self-denial was valued by these men above any immediate or even long-term sensual gratification, though present work and privation would bring later reward. The managers of small stations were poorly paid cattlemen, some suffering great privation, danger and depression. Their black companions were an integral part of their endeavour. Even the humblest drovers could sometimes participate imaginatively in the glamour associated with pastoral life, and more significantly, the poorest owners could take pride in sharing the white man's burden of managing the blackfellas who were an organic part of station communities.

Bert Nixon spoke with admiration of the moral qualities of the Aborigines who had worked for him. His authority concerning 'his' blackfellas demonstrates the way two cultural domains were drawn into one. Difference and contradiction were hidden beneath the facade of the single station community, with the racial hierarchy and the physical separation of the 'blacks' camp' the only evidence of the specificities of Aboriginality. The oneness of the station community was echoed in the notion that blackfellas belonged in the outback, so their station work was 'appropriate and appealing' (Gibb 1971:3). While their skills in the bush and as trackers were valued and recognised by stockmen and the police, the pastoralist's self-conceived world of pragmatism and rationality left no room for any recognition of the symbolic and psychological power of what was called primitivity. It was outside the stations that the exotic or spiritual qualities of these 'others within' had symbolic and imaginative value for the nation in enhancing the colonial imagery of the authentic Australian outback.

Alongside the intimacies of their intertwined identities and the common purpose of the mustering camps, we saw above that domestic life was racially separated. Rembarrnga people cooked and talked and the children interacted in communal space around fires in the camp and out in the bush. They arranged ceremonies, initiations and marriages away from the scrutiny of the whitefellas who were up in the house. The unity of the station community was in the hierarchically structured inter-relatedness of black and white Mainoru residents, as well as the logic of their discursive and physical separation. This was illustrated in the alacrity with which information was proffered to me about the character of the erstwhile 'Mainoru mob' by the erstwhile owner, who knew me only as an anthropologist from Sydney University. When I wrote to Heather Dodd in 1976 with some general enquiries about the history of the Bulman community, I received what amounted to a moral map which positioned the individual members thus (I spare them the knowledge of who was so judged):

> [A] is very intelligent and literate and you should talk to him if ever you can . . . He's eligible for an invalid pension but prefers to work. So does [B] and so incidentally did his father.
>
> By the way [X] is a rogue. His wife [Y] is a rogue and a liar. Her brother [Z] is a rogue and a liar and a very bad man. Don't believe anything [Y] tells you. If [Z] ever tells you the truth it's probably something you should not know. As a seller of secrets he nearly broke his father's heart. The cousin [M] is a fine person, so is his sister [N]. Brother [P] is a good guy and so is [Q] (letter, 1976).

In the next letter she said, '[Q] has always had a very low tribal ranking. Due to his physical disabilities he could not dance or hunt. Any esteem he has is due to his European skills.' Heather Dodd's willingness to assert such moral judgements about a group of black people to a complete stranger reveals the way white people conspire to own the knowledge of the nature of black people. She was directing me to choose my informants from those who could be trusted to speak about Mainoru. Access to this personal information would guard against a white truth being contaminated by black lies. The authority with which she could make and share these judgements stems from the colonial regime, bolstered by the science of anthropology, and it differentiates her from, and elevates her above, her black co-residents of the station. Markers of authenticity, such as the mention of secrets being sold, were included in her letter.[2] We whites, she implied, can recognise the need to protect what is sacred to Aborigines, and our moral sensibilities allow us to share an abhorrence of treachery and to deplore the disloyalty of the son who sold secret material. Heather also added that 'anything that is purely aboriginal you must get from the people themselves. If they want you to know it, they'll tell you.' Here she is framing the 'purely aboriginal' as a domain she and I should recognise and respect, but one that remains outside the reality of the present, irrelevant to other social conditions. Thus Mainoru, in its owners' imagination, consisted of an intimate community composed of black and white people who were intertwined in a naturalised hierarchy.

Rembarrnga also expressed loyalty to this domain, and their affection towards old pastoral bosses is typified in Peter Lee's story about 'my old Jack' in the days when poddy-dodging was a regular adventure:

> Oh, old Jack McKay drank any kind, rum. Poor fella. My old Jack he saved my life. Two, three policeman been after me, trying to get me. But my saviour [was on] one side, Mr McKay. From Mainoru we were chased around, me and Bandy, and another dead fella, all the stock boys. Diver, Slippery, all that. Four dead men and me and that old man alive, old Bandy (1989).

The sense of a shared intimacy and history was lost when the newcomers from the world of international capital speculation, which shared no relationship with old Jack, bought both Mainoru and Mountain Valley.[3]

If we think of Mainoru as a single cultural arena, then the selling of the station exposed its hidden fault line. The ties of social identity that bound the community ceased to be expressed when the deaths, departures and the walk-off occurred. The reversal of the economic logic of cheap labour and the loosening of the protective arm of the state meant that the social system which had grown up around these structures was shattered and fell apart.

The constructed and contingent nature of 'culture' is difficult to perceive when social life proceeds apparently uncontested. The unself-conscious style and everyday meanings of social life come most starkly to consciousness when faced with challenges, in this case the state's renewed pursuit of racial equality. The new demands caused the destruction of what had become normal station life. At least that is the view of those known as 'rednecks' who saw the state forcing them to relinquish their property, the blackfellas. Their moral authority within their cultural universe was broken when those customarily treated as inferiors were given equal footing in the law. These 'rednecks' were ill equipped to defend their obsolete practices. For many Aboriginal people, being freed from quasi-serfdom had painful consequences, as they lost access to their own country and had no place of residence except government stations, and no source of subsistence except what they began to call 'sit down money'. For the Mainoru mob the consequences were more ambiguous.

Rednecks betrayed

Heather Dodd's discovery that Mainoru station had been an economic failure, and that her uncle had 'left the place in a mess and with huge debts', far from leading to disillusionment with pastoralism and its use of Aboriginal labour, enhanced for her the heroism of Jack's struggle, the romance of outback poverty and the selflessness of the station's tutelary task. Heather emphasised the moral significance of her family's role, saying that 'the station would have been a lot more profitable if we'd done the way some did. The Aboriginals kept us poor in a sense.' She painted a rosy picture of the Aborigines' quality of life, which was due to the fact that:

> Everyone had some sort of job. And they had to do the job to get whatever they got for it. It wasn't much but the point was that nobody was freeloading. And for the young men there's nothing better than being a stockman for a young fellow of any kind . . . when we went, there was no more motivation. There was no one to chase them back (1988).

The assertion that people had to be chased back to work indicates that the pastoralist's task was incomplete because lessons of labour were still being learned. In this discourse of disappointment, provision of government funds leads to a debilitating psychological and social dependency. The Aborigines are seen to be the tragic victims of government policy. In her first letter to me Heather asserted:

> Wholesale government cuts could be the saving of the [Bulman] group. They have learnt nothing but how to 'be blackfellows' and accept handouts. They had been a fairly proud and capable group that had never received one penny they did not work for. They now are convinced that they have a right to be cosseted and looked after for the rest of their days. Bear in mind that my earliest and closest friends are among these people . . . These men never wanted something for nothing. They are being ruined by the government's policies (letter 1976).

In Heather's account, Aboriginality becomes insignificant once certain desirable qualities are donned by these 'closest friends'. Mainoru had successfully nurtured the virtues of pride, work and never wanting 'something for nothing'. The exploitation of the labour of one's 'closest friends' was turned into a necessary evolutionary step towards economic independence and the virtuous pride that accompanies it. Heather felt herself and her mother's teaching to have been betrayed by a government which has 'cosseted' and 'looked after' these people, thus allowing them to revert to childish dependency. She attributes fragility to their newly aquired virtues in that they quickly succumbed to soft treatment. The romantic affirmation of the pastoralists' own regime is also an affirmation of Heather's family's self-image as nurturers of the nation's new children.

In fact the assertion that they 'never received one penny they did not work for' is not accurate. Not only did they often work for no pennies, but the statement disguises the way government allowances were claimed to support dependants. 'Larry didn't work, but we tried to keep him occupied so we could feed the [eight] children,' Heather said elsewhere. That is, Larry had to be employed if the station was to receive the allowance for dependent children. Thus, while the pretence that Larry was working served both the station's and Larry's financial interests, the deception was attributed to the need to protect Larry's pride. Heather constructed an account of what Chuckerduck gained from his employment at Mainoru: 'He gained job satisfaction and good health, and a current position of esteem that detribalised elders don't have these days unless they have job skills that the younger ones value. It has given him pride' (letter 1976).

This statement encapsulates a story of difference being over-ridden by modernity. It represents the Aboriginal individual as *tabula rasa,* a blank slate on which have been inscribed the universal values of the unmarked category of 'worker', one who enjoys 'job satisfaction and good health'. The 'detribalised elder' would not receive esteem without resources valued by 'the young ones'. His pride in this work is the source of his identity. Characteristics of opportunism and an a-historical material rationality which rations respect on the basis of productive value are attributed to these young ones. Chuckerduck's 'job skills' in cattlework are represented as the basis of his current esteem, and thus Mainoru has left a legacy of value. As with the man whose only esteem was said to be 'due to his European skills', there is a racialisation of skills and emotions here. Anything of the modern world is assumed to have value collateral for blacks, credit for which is owed to Europeans who generously taught to others the skills that they owned.

Heather echoes a common discourse among old or erstwhile pastoralists who see their 'boys' as being spoilt by government policies of 'handouts' to blackfellows. Reliance on government money is associated with dependence, social inferiority and shame, while the previous state of dependency on pastoral stations is construed as a situation of healthy hard work and independence. This is a version of a standard discourse on welfare dependency and social disadvantage which is authorised by certain scholarly work and circulates as an accepted set of diagnoses in the media and in discussion. The familiar disappointed reaction of the colonisers to the decolonisation process does not rely solely on the belief in productive labour and other features of capitalist relations as the only proper form of social relations. It also claims superior knowledge of colonial subjects. That is, the pastoralists responded to the events of the self-management era as if they provided yet more evidence that it was they who knew the Aborigines rather than the bureaucrats, the eggheads or 'those people from down south'. The Land Commissioners who were appointed to implement the *Aboriginal Land Rights (Northern Territory) Act* epitomised for them the worst of this new madness.

Pastoralists who raised objections to Aboriginal land claims before the Land Commissioner did so in the name of a cultural tradition which had previously enjoyed explicit support from the state. Yet times had changed and Bert Nixon was reduced to an object of mockery in the hearing of the Nitmiluk (Katherine Gorge) claim in Katherine, due to his misunderstanding of the procedures in their formal aspects, in their intent, as well as in the kinds of knowledge that they privileged. He said incredulously, 'I put the first pair of trousers on those blackfellas. It's not them that asked for land. It's the Land Council that's told them to ask. I tell you they never owned Katherine Gorge' (1987 transcript of hearing).

His opposition to land rights was grounded in personal and particular knowledge, not the kind of abstract, formal and analytic knowledge which dominates court processes. He was one of many land owners in Australia who did not know that Aborigines had kinship systems (Chase 1984). His experience had made certain facts clear to him, and he was confident and proud of his form of knowledge which had been, in the past, legitimated and indeed relied on by the state and by society more generally. He saw an absolute contradiction between the priorities of land use for production and profit, and land rights for Aborigines. His own use of the land had brought him few material rewards, but this did nothing to undermine his faith in the superior worth of his enterprise or the accuracy of his perceptions.

The shift away from assimilation towards self-determination meant that the focus of bureaucratic attention moved to the 'tribal' or 'outback' people who lived in 'communities', and away from those Aborigines who had already fitted in with urban structures by adopting nuclear family households (cf. Collmann 1988). A shift in forms of social legitimation was illustrated in the juxtaposition of two items in a bicentennial register of notable Northern Territory women. Mrs Dodd, the remarkable outback teacher of Aboriginal pupils appeared in the same list as Nelly Camfoo, who remained illiterate, and so could be deemed Mrs Dodd's failure. Mrs Dodd was credited with 'creating' a literate community of 'trustworthy and honest' Aborigines. The register recorded her as:

> A dearly-loved and widely-respected pioneer of isolated education in the Northern Territory who for nearly 20 years tutored generation after generation of Aboriginal students . . . Perhaps Margaret's most outstanding contribution . . . was her active demonstration that Aborigines, like any other human beings, respond to being treated with respect and dignity (Lea 1988:45).

This same register also listed Nelly Camfoo as outstanding: 'As with many other members of the community Nelly was schooled in stock work and domestic service at Mainoru station (see Margaret Dodd this register)' (ibid.:20).

This placing of an individual black woman in the equivalent position to the pioneering white teacher contradicts the established racial hierarchy. The twelve years of Mrs Dodd's school is mythologised to 'generation after generation' of students. The attribution to Nelly of 'ample leadership qualities' represents the hope, widespread among well-intentioned whites, that authoritative Aboriginal leaders will emerge who will conveniently lead the people along the path to independence, where they will cease to burden our consciences. Here is illustrated the paradox of imposing self-determination and imputing the necessary personal qualities for its fulfilment.

The new discourse which emerged from the sudden demand in the early 1970s that Aborigines become self-managing was marked by an extreme and explicit polarisation of whitefellas. A widespread and self-righteous condemnation of the changes, sometimes with an undercurrent of racist contempt, emerged as one orthodoxy, which was countered by a defensive reliance on fundamental egalitarian and anti-racist principles in the name of justice, progress or humanitarianism. The former was identified with the outback, while the latter was generated among the urban bourgeoisie. The public confrontation of these two positions left little space for any critical assessment of the social circumstances and priorities of Aborigines, let alone for any examination of entrenched racialised social relations and their ambiguous forms of interaction. The new progressive policies and the flourishing new bureaucracy could not be criticised without the risk of giving succour to the redneck enemy of racial equality.

'Southerners' are familiar bogeymen in the conservative discourse of the Territory, and from the local's point of view they reached plague proportion in the early 1970s. New staff were appointed to implement policies of the new Council for Aboriginal Affairs (CAA) set up by the Liberal government after the 1967 referendum.[4] The CAA was replaced by the Department of Aboriginal Affairs (DAA) under Labor in 1972. Harry Giese, the powerful and energetic Director of Welfare since 1953, complained that in 1972 he was 'shut out of any Aboriginal Affairs by Dexter and Coombs, and not allowed to visit communities'. He called the new officials 'those stupid individuals from Canberra' (interview 1989). Their 'stupidity' consisted of no longer taking the difference of Aborigines for granted, but rather depending on a similarity; that is, a shared vision of the future. Not only was the state again out of tune with the outback, but, more importantly, the invisible cultural under-pinnings of new progressive policies meant that they busily reproduced the racial inequality they wanted to expunge. Before explaining how that came about at Bulman, we will explore further the historic betrayal of those the policies were supposed to benefit.

But first Heather Dodd's sense of betrayal is revealing. It is not only on behalf of her mother but also on behalf of her childhood companions and friends:

> By the time the school got rolling Mum got in these vitamin drops and we grew a lot of fruit and goat's milk. So every day the kids had this appalling brew of goat's milk with added vitamins and all this sort of stuff which was forced down them . . . Their living conditions were atrocious by 1980s standards. They didn't have housing as such. We eventually managed to get them huts. But they were healthy and strong. They had direction and motivation. They were all terribly important. Yet of the nineteen kids Mum started school with I think ten are dead (1988).[5]

To Heather the deaths confirm the wisdom and virtue of a regime where the significance of individuals, as well as physical health, had been paramount. Her bleak story could be seen to expose her own and her mother's claims about the health and contentment which resulted from the care they provided as a neo-colonial fantasy, proven hollow by the subsequent deaths. But the deaths also illustrate a real betrayal of the promises made to Aborigines at Mainoru, promises which involved a much wider cast of characters than these pastoralists.

The regime at Mainoru was not some isolated fantasy, but was in harmony with the state's intentions and the nation's desire to educate and assimilate Aborigines. Their solicitude illustrates Fanon's metaphor of colonialism's unconscious desire to be a mother 'who unceasingly restrains her fundamentally perverse offspring from managing to commit suicide' (1986:170). Perhaps, having lost the capacity to reproduce their society independently, the offspring reverted to being 'perverse' and are no longer restrained from suicidal impulses. Thus the story of white solicitude and its reversal, followed by an era of premature black deaths, contains a much bigger and more difficult truth about the colonial covenant and its destructive potential, especially when changes are sudden and blind to the past. The subsequent era of race relations is replete with ambiguities and contradictions, with desire and dismay, myopia and unintended consequences, many of which will be explored in the rest of this work.

Heather was living alone in Darwin when Nelly expressed concern about her well-being: 'Heather Dodd got nobody there to talk to. Eileen [Cummings] told her one time, "Go up to Bulman and go and see all the people that you know, that grew you up." But Heather never came' (1987).

The notion of living alone in a world without kin was strange enough, but Heather's distaste for visiting Bulman baffled the people she affectionately called 'the mob'. However, her contacts with them remained alive because members of 'the mob' would telephone, particularly to let her know of deaths, of births, but also of other events. She had occasional visits from those who came to Darwin for school, jail, hospital or some other chance event. At these visits the dozen large volumes of Mainoru photographs would be laid out on the tables and floor for children and adults to examine. I went there with some Bulman people several times between 1979 and 1989, when Heather moved to Queensland. She had a sense of authority concerning the past both because she owned the photos and because she was always the first to identify the subjects and the events surrounding them. Her authority was not challenged by the mob, and great pleasure was taken in viewing these old photos, though there were hints of resentment that Heather owned them.[6]

Blackfellas betrayed

There are many effects of what I am calling betrayal, where earlier promises and trajectories were reversed for no reason that was apparent to people in the bush, black or white. Part of the betrayal was in the state's envisaging fine new possibilities without recognising the value the past had for those on the racial frontier. Aborigines were betrayed by the changes in more complex and contradictory ways. In Collmann's words, the 'meaning and utility of the adaptations [Aborigines] were earlier forced to make' were negated (nd:29). The vicissitudes in dealing with government departments, whose presence became so pervasive in the following years, threw up deeply ambiguous situations and meanings for Rembarrnga people, and caught them in contradictory discourses and experiences of modernity, of autonomy and of tradition. Thus the unrecognised and unintended betrayal of blackfellas lay, not primarily in the break with the stability of the past, but in the confusion and misunderstanding inherent in the conception of 'self-determination'. The way 'self-determination' operated at Bulman will be detailed in the next chapter, but here I will describe some of the conditions to which the new policies were blind.

Heather Dodd saw Mainoru as replacing the domain of the primitive, something people left behind when they came in to the station: 'There was little that was really traditional about the station people, though we won some really wild kids when the school opened, and there were always nomads wandering by' (letter 1979).

To Heather, meaning was monopolised by modernity. Because ceremonies and walkabout were seen as recreation rather than as important expressions of faith or identity, they could coexist with modern understandings. Tradition did not occupy any significant social space. The domain of the primitive still existed, but it was beyond the station borders. Willy Jailama Martin also believed tradition (or culture) and station work were not incompatible, but to him tradition remained the salient factor. Reflecting on conditions at Mainoru he said:

> We still had bush tucker every time. And ceremony. That didn't stop from that day right up to here now, still going. That's the biggest block for many tribes, if the station tried to stop ceremony. But at Mainoru Station; Jawoyn is there, Ngalkbon is there, Rembarrnga is there, Nalakan is there.
>
> A lot of people used to come out to Mainoru River from Katherine, walking. Ngalkbon people they used to come. We used to have a lot of ceremony, very important thing, sacred. And initiation for the young men (1989).

Willy is asserting that tradition, signalled by bush tucker and ceremony, remained alive within the pastoral setting without pain or difficulty. But when the new policies began to speak of tradition and culture, they were not intending to encourage corroborees in the camp or ceremonies in the wet season, let alone brother–sister avoidance. These terms had become part of a different discourse entirely, one of self-determination, and what 'culture' meant in this context only gradually became apparent.

A reassessment of the past has been generated among Aborigines in the bush. Previously muted views about whitefellas' deceptions, betrayals and incompatible interests have emerged. For instance, the illegitimacy of the pastoralists' claims to ownership can now be confidently asserted. George Jaurdaku named those who owned the country before, during and since the Territory's cattle station boundaries were drawn:

> We worked all around the country. We built up stations, made paddocks. We stay here now, at our station [Barmedakola, Mt Catt]. It used to belong to Billy Farrer, but it belongs to me. It's my land, from my father. Billy Moore had a station here. He was going to build a house, but Larry and Dick kicked him out from that country. They said: 'You can't build a station. Another man owns this.' They told him, 'You can't cut this up. It's our land, one man owns this.' He said, 'Who owns this?' Larry told him, 'It's Georgie owns it—my uncle, my father.' Billy Moore was frightened of Jack McKay. He couldn't tell him. He was hunted away and he got Mountain Valley after. Lot of cattle too. He was a good old man that old Billy Moore. Half-caste bloke. Aranda. He could speak Aranda language and Pitjantjara and Walbiri (1989).

Here the 'half-caste bloke', Billy Moore, recognised what Jack McKay did not; that is, that the country had other owners. 'He couldn't tell' Jack McKay because Jack was not receptive to any assertion of ownership by George Jaurdaku. Billy Moore's awareness of Rembarrnga meanings may have made him reluctant to assert his rights and acquire land under leasehold. Thus the stockmen's tale of Billy Moore's acquisition and subsequent loss of Mountain Valley station in a poker game (see Chapter 3), may have another meaning in the light of his knowledge of other owners.

There was a retrospective sense of betrayal in Alma's memories of never being paid for her work:

> That first lot, we worked for food, for handkerchief, for tobacco. That's the law again. Never pay. Then he [Neville Hood of Mountain Valley] went away altogether, forever. I don't know where he went. Maybe he

went to Queensland, inside, hiding. We only just worked for food, anything, spur, whip, blanket, pillow slip, mosquito net, calico, towel.

Alma suspected that this man was hiding because he was ashamed or fearful of the consequences of having cheated people. Even accepting that it was 'the law' at that time, Alma knows it was wrong not to pay people.

FOOT WALKING TO BULMAN

Florry's account of reaching Goinjimbi illustrates the naturalness with which relations of care and dependency surreptitiously established during the Mainoru years shifted from the pastoralists to the government. She did not see the departure from Mainoru as severing relations with the station but assumed the Mainoru manager would continue to be concerned about them. In fact he handed responsibility over to the Welfare Branch in the person of Danny Watson:

> We waited to see whether that man was going to come, but he didn't come. We sat down. We looked around for sugarbag. We tuckout [ate] sugarbag, tuckout kangaroo, tuckout goanna.
>
> 'Righto. We'll go up that way now,' and we went to Horse Creek. We camped there. We got goanna, we ate it all the way. We camped there two days again . . .[7] Everybody walked with that much swag. No motor car. Ronny Lindsay, my son walked too. Don Forbes, Rexy, Ricky, Kevin, Eric, all that lot of married men. Geoffrey Campion, Henry, my husband, Willy, Lucy and me.
>
> We camped one night and early we kept going to Mt Catt river crossing and there was big rain. We made a big house, paper bark house. Danny Watson went past. He knew we were walking, with piccaninny. He carted up tucker for us to here now. There was no house here, nothing here. We had tucker now (1989).

Danny Watson was employed by DAA as the manager of a cattle project already planned for Bulman in cooperation with the established Aboriginal settlement to the north, Maningrida. He took stores out to the people because the Mainoru manager had let the administration know about the exodus. While the walk to Bulman waterhole was a matter of pride, and has now acquired historical significance, it was far from unmitigated pleasure for people used to a regular supply of flour, sugar and tea. Susan Murray recalled her suffering, partly due to her pregnant state:

I cried on the walk to Bulman. I was sixteen years old, and pregnant, I wanted to go back 'cause I was hungry. We only had goat milk, and not enough flour. After two weeks living on fish, yam and wallaby, I was really sick. Chuck and Aunty [Florry] took turns to stay with me in the humpy each day. Then the Welfare discovered I was one of the runaway girls from Kormilda. Mrs Watson was asked to keep an eye on me. Rhonda was born there at Bulman waterhole (1993).

Thus the beginning of the new relationship between Rembarrnga people and the state was marked by a continuity of paternalistic solicitude. While Florry, Chuckerduck and others continued to claim they could subsist entirely on bush tucker, and while that may in fact be true, people had come to need flour, tea, soap and tobacco. Sometime after the exodus from Mainoru, Lorna Martin sent a letter to Heather Dodd of Mainoru complaining that: 'We always foot-walking from Bulman to Mainoru for shopping we always take one day to walk to Mainoru but from Mainoru to Bulman always takes 3 days, carry lots of load' (E460 72/1003 Dec. 1971).

Lorna turned to the old patrons to seek help, but of course the McKays and the Dodds were gone from Mainoru and had no power over such matters. The letter made its way to Heather in Darwin, and she sent it to Harry Giese, thus confirming in Aborigines' eyes the common purposes of state officials and pastoralists, and the unitary authority of white people. This scrap of paper with its hand-written plea provoked a number of memos, a serious bureaucratic debate about the future of this group, and a letter to Lorna from Harry Giese who was on the point of being ousted as the Director of Welfare. His formal and long-winded account of current plans and policy concluded: 'I have asked Mr. Lovegrove and Bishaw to look at the question of providing some assistance to you and will write to you as soon as I have their report' (E460 72/1003 Jan.–Feb. 1972).

Giese apparently disapproved of the mendicancy which lay behind Lorna's cry for help. The specific immediate need for transport was ignored in favour of long-term plans. Giese was still encouraging attitudes of self-reliance in the individuals rather than adopting the new discourse of 'the community'. In contrast, the response of an officer of the newly established DAA illustrates the shift in policy:

Mrs Martin is one of the group of Aborigines who elected to stay at the Bulman . . . people are demonstrating their determination to make the Bulman their home and we must be prepared to service the population that is going to assemble there once the Gulperan [cattle] Company begins to operate (E460 72/1003/4 Mar. 1972).

The orientation here is towards the 'group of Aborigines' who have shown 'determination', and they will be rewarded with the provision of 'services'. The community is being established discursively in order to be made the target of the government's efforts. 'Community' was seen as embodying tradition and culture which were now to be respected as legitimate parts of the nation. The wish to 'make the Bulman their home' was the kind of communal desire that could make self-determination a reality.

The vanguards of self-determination eagerly condemned and repudiated the official past which had shaped people's lives. Much of what Rembarrnga people had previously been rewarded for, such as habits of deference towards whitefellas, was now wrong. Some other lessons, such as speaking English and cattlework, were valuable, but they had little experience of money or management. New freedoms were being welcomed but old and new constraints and limitations were unrecognised. Like earlier policies, self-determination was a palimpsest, being situated on a much reworked surface of overlaid intentions and overwritten policy designs.

Self-determination was to herald a radical change to a new era of racial equality. But equality could not be suddenly conjured into being by brave words. Differences which had been constructed and confirmed by inequality at every level through inter-racial history were in fact constitutive of the black and the white people being governed, and also part of the governors themselves. Thus hopes and plans were confounded by a series of unrecognised conditions deposited by history.

The discourse about racial character and the management of race relations was always unstable, composed as it was of a series of contradictory stereotypic representations. The assumption of essential Aboriginal inferiority or backwardness had competed with the presumption of a universally available but dormant rationality which would enable them to respond to tutelage. The existence of this potential rationality was challenged as the new focus on tradition and community began to take hold. As self-determination faced difficulties, old beliefs about Aboriginal inferiority or specific incapacities re-emerged. Thus racial thinking was not simply fixed, historically prior to the Territory's racial policies, but was, in each new era, revamped and reinforced by the failure of plans, a failure often attributed to

Aboriginal non-compliance with practices that were meant to advance their interests.

Significant continuities from the past were overwritten and concealed. For instance, Aborigines could not avoid the economic logic of capitalist enterprises, a logic around which the established welfare policies had been developed. The Welfare Branch had aimed to make government settlements economically independent through commercial enterprises, with training programs to increase Aboriginal participation and eventual management. Now the same process was to occur, but chosen by, and under the direction of, Aboriginal communities.[8] Far from self-determination leading to the departure of whitefellas from Aboriginal affairs, an army of new senior public servants was appointed to spearhead the progressive policies. Some of the new DAA officers openly demonstrated their ignorance of Territory traditions. A patrol officer who visited Mainoru, for example, was puzzled that the manager 'for some reason did not want to see us'. They were able to 'discuss the Gibb report with him', but the manager was not happy that the patrol officers would visit again (83/441 June 1973). This official desired 'to get as much exposure to the pastoral way of life' as possible in order to 'improve liaison and communication'. Unaware of the history he was stepping into, he was blissfully unconscious of the significance of entrenched practices on the racial frontier.

Another condition retained from the past and overlaid with new words was the need to manage money on behalf of Aboriginal people, especially with the expanding of Aboriginal projects. Communities might not know their own interests or recognise that white people might be cheating them. Nelly sang the praises of Danny Watson because 'he always gave money when we went to ask in town. He'd give $50 or $80. No matter he took it from our wages later. That [DAA man] in Katherine is no good. He'll only give $2 or nothing (1985).' Such judgements were seen by officials as naive, inviting dishonesty from trusted whitefellas on the one hand and wastefulness on the other. Here the cultural difference that threatened self-determination was not some esoteric ceremonial practice or particular behavioural propensity, but rather a different moral order, a contrasting sense of responsibility towards human relations and material goods. New habits had to be put in place. There began the production of a whole new system of bureaucratic practices, techniques of accountability and rituals of responsibility directed at Aboriginal communities. A new moral order was being installed, grafted onto a new discourse of concern for community autonomy and pursued through the formation of corporate bodies.

Aborigines were coerced, as Sansom says, 'by a pervasive and perduring imperative of Western political culture: the requirement that to have discourse with the state, an assembly of men must be made over into an entity' (1985:70). The demands of the expanding bureaucratic culture led to complicated and volatile responses from those who lived under the much reworked surface of policy intentions.

While the need to don the cloak of proper bureaucratic processes acted as a brake on the immediate possibilities of self-determination, the official recognition of Aboriginal history and culture in a range of forums allowed for the emergence of another discursive arena which positioned Aborigines within the nation and with a legitimate voice.[9] Local forms of Aboriginal expression in which Bulman people are involved include the annual Barunga Festival, the production and sale of art and artefacts, and the performances of bands such as Blekbela Mujik, which was based at Bulman under the leadership of Peter Miller, Town Clerk. Further, there was an urge to reverse some of the separations. Just after the walk-off from Mainoru, Florry's daughter Eileen Cummings began to revive her own and her children's association with the whole cultural domain of Rembarrnga at Bulman. In this case, policy changes provided the means to establish a continuity of kin connections which previous policies had ruthlessly denied her. What remained constant was the capacity of the state to overwrite and rewrite their lives for better or worse.

The Mainoru mob now became the Bulman mob and gradually became the focus of more attention. The combination of their authenticity as 'tribal' Aborigines, their experience with cattle, and their schooling made them 'ideal clients'. Old Welfare Branch staff spoke highly of them to the new officials. Strange *mununga* began to appear at Bulman with new proposals and promises, particularly suggesting that the government would help the people by providing funds for their own cattle station. Some of the Mainoru ex-stockmen, such as Chuckerduck, Don Bununjawa and the three Forbes brothers, were enthusiastic about the idea of running their own cattle station. For Tex, who had gone to Roper with Nelly after Foster bought Mainoru, it was as if his dreams were coming true.

Nelly can introduce the subsequent events at Bulman and the beginning of Gulperan:[10]

> This mob walked from Mainoru, sat down here.
> Then this bloke named Danny Watson, he was Welfare, working under a Welfare bloke named John Hunter. Danny was fighting for

Rembarrnga tribe. And John Hunter was fighting for the Maningrida mob. Maningrida mob was going to come up here and stay here but Danny Watson said that this place belongs to these people, tribal people. He told us that he was going to start that Aboriginal station for us. Danny was waiting for me and old Tex to come from Roper.

When Welfare didn't like Danny to help us, he took all those cattle and horses to Beswick, to that other welfare country. My old man [Tex] and my brother Willy they went to Darwin with the directors who belong to this place, but some of them died now. Those blokes asked Mr Giese, Aboriginal Benefits Trust Fund, to start up a station. We got it, we came back and started it then. You used to walk around down the first station with us (1991).

Nelly attempted to make sense of these events by recognising what her brother Willy called 'white man politics'; that is, the struggles within the Welfare Branch and the DAA. But the full force of those politics was only revealed as the self-determination era came to fruition. Bulman, home to less than 80 people, became the target of fantastic new plans, including cattle stations and shops, towns and service organisations, all of which were to be managed by Aborigines. The files on Weemol Inc., and Gulperan Pastoral Company are fat and full of the confusion of a bureaucracy which conceived the way ahead as the road of 'viable commercial enterprises'. It is to these matters that we now turn.

8

〇〇〇〇

A Viable Enterprise

The business acumen of the Directors still leaves a lot to be desired.

—*DAA memo, 1974*

If we don't speak up we can't win. We've got to tell them all what we mean.

—*Smiler Martin 1985*

IMAGINED COMMUNITIES

When I set out to understand the genesis and structure of the racialised society which I encountered during field work in the Territory, academic anthropology was of little help. For me the spatial adventure of anthropology in unfamiliar places has been transformed into a temporal exploration which depended not only on an ongoing familiarity with Bulman but also on the use of documentary material beyond the observable phenomena of field work. What appeared to me in 1975 as bizarre discordances and misunderstandings, revealed themselves on the one hand as the products of a rational program for progress which was generated in other places, and related only tangentially to the history, experience, practices and desires of Rembarrnga and other people of Arnhem Land. On the other hand, it was the Rembarrnga people's responses to this program that continually surprised and upset the whitefellas—rednecks and pen-pushers alike. Now, using policy statements, funding guidelines, plans and reports of governments, as well as Rembarrnga people's comments and my own experience, I will follow the Bulman story as it evolved in the era of Aboriginal self-determination in the 1970s.[1]

Fantasies of progress

There was an idealistic zeal among the new state officials of the 1970s who saw themselves as the antithesis of racist whites. The opposition between civilisation and savagery was inverted into oppressors and oppressed; racist whites were seen as the enemies of progress and the way was being paved for the waiting blackfellas to welcome their liberation. Further, the local, sceptical audience for 'self-determination' became a constituent feature of its implementation. While certain imagined virtues and desires were attributed to Aboriginal people, local whites were seen as burdened with ideas of racial superiority, either as backward·rednecks or carrying the old paternalistic 'welfare mentality'. The previous Director of Welfare and active reformer, Harry Giese, came to epitomise this welfare mentality which was to be swept away, allowing Aboriginal communities to engage in productive projects under the benign and helpful eye of the Department of Aboriginal Affairs (DAA). The narcissism of the vision is revealed in the mythic dimensions of 'self-determination' which was supposed to usher in equality and freedom.

Enthusiasm and energy among new state officials and Aboriginal clients marked the beginning of this era, but the delusions within the plans for development became rapidly evident as ambitious and expensive projects began to collapse in a series of tortuous and often bizarre events marked by bankruptcies, debts, scandals, and sharp policy reversals following public outrage. The faith of state officials, liaison officers and local managers was in rationality and instrumentalism, familiar features of a specific cultural domain which was taken to represent a universal 'common sense' (Gramsci 1971). Ideas of economic progress and social development were taken to represent every man's aspirations. The development of whole communities under the principle of self-determination was in fact an unprecedented policy and the nature of these communities was misunderstood. The fantasy and fetishism in these plans is concealed under a rhetoric of rational pragmatism, which shows that the state, while excited by its own ambitions, was secretly made uneasy by signifiers of racial difference.

An illustration is the numerous brochures with images of individual, smiling, well-dressed, young, educated blacks engaged in industrious or educational pursuits which were put out by the DAA and ADC, and which mimicked the earlier Welfare Branch advertisements. These 'positive images' deleted from view the older illiterate Aboriginal men and women, and members of 'the camps' in the bush and on stations, as if images of real communities were the mark of a difference and inequality that had to be hidden from public view. The intellectual climate in which these state officials were immersed is evoked in Castoriadis' criticism of 'intellectual boy scouts' who erect a facade which celebrates cultural difference while camouflaging the assumption that 'the steam-roller of "progress" will lead all peoples to the same culture (in fact to our own)' (1992:10). The hallmark of this new policy was supposed to be the recognition of Aboriginal tradition and community autonomy, and difference was to be no barrier to Aboriginal participation in the wider society.

But while a notion of difference may have been accepted, much actual difference was not recognised. On the one hand Aboriginal ceremonial life was treated with formal respect but given no space in which to operate. On the other hand the stark difference of illiteracy, which implied a more recalcitrant inequality, was not discussed openly. Literacy was not defined as a cultural matter but rather a temporary disadvantage, a mark of inferiority which was already being overcome with schooling. Of course the literacy of whitefellas, and the proliferation of the written word in an oral culture, was never perceived as a problematic difference, and no mention was made of social and domestic practices which became stumbling blocks in the relationship between Aborigines and their new patrons. Thus the eyes of eager state officials and bureaucrats were averted from actual systematic differences between the way Aboriginal people and white people lived and interacted, and from established and habitual racial inequalities and awkward incompatibilities.

Aboriginal culture was now to be incorporated inside the liberal democratic nation. But the actual culture, the social world which Aborigines inhabited, was seen as a deficient social space, which required ongoing tutelage. This actual social life was not defined as 'culture'. Historically constructed deficits and racially marked hierarchical deficiencies became of crucial relevance to the policies of the state. What needs to be understood is the way the idea of preserving an autonomous sphere of Aboriginality became a token incorporation, a rhetoric which ignored, over-rode or tried to reshape what it could not recognise as 'culture'. The space of culture was purely esoteric. The recognition of sacred sites and the paying of royalties to traditional owners were the formal practices which proved the rules and allowed all else to remain the same.

This culture was not to disturb the nation. The Gibb report warned that, 'The concept of separate development as a long-term aim is utterly alien to these objectives' (i.e. identification with Australian society) (1971:2). This distaste for 'separate development' was taken to be self-evident, forestalling any consideration of the difficulties of situating a different body of social practices into the nation, and precluding any concern with the way systematic separations of the past had constituted specific, intricate, racialised relationships between whitefellas and blackfellas which would somehow have to be re/formed. What the state wanted was absolution from the past, not recognition of its effects.

Yet continuities with the past were legion. The demise of the Welfare Branch[2] in the early 1970s did not alter government practices fundamentally. While patrol officers became field officers, they produced reports, memos, meetings, budgets, advisers and arguments in Darwin and Canberra offices. These same practices were redirected towards producing communities with the characteristics needed for them to become self-determining. State officials had now to engage in a particular kind of productive work, work that was both imaginative and embodied, work on Aborigines. This 'people work' had the contemporary purpose of establishing 'self-determination', and it was conducted alongside the established system of embodied race relations practices, which continued to operate largely undisturbed. The aim of this work was to construct conditions for community autonomy, initially through dialogue between communities and the government agency, the DAA. The community was the entity which had to be produced and targeted to fulfil the ideological demands of self-determination. Aborigines would ultimately administer and service their own community needs. The nature of the needs and the *modus operandi* of their administration were to mirror that of bureaucratic culture. In return for a system of self-management and self-policing, the community would continue to attract the government's support and funding.

A new aspect of *mununga* culture became apparent to Rembarrnga as they interacted with different kinds of whitefellas (cf. Beckett 1985:104). A characteristic rhetoric emerged, as well as habitual ways of mediating the vast cultural gulf that did not merely consist of inherited cultural differences, but had been engineered by particular responses to these differences. The matter of race was rendered irrelevant by these planners, but it was dealt with by stealth behind the facade of progressive fervour which imbued the plans and programs for Bulman's autonomy.

Gulperan Pastoral Company[3]

The development initiatives at Bulman in the 1970s were intended to overcome 'the economic vacuum that faces the Aboriginal communities of the area' (E460/72/622). The development of the 'Bulman waterhole area' as a cattle project was first embarked on by the Maningrida Progress Association and the Bamyilli Social Club in 1970. The names of these organisations show them to have been historically situated at the end of the welfare/wards era. They still employed local white men who had experience with cattle and with the local Aboriginal people. One such was Danny Watson who asked Tex to return from Roper River after he brought the first cattle down from Maningrida. Tex recalled:

> I was working there and all of a sudden I got a letter from Danny: 'Tex, you interested in running a camp here at Bulman? Because you know this country.' I took the job straight away. I rang up from Ngukurr, I rang up to VJY [radio telephone] and said, 'Get the horses ready and I'll be there, in two or three days time.' I got an old Land Rover. A big mob jumped on there including my uncle Charlie. Dawson Daniels said, 'Oh, I'll come too.' Only the front wheels were working. The back ones were all eaten out and the fanwheels were all broken. But we ended up here and put the camp up straight away (1989).

Florry Lindsay also spoke of Danny Watson's involvement soon after they walked from Mainoru, and of what it meant to them in terms of race relations:

> Danny Watson came down with a big truck for us two. We were at Bonijako, with my nanny goats.
> 'You twofella can work now,' Danny Watson said.
> They loaded up all our swag and brought it here [Goinjimbi], just down to the little creek there. We had to walk with dog and nanny goat. They built a yard for my nanny goats and made a camp for us. The boys worked here then. We wanted to work for that Danny Watson seeing that man at Mainoru didn't want us. He's for Aboriginal people that Danny Watson, he's different. He's with blackfella. They sent him

to Beswick then, the welfare. He went away then, Danny Watson, took his swag and everything. He left us. He left tucker and everything for us. They took him to work for another mob of people.
We sat down here all the time (1975).

Danny Watson's status as the hero of these first years of the Bulman community typifies one role played by whitefellas in this drama. He was 'for Aboriginal people', yet he belonged to the outback, redneck domain of Territory cattlemen. The community's liking for him disturbed the progressive DAA officials because he took his position of authority over Aboriginal people for granted. He would punish people for disobedience, was not averse to blackfella jokes, and would speak of Aborigines in patronising or stereotypical ways, garnished with a jolly and humorous manner. Further, he did not pay homage to ceremonial life or kinship, which to him were merely markers of primitivity. Thus he transgressed the two principles which fuelled the new policies, the assertion of egalitarian principles and the declaration of respect for what was defined as Aboriginal culture. Yet he was judged by these Rembarrnga people to be 'with blackfellas', a familiar friend who not only worked on the early project but encouraged Tex and others to apply for funds for Gulperan Pastoral Company. I stayed with Danny Watson and his wife once when he was managing Beswick station for the government in the mid 1970s. They were puzzled by the kinship designations they had been given, and asked me what the 'skin business' meant. They were impatient and dismissive of my explanation of the subsection system named by these 'skins' (figure 1). Ultimately, in the context of what was now called Aboriginal Affairs, Danny Watson was judged to be an anomaly, and did not remain as manager of Beswick station.[4]

The Aboriginal Benefits Trust Fund (ABTF) was initially asked to fund the newly formed Gulperan Pastoral Company to the tune of $73 000 (E460 72/622; 71/3516). The supporting documents generated in the DAA offices claimed that the station would achieve both social and economic aims by 'providing paid employment' and 'training', and also by generating 'income for the settlement'. While accepting advice on the economic viability of enterprises, government officials were assumed to be experts in the social domain, and spoke with ease of what was needed:

The Gulperan Company will require a competent European manager . . . With him will rest the responsibility of creating the actual working project . . . the Aborigines will own Gulperan lock stock and barrel . . .

they will need to participate in the operation and be supported by it if our ultimate goal is to be reached. [They] are capable of providing good quality and stable work force . . . eventually providing managerial talent (E460/72/622).

One fault line in the logic is apparent in the comment that 'the need to involve the largest number of people possible' had to be 'commensurate with economic viability' (ibid.). The conflict between these principles is precisely what Mainoru station had overcome by ejecting 'unnecessary people'. The frequently repeated hope that Aborigines would become 'free of European oversight and domination', a new objective in historical terms, is ironic in the light of what was envisaged and what followed. History and race relations and the deficit culture they had constructed, became the rationale for progressive whites to continue European oversight and domination of decision making in the communities which replaced individuals as the focus of moral evaluation and hierarchical ranking.

What began as a small cattle project became the target of plans for a large ambitious two-pronged initiative. A full-scale cattle station would be complemented by a township to be built at Weemol, about seven kilometres from Bulman, to house and service the community. The formation of Weemol Inc. to cooperatively build the town was an unmitigated expensive disaster (Cowlishaw 1998). The expansion of the Gulperan Pastoral Company was the pet project of a particular DAA officer whose departmental advisers recommended a modest development. With a fine disregard for the parochial and personal matters of concern to Bulman residents, and after many budgets, projections and differences of opinion, the expert view of a firm of pastoral advisers that 'The low key operation . . . would not work in this case' (E460/51 74/180), was accepted.[5] Generous funding of $612 909 was approved in late 1974. A resident full-time European adviser was to be appointed and the firm of pastoral advisers retained to manage the financial functioning of the operation. Thus the DAA retained control of management and funding decisions.

Two years later the newly installed Liberal government froze the funding of all Aboriginal enterprises, viable or not. Thus, after several years of consultation, of extravagant promises and moral exhortation to the Bulman mob to be loyal to 'their' project, the funding was suddenly cut for about a year, after which it was restored on a modest scale. In the meantime the European adviser had left after two years dedicated to building the project, the stock workers had taken jobs at other stations or were receiving unemployment benefits, the store had run up a huge debt which burdened the community for years, and some people had moved away.[6]

Analysis of these events reveals the national significance of self-determination and the moral investment of the public servants involved in these projects. For instance, the pastoral advisers saw themselves as facing a challenge 'to prove that the aboriginals at Bulman, *properly guided*, are capable of running a cattle station' (E460 73/7229, Nov. 1973, emphasis added). In a commentary on the moral worth of communities, the Bulman people were compared favourably with the Weemol population after Weemol Inc. failed: 'This is the group of people who wish to get ahead, do something constructive and are showing some sense of responsibility . . . unlike the Weemol community they would be quite willing to assist in the erection of their houses' (E460/51 74/2249 June 1975).

The DAA asserted that the community was motivated 'perhaps more than any other Aboriginal community in the Territory, by the desire to have its own cattle station . . . A decision . . . not to support the project . . . would be a bitter disappointment and one it would find hard to accept' (E460/51 74/180 July 1974). These sincere and seemingly innocent judgements represent an alien set of assumptions. Far from referring to some existential reality, they are based on notions of community interest and common striving that have the moral purpose of demanding or stimulating community loyalty. Whereas in the past individuals were offered training and the opportunity to shed their community identity, now the community and its culture were offered the chance to flourish with the assistance of the state. Communities would produce, police and stabilise their own subjects. The transformation to a social and economic autonomy within the national identity was founded on a postulated but absent community consciousness, and led to the piecemeal flounderings of the state in response to the situations it had generated.

I am arguing that, rather than merely a sign of local incompetence or a result of changes of government, the disasters, reversals and changes of plan at Weemol and Bulman were consequences of the shift in the ideology of race relations. They revealed a fundamental hiatus in the state's approach to 'self-determination', with management of the 'social' domain severed from the 'cultural'. For one thing there was no recognition that the new conditions of possibility for Aboriginal communities posed challenges for old social forms, such as those stemming from Aborigines' previous relationships with whitefellas as recipients of rations, as underpaid or unpaid employees, as hospital patients or school pupils. They were now to express their desires and aspirations openly in accordance with the wishes of field officers who did not appear much different from the patrol officers who had not wanted to hear them in the past. Many people did not speak, let alone read, standard English, and it was never suggested that bureaucrats should learn local languages or even Kriol. Further, the bureaucratic requirements of budgets, guidelines and accountability, and the nature of large incorporated companies, were quite outside Aboriginal experience. Repeated vague references to 'training' hinted at a recognition of barriers to Aborigines taking advantage of what the state was offering; the training, as in the past, referred to a one-way process of learning, flowing from the white to the black domain.

These were also new conditions for whitefellas who were involved in the new Aboriginal enterprises, and some cynical and obstructive bureaucrats emerged among those who saw the spending on community enterprises as government folly. A network of deception developed, sometimes at the level of crude lying and cheating, but more often in the form of hypocrisy and impression management, which pervaded local institutions, both government and private. Whitefellas often felt they had to conceal their real relationships with blackfellas because they conflicted with their official role. Others hid from view the pecuniary advantages they gained from their positions, in some cases by blatant misappropriation of funds.[7] The lack of response or wrong responses from Aborigines also had to be hidden from public view. Many government officials became engaged in constructing the facade of self-determination as if, perhaps by sympathetic magic, the real thing could be brought into being.

It was difficult to render profitable what were in fact marginal businesses at the best of times. The added costs of white managers and advisers were made more burdensome because many gave bad advice, having never run successful businesses themselves. Further, managing government-funded Aboriginal businesses did not call forth in these employees the self-discipline to work long hours and practise parsimony for their own advantage. Then there were those who felt they should engage in generosity, if not profligacy, in the pursuit of Aboriginal equality. Yet others sought to line their own pockets. Add to this the loneliness of remote communities and the alienation from the Aboriginal residents, and it is clear that such pastoral businesses, which had relied in the past on a good deal of unpaid labour, could never seriously have been expected to make profits. Finally, the conflict between managing a business for profit and running an enterprise to benefit the community in more general ways often sank such commercial enterprises.

Before discussing the complex place of both the notion and the facts of culture in these events, I want to illustrate some of the particular practices which *mununga* developed in relation to blackfellas in the mid 1970s.

MANAGING STRATEGIES

A number of techniques were developed within the bureaucracy to manage self-management, and four areas will provide illustrations.[8] Meetings, which were highly ritualised, were one of the most characteristic techniques. Then there was ventriloquism, an interpretative practice which operated to conceal the lack of 'self-determination'. Third, at the conceptual level, the notion of 'culture' was deployed as a token respect for tradition. Finally the conceptual and behavioural technique of separating private from public matters operated to disallow many Rembarrnga attempts to take control of their own domain. Many absurd little dramas of cultural politics were played out on this racial frontier as it was reshaped to fit modern demands for racial equality. One such concerned the tractor and attached backhoe, left after plans for a town at Weemol were abandoned. This machine was all that Willy Martin retained after the extravagant plans and promises with which he had cooperated. When he discovered that DAA officers had taken it away while he was out hunting, he shouted furiously, 'That's my backhoe. When blackfellas give something we don't take it back again.' He asserted here a moral superiority, a distinct cultural identity which contrasted favourably with the treachery of whitefellas. He is also identifying a moral struggle where the opportunity to assert another legitimate cultural identity was being smothered by a new form of cultural hegemony. Such Rembarrnga assertions were mostly cloaked and choked by new demands to bureaucratise, to remake the relationship with the *mununga* domain still from a subordinate position, in language which assuaged the white liberal desire for appeasement.

Meetings

The frequent meetings in isolated Aboriginal communities[9] which characterised this era were both a measure and a source of alienation (von Sturmer 1982:89). These meetings bore little resemblance to meetings among the Bulman mob, where the emphasis is on expression rather than decision, and where criticisms are muted in order to avoid overt conflict (Myers 1986b:432). A literate culture tends to discourage such 'time-consuming' practices. Gulperan meetings were minuted and decisions recorded.

At Bulman in 1975 the sound of a small plane would evoke excitement, but when someone called out 'DAA mob', or 'pastoral mob', it prefaced a boring and frustrating meeting. Strangers, some dressed in long white socks, would shake hands and announce which department or firm they represented, while their real motives remained a matter for suspicion among people for whom minding someone else's business in someone else's country is, to say the least, somewhat distasteful. A protocol developed which saw the visitors seated on the few plastic chairs, while members of the community—men and women, children and adults—would sit cross legged on the ground, coming and going from the gathering, some trying to make sense of the foreign, bureaucratic processes. The mystification was not confined to the Aboriginal participants. These state officials were neither economists, accountants nor experienced entrepreneurs, and explained funding guidelines and economic projections in terms imbued with enthusiasm rather than realism.[10] Their lack of economic prescience became increasingly apparent.

After outlining changing plans and budgets, an official would try to prevail upon members of the community to make some response. But how could Chuckerduck agree to plans for his country which involved leases, square miles, and 'considerations' like 'securing finance', the 'takeover of Commonwealth assets on the lease area' and 'registration of the Company' (E460 72/622 Aug. 1972)? Officials' attempts to modify their speech resulted in loud repetition and infantilised English. In the end someone would shout 'Come on you mob, speak up', or 'Do you mob agree to that?' and there would be nods or grunts which were sufficient to record a vote in favour. At a meeting of the Bulman mob, Smiler Martin, a man with little sophistication in the world of whitefellas, made a speech saying, 'We mob have to speak up, and that way we can beat them. If we just sit down quiet, they all the time beat we. If we don't speak up we can't win. We've got to tell them all what we mean' (1976). Others also tried to cooperate, excited by visions of the future or seeing possibilities for themselves. When asked if they wanted their own cattle station, it is not surprising that no-one spoke against it.

DAA officials assumed that they could explain the plans and the project and obtain rational decisions quickly, but there were misundertandings at every level. For instance, living in a densely interacting community, Rembarrnga people habitually avoid sharp disagreement and personal criticisms unless setting the stage for an open fight, but their subtlety and careful expression in trying to negotiate delicate situations of personal dissatisfaction with staff or advisers were overlooked by DAA officials. When frustration led to anger and explicit criticisms, Rembarrnga attempted to mimic aggressive whitefella talk and sounded crude and emotional, so were not taken seriously. Complaints were never 'correctly' expressed, so the profound dissatisfaction which existed in the community was not recognised or registered.

The experience of being misinterpreted was another reason for reluctance to speak at meetings. Expressing oneself in a foreign arena is fraught with danger because the significance of one's words is beyond one's control (cf. Berger 1975). Rembarrnga people knew that *mununga* would make unintended meanings of their words. The Gibb report had concluded sadly: 'The point of view of Aborigines is difficult if not impossible to obtain by direct communication' (1971:25).

At the meeting after the manager of Mainoru was caught stealing Gulperan buffalo, community members wanted charges laid, but matters such as this were outside the official guidelines. Other requests were deemed inappropriate, and sometimes led to meaningless formal resolutions such as that the station vehicle would be allocated 'according to need'. The 'need' for transport was constant and urgent: the needs to get stores, attend ceremonies and funerals, visit kin, go to hospital, hunt and fish at distant places. Rather than a solution to the transport problem, such resolutions provided instruction in the protocol of self-management. 'The wishes of the community' were thus rendered trivial compared with the large commercial enterprise of Gulperan.

These meetings achieved something else. By putting the state's resources into producing meetings, credence was given to the notion of self-determination through consultation. Teaching the discipline and etiquette of meetings and consultation became an end in its own right. It was in meetings that the goal of consultation was to be realised, but always imperfectly. Meetings were produced repeatedly as self-determination rituals. Yet, as will be explored later, this facade created embarrassment among white officials, and the community members who were being gradually coopted into this process often subverted the mantle of correct procedures even as they donned it.

Ventriloquism

Government officials, pastoral advisers and accountants acted as ventriloquists in relaying to each other and to their superior officers the views and wishes of 'the community', which in fact originated in their own minds and were formulated in their own style. While meetings were ostensibly to consult and discuss projects, in reality they were to gain authorisation to run the projects in ways that appeared 'rational' and 'efficient', and in accordance with budget guidelines.[11] The phrase 'the community's wishes' became a mantra for many purposes. Typical is the assertion that 'Consultation with Aborigines has led to a decision to form a company' (E 460/T4/77/87), where 'company' is a legal term entailing complex obligations, structures and procedures of which the officials themselves were only vaguely aware. The systematic facade which was erected to give the impression that Rembarrnga people made decisions about Gulperan, relied on their acquiescence being signalled by nodding or raising a hand when urged to do so. Repeated assertions that the community was itself planning and determining the project's future were openly deceptive. In reality community members were participating in alien forms of interaction and discourse, and were assenting to an agenda formed elsewhere.

When the Gulperan Pastoral Company was set up under the laws governing such things, with shares, directors and a constitution, five 'traditional owners' were named as directors in a process of generating the representivity that is required by governments (Beckett 1985; Weaver 1985; Sansom 1985). Initially there were also three European directors,[12] and when the officials from Darwin flew in to Bulman for meetings, they picked up the neighbouring leaseholder on the way, a tacit recognition of the need for local knowledge of the kind represented by experienced officials of the old Welfare Branch and by local pastoralists. However, in line with 'Aboriginal self-determination', and the suspicion that all local whites were 'rednecks', DAA removed the Europeans (E460/72/622 1972), and the shareholders and directors of the Company were six 'traditional owners'. Despite being illiterate, the directors were said to have 'endorsed the articles of association' for Gulperan Pastoral Company, one by signing his name, two by printing their names, and the other three by appending their thumb prints. One company share was issued to each director. The dissimulation embedded in this 'self-determination' was revealed when the unsatisfactoriness of thumb-prints was brought to the attention of the Bamyilli superintendent. He was asked to: 'Enlist the aid of your Head Teacher in an effort to teach the men to write their own names. It would be preferable if they could be taught to write their names rather than print them' (E460/72/662 July 1972).

Why did the officials want to conceal the fact that these men were illiterate? Was a signature supposed to ensure the signatories' real agreement, or does a signature carry a weightier legal meaning? Perhaps the directors were being protected from the contempt of the 'rednecks' whose shadows often fell across these projects. Signatures, like nodding heads, protected the ventriloquists from revealing their own role in managing the enterprise and managing the voices of others. While officials observed that 'literacy is still the major problem for advancement' (E460/64 76/25 May 1976), they continued to act as if meeting agendas and minutes were read by the participants.[13] The Bulman community saw their own illiteracy as a serious lack and repeatedly requested a school. However they did not accept that the lack rendered their control over the enterprise illegitimate.

The enthusiasm of the officials was attributed to the community:

> Interest in the Gulperan project is deeper and more effective than the mere desire to make a living . . . the project is seen by them as providing a real opportunity to establish themselves on land they once owned and to establish themselves free of European oversight and domination . . . they understand the need to purchase European management skills in the first instance (E460/72/622).

Who could fail to be inspired by such a reasonable proposal with its allure of liberation, yet who would doubt that this vision of the future was written for a funding application? I am not denying that the words may have been the government official's understanding of Rembarrnga wishes. But when reproduced in a government document they have entered a different discursive arena and take on different meanings. In fact it is desire itself which is being privileged and produced here, the desire for autonomy. Paradoxically, further dependence was required to achieve independence; management by whites was needed to realise self-management. The self-perpetuating and parasitical nature of European managerial systems is in their being always temporary but always there. The management consisted of harnessing certain impulses for autonomy and desires for independence, and shaping them towards self-policing practices. This shaping of the community was spelled out in the Gibb report: 'We believe that to coerce them or to nurse them through the change would be to rob them of the opportunity for and the experience of *evolving structures and leadership* which are absolutely essential if they are to be involved in the economy with a degree of *autonomous self control* (1971:3, emphasis added).

Quintessentially whitefella logic was often apparent in decisions attributed to the Gulperan directors. For instance, the directors were said to have requested that 'the initial manager should be a young active man with leadership qualities who would be prepared to live and work on the lease . . . for a short period' and that later, when housing, finance and cattle came, 'a more mature and capable manager would be sought' (E460 72/662 Aug. 1972). The lack of accommodation, and indeed the lack of cattle, fences or yards, meant that only an inexperienced junior was likely to want the job.

This notion of helpful whitefellas available to fulfil these unprecedented tasks was another fantasy. Any young and eager European of goodwill was presumed to be capable of managing an Aboriginal community project. 'A competent European manager' would be able to 'gain the confidence of the Aboriginal people and guide them in the correct methods of cattle station management', 'train the people' in various skills and techniques and 'generally guide the people along the lines of self help' (E460 73/7229, 1973). The large investments in community-based commercial enterprises were being managed by DAA officials who lacked skills in business, accountancy or management, though they believed they understood Aboriginal community needs. The experts and the managers they appointed were often manifestly naive and incompetent. They were protected by the notion that the knowledge and skills to run a business are possessed by all white people because these skills belong to white culture; the progressive arts of funding and enterprises were thought to be familiar to all modern men and women. There is here a racialisation of work and knowledge which sustains the tutelary system. A more explicit racial logic was evident in the appointment of a European manager of Gulperan who had run a cattle station in Kenya. The fact that he had 'worked with blacks before' was seen to be a valuable qualification for the job, and indeed the racial logic of colonial relations did make his experience relevant. He often compared the colonial subjects in the two continents, nostalgically wishing for his previous African workers who had, he thought, been better schooled in their role.

Those officials who had the imagination to grasp the depth of the conflict between social and economic aims were nonetheless swept along by the urgency of the ideal of racial equality. For instance one DAA officer said of Gulperan: 'There will also be difficulties for some time in acquainting some of the Aboriginals with the objects of the exercise and in them being prepared to discuss their ambitions with unknown visitors' (E460 72/622 1972).

To this admission that the people did not understand the project is added the implication that the people were too shy or too estranged to discuss their 'ambitions'. Ambitions too had to be managed, their expression had to be encouraged and produced in a suitable form. In fact I shall show below that the 'ambitions' that Rembarrnga people initially expressed were not recognised as such—they were the wrong ambitions. One administrator in Darwin commented on the unexpected difficulties being faced by the self-determination process, and confessed to Canberra that: 'The painstaking processes which are necessary to get their views and the lengths we have to go to to ensure they are fully involved in all of the management processes . . . [mean] we are only paying lip service to legitimate community demands' (E460/14 82/164 July 1973).

The consultative process produced in meetings required a certain kind of subject, a consulting subject. Such subjects were supposedly being produced by being rewarded when they reproduced the ventriloquist's discourse by expressing 'legitimate community demands' under white men's tutelage. Another report confessed to the nature of this 'self-determination':

> [I]nordinate pressures are being exerted at all levels to effect change in Aboriginal communities, not least from those who want to force on communities facilities which they may not want. As a division we are finding it most difficult to live by the accepted policy statement approved by the Minister on 'self-determination' (E460/133 83/103 Sept. 1973).

Recognising culture

The discursive recognition of minority cultures is a common feature of modern complex societies, but in the Northern Territory of the 1970s such recognition functioned to obscure the place of race and mute the ability to celebrate existing difference. This turning away from the living cultural realities, which were inextricably intertwined with social inequality and racial identities, occurred partly because of the presence of an aggressive public rhetoric which decried self-determination as 'waste', ridiculed the enterprises and openly predicted disaster. To protect the projects from this hostile discourse, many involved whitefellas muted their own anxiety that Aboriginal alienation from the ordinary processes of modern society was so extensive as to represent an insuperable barrier. The fear that any failure might mean the planners were mistaken about Aborigines' desires and abilities remained unspoken, and the mystification of difference was thus exacerbated.

The state's difficulty with difference is apparent in the narrow and particular place accorded to the idea of Aboriginal culture. Aboriginal culture was restricted to an indigenous version of elite culture, with ritual and ceremony privileged, but severed from their social conditions. Collmann showed how white officials in this era used knowledge gained from Aboriginal elders opportunistically to authenticate their own positions (1988:31–32). The role of cultural broker required appropriate knowledge of 'tribal' matters and of Aborigines' intentions:

> Weemol Springs is a site of tribal significance in the Bulman area and the site of the Community's proposed township . . . The community is also establishing through its wholly owned operating subsidiary company, the Gulperan Pastoral Company Pty. Ltd. a cattle enterprise . . . it is expected that many . . . will return to Bulman as further employment opportunities become available (E 460/51 74/180 July 1974).

These knowledge claims reveal the opposite of what was intended. They show a lack of familiarity with the cultural priorities of Rembarrnga whose future was being planned, as well as a lack of economic insight. Areas of 'tribal significance' abound, and such significance would be more likely to preclude than invite the building of a town. Moreover, it was not primarily 'employment opportunities' that were drawing people back to Arnhem Land, but rather the opportunity and desire to escape from the large government reserves of Bamyilli (now Barunga) and Beswick and the decision, as Alma said, to 'give away white man now'.

The state's impoverished understanding of Rembarrnga relationship with country is evident in the lack of attention paid to traditional owners and managers in all the planning and disappointments associated with the Gulperan project. A detailed report in 1977 showed no awareness that discussion and negotiation concerning the cattle station had been taking place among various clan and language groups with authority over this country. 'Internal rivalries' and 'personality clashes' were seen as merely obstructions to planning and progress, rather than clues to a different social tradition through which creative responses to present conditions were emerging. A meeting of Aboriginal people responsible for the country took place in 1976 at Weemol, with no *mununga* other than me present. It was attended by about twenty adults from Barunga, Beswick and Bulman, and began with a long exegesis on 'what's going on from beginning' in Kriol and English. The speakers each stood and spoke at length reviewing what others had said, emphasising points of agreement, putting a different emphasis, or asking a question that had not been satisfactorily dealt with. The theme was, who is 'boss for that country', but all the speakers emphasised that Gulperan could be run and managed by 'that yella-fella', Tex, and that 'all family are welcome here'. Bruce and Kenneth were to help Tex and do the bookwork. Willy Martin was to be manager at Weemol. Some tensions about particular people were aired. For example, 'We can't push him out. If he wants to go he can go. We can't say, "You go away", that's giving cheek.' The meeting lasted all morning, and only broke up when it was assured that everyone had said what they wanted to say, and that Tex Camfoo's position as manager had been authorised. As we saw in Chapter one, Larry Murray said that they would talk about 'country only, not ceremony, because government department doesn't understand'. A brief sketch of the things that 'government doesn't understand' is needed here to augment earlier discussions.

Much of Rembarrnga country is to the north of the settlement, and many Bulman people are Ngalkbon, Jawyon, Nalakan as well as Rembarrnga. Kin and genealogical ties, conception and birth sites and historical association give individuals authority and responsibility in relation to various sites in various areas, and debate and discussion of these flexible rights are the stuff of everyday life. Ceremonies in the area are arranged and authorised by mutually dependent clans and lineages involving large networks of intricately related individuals who negotiate endlessly about these things. Larry Murray and Chuckerduck Lindsay shared responsibility in the 1970s as the senior 'manager' (*Jungaie*) and 'owner' (*Mingeringi*) respectively in relation to the Yappaduruwa ceremony at Bulman waterhole. Sophisticated management of these matters is necessary where nothing is set down in rigid form but where everything is negotiated anew in relation to certain principles and ever changing circumstances (Sansom 1988; Tamisari 1998). An example is the way that people who stressed their links and rights in the Bulman area when Gulperan was discussed, would begin to speak of their consciousness of living in others' country when there was conflict, and would plan to go to their 'own country' at Nungalala, Malyanganuk or Ngukkur.

Equivalent complex and flexible sets of rights and responsibilities to country have been described for many areas in Australia (Hiatt 1965; Myers 1988). They are incommensurable with the Australian law which recognises individuals' own specific, bounded areas to which others do not have rights. There is also incommensurability between, on the one hand, the conception of land associated with commercial exploitation which renders land as the passive object of human agency, and, on the other hand, the Aboriginal understanding of the inter-dependent relationship between people and land which is itself productive. Sitting in country and walking through country are actions which generate meanings and events. The sentient country responds to people and people respond back to the land (Povinelli 1993). When Nelly Camfoo says of the Djarada ceremony, 'If we don't do this we will all die', she is asserting that this interactive, ceremonial, productive relationship with country is necessary for the continuation of Rembarrnga life. State officials and pastoral advisers spoke of country as 'pastoral' land, and when they were trying to express their sensitivity to Rembarrnga concerns, they would stress its aesthetic qualities or the wonderful barramundi in the rivers. Most were unaware of, or misinformed about, the ties to country and ceremony, the genealogical and affinal links among the Bulman mob, the clan and ceremonial ties between these groups and others, and even the broad outline of the local peoples' history. In general, they were less aware of Rembarrnga traditions than earlier patrol officers who had attended classes at Sydney University and had long-term relationships with the people in their patrol area.

While official discourse registered 'culture' with formal respect, it was given no systematic place in the planning or the structure of the enterprise and did not entail the administration in any dialogue. 'Culture' was the icing on the cake of the more important 'social' matters to do with the 'viable project' and with the provision of housing and services. Well-meaning bureaucrats had replaced the myth of a fragile Aboriginal tradition with its opposite; now Aborigines could become part of capitalist culture without tarnishing their own cultural identity and lifestyle.

Seemingly irresolvable conflicts became apparent on occasions such as the long-planned major DAA meeting at Bulman, at which only two Rembarrnga men turned up. No-one had warned the officials that the community had to travel to a funeral. Bureaucratic recognition of culture took specific forms, such as appointing traditional owners as directors of Gulperan. Perfunctory gestures towards those things recognised as culture sufficed because they were now the responsibility of Rembarrnga to maintain autonomously. The planners' alienation from this social environment is illustrated in their interpreting the absence of the directors of Gulperan from the Bulman camp as a loss of interest in the project. The fact that community populations fluctuated always made officials anxious because it contradicted the system of rewarding domestication with infrastructure investments. They saw nomadic behaviour as temporary and problematic, rather than a characteristic expression of attachment to kin and country. 'Tribal matters' were never seriously considered when planning a town or a cattle project. One rare mention of sacred matters was made at a meeting: 'It was further decided that Chuckerduck Lindsay and Tex Camfoo would go to Bamyilli and Beswick almost immediately to get the tribal elders who would mark the tribal trees and ground areas at Weemol that were not to be cut or graded in the work done on that project' (E 460 73/7229 Dec. 73).

Such gestures could not secure respect for sacredness because those who drove the tractors and graders remained white. Thus even when official recognition of cultural priorities was achieved in the 1970s, Rembarrnga ability to enforce them was limited. An impoverished view of cultural matters continued to pervade official discourse, yet this limited acknowledgment of tradition was enough to sustain the credibility of its ideology. Because previous welfare regimes were seen to have failed due to their refusal to acknowledge Aboriginal traditions, the token incorporation of 'tribal matters' gave state agencies faith in their own ability to sustain and manage Aboriginality.

The domain of 'tribal matters' was aligned with racial identity, as illustrated in the positioning of Tex Camfoo and his wife's brother Willy Jailama Martin. Tex's Chinese father meant he was light skinned and his schooling had made him reasonably literate. But it was his social classification as 'half-caste', sometimes legally 'exempt', and later 'European', that made Tex seem to be the ideal link between the bureaucracy and the community. He was appointed manager of Gulperan with the planners claiming that 'part-Aboriginal Mr. Tex Camfoo . . . has the necessary experience and level of responsibility to handle the position' (E 460/51 74/180 July 1974). This extraordinary claim was made on the basis of Tex's level of literacy and eagerness to cooperate with the planners. He had no accountancy skills or experience of bureaucratic accountability. The 'necessary experience' for managing a pastoral station with a $600 000 budget and a community of a hundred people, was as a head stockman on a marginal pastoral property on Aboriginal wages!

Tex was seen as a modern man, positioned inside the domain of the state, beside the bureaucrats, assisting them with his useful links to the domain of Aboriginality. Bureaucratic hopes were vested in him because he saw Gulperan as a chance to reinstate his life as a head stockman, and he reassured officials with his familiar jocular style of interaction. In contrast, Willy was the authentic Aborigine and represented the tribal arena. He was to 'be responsible for all matters with respect to Aboriginal Tribal Law and he is to assist Mr Camfoo . . . Both Mr Martin and Mr Camfoo are to be responsible to the Board' (E 460 73/7229 Oct. 1973). Tex was also fully involved with 'Aboriginal tribal law' and the ceremonial domain, though it has suited both himself and most whitefellas to conceal this fact and to keep the two worlds of meaning separate. This has been so since he was physically separated from his mother and from the ceremonial business of the community which he nonetheless continued to identify with. Thus he speaks of being a knowledgeable law man and also of having 'sneaked around' to the ceremonies, believing it to have been illegal for him to be there (Camfoo, in press). While Willy and Tex were promoted as leaders at various times, and both tried to mediate across the cultural frontier, officials were repeatedly disappointed in them.

Rembarrnga people were reluctant to take on management roles in relation to the cattle station or even the store. Though Tex and several others became overseers of Gulperan for varying periods, the necessity to exert authority without regard to kin connections was difficult, and especially distasteful in the presence of the official disapproving gaze directed towards the business of ceremonies, funerals and kinship which threatened the priorities of Gulperan Company business. Rembarrnga eschewal of the discourse of community duty and public service, and the apparent refusal of these 'leaders' to 'do something for their people', seemed like an irresponsible lack of maturity to officials who took their own expressions of social responsibility to be universal moral principles.

The bourgeois ideal of autonomous subjects took a particular form in this era of governing Aboriginality. Subjects were now required who were autonomous and self-willed and who represented the community. Continuing government interventions and particular regimes of dependency were justified by the need to produce communities that would eventually achieve independence when they had the prerequisite skills. Thus ideas of the individual merged with anthropological and sociological understandings of culture and community, and together they created new forms of governing.[14] Aboriginality was no longer to be broken up into autonomous self-policing individuals, but would be expressed in autonomous self-policing communities. These communities would be taught the value of independence and self-management by young white men, including government officials who flew in and out, service providers who visited regularly, and local managers appointed by the administration.

Public, private and personal

The entity targeted by these policies, and the entity which was to be self-determining—that is, 'the community'—did not refer to a self-conscious, pre-existing entity to be found at Bulman or anywhere else. Rather, it referred to an imagined sense of community consciousness and loyalty that had to be simulated where it was found to be absent. While western urban citizens, especially public servants and administrators, take for granted at least the *expression* of civic duty and good citizenship bracketed off from private life, Rembarrnga people do not experience the division of community from private, family matters, so that the demands for loyalty to 'the community' could not draw on an indigenous tradition. Visiting officials invited mimicry of their own enthusiasm for the project and for the community's future. The entity 'the community', which was to be brought into existence, threatened to fracture the network of families which reached far beyond this residential group and whose interdependence had nothing to do with the Gulperan Pastoral Company.

The Bulman mob's refusal to separate 'private' and 'public' matters was anathema to officials. The minutes of one meeting recorded that 'The Directors discussed whether Bruce Murray's mother should be permitted to return to the Bulman' (E460/51 74/180). The raising of a 'private' family conflict at a meeting was not taken to be a sign of a different sociality. Rembarrnga people insisted on interpreting relations with bureaucrats as personal, greeting a remembered face with 'You know me, eh?', and 'He really helped us mob', and pressing officials to recognise the particular needs of local families. Such ordinary cultural practices embedded in everyday interactions became a political response, an attempt to redirect the priorities of those who made decisions. Relationships developed not between 'the community' and the 'the state', but between particular individuals. In return for help in dealing with the alien, bureaucratic world, friendly whites would be shown a concern for their social and physical comfort while they were at Bulman.[15]

Young anti-racist officials tried to bridge what they perceived as the cultural gap by such means as wearing casual dress or exaggerating their colloquial speech. Some began to appreciate Aboriginal people's different manners and to enjoy them as equal human beings. They learned vernacular expressions and local protocols, identified a *bunji* and accepted a 'skin' designation,[16] though few had the time or the tools to grasp their significance. They accepted being called 'old John' though only 30 years old, recognising that the affectionate and respectful epithet refers to maturity rather than old age. This common Rembarrnga practice frequently causes whitefellas to bridle or protest. Even Heather Dodd exclaimed that 'old Smiler' was inappropriate because, she said, 'he is my age, only 36'.

When more substantial relationships formed, and whitefellas were drawn into the warmth and humour of Rembarrnga sociality, it was often differing assumptions about reciprocal obligations that broke them up. The potential of such relationships to bridge the social gulf was thwarted by the turnover of staff. That meant there was no long-term involvement of individual officials, precluding any follow through, planning or accountability.[17] A further common source of breakdown was the difficulties associated with having an extended family from the bush camping in the official's suburban house.

The plight of the white officials was revealed in their attempts to avoid expressions of their superior power and disguise their access to resources in order to assert their egalitarianism. They found it hard to recognise that they could not shed their own history, let alone divest themselves of the power they wielded. Their attempts to culturally adapt often appeared as patronising gestures.

Finally, while the demarcation of public, community concerns from personal private ones is arbitrary, and culturally specific, this does not mean it is superficial or easily modified. Government funding is prefaced on such a separation and breaches will be interpreted as incompetence or corruption. Thus the DAA refused Gulperan's claims for reimbursement for 'expenses of a personal nature', including flights to hospital and transport home from hospital, opening of saving accounts, visits to law courts to pay fines, delivering cash to a boy at Kormilda College, preparation of personal tax returns, arranging for bail and payment of court costs (E460 73/7229 Jan. 1974). These are glimpses of the needs and concerns of a people whose lives are linked inexorably with the institutions of the state, and yet are structured around different priorities and meanings.

LIBERAL PLURALISM AND DIFFERENCE

When the administration tried to turn the Bulman mob into small businesspeople, they were encouraging a form of mimicry which they took to be a natural evolutionary process. They did not recognise that these people's own cultural domain with its moral contours and forms of sociality would not, indeed could not, be abandoned. Rowley said 25 years ago, 'the idea of a non-literate culture having values that could charm and hold those socialised within its framework . . . took a long time to develop' (1972a:225). It was developing slowly as notions of culture and multiculturalism were being incorporated and re-deployed within state apparatuses. A form of pluralism, derived partly from the cultural relativism of social anthropology, now had a place in establishing the moral authority of white officials who were anxious to differentiate themselves from the cultural ignorance of past bureaucrats.

Moral agendas

Tex, Willy and anyone else who responded to the offers and promises of the era were soon made aware of the kind of regime they were entering into. The administration's moral agenda and coercive weapons are apparent in this internal memorandum concerning the Gulperan project:

> The *business acumen* of *the Directors* still leaves a lot to be desired, however we are making *concerted efforts to teach them* to keep within their budget and that *they have to work for what they are getting and not have things just because they want them and the government is paying for them*. This unfortunately is the attitude that has developed since the inauguration of the ABTF and the Loans Commission. The *standard of discussion* at Board Meetings is still rather *withdrawn* (E460/51 74/2249 Dec. 1974, emphasis added).

The language of commercial business management is used here to express a sense of disappointment that the community is morally wanting, having developed an attitude of dependency and opportunism after two years of funding. This white official produced in the community a mirror of his own expectations and motivations. The dependence of white officials on black problems for their jobs, vehicles, offices, travel and accommodation did not, of course, raise the same moral concerns. Further, the political force of the officials' moral judgements was obscured by the ideals and language of self-determination.

Cultural insensitivity was mutual. While whitefellas were oblivious of the real nature of Rembarrnga priorities, whether stemming from religious anxieties, emotional desires or more pragmatic needs, Rembarrnga commonly transgressed the sensitivities of whitefellas by asking openly for Toyotas, tractors, cattle, fences, houses and a host of other things. They had been encouraged to express their views, but the *way* they did so was taken to expose a moral failing, denoting a wrong attitude to government funding. Their requests and demands were not recognised as rational responses to the policies of self-determination, but rather as corruption by them. Their responses were certainly not interpreted as cultural; that is, reflecting a specific, historically constructed relationship to material goods, different understandings of responsibility, or a specific patterning of authority relations. Rembarrnga people were insensitive to the fact that government funding entailed a relationship of mendicancy.

The lack of expression of loyalty and commitment to the Gulperan project, and the absence of expressions of communal pride or disappointment at appropriate times, puzzled and upset the officials. No shame was evinced when equipment was lost or funds 'wasted'. Few Rembarrnga had much idea of the way funding worked, and the 'bottom line' was not something they read.[18] Further, they did not recognise that they should be grateful for the selfless and impersonal duty being performed by those who represented the government's generosity. Bureaucrats were baffled by the lack of fetishisation of goods and by the ineffectiveness of money in enforcing moral priorities. Rembarrnga shamelessness astonished, angered and embarrassed some of their supporters, who found it increasingly hard to maintain the smiling altruism of the dedicated anti-racist public servant when meeting with the black communities in the outback.

These discontinuities created crises of confidence in the Gulperan project among officials and advisers in the early years. For instance, in relation to drinking and the misuse of community vehicles, the officials admitted to their own concerns. The pastoral advisers reported that the 'biggest disappointment' was the over-indulgence in alcohol by the Aboriginal manager 'who is setting a bad example' (E460/64 76/25 May 1976). They complained to DAA that 'It is an extremely hard task to make *the Aboriginals* realise that machinery has to be serviced properly and not abused' (ibid. Dec. 1975, emphasis added).

> During the European Supervisor's absence . . . the Aborigines . . . showed a total disregard for the welfare and maintenance of their machinery and vehicles . . . In an endeavour to get to Katherine they drove or pulled vehicles and a new tractor through creeks and rivers and at times completely submerged the tractor . . . motor is completely 'blown up'. They have been told no more vehicles will be purchased (E460/64 76/25 April 1976).

It should be explained that this is an exaggerated and generalised account of an event that occurred at the end of the wet when there was no food at Bulman, although a supply of alcohol had come in by plane. Two young men were sure they could beat the floodwaters. Within the moral discourse of the state the apparently careless destruction of vehicles, like the illiteracy discussed above, could not be analysed as a clue to a domain of valid cultural difference. It had rather to be condemned or excused as a moral lapse, a temporary and reversible aberration, identified with the pathos of prior marginalisation. Drowning a vehicle was a crime against all good sense, not only to government officials but to community members who were immediately disadvantaged. To embark on a search for some different evaluation of community vehicles, or for some specific cultural form to explain this apparently wilful destructiveness would seem irresponsible and perverse. Myers' argument that 'the use value of rights to "things" is not at all obvious' (Myers 1988:52), would seem irrelevant in the context of a resource management policy meeting.

Within the community the shock, anger and dismay at the destruction of these crucial vehicles was followed by laughter as jokes developed about the events. The incongruity with white values was a source of daring humour, and the surrounding events were mined for all the enjoyment they could offer. Later Florry chuckled as she talked of her nephew's[19] drunken exploits: 'Kenneth told me, "This motor car, 'im toy one. 'Im only swim swim." He was going to take him in the water. I think he made it into a toy one, this Toyota. We were killing ourselves laughing' (1976). Conscious of my *mununga* sensibilities, Dorothy added, 'That Kenneth don't know what he's doing when he's drunk,' and laughed a little nervously.

While grants for purchasing 4WD vehicles soon began to be more closely controlled, such disasters were concealed and official anger swallowed. The administrators had defined the Bulman people in terms of their collective desire to own and run a cattle station, but when they repeatedly failed to conform to this image by not playing out the roles presented to them, the political weight of the state's disapproval was gradually brought to bear. The management of self-management depended not so much on the administration's judgements about the project, but on its judgement of the Rembarrnga people's ability to understand, accept and internalise the moral order within which these judgements were made. They had to be able to judge themselves in terms of the administration's need for responsible participants in a government-funded enterprise.

Consciousness of the whitefellas' moral evaluations of common-place responses shaped the self-consciousness of the Bulman mob. Yet these conditions failed to produce a general conformity. The inversions and subversions which were apparent in the jokes and laughter about non-conformity, including drunkenness, comprised an endemic form of resistance which was secreted from white eyes.

The state's management of self-management escaped scrutiny and evaluation by the criteria of accountability which it wanted to teach others. Secret anxieties energised the 'people work'; that is, the work of producing people with certain kinds of speech practices, motives and desires that would reflect back to the well-intentioned white officials their own community-focussed designs and desires. But those engaged in this work were never permanent. Their jobs lasted a few months or a few years and then they were replaced by others in a kind of nomadic professional culture where the wish of individuals to get ahead and improve themselves legitimised constant movement known as upward mobility or spiralling. A more immediate cause of mobility in what are seen as stressful conditions is known as 'burn out'.

What sustained the administration in the midst of this discontinuity and fragmentation was an ideology and a use of policy which gave the illusion of coherence and continuity. The serious and well-intentioned young bureaucrats, as well as school teachers, nurses and local managers, were nourished by their participation in the liberating rhetoric of self-determination. Good intentions smoothed over the changes in personnel, and the lack of historical depth in personal relationships which would have been necessary to achieve a serious dialogue with Aboriginal people. In structural terms, the asymetrical relations of power between the two participant groups explain the sustaining of contradictory views of the project. For the bureaucrats, accountability, justification and success did not reside in the judgements of the community but in the hierarchical relations of the bureaucracy.

Ultimately they were not accountable to the 'community' but to their superiors.

Bureaucratic culture

The failure of the Gulperan Pastoral Company was attributed to the unfortunate deficiencies of the Aboriginal people such as the lack of English and the insufficient grasp of policy, funding and management practices. But the deficiencies of the bureaucrats need to be spelled out, not in terms of individual ill-will, ignorance or deliberate bad faith, but as the cultural characteristics of those positioned structurally within the realm of state power. We have seen myopia, mistakes and misinterpretations at every level of official practice. All this needs to be understood in the context of the cultural domain of liberal pluralism which I shall describe by personification. The liberal pluralists are imbued with good will towards the marginal and disadvantaged and want to recognise cultural otherness in all its manifestations. But real otherness is usually also marginal and disadvantaged, unless it has been appropriated by that cosmopolitan minority who delight in a sophisticated appreciation of varied cultural manifestations.

The only way the liberal pluralists can deal with the different and the marginal is to coopt and incorporate them. While this incorporation may be inevitable, or arguably even valuable for the disadvantaged, the process is so cloaked in unrelated fantasy and mystification that the self-assertion and domination of liberal pluralist values is difficult to recognise. The result is that the particular character of those classified as marginal cannot be retained. Liberal pluralism engages with the marginal in order to correct injustice and it does so by 'correcting' the lives and the otherness of marginal populations. Thus marginality and the character of the marginal can only ever be temporary and partial; it is alway headed towards the mainstream if redemptive strategies are correctly shaped. The onus for change is inevitably one-way.

It should not be assumed that an insufficient grasp of policy, funding, management practices and so on meant that the Bulman mob were incapable of understanding the plans and taking control of them (cf. Thiele 1982:34). While there is evidence of naivety concerning the domain of commercial and government matters among Rembarrnga people, this naivety was matched by the ignorance of many state officials, not only of pastoralism and commerce, but of the people they were dealing with. We saw how the illusion of coherence was maintained in the face of discontinuous policies and personnel by a progressive and modernising ideology encased in a body of good intentions. Throughout the Territory, good will was the stand-in for dialogue, debate and negotiation with Aboriginal people.[20]

The following examples show first that Rembarrnga people tried to participate in the plans for their future, and second that the resilient and resistant forms of social practice in the Aboriginal community did not give way before normalising forces. Though conscious that Gulperan was important, many of my black companions in 1975 and 1976 did not attend the meetings, felt or feigned disinterest in who the whitefellas were, and certainly did not consider their lives to be dependent on the government's plans. White men often appeared who wanted something. Rembarrnga sometimes speculated about their personal characteristics but were seldom ready to indulge their desire for eager responses. As we saw in chapter one, Rembarrnga often felt humiliated by encounters with whites, and many tried to avoid them.

A counter-discourse began to emerge in the bush which can be seen as a commentary on the dilemmas created by dependence on an alien state apparatus. Examples are the Rembarrnga emphasis on personal relations with bureaucrats described above, and their attempts to take control. Despite the need for community participation, attempts to participate were not necessarily applauded. At one meeting 'Mrs Camfoo said that Aboriginal people are not having enough say in the day to day running of the cattle project' (E460/64 76/25 Dec. 1975). She requested that DAA provide timber and iron so that the members of the community could build their own houses. Such an individual and personal request was too modest for the state officials to respond to.[21] Complaints from the community that they lacked control over the money were met with repeated recording of resolutions that 'there should be more consultation with the resident European supervisor'. That is, they had to reform their interactions with whitefellas in general and with their manager in particular.

The letters to the government from community members conflicted with bureaucratic practices, not only in their modesty and localism, but in combining requests in unexpected mixes for what amounted to an overall plan for community development. One list written by Tex includes schooling and fencing, horses and houses, a little dispensary and 'a man to run the book-work' (E460 73/7229). As well he says, 'I like to go Forward' and 'I would like to be Proud of Things and land that we owned'.[22]

Demands that the people be heard and that self-determination be implemented were made in a letter, actually written by a visiting white man in cooperation with Nelly and the signatories:

> Dear Mr McHenry,
> Mr Bryant [the then Minister] says that we aboriginal people are going to be encouraged to make our own decisions and run our own affairs. We appreciate the help the welfare people give us, but we do feel that we are not given a chance enough of our own decisions and want to change things so that we can do so. At the moment we want two things that are very important to us.
> First we would like to change our Secretary who was chosen for us by welfare and not ourselves . . . [23]
> The second thing is that we want to know when the consultant people are coming from Canberra to see us. We have come here from other places and would like to get this place of ours operating quickly before some of our people lose interest and move away.
> One more thing is that we urgently need a school as we have 11 children here and no school.
> Yours Faithfully,
> Tex Camfoo, Chuckerduck Lindsay, Smiler Martin, Tommy Kelly, Willy Martin. July 1973 (E460 73/7229).

Each name has been written or printed, indicating that the earlier instruction about writing had been put into effect. Deploying these notions of 'this place of ours', expressing pride in 'the land we owned' and in 'going forward' represents an adoption of the language of community and community interests in accordance with bureaucratic discourse. There is a shaping of consciousness and desire around the notion of community and its place, a strategy which answers the official requirement for a particular attitude and form of expression, and which diverges from the more fluid boundaries of social identification characteristic of Rembarrnga sociality.

Deep conflicts between the community and the state were camouflaged in official discourse by being interpreted as conflict between 'what the community wants' (vehicles and houses) and 'the interests of the cattle project'. But Rembarrnga recalcitrance continued to be expressed in the behavioural dimensions of their sociality which are not mentioned in official records. For instance, the practice of openly sitting and playing cards for hours on end contradicted the moral language of 'a good day's work', of 'getting things done' and 'making an effort', and was seen as shameless public laziness. To Rembarrnga, simply being busy did not demonstrate responsibility or moral worth.

Whitefellas disapproved of men 'lounging about in the camp', and some would offer a good example by hurrying about their work, displaying an exaggerated sense of urgency and an air of busy purposefulness, which caused amusement among those it was intended to instruct. Whitefellas' lounging was done out of sight, in private, at home, after hours, and any interruption of this privacy by 'demands' from Rembarrnga people was greatly resented.

These events do not merely reflect local neo-colonial forms. There are common elements in the experience of modernisation among those who neither generated nor controlled its initial entry into their space but who later began writing their own requests, organising their own meetings, and supervising the presence of modernity for their own benefit. This complicity of people in their own domination takes place through the creation of desires to participate in the arts of government, the legitimacy of citizenship and the wealth of modern life. When they try to participate, the irrelevance and naivety of their immediate desires can soon become apparent. At Bulman, after a directors' meeting had completed a discussion of 'securities', 'insurance' and 'further encumbrances', Willy Martin made the suggestion that the road between Weemol and Bulman would be ideal for a 'take away' roadside cafe (E460 74/2294 Nov. 1974). This is a bush road between two small communities, which also carries a little dry season Katherine–Gove long distance traffic which does not pause in its rush from town to town. When Willy Martin suggested a roadside stall at this place, he displayed on the one hand his willingness to participate in the visions and promises which the state officials seemed to be offering and also his 'innocence in the realm of capital' (Srivastava 1996:120). The seductive assumption that the simple act of entrepreneurship, whether it be in a block of land or a roadside stall, is sufficient for successful participation, is widely shared across race and class lines.

An agronomist who is an old and intimate friend of some Rembarrnga people typifies the white sympathetic view of this history in his assessment of what went wrong:

> There's good potential. I don't think any Aboriginal people have had the background and traditions to do something as complicated as managing a cattle station and handling the bookkeeping and the management decisions involved in buying and selling—as well as figuring out how to overcome the problems of the family and the clan and the problems of managing people on the spot. I think that will take a long time and I don't think it's paternalism to say they'll need outside help for probably

decades to come. Maybe it takes two or three decades of self-management before you start having the traditions to overcome the problems. You can't force or rush these things through. You can never say there's a time when you hand over that authority. You've got to do it in dribs and drabs, and they've got to be able to hand it back [to others to manage] (Smith pers. com.).

Here the problem is defined as a lack of appropriate social resources and skills for managing people. Their communal, democratic forms of decision-making preclude the hierarchical structures needed to make business decisions and to wield authority over labour power. There is a lack of cultural capital, an absence of certain kinds of relations for managing and deploying people. That is, Aborigines have to produce an alternative social order within their own arena if they are to progress. They must overcome resilient and resistant forms of social practice; that is, the 'problems' of the family and the clan. Government planners made continual references to the necessity for self-help, which referred obliquely to Aborigines' moral inability to help themselves, as manifested in the failure of government projects. These failures thus reinforced the new forms of moral and cultural hegemony.

While there has been much analysis and criticism of the logic underlying government policies, an examination of the problem-solving mentality itself exposes aspects of the cultural process which produced such savage and sometimes bizarre results. The allocation of a $600 000 budget to a business project to be run as a community enterprise by non-literate and non-numerate directors on land rejected by previous pastoralists, required a good deal of courage and foolishness which made sense at the time as a solution to a particular historical problem. It required considerable sympathy for Aborigines, and a commitment to the task of self-management no matter how destined to commercial failure. Indeed failure could confirm a romantic portrait of Aborigines as too democratic to succeed, too anarchical to create hierarchy, too sharing and caring to run a capitalist enterprise.

'This country owed DAA a big debt'

The search for the viable enterprise at Bulman was interrupted when funds for Gulperan dried up soon after the white manager's substantial house had been built at the planned new site at Gulin Gulin. The DAA reports after 1977 were imbued with a sense of sorrowful disappointment, and the need to be hard headed. Self-determination rhetoric was modified, and it was admitted that decisions had 'not taken place at the request of the community although with its knowledge'; the pastoral adviser's contract was terminated and the company placed on a limited budget (E460 75/25/1). A DAA pastoral expert's report expressed sadness at the project's failure, tempered by a desire not to blame the Bulman people for the waste of money. He found only one paddock in good condition; only 30 people in residence; only three people employed as stockmen. The shop was $700 in debt, owed by people, many of whom were no longer residents. Because 'a large amount of time each day is wasted on organising themselves and their equipment . . . productivity is severely cut and thus wages reduced'. With pained sympathy the bureaucrats could find 'no alternative' but to have the station try to pay off the store's debt. This was because the community might be taught bad habits were they to be excluded from the same accountancy rules as other recipients of government funding (E460/64 1976/25/1).

When I returned in 1979 a series of temporary white managers with various levels of honesty and decency[24] had come and gone and the store had accrued debt several times. Rex Campion, Kevin Forbes and Bruce Murray each had a period as supervisor of what became a low-key cattle harvesting project. The financial situation became truly chaotic due to mismanagement by the service organisation that had been set up in Katherine to manage the provisions and finances of remote communities. The white manager of this organisation wanted to establish racial equality by spending money freely, as prosperous non-Aboriginal enterprises did. This manager had lost several hundred dollars to Kevin Forbes in a card game on a visit to Bulman; he tried to expunge the debt by buying Kevin a car which had broken down at Bamyilli. A DAA field officer exposed the manager, complaining that 'his gambling forays tend to build up friction and resentment against whites which makes the cattle consultant's job even harder' (E460 75/25/2).[25] The manager ignored DAA's direction and warnings, and when eventually charged with misappropriation of funds he was able to demonstrate to the court's satisfaction that his spending was authorised by the Aboriginal board of directors.

The reshaping of responses continued. At one meeting it was reported with warm approval that 'Rex Campion read out a list of matters . . . which they required advice on'. The DAA field officer found it 'encouraging that the community has become sufficiently organised to the extent of presenting a written submission of what they required'[26] (E460 75/25/2 Aug. 1979). By 1980 field reports were more openly focussed on commercial and management issues. 'Tribal matters' were no longer mentioned, and the ordinary and ubiquitous negotiations about rights and authority over country were still interpreted by officials as 'controversy': 'The ownership issue still continues to be a controversial one with a reversal of previous findings with certain members of the Nalakan/Rembarrnga group, e.g. George Djadiku, claiming that the Ngalpun's sovereignty over the Golung golung area is not valid' (E460/54 83/363 (2), orig. spelling).

There was an alternative understanding of the trajectory of Gulperan: 'We worked and made this country big. That place where we camped before, Goinjimbi. *Mununga* called it Gulperan Pastoral Company. Now we've got this Gulin Gulin. Why they changed this place is because this country owed DAA a big debt' (Nelly Camfoo 1982).

At Mainoru a new manager and his wife encouraged and assisted the remains of the Gulperan project and supplied services to Bulman residents. A small community of about fifteen Rembarrnga people was re-established at Mainoru for a few years. The Mainoru school had been closed in 1972, but Annette Murray, who had completed her schooling at Kormilda College, began to teach the children regularly. A DAA report on Mainoru found that 'Annette Murray takes classes for seven or eight students. She is helped by the manager's wife . . .'. The manager requested that Annette be paid some sort of wage for her initiative as she spent 20 to 25 hours a week teaching, but because the school was not registered and Annette was not then a trained teacher, the Education Department said it was unable to pay her. The field officer said of the manager: 'Overall I was impressed . . . makes a difference to be able to talk to somebody with constructive criticism and opinions rather than receiving a stream of racist comments and jokes directed to us and the resident Aboriginals' (E460/54 83/441 Apr. 1978).

This official appreciated this manager as they shared progressive views, both making voluntary efforts to engage an Aboriginal person in educational activity which is undeniably of benefit to the community. When this manager and his family left Mainoru, Dorothy Murray went with them, spending two years at a station near Daly River, 1600 kilometres away. She took her brother's daughter Sonia Martin with her, but finally returned to Bulman because, she said, it was too lonely for them so far away from family.

In 1981 Mainoru returned to the more typical Territory style of management. Mr Foster sold the property and it was amalgamated with

Mountain Valley under the ownership of one man. The departing manager warned the DAA that the new owner 'was not favourably disposed towards Aboriginal people' and had made 'veiled threats to withdraw services currently provided to the community . . . power, water, store, canteen, and locally killed beef'. A field officer visited and reported that 'Most [Rembarrnga] returned to Bulman, though some of the stockmen continued to be employed under contract for specific work such as the annual muster' (E460 54/83/441). This work dried up when the owner began to bring in seasonal workers, picking them up at Mataranka in a truck, providing for them on the station, and delivering them back when the muster was completed. This was a means of confining interaction with Aboriginal workers to the task in hand. It represented a complete severance of the reliance on Rembarrnga workers, many of whom had been born on Mainoru or Mountain Valley stations and some of whom had worked there since they were small children. But that is by no means the end of the Bulman or the Mainoru stories, let alone that of the Rembarrnga people.

9

⌀○○○○⌀

Enjoying Democracy

My brother got that land, he never forgot. He said, 'I got that place for you. You want to give away white man now, don't work. I want to show you that place. I've got good country.'

He said, 'You want to still hang on with the white man yet?'

I said, 'All right, I'll go.' I couldn't believe that place!

—*Alma Gibbs 1989*[1]

Rather than a creative interaction or melding of the characteristics of two cultural domains at Australia's cultural frontier, whitefellas appear to be repetitively painting over the surface of blackfellas' lives but failing to efface the existing dynamic pattern. The new designs do not take easily. The ascendancy of whites, and the body of moral judgements which they spread over their surroundings, are subject to systematic, if muted, judgements from the shadowy realms underneath.

A clue to these judgements is when Rembarrnga comment with distaste on whitefellas' practices: '*Mununga* don't like kid or family.' '*Mununga* don't have skin. I hear you marry your second cousin.' Another example at the level of everyday interactions is the shock expressed by Lorna and Dorothy at the physical immodesty of two white women who sat at a meeting with their knees bent up, seeming to invite attention to their genitals. When a resident manager, in the presence of Nelly and Tex, gave as a reason for his daughter not going horse riding that she was menstruating they were acutely embarrassed, seeing his display of this knowledge as implying awful intimacies.

It is the ongoing living force of the underlying Aboriginal cultural script which leads to Rembarrnga distress when they observe punishment rather than affection being meted out to white children who cry, and to the expression of curiosity about a society which appears to operate in the absence of kin categories. Such generalisations and judgements are clues to a realm structured around different values from those of white society, a realm where personal actions and attitudes are rarely the target of a moralising discourse. Others' peculiar practices tend to evoke laughter and teasing rather than censure.[2] The racial hierarchy has left deposits which disfigure the surface of social life, so that such laughter or shock, and the judgements they represent, must be muffled. The critical discourse generated among black people is rendered invisible to whites.

Nor can Aboriginal dissatisfaction with self-determination be expressed because the language of autonomy, which gives the appearance of voluntarism, choice and lack of constraint, and which provides popular explanations of contemporary conditions, cannot be easily ruptured. The changing conditions under which Aboriginal people have been invited to be part of the state, to join the nation and to become dependent upon goods and services from the government have always been both naturalised and idealised as progress. Many whitefellas and blackfellas are, innocently or knowingly, complicit in the government's forward looking projects, whose boundaries and contingencies are difficult to identify as lives become embroiled in them. Traces of prior orders and designs are apparent in the ordering of Aboriginal social life.

In previous chapters I have tried to give an ethnographic account of the conditions under which Rembarrnga participate in the nation's discourses and the state's practices. Put simply these conditions include, first, the lack of any white adaptation to Rembarrnga practice and thus the rarity of ongoing dialogue between the two worlds of meaning. Then there are the insistent invitations and seductive rewards on offer to those blackfellas who take part in community development projects. Finally there are the manifold pleasures—material and symbolic—for those who become actors in both worlds and who can explore the possibilities and rewards of modernity. Varied responses to these conditions have created new interests and alliances, and have caused fissures and cracks to appear among clan and lineage loyalties.

These conditions are not part of a lively public discourse about the successes, failures and disappointments of Aboriginal development policies. Rather, interpretations are smothered in assumptions, anxieties and orthodoxies. Both the hostile or moralistic deploring of misdirected government policies and the sympathetic explanations of what is perceived as the Aborigines' plight are embedded in a political and moral quagmire. Local officials cannot admit to their own part in the kinds of failures and flounderings I have described above but they must protect Aboriginal people from the racist environment. The silences surrounding these situations stem from the ambiguity and confusion about whose identities are being protected in this essentially, potentially, hostile context.

Also conspiring to confuse the scene is the post-modern and popular celebration of difference which wants to affirm all forms of Aboriginality as valued expressions of otherness which the nation should value and protect. Anthropologists and cultural studies scholars share this stance, and agree that the state created oppressive conditions causing immense suffering to indigenous people throughout Australia. These orthodoxies lead to the dismissal of any critiques of progressive government policies and receptive Aboriginal responses as malicious or misinformed. Seldom are Aborigines' attempts to embrace modernity understood as a dialectical process. Silencing of critical views has meant that secret explanations circulate unchallenged, and these secreted truths are about the refusal or inability of Aborigines to become modern, and about their opportunism or corruption which is variously disapproved of or, cynically or benignly, understood.

My own moral aim has been to scrutinise the consequences of state power being ostensibly wielded to overcome the existing racial hierarchy. As we have seen, forms of power exist not merely in the state, but in all kinds of places and peoples. The moral power now exerted by aspects of Aboriginal culture which are privileged in certain contexts is one example. The distressing prevalence of internecine struggles within Aboriginal communities is another. Individual Aborigines can accrue considerable power in their community. Each of these forms needs to be understood in its specificity; such power is hedged with conditions, and itself becomes the target of resentment as well as complicity among white officials. Growing internal inequalities in Aboriginal communities, structured around differential access to resources, are evident even in remote outstations. Changing efforts of state officials to solve 'the Aboriginal problem', and the endlessly varied responses to these offerings, make this a difficult story to end. I will make an attempt, not to complete a comprehensive interpretation of Bulman today, or to set out the definitive lessons to be drawn from

Rembarrnga history, but rather to show how the unresolvable tensions of the self-determination era are still being worked through. The moving racial frontier continues to create painful and persistent dilemmas that are hinted at in every event. Using a notion of levels of social existence, I will give examples of how these dilemmas are played out at the material, the political and the symbolic level.

MATERIAL MODERNITY

Since 1976, when the Gulperan manager's two-storey house was constructed at Gulin Gulin, there have been remarkable changes in the material conditions of the residents. In 1977 three flimsy houses were built at the new site where ample bore water was available, and some of the community moved there. Intermittently a town has been constructed where there had been grass, stony red earth and a symbolic plane of marks, tracks and sites. Each year something was promised and something appeared: new solid houses, a store, a mobile school, pumps and an all-weather road to Weemol were all in place by the early 1980s. By 1998 there were formed roads in the township, a larger store, an adequate generator, a clinic, a permanent school, a mechanics' workshop and an administrative building as well as eleven houses and a number of shacks in the main town, and six houses and a few demountables for staff in a partially separated area (plate 24). After years of inadequate, overflowing septic tanks, a sewerage treatment plant was being installed. There were about 120 residents and many others visited. There was an area of makeshift huts and humpies where those unable to return to their outstations lived. Four-wheel drive vehicles, mostly owned by organisations or supplied by government departments as part of the job, were parked outside staff houses. A few unregistered cars in various stages of deterioration were in intermittent use for bush travel, kept going by the ingenuity of bush mechanics. Tex and Nelly had their house built at the old camp, Goinjimbi, and had their own vehicle.

Buildings and equipment are evidence that the Bulman mob has participated in the inexorable encroachment of certain modern forms.[3] They are now producing within their own cultural space a social order, authorised by the state, which has a hierarchical structure and relations of authority which mimic those of the white world. This social order is not yet properly installed and its instability is a focus of anxiety among those state officials who are responsible for various services and operations, while within the community it is a focus of gossip and politicking. The knowledge that many schemes and projects have failed, and that new ones can only hope to achieve partial success, means that a sense of pathos binds the well-meaning bureaucrats to the Aborigines they serve. There is a shared recognition of the informal requirements and the limits of the contradictory programs in which they are all engaged.

Avoiding whitefellas

Scattered sparsely throughout Arnhem Land, hidden among the trees and scrub, are little 'outstations', the homes of small communities, usually not discernible to the outsider until one is right there. Bulman was an outstation in 1975. By 1990 it had spawned seven outstations and the incorporated body, Gulin Gulin Resource Association, with its own vehicle and equipment, provides facilities and services to them (map 2). In 1971 Weemol was one of the first to take advantage of the outstation establishment grant of $20 000. Other outstations rapidly appeared throughout Arnhem Land, mainly serviced through the older, larger settlements. Many have only two or three related households, ten or twenty people, and initially had little more equipment than a 4WD vehicle. Since then, most have two or three houses, a generator, a solar-powered pump and telephone. Goods, especially the staple foods of flour, tea and sugar, as well as tobacco, soap and dozens of other things, are trucked in fortnightly in the dry season. Television sets, video players and tape recorders are purchased and, when they work, provide a peephole into the world of the mass media. The main work and play consists of fishing, hunting, gathering bush foods and other materials. Some outstations produce artefacts or bark paintings. Social life is characterised by dense social interaction among extended networks of kin.

The little outstation communities have had varied histories in consciously establishing new ways and incorporating old ways of living, but under shifting and unpredictable conditions of support from governments. Some outstations are only used in the dry season. Others have airstrips for the use of the planes which traverse Arnhem Land regularly. Some outstations have had no resident population for some years, though they are not 'abandoned'. Bulugadru (map 1), a Maningrida outstation, is where Smiler and Lorna's daughters live, married to two Gunwingu brothers. A teacher visits for several days a month to help Michelle who is undertaking the teacher training

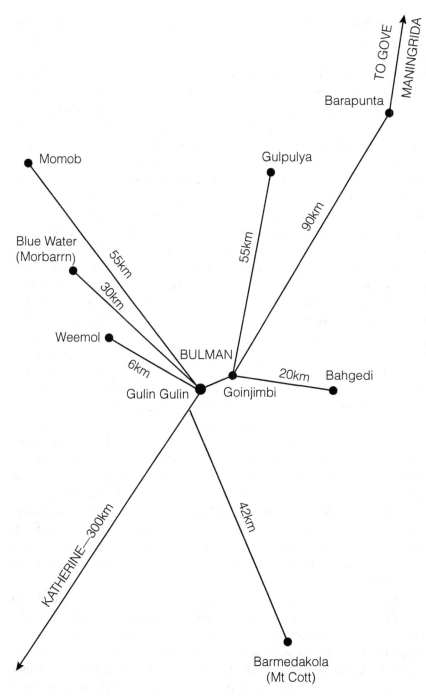

Map 2   Bulman outstations

course at Batchelor College. Thus, as Aborigines retreat into the bush, they beckon elements of educational and medical institutions to follow them. Such a thin overlay of desired, foreign, cultural practices can be moulded to what is already there, reshaped to harmonise with the patterns of these bush places. Far more than Bulman, outstations offer the space to explore and establish a modern Aboriginal identity away from the scrutiny and judgements of whites. Yet it is not possible to escape interaction with the state's institutions and personnel. For instance when someone dies, institutions such as the hospital, the mortuary, the coroner, the funeral director and the police have to be involved. The knowledge and skills needed to conduct these interactions with confidence and dignity are increasingly evident.

The state had an ambivalent view of the outstations movement from the start (Palmer 1990) and funding was resisted (Gillespie 1982:5). The eagerness with which Aboriginal people returned to the bush surprised white observers, and many believed that outstations were a temporary fad rather than a serious social movement and that the unserviced camps would be soon abandoned. Others, such as this government official, developed more positive theories: 'There is a transitional period whereby people stagnate before they throw off the yoke of settlement expectations and realise things only happen through their own initiative and effort. This is also tied in with finding a new sense of direction and purpose' (E460/16 83/363 Oct. 1979).

The metaphors of 'stagnation' and 'yoke' for social and psycho-dynamics entailed a new critique of the past. Unlike the erstwhile Mainoru owners whose images of the past took on a rosy glow in hindsight, the state was judging its own past harshly, confessing that settlement expectations had been a 'yoke' which had submerged 'initiative and effort'. The state could do this because, as we saw above, a new form of racial consciousness was integral to the sense of self and the political identity of the personnel who saw themselves as part of a new era, with the redemptive task of correcting the errors of their predecessors.

Among bureaucrats, positive visions of outstations as emblems of an autonomous future competed with concern about the material conditions of the residents, and about the practical problems of supplying them with goods, schooling and medical services. As a report about the Bulman outstations said: 'All of the communities are seriously disadvantaged . . . a number of Aboriginal groups have made genuine attempts to establish permanent outstations but the area's isolation, wet season factors and lack of physical support has frustrated them in their efforts' (E460/37 85/133 Aug. 1985).

Lurking behind the concern is a notion of permanence and settledness that is at odds with the priorities of the outstation residents. The anxious gaze of a colonial official regularly accompanied government funding. To their client Aborigines, government officials seemed capricious, mean and liable to be unexpectedly hostile. 'They've taken the tractor and trailer off Paddy', someone said at Bulman one day in 1976. Paddy Fordham Wainbarrnga was the driver, in both a metaphoric and literal sense, in setting up a new outstation at Bamdibu about 115 kilometres from Bulman. He had driven from Barunga on his new tractor with a trailer full of family and their swags, returning the following week to replenish the stores. But with all the people in the trailer there was little room for the flour, tea and sugar. After two more such trips, two new tyres were needed and the money in the Bamdibu account was finished. The government adviser said with a tone of cynical but disappointed resignation, 'That's the end of Bamdibu!' No-one at Bulman understood what he meant. They would wait until the government gave them more money, perhaps next year. Their country would wait for them as it had been waiting for so many years.

The 'outstation movement' is a movement away from reserves and institutions, away from whites' designs. It is a movement towards a future of materially modest but socially ambitious proportions. This is not an escape from modernity; modernity is part of Aboriginal tradition. Cultures require space as well as time to organise their boundaries and articulate their concepts of order and desire (Bachelard 1969). Aboriginal communities crowded into limited camps and settlements under the judging gaze of white masters had no room to develop their own mimetic and alteric responses to modernity. The physical proximity of different clans and language groups had also created conflicts such as the disruption of marriage rules. Outstations are providing space, physically, socially and psychically, to develop another kind of relationship with whitefellas, as well as time to assess, filter, appropriate and refuse a range of possibilities.

But outstation residents still depend on whitefellas, even though they might now employ them. The hierarchies of employment and race, while complementary before, are often at cross purposes in the modern world, partly because of the control white people are able to exercise over material technologies. This was illustrated in a typical incident concerning the crucial and scarce resource of transport. One morning in 1995, the Barapunta mob, who had been camped at Bulman for some weeks, heard of an impending government inspection of their outstation school and were desperate to get back home to prepare for the visitors, fearing official disapproval of its deserted appearance. The resource centre manager refused to take them because they had not arranged the trip earlier. The Barapunta people sat on the hill nearby, swags ready, angry that their recently appointed employee would not accede to their urgent request. At their request I spoke to the manager. He was adamant; at a recent meeting everyone had agreed that he'd take a run once a week to each outstation, and he sat in the little fibro office firmly explaining to me that 'these people must keep to agreements if they are going to get anywhere. I can't run around everyday just when they suddenly ask.' To him the demand was stereotypical irresponsibility on the part of the man he saw as the leader of the group. The white man was unaware that this large kin-related group was constantly engaged in a process of nego- tiating the needs and demands of its various members—mothers and babies, old or ill people, children, as well as those who were robust and energetic. In this case, the racial hierarchy aligned with the dominant culture's ordering principles was more powerful than employer–employee relations.

Suitable houses

The common notion that material culture is purely instrumental, rather than a repository of emotion, imagination and loyalty, is again given the lie by the bureaucratic dismay and public denigration when Aborigines adapt houses for a different use in a differently defined social space (Morris 1989:176). Much could be said about the place of the building known as 'the home' in race relations. The desire to provide suitable Aboriginal housing has attracted many designers and architects (cf. Cowlishaw 1988:141; Heppel 1979; Myers 1988). The housing initiative at the outstation Barramakola (Mt Catt) illustrates the pitfalls of good intentions. A contract builder in Katherine designed houses with a simple structure which seemed to blend with the bush, and he was commissioned by the DAA to oversee the building of several of them at Barramakola. Logs were used to frame walls made of local stone, clay and cement composite which required only basic skills to construct. The use of local materials and labour made this seem like the ideal, inexpensive, self-help project, but these economic, social and aesthetic advantages were apparent only to whitefellas. The residents saw the houses as obviously inferior to the usual houses of whitefellas and called them 'rubbish houses'. When George Jaurdaku was heard to say, 'I suppose it's better than living in the mud' (E460/37 85/133), officials were deeply offended, failing to recognise that in this wry and humorous remark was a comment on their own enthusiasm and emotional involvement in houses they would not live in themselves. They saw George's apparently careless judgement as a sign of irresponsibility and ingratitude towards the generous state coffers and aesthetic sensibility that had indulged his family's desire to live in a remote place.

Contemporary houses involve furniture and a whole range of services as part of the way they function. When the Bulman mob was provided with their first three houses in 1979, they continued to sit down around the fire outside in the lee of the houses. The houses lacked furniture and electricity but this was not the main reason they sat outside. Rather, the fire was loved, and was an essential part of sociality. When a bullock was killed, a large section of the raw carcass was deposited inside on the built-in kitchen bench. To get some beef for supper one would take a knife and a torch to go inside and, slapping aside the gnawing cats, slice a piece off. Children of all ages took turns to hack at the meaty part of the huge hind quarters. When a sliver was detached the child would give the knife to another and take the meat outside to roast in the ashes. The scene appeared bizarre and chaotic to one used to kitchens and their intended use. However, it was of course ordered: the bench was useful, replacing a tree branch to keep the meat off the ground. Such 'misuse' of the government-funded houses is a constant source of sorrow or suppressed irritation to whitefellas, especially to those who have identified in some personal way with having provided for Aborigines' housing needs. The public servant reluctantly concludes that Aborigines have not yet evolved an appreciation of the forms of domesticity the rest of us enjoy.

At Bulman, houses are treated functionally and flexibly, with no great pride invested in the ownership of the building and less on maintaining an ordered aesthetics. They are still being tried out. Practices in relation to houses have not become weighty responsibilities demanding elaborate and endlessly repeated housekeeping rituals and maintenance. The vast emotional and financial investments which are regularly made in the home by whitefellas are absent here. Modern people have problems in recognising that modern goods are 'sacramental of other meanings' (Dening 1988:9). While anthropologists may recognise that changes in the use of material goods express different cultural priorities, a conscious rejection of foreign values, or a form of 'creative bricolage' (Levi-Strauss 1966; Morris 1989:74ff), the bureaucrats who stand before the Aboriginal people do not appreciate their 'misuse' of the valuable things with which they have been provided. The incongruities associated with putting things to unintended uses can have other purposes and effects, such as offering a space of freedom in this subordinated social sphere. Nelly's conversion of Rinso soap powder to shampoo (Chapter 4) has the potential to evoke ridicule, but on the other hand it expresses the pleasure of flouting white propriety. The self-parodying humour which often accompanies the subverting of whitefellas' order can confirm the worst white fears.

Morris (1989) has shown how new material resources such as houses can invite creative responses but can also disrupt stable practices and social habits. By changing the ordering of space, they create new social conditions. For instance, while houses inevitably provide privacy, they interfere with more flexible interaction when people sit in the open, able to see and communicate with others at a distance (Sansom 1988). The sociality practised when sitting around fires outside cooking food, making tea, watching people as they come and go, playing cards, fulfilling daily tasks, being available to kinspeople, and communicating discreetly with signs and finger talk are all interrupted by buildings, and indeed by a house, which marks a specific family's space off from the network of kin with its graduated levels of distance from other points in the network.

My argument is not that houses are not valued by Rembarrnga people. More people have come to want and need privacy more often, and the facilities for washing, cooking and for storage become ever more important with reduced mobility. Modern technologies are being incorporated into social life and some, such as the telephone, have facilitated and lubricated social interaction in ways that enhance Rembarrnga society's ability to reproduce itself. Solar-powered pay telephones in outstations allow people to be informed of others' whereabouts and well-being in a way unimaginable even in the mid 1970s.

However, increased access to vehicles, planes and telephones does not simply increase travel and communication. Paradoxically, they can decrease familiarity with the land, create barriers to travel and interfere with accepted forms of communication. Planes pluck people out of one community to another in minutes, and visits to attend funerals need last only hours. Many young people have never walked over the land with which their grandparents were intimately familiar; their relationship with country is based on different experiences. Further, motor cars and plane fares are not as equally available as walking. In the 1970s huge communally owned cattle trucks transported whole communities to ceremonies, but now individuals own or control the private and community vehicles. Private ownership and varied incomes mean that it is the educated and employed men and women who have access to more resources, and other kin must rely on them.

GOVERNING AUTONOMY

We saw above how the paraphernalia of everyday life on a station was a compelling element in the pastoralists' domination of their untutored workers; the mastery of pragmatic technology confirmed their grasp of the meaning of the world. But capitalism has moved on, and those techniques have lost their primacy. It is technologies of governance, systems of political representation, of funding, of accountability and practices known as democracy, which are now being taught with the same assumptions as were attached to farming technologies in an earlier time. These are the necessary tools for the Aboriginal people's future, an invariant reality, a morally neutral common sense. Aborigines are now being enticed into exercising the same rights as whitefellas, rights which are supposed to ensure that we are all equal citizens.

Replacing whitefellas

In the 1970s the common view was that Aboriginal people would soon take over the management of communities. Whites wanted to complete their liberating project and Rembarrnga people wanted to be rid of the intrusive presence of whitefellas. But, while community members have further schooling and some of the jobs, there are ever more whitefellas needed to staff the organisations and institutions which sprouted vigorously as DAA was complemented by ADC (Aboriginal Development Corporation)[4] and then both were replaced in 1990 by the elected body ATSIC (Aboriginal and Torres Strait Islander Commission).[5] At Bulman a larger, more stable population has congregated and increased services have been provided for what is now a town, officially named Gulin Gulin, managed by an elected body called Gulin Gulin Community Council.

However, nearly all senior staff positions in the community—accountant, store manager, bookkeeper, resource association manager and the senior staff of the school and clinic—were held by white staff or outsiders in 1997. The term 'white' refers to a cultural domain rather than a skin colour; the Gulin Gulin accountant in 1995 was Indian, but was defined as a 'whitefella'. However, Bulman people held many junior positions and worked as assistants to the white staff in the Council offices and the shop, and as outside Council staff. Furthermore, two community members held powerful positions. In 1990 Annette Murray was the elected Chair of Gulin Gulin Council and her husband, Peter Miller, originally from Central Australia, was appointed Town Clerk. Each has a teaching degree from Batchelor College and Deakin University (Bulman Oral History Series: 11). They were in a position to exert direct control over both the white and black employees, and could also wield a wider influence on the decisions of government agencies.[6]

Is this, then, the gradual achievement of self-management? Perhaps it is, but both the 'self' and the 'management' of Aboriginality have changed. The need for moral and financial accountability has shaped self-management to the demands of bureaucratic practice and the policy discourse of the state. The needs and desires of Rembarrnga people who take staff positions have only occasionally and temporarily disrupted or subverted official plans. The discourse of 'self-management' is now employed by individual Rembarrnga people to construct an entity towards which funding can be directed. This entity, the community, takes various organisational forms such as the Gulin Gulin Council and the Resource Association, which can now be held responsible for the outcomes of the state officials' plans.

Replacing the white staff in communities and in government agencies entails more than merely putting Aboriginal people into certain positions. Technological and organisational paraphernalia which demand specific skills have been everywhere incorporated into Aboriginal social life. To work in the shop it is necessary to properly understand the till. To take part in established institutions, even the humble local cooperatives and corporations, one must operate within their parameters. Constitutions of incorporated bodies, rules of organisations, accountability as well as the force of established practice, all function to conserve the form of institutions, but also to promote and perpetuate certain forms of subjectivity. The myriad technologies of power directed at the community by the state increasingly appear in the guise of Aboriginal organisations, corporations or enterprises.

Self-management then does not mean that Rembarrnga staff can introduce Rembarrnga practices into these activities. The lack of meetings and flouting of proper procedures can indicate that the meaning of these bureaucratic structures has not been internalised; many community members are indifferent to them. The structure of Council and committees sometimes appears to be a non-functioning shell, and yet in other contexts Rembarrnga notions of time, place and discourse are being forcibly modified to harmonise with the relatively inflexible institutions of the state. For instance, the school and the clinic are funded and controlled directly by government departments which ensure they continue to function within the framework of standard practice, though slow time frames and shoddy outcomes are expected.

The new sense of community consciousness creates a discord between social responsibility and the personal and family responsibilities which a kin-based sociality realises in everyday interpersonal interchanges and interdependencies (Robinson 1995). The need to speak of funding budgets, town plans, census forms, provision of state resources and employment programs, has created a consciousness of the township and its residents as an objectified entity which can become a rival to kin for loyalty and identity. As the Barapunta incident showed, residents of a community become conscious of the demand that they form a stable population to ensure the provision of services and the fulfilment of long-term plans. Individuals who wish to gain the rewards for complying with the state's demands are prevailing upon their relatives to obey the rules and disregard conflicting demands from other kin who belong to another community. In this way a sense of community is being reconstituted around a specific locality and group which commands loyalty and which can deliver stability to the state in return for a stable supply of resources and personnel.

The designs of earlier regimes to paint Aboriginal existence out of the landscape have left their mark. The economistic designs of the more recent Gulperan era have also left traces on the Aboriginal culture which was to remain visible in specific discrete forms under the whitewash of modernity. Now individuals who are authorised as power holders and who represent the community and liaise with government, are cloaked in new roles and armed with new skills. They must speak to state officials, make demands on governments, and express community wishes. The material conditions of white service providers go with these jobs; such people suddenly find they have vehicles and good wages as well as larger and better equipped houses in areas somewhat separate from the bulk of the community (Howard 1982; Sackett 1990;

Thiele 1982:26). Thus, an often uncomfortable internal stratification is being established as a necessary adjunct to community autonomy and self-determination. This is part of a process whereby communities became increasingly drawn into the bureaucratic promises and patterns, and thus more dependent on government funding. Some individuals are eager to comply with bureaucratic demands and become shamed by practices characteristic of their Rembarrnga kin. But, contrary to the assumptions of many *mununga*, underlying alterity is not automatically or completely replaced in these conditions. The potential to uncover and express a deeper living subjectivity and sociality remains. The power of *mununga* employees and Rembarrnga authorities is thus being played out in complex and ambiguous ways.

Employing blackfellas

The process of 'Aboriginalisation', begun in the 1970s, was intended to remove neo-colonial whites from positions of power over Aborigines. Organisations across Australia began to recruit Aboriginal staff.[7] In the Territory, Aboriginalisation meant an emergence into official and liaison positions of brown rather than black Aboriginal people, though of course it was not the colour of the skin which led to their being employed. It was the Territory's history rather than any current intentionality which created the conditions for another form of colour coding to be insinuated into the process of self-determination. While race was no longer mentionable, notions of race were present in historically produced social identities. The dynamic and shifting discursive power of race had earlier placed blackfellas and whitefellas on either side of a fault line, giving a peculiar meaning to their interactions. 'Yella-fellas', as those of mixed parentage were called at Bulman in the 1970s, had fallen into the fissure created by the state, and the state in the past had forced them to climb out on the white side. After 1970 the state encouraged them to cross over to the black side, where they are accorded a valued place on the contemporary racial frontier.

Many of these people have had a history of social intervention into the fabric of their primary relationships and social identities. They have now entered the public imagination as victims of extreme deprivation, though there is more ambiguity and complexity in their condition than the public imagery allows. The comprehensive policy of removing what were known as 'mixed-blood' children from the 'blacks' camps' (see Chapter 5) created a split between such children and their black kin. Their racial identities were reshaped through an explicit, if disordered, retraining program which forced brown people away from black parents into white institutions or homes, which seldom fully accepted or assimilated them. Bonds were formed among the inmates of these institutions, and over time a distinct social grouping developed in the towns of the Territory consisting of light-skinned Aboriginal people with distinctive social experience and identity (Cummings 1990). However, the connections between the children who were removed and their primary black kin were not obliterated. The Bulman mob knew exactly who was taken and used the sparse information about these absent children to keep alive a social space for them to be reinserted some day inside the ubiquitous kinship system. Now that this reinsertion has been made possible, some individuals have actively attempted to reverse the effect of enforced separations, but the changed nature of these subjects has made this a troublesome process.

Eileen Cummings is one such person.[8] Another is Sally-Anne King, born in Katherine, whose parents were both designated 'half-caste'. When Sally-Anne and her white husband were appointed to manage the Bulman store in the late 1980s, Nelly identified Sally-Anne's genealogical connection to herself and others, thus positioning the couple as both insiders and outsiders. As such they have been embroiled in conflicts and rivalries, though their long-standing familiarity with the community as well as their dedication and hard work have made them highly valued. Sally-Anne took an enthusiastic part in facing up to the tensions concerning authenticity and authority to decide who should be at Bulman. Once, in the course of an argument about permits to be inside Arnhem Land, she shouted, 'Well, I don't need a permit; I'm a fucken blackfella too.' The alliance between Sally-Anne the employee and mediator of institutional demands, and her sponsoring kin, became a powerful tool in the political arena.

The Bulman mob's sense of social identity has more to do with personal knowledge and kinship than skin colour, but whitefellas' identification by colour is familiar. When a huge truck was loading Gulperan cattle in 1975, I asked Florry:

'Who's that blackfella driving?'
'You must know. He's your mob, *mununga* one,' said Florry.
'Might be yella-fella,' we both said and laughed.

The term 'yella-fella' has been dropped from the vernacular, at least in public, since its denigrating meaning in the white world has been recognised. The permeability of racial boundaries is nothing new, but the legitimacy of racially ambiguous people has increased as their old role in the racial hierarchy has been refigured as one of liaising between the state and Aboriginal communities.

The state now recognises the authentic Aboriginal identity of brown people they previously wanted to 'assimilate' because of their skin colour. Such people are being encouraged to positively identify as the same as the black parents or grandparents they were forced to be different from. While appearing to concede that Aboriginal identities cannot be fractionally apportioned, the state's practices are such that these people are delegated a task for which they are seen as uniquely suited, the task of teaching their estranged black kin lessons of autonomy and assimilation. Their formal status as Aborigines means they can be made to carry the burden of a racial boundary once legally constructed and now ostensibly a voluntary matter. The racial heritage of those who were removed is supposed to confer an identity which gives them automatic insights and understandings of the domain they were severed from. The state is embracing a form of identity politics which elevates racial heritage as the crucial marker of identity, at the same time as it acknowledging social relations, social practice and history.

Racial and cultural boundaries remain the subject of an intense and contentious public discourse.[9] The racial boundary is aligned with the cultural boundary by reserving the designation 'Aboriginal' for those in the bush as typified in the comment: 'It's an absurd definition of Aborigine that just lets everybody be called Aborigine. A policy that allows a sixteenth-blood Aboriginal person who was born in Darwin to talk as if they are the same as a full-blood who was brought up on Wattie Creek is just absurd' (Robert Smith 1989).

The use of the words 'lets' and 'allows' is significant here, appealing as they do to authority vested somewhere outside those claiming the identity, but wielded, it is implied, in the interests of protecting the specific social character of the 'full-blood . . . on Wattie Creek'. This popular reification of pure racial categories is specific to Aborigines in remote locations; there is no equivalent public discourse about other minorities who are racially identified, such as the Chinese community which forms a large and long-established part of the Territory's population. The state's attempt to allow Aborigines with a racially mixed heritage to choose their racial identity offends those who see the category of 'full-bloods' as an exclusive one. For many, the racial, cultural and class boundary between 'real' Aborigines and those with 'a sixteenth Aboriginal blood' is so salient as to make the common Aboriginal ancestry trivial. The latter group are too much like 'us' to be in that highly significant category 'full-bloods'. It is not the obviously disparate nature of the Australian population which is at issue, but the protection of a category which attracts state funding, which is served by a special administrative structure and which has accrued legal indigenous rights to land. Perhaps most important, it is also a category bound up with Australia's national identity in emotionally and morally complex and ambiguous ways (Hamilton 1990; Lattas 1997; Marcus 1997; Muecke 1997). We all need 'the full-bloods' to occupy a symbolic cornerstone of the nation.

The right white

The state is not a mechanical agent which imposes a colonial structure. It operates through officials whose inchoate and contradictory reasons and emotions accompany the forms of race relations experienced by diverse populations. As state officials engage in the mundane struggle to think well of themselves and to be thought well of, trying to live with honour and without shame, and in this case, trying to pragmatically assist Rembarrnga people to manage their own community, they are aware that what they are trying to achieve cannot work as it should. The pride of these white people stems from doing good, but it is constantly under threat of exposure both from those they see as rednecks who reject their efforts, and from blackfellas whose ever present gaze has the potential to expose the whitefellas' sense of superior moral worth and to unmask their self-interest and hypocrisies.

A steady stream of white men and women come to take up employment at Bulman in various capacities. Rather than taking direction from their employer—that is, the community—they believe they have come to help the people change, and do so through explanation and example. In the past, the dearth of applicants for jobs in remote Aboriginal communities meant that those appointed were often themselves somewhat marginal.[10] Today those who work at Bulman are more conventionally middle class, younger and confident of their ability to do the job. However, apart from the now established public knowlege of the violent nature of Australian colonialism, they are usually ignorant of any specificities of Aboriginal lives or history. Proximity to people whose manners and social practices are unfamiliar and in conflict with their own can lead to discomfort and unease. Often ambiguous responses develop, emotional distress competing with ill-concealed contempt for what they see as Aborigines' bad, inferior habits.

This was epitomised in a conversation over dinner at Bulman in the early 1990s. A young white man I will call David had been at first enthusiastic about his job of running a six-month training scheme at Bulman for about sixteen young people. After six weeks he spoke about the community in a way at once derisory and anxious. He was showing off with a knowing sly 'humour' for the enjoyment of his visiting girlfriend and another employed young couple at whose demountable staff house we had gathered for a meal. When the host complained 'they go off for smoko and don't come back for twenty minutes', David pretended amazement: 'You mean they come back!' he said. He recounted an event which he saw as epitomising his problems. He had been called away from his job to pull the station vehicle out of a bog and found the petrol tank was almost empty. He concluded scornfully, 'They drive those vehicles in the scrub for killers [bullock for station beef], and no-one cares for them. They let the kids break the upholstery. They took off the air filter 'cause it seemed unnecessary. And they don't even check if they've got enough petrol!' Then there were exclamations about the long distances 'they' walk in the bush.

The woman, who was employed at the women's centre which provided school lunches, joined in: 'The children will eat one hot dog and come back for another and then another.' 'Well,' explained her partner with authority, 'when there is food they will gorge and then they can last through times when there is nothing.' 'They' referred to Aboriginal hunter–gatherers. With a combination of mirth, disgust and pity these four white people outdid each other in describing the condition of particular peoples' houses; the floor of one is half gone; another has walls that flap and the toilet rocks. They glanced at me and began to speak in praise of particular individuals. 'Richard is a really top worker'; 'I've got some really good blokes there'; 'Laughlin works on that car of his every day.' Astonished admiration was evident in the comment that, 'Those blokes crashed one vehicle and removed the engine and put it in another body.'

These white people had been disappointed. They came to help, and tried to establish camaraderie with the Bulman mob as if they were equals. The young, black, schooled men and women they worked with were, in Homi Bhabha's phrase 'almost the same but not quite'. The whitefellas regularly construe the stress of their jobs as due to intransigent blackfellas whose challenges to normal white practices are ridiculed and mocked or else sympathetically explained as due to some essential quality or evolutionary adaptation. There is faith that, in the end, they will adjust and become more responsible. The celebration of difference evident in the texts of post-colonial theorists and progressive social scientists is absent here. Instead, white men sometimes have to forcibly defend proper, responsible practices of accountability against their erosion in the face of local demands. An example was when wages began to be paid according to hours worked, rather than by a standard weekly wage. Rembarrnga workers construed this as getting 'short money', and there was anger and a violent argument about the time-sheets which seemed to have a power beyond the control of either the trainees or the trainers. The white foreman was accused of cheating the workers, and two refused to return to work. In other cases, David docked trainees' wages when family demands or trips away interfered with the time at work. The trainees challenged the logic of this. As the trainee was not at fault, needs were not reduced, no necessary task had been left undone and he still had the job, why, they asked, was the pay reduced? These young Rembarrnga men and women were sceptical of David investing their very presence with such weighty value. They did not accept that a major element in the training was regular, punctual attendance, quite independent of what work needed to be done. Thus, as bureaucratic order and financial responsibility were enforced, other forms of irrationality became apparent.

David was aware that his denigrating humour was at odds with official rhetoric and with his own employment specifications. He confined his true opinions to exchanges with his peers in the evenings at home, in an atmosphere of glee at abandoning political correctness, in the same space where drinking exploits, dangerous driving and other irresponsibilities can be joked about. Though not enunciated in public, Rembarrnga people were aware of his opprobrium. There is now a hidden double standard at work, because the form of racism which used to occupy the public arena of policy has, it is claimed, been eliminated. With formal equality in place, David's views were legitimated as his private opinion about other people. But though an employee of the people he denigrates, he also had access to, and influence over, their personal daily lives. This is an example of the privatisation of racism which is protected by the right of every individual to hold any belief or opinion he or she wishes. A different code governs the circulation of this racism from that which applies to public expressions of the kind of racism which is universally condemned. This private racism occupies the privileged arena of personal belief which is there in the bar and at the barbecue and at the dinner party in Canberra or Arnhem Land. It is there also among long-serving public servants in Darwin where there are those who, in private, enjoy the use of terms such as 'coons' or 'gins' (Smith, pers. com.). Such crude racist terms were not used at Bulman, but racial hierarchy was present in the consciousness of whitefellas such as David who has returned to Darwin with his stories. The more immediate effect of David's private racial opinions was that the training program was undermined by the lack of personal trust and understanding between the white trainer and the black trainees, weakening the value of his classes in building, carpentry and gardening.

The state, in the form of ATSIC, now accords the Gulin Gulin Council the right to hire and fire its staff, but that process is by no means straight forward. While members of the Bulman community are able to interview job applicants, this process is largely an empty formality, not only because they find asking strangers personal questions virtually impossible, but because the terms of the contracts are not theirs to determine. ATSIC officers in Katherine make the appointments after consultation with the community. But ATSIC officers cannot protect the community from the contempt of those who are appointed on the strength of their skills and knowledge in ordinary domains of everyday life.[11] Different manners have become problematic with the development of close relations across a cultural barrier because of the systematic organisational and structural authority which underpins the work and thus the culture of whitefellas as they execute government policy.

When there is a convergence of manners and practices on the surface, always of course in one direction, the problem may be exacerbated rather than solved, for disparate meanings may be concealed and disguised. For instance, the appearance of conformity in dress does not mean that nakedness assumes the shameful or sexual dimension it has in societies where clothing has a more embedded place (Povinelli 1993:124ff). It is easy to assume that common practices have common meanings, and thus state officials can operate as if modernity already exists in the form of literacy, future orientation, financial awareness and knowledge of bureaucratic rules. Heather Dodd also assumed that once conformity to white practices was established, nothing other remained to disturb the new habits. She stated proudly: 'The Bulman people know. They worked certain hours; began at 8 am and worked until twelve. Two hours siesta and then 2 pm to 6 pm. Punctual and regular. So they should know . . . People have funny ideas about Aborigines.'

She meant that Aborigines are not locked into a set of ideas inherited from the past, but can adapt to modernity with ease. But to David, it was the Bulman people who had 'funny ideas' because they still expressed other, strange values. Like other whitefellas, he adopted a habitual, defensive stance, reasserting his own values, and perhaps his own failures, in relation to practices which appear as areas of Aboriginal deficiency, ignorance or some other lack, rather than as cultural differences.

While the sons and daughters of Larry and Dolly, and Chuckerduck and Florry, have positions on the Community Council and can demand that officials answer their questions in meetings, they see themselves as loyal to the law of their parents. Annette says: 'Before when we worked for whites, they told us what to do. Now they can work for us because we are on our own land since the Land Rights Act.' But the conditions of 'working for us' are ones determined by particular services and institutions, making the boundary between 'us' and 'them' less visible. There is impatience and frustration on both sides because, despite formal lines of authority, the racial frontier remains disorganised. When David complained that four of his trainees were still not turning up for work two weeks after the funeral of Annette's young sister who was killed at Bulman, Annette responded angrily, 'We don't just mourn for a couple of days like you mob. We might take two weeks or a *month* off. This is *our place* now.' She was aware of the disruption to David's plans and to the department which funded the training program which she helped put in place, and she felt burdened by the need, while herself in mourning, to explain the legitimacy of Rembarrnga mourning practices to these outsiders. She was at once defensive and angry in the face of these whitefellas' judgements.

Whitefellas who meet with Aboriginal people see them as being on the way to modernity. They have given up their spears and digging sticks, and as they can join us, it is assumed that they are trying to. Thus, at the same time as difference is beginning to be recognised and respected, Aborigines are being more firmly vested with the same aspirations as whitefellas. Signs of blackfellas' remaining differences are disturbing; a breach in what is taken for granted may be a glimpse of absolute difference. At any moment the gulf of incomprehension can yawn, and hysterical mockery threatens to erupt. Thus the mimetic process is never stable, but is constantly under suspicion and review.

Commerce and kinship

It is popularly believed that commerce and kinship are, in some way, incompatible. But on the other hand, practices and ideas associated with these two terms co-exist everywhere, especially among the rich and powerful. What is not recognised is the fact that commercial activity is imbued with an irrationality which is starkly apparent to those yet to be seduced by its charms. Early in his career, Elkin suggested making use of 'the native institution of gift exchange' to explain about raising cattle for the market: 'If those of us who are employers took the trouble to explain to our native employees that we have our "exchange routes" and exchanges of goods, we should have less reason for complaining that they do not take any interest in their work. Why should they . . . if they do not know its purpose . . . method . . . or results' (1934:12–13).

He made the common assumption that knowledge of the purpose, method and results of commerce would lead to its being embraced. Bureaucrats have struggled to inject an understanding of the profit motive, and the motive itself, into self-managed Aboriginal organisations which often seem oblivious of the rules of commerce. The experience of Rembarrnga ringers at Mainoru was of the demanding and dangerous work of mustering and branding stock, but not of the business enterprise of pastoralism. Commercial interaction entails specific orientations and forms of subjectivity which are just common-sense among whitefellas. For instance, buying and selling are accompanied by close attention to specific prices and by a suspicious orientation: *caveat emptor*. Other commercial activities, such as accounting for moneys spent, investing capital and accruing interest, require a calculative orientation and a valorising of money in ways that are inimical to Rembarrnga as to the Aborigines of Darwin whose transactions Sansom (1988) delineates with such skill. Rather than arguing that such subjectivities are quite absent or always resisted by Rembarrnga, it would be more accurate to say that they learn or reject them through experience. Unlike the peasants among whom Taussig (1980) found a series of mythic and symbolic responses which associated capitalist enterprises with the devil's work, Rembarrnga experiences with capitalism and the money economy have been brief and contradictory. But, while not sharing the western notion, fuelled as much by economic theory as by a crude socio-biology, that all human beings are basically greedy and selfish, they have learned that some whitefellas cheat. Those who have been sold dud cars in Katherine soon learn a necessary suspicion.

When Rex Campion was manager of Gulperan in 1980 he did not hesitate to telephone the abattoirs and arrange to sell a load of cattle directly when the community was short of money. He was questioned about this action by DAA staff who were trying to protect him from making unwise, unprofitable sales. When told that he should first have gained permission, Rex was angry at the interference, saying the community had the right to sell its cattle. His wife Susan recalled their being hurt by the official solicitude and the assertion that they might have got a better price elsewhere. More recently, rules about sources of funds and budget constraints are difficult to understand and take seriously. When an annoyed official asked questions about money spent on beer at Weemol, Willy Martin assured him that the beer was bought with 'artefact money', not 'welfare money', wrongly assuming that the official's annoyance would be mollified (E460/37 85/133 Aug. 85).

The notion of resistance is too often associated with overt consciousness, intentionality and explicit, formal, political struggle. As discussed in the Introduction, resistance has a more passive meaning, such as that exhibited by a wall when leant on. This is a conservative resistance, a resistance to change or perhaps a protection of what exists. This kind of resistance is often misinterpreted as stubbornness or stupidity. It is not conservatism for tradition's sake, but a 'stubbornness' that enables a people to survive in conditions of oppression. The difference between conservative and more deliberate kinds of resistance is blurred, and in fact there are many tacit ways indigenous social processes can be seen as resisting cultural hegemony, ways which have little to do with a consciously political intentionality.

Retaining established everyday practices and the refusal, or perhaps the inability or unwillingness[12] to fetishise material goods in ways that would interrupt interpersonal relations, are not articulated strategies but are resistance nonetheless (Taussig 1980). While Rembarrnga have accepted some aspects of capitalist social relations, such as monetary payment for labour and goods, commercial principles have a limited place in intra-community social relations in Arnhem Land. It is not merely a lack of information at stake when people appear ignorant of commercial realities. In some cases the appropriate and necessary moral convictions and internalised principles for running a commercial enterprise are rejected as alien. Whitefellas' interest in wealth is understood to be different from Rembarrnga interest. Nelly speculated about why white people come to Rembarrnga country:

> It's because we're rich, up here we're rich. All different company, mining for manganese and diamond, they came up and ask us. We told them we don't want mining. We were born with bush tucker, we were born on the ground, we never wore clothes before, we don't know wireless, we don't know even know motor car, we just learning from you people. We don't want that mining (1982).

Hitler Katcherelli had a different view, seeing wealth as something Aborigines had not known how to take advantage of, though any value it might have was overridden by the necessity to guard the country/culture from harm:

> Blackfella has got more land, more money than whitefella, but whitefellas know about that mining. Whitefellas find that money. We don't know and we don't worry about that money. We worry about culture. We've got to have sacredness, and can't allow white man to come through because dreaming is inside, underground. You never know when the mining can kill it inside. The family watching might spear that man [who gives permission for mining]. We know there's money there but we can't touch it. We've got this heavy thing called culture. Nobody can touch it, no matter who it is (1991).

Smiler Martin worried that 'some people go slack and allow that mining', and emphasised two principles which must be adhered to if mining was to go ahead. One is that everyone involved must be consulted and unless everyone agrees there should be no mining. Second, if the sacred areas could be avoided, then the mining could be agreed to. To ensure this avoidance there must be knowledgable elders present with the surveyors and the bulldozers. Smiler has given much thought to these problems. He has been told the government is short of money, and suggested that, if mining were allowed, some of the money should be given back to the government.

The use of money as a universal, inert means of regulating exchange is sometimes wildly misinterpreted, revealing that commercial principles are neither logical nor self-evident. Stories of this nescience abound; when a shopkeeper admitted that the wholesaler had already been paid for the goods in the store with a cheque from the community account, a community member angrily demanded to know why the Aboriginal people had to pay for their groceries again (Thiele 1982:44). When another community was being told of their debt to the bank, someone suggested they write a cheque to pay it off. These could be seen as an example of that 'innocence in the realm of capital' (Srivastava 1996:120) which we encountered in Willy Martin's wish for a take-away stall on a bush road (Chapter 8). Or they might be samples of blackfellas' humour at the expense of whitefellas who are seen to worry inordinately about money. Blackfellas are having to take up such worries as commerce inexorably makes its mark at Bulman, as it did in the Gulperan years, and continues with local tourist operations and joint venture mining agreements.

Those socialised into the underlying logic of a capitalist economy seldom perceive its counter-intuitive and illogical aspects. It was difficult to explain to Chuckerduck the vicissitudes of the national and international market which led to the closure of the Katherine abattoir, and which determine beef prices and royalty payments. Further, Rembarrnga perceive the valuing of physical labour above ongoing responsibility for the law, ceremony or knowledge, or for keeping the camp in order, as irrational. The 'irrational' Rembarrnga view is supported by their observation that the rewards people receive for their work do not appear to be based on the value of the work or what it produces, but on performative skill and character acting, despite all the assertions of whitefellas. The government's accounting makes no sense to Nelly. When her pension was reduced because Tex was being paid a wage for running a small saddlery business and training others in his skills, Nelly asked me, 'Why does the government take my money to pay Tex?' These few examples of the opacity and illogic in the cultural domain of money could be multiplied many times. On the other hand there is another kind of logic in the Rembarrnga view that if the boss is a friend he will pay you more rather than less for your labour, just as the large price that a friend will pay for one's artefacts is a matter of pride; the status of friend or putative relative is confirmed by their generosity with money. This contradicts whitefella's tacit rules for nepotistic relations where a friend or relation is meant to charge 'mates rates'. Thus the managers of projects who try to enforce strict accountability are seen as expressing enmity rather than responsibility.

Women's centres, which were established in the 1980s in Aboriginal communities, were also supposed to engage in commercial activities. Imported practices and concepts about profitability and gender roles drove them forward. At Bulman the old manager's elevated residence was redesigned as a women's centre and renamed Chupalara. It was asserted that 'The women wish to prepare mainly traditional foods involving cost of bullets and fuel' (E460/37 85/133 1986). In an astonishing leap of the imagination, a government official calculated that the centre's budget of $3000 would generate an income of $5040 in 1988, $20 160 in 1989 and $69 660 in 1992 from the sale of take away meals, artefacts, clothes and vegetables (ibid.). This projection reflects enthusiasm for commerce, a tenuous grasp of its nature and the willingness to deceive with rhetorical flourishes in order to gain funding for a fashionable project. The centre was to provide a place for women to gather and be taught certain arts associated with houses, housekeeping, cooking, cleaning and caring for children. These lessons are seen as necessary because houses are 'not part of their traditions'. A public servant was seconded from Katherine to run Chupalara for a year and, according to a glowing report in January 1989, the venture was already on the way to becoming a permanent success (ibid.).

Mimicry of the language of enthusiasm for commercial enterprise and for independence can mislead the officials into accepting that the knowledge, intention and underlying orientation reflect their own. Nelly remained enthusiastic about the centre and demonstrated a command of the language in which the logic and beauty of commerce is expressed, but her grasp of the principles of government funding and profitability have a mythic dimension which differs greatly from the myths perpetrated by the bureaucrats.[13] She said:

> First we set it up with all the women chucking in $20 and we bought the food and make money with that. I made $7000 in three months from cooking outside, when contractor was still building up this place. I went into the black. I got a shock that I got $7000 and DAA and ADC got a shock too. Then DAA were really interested and they chucked a lot of money to us and DEET was running it. Well it was on top then . . . We are employed by DEET at the moment. But in two or three months we will go on our own . . . I brought this up to make lively station you know for these young people to work. When they come back from Kormilda they've got to come up and work at the women's centre and make money to go back to Kormilda or anywhere (recorded 1989).

When Nelly took over Chupalara in 1990, she established some different practices. Strict accounting for small amounts of money between close kin ceased, and pockets often substituted for the till. The irrational practice of refusing to provide the food one had prepared for a hungry child or indeed an adult, merely because they did not have a particular coin, was abandoned. Leftover food was often given away, a practice which substituted for the rules about keeping food hot or frozen for particular lengths of time.

The operation of the women's centre had again changed when I visited in 1995. Four Rembarrnga women, who had learned as children to make damper and bread, and do so regularly in camp ovens on open fires, spent a whole morning being taught to bake scones in the electric oven under the inexpert tutelage of a young white woman, Cathy, who confessed to having no liking for the domestic arts. She had the job because her boyfriend worked in the Council office, another example of the racialisation of knowledge. Her scone making was strained and elaborate with use of a recipe book and careful measuring of ingredients. Only a few small scones were produced. Scone making may be of little consequence in itself, but it neatly typifies the way skills and knowledge already in place are over-ridden in minute and multiple ways, and community members are assumed to know nothing of value.[14] Under a training scheme at the women's centre, eight women worked daily to provide lunches for school children as well as anyone who wanted to buy them. Cathy and the head teacher instituted new practices to avoid what Cathy called 'chaos' when mothers and children had come up to the women's centre at midday and 'milled around' in the rooms. Now the children were lined up at the school and their names marked off a list as each was given a packet of sandwiches. This allowed for both the amount consumed and the payment to be controlled and order to reign. No space or time was left over for other manners.

The dilemmas of such employees as Cathy can be acute. She enjoyed her job and liked the young women she worked with, but she confided to me, somewhat shamefaced, that she had serious difficulties in relation to hygiene and to domestic violence. The sight of her dish cloth being used as a handkerchief was something she could not stomach, but she was unable to mention this to the woman concerned, let alone reprimand her. Unlike the Mainoru days, the interactions across the racial boundaries are supposed to be based on fundamental equality, and that supposition would be breached by instructions about personal hygiene. Cathy asked my advice, and I tossed up between informing her of Mary Douglas's work on pollution, discussing the history of the germ theory of disease or discoursing on cultural relativism. I told her that Bulman cloths were not confined to one purpose but were discarded or washed frequently and further, some whitefella's habits, such as carefully wrapping snot in handkerchiefs which are placed in pockets to be used again and again, appear repellent to blackfellas. Cathy also got into trouble about time-sheets. Having defended her practices by appealing to the rules which were outside her control, she then allowed one woman leave without docking her pay for fear the husband would not allow his wife to return to her job. Then she worried about creating a precedent and encouraging more absences.

Working for or towards viable enterprises entails more than a cerebral understanding of commerce. There is the need to accept the authority of things above people, the principle of possessive individualism above fulfilling duty to kin, and the value of being 'economical' above desire. We saw the pressures to adopt such practices in Annette's description of Mrs Dodd's lessons about not wasting food. Many younger people now take pleasure in possessions such as clothes and taped music, and have acquired desires that were alien to their parents. There is a complex play of desire and distaste, of loyalty and betrayal in relation to older traditions, being lived out at Bulman and elsewhere in Aboriginal Australia.

A WHOLE WAY OF STRUGGLE[15]

Like Chuckerduck in 1975, Tex in 1995 worried that the young people would not sit and listen to the old people. And Annette, like many before her, worries that the children do not speak language (Rembarrnga), and are not knowledgeable about specific traditions. Such concerns are the overt signs of conscious desire to resist or limit assimilation, and are endemic in Aboriginal communities. There is, however, a wealth of distinct but less visible and unnamed social practices which resist change but go unremarked. These practices and habitual orientations, which I have stressed as one field where race relations are being played out, are subtly and systematically affected by outside forces bearing on the community. On the other hand, much has been protected by being deliberately hidden under the cloak of alienation. Everyday social life at Bulman appears to be dominated by the cycle of the working day, the school day and mealtimes, but beneath the surface powerful shapes of other resilient social forms move to other rhythms.

Keeping culture

The notion that the Bulman people are faced with a choice between two worlds is only true in the weak sense that there are competing values and laws stemming from two different traditions which command various loyalties among different individuals in the community.[16] I have shown how rival understandings of the world constantly compete for legitimacy, but the competition is played out in specific events; that is, the competition is between particular practices, judgements and priorities. Dolly's affirmation: 'I believe in that old man' (Chapter 1) contained a recognition that 'that old man' does not command everyone's faith. When Dorothy repeats a phrase from her previous employer that 'children should eat more tucker', she is affirming a form of knowledge which is at odds with the autonomy of Rembarrnga children. Though Rembarrnga are not hostile to modernity, modernity seems hostile to them, and certain forms of knowledge, such as the divining of who was responsible for a death, are habitually concealed.[17] These are *rival* understandings of moral and pragmatic orientations, and the revealing and concealing of them in various circumstances have become part of everyday life.

The innocent terminology of the English language represents a threat to social forms. There is no diminution of the implacable force of standardised language, so *mununga* constantly ignore and over-ride Aboriginal kinship practices, confident in their knowledge of the distinction between a sister and a cousin, and of the meaning of 'aunt' and 'uncle'. But the English terminology works in terms of the nuclear family, differentiating father, mother, brother and sister from other nuclear families. It lacks a whole series of distinctions which are crucial to Aboriginal kinship categories.[18] It also emphasises some distinctions, such as age and gender, which are less significant in Rembarrnga terminology.

Practices adopted by Aboriginal people which serve to ease such awkward incompatibilities include the use of English names which do not bear the sense of secrecy or the weight of meaning that Rembarrnga names have. Rembarrnga people's sense of self has come to be mediated partly through the English language, including names, and great pleasure is taken in finding new names for babies. Also there is, in some cases, an erosion of meaning attached to certain kinship rules. Avoidance practices, such as brother–sister avoidance, and the avoidance of the names of deceased people, are now brought into operation according to circumstances. Some people easily switch from blackfella to *mununga* conversational conventions, but over time this means a loss of the intensity and emotional power of the Rembarrnga rules.[19] For instance, while old Larry's sense of discomfort led to him carefully positioning himself out of the way of his sister Florry when they travelled in the same vehicle in 1975, some young Rembarrnga people no longer evince that emotional response when speaking with or being near their real or classificatory siblings, who are sometimes called 'poison cousins'. As in all social traditions, each generation experiences the world differently and thus the subjective significance of certain cultural elements changes over time. But not quickly or completely enough according to the manager of Gulin Gulin Council. He complained that after he had hurried to Weemol to pick people up to come to work, 'they all get in, then someone comes up and they all get out again'. Someone explained to him 'poison cousins', and he had to wait impatiently while they stood there deciding how to overcome the problem. The internalised anxieties of the nation's white representative about the proper ordering of time came into play when he was brought up against this difference, and his job as well as his place in history made him confident that the delay in starting work was a more dangerous threat to social order than the non-observance of an avoidance relationship.

While these incompatibilities on the cultural frontier continue to produce inequality, the greater significance and legitimacy now accorded to certain explicit forms of Aboriginal culture have encouraged their bold assertion in some contexts. The increasing room for the expression of black tradition within white institutions was evident after the death of the Yolngu Member for Arnhem in the Territory Parliament, when the building was smoked in accordance with the practices of his constituents. The rights recognised in the land rights, native title and Aboriginal heritage legislation have given a strength to the assertion of other forms of Aboriginal culture (plates 25, 26). The annual Barunga Festival, the making and marketing of paintings and artefacts, and the quotation from Nelly Camfoo about Aboriginal stockwomen which is featured at the popular tourist venue at Nitmiluk, Katherine Gorge, all indicate a new legitimacy for a certain aspect of Aboriginal practice. But in the main these expressions are symbols at the margins, set aside from the 'steam-roller of progress' and able to flourish only when they interrupt nothing more important.

The cultural future

Anthropologists Strehlow and later Stanner agreed with Aboriginal elders that young Aboriginal men were not worthy of their trust (Stanner 1979:91; Strehlow 1947). Strehlow saw himself as a more worthy recipient and conserver of that knowledge. Older Rembarrnga people of a generation later express a general anxiety about the ability of the young to uphold the law. The sense that the old body of law and knowledge is under threat is evident in many impassioned statements such as Peter Lee's:

> We've got to hold up culture. If you leave it now, no good. That's you and me [our] grandma, granddad, nephew, early days. You and me have got to hold it, not forget it. Not be slack. You and me together, white and black.
>
> You've got to know your own business. Young fella got to learn that culture now. He can go back drink beer, but he thinks about culture too. He can sit down at school, still think about culture (1989).

This is a Kriol expression of the desire to keep alive the culture of parents and grandparents; that is, the knowledge passed on orally and through ceremony and practices of all kinds. The vulnerability of this oral–aural tradition is not perceived as due to the presence of schooling or beer. Peter Lee asserted a new state of being, level with white people, saying, 'We got own station now, whole lot. Same as white people now, we all level now. 50–50.' Peter is here using whitefella's knowledge to proclaim blackfella's legitimacy, with equality and cultural pluralism the basis of a plan for the future. He took great pleasure in emulating social forms of behaviour which are considered good manners among whitefellas. One day at Beswick, after taping a conversation, Peter asked if I would have a drink with him and his friends. We sat on the benches in the 'canteen' and talked and sipped our beer in a manner which was not at all usual in that environment. When a drunk man lurched up to me and asked for money, Peter was mortified. His disappointment and sense of shame were palpable. Thus the revived urgency in the desire to hold on to the law is not a form of nostalgic yearning for a past which will exclude European law and practice, but is driven by a sense of the failure of life under the rule of *mununga* law, and the present distress apparent in young people: 'Too many young boys gone. They just drink in the bush, killing themselves. All that trouble. We can turn some around, make them good men. Put them in job' (Peter Lee 1989).

There is considerable social distress evident on the larger government stations, with high levels of alcohol use and violence, and at Bulman such things regularly disrupt and disturb everyday life. While many community members neither drink nor fight, and see the community as a normal, functioning social world, others are conscious that the community is troubled, not only by such palpable conflicts but also by less tangible problems such as a sense of shame and a lack of conviction and direction. Forms of violence have arisen here that are totally alien to the white people who staff the community. Cathy was troubled about how to respond when one of the Bulman women was repeatedly beaten by her husband. The attempts of others to assist this young woman were invisible to Cathy, and she was particularly shocked at the apparent lack of condemnation from community members whose reaction to interpersonal violence was different from hers.

Bandicoot also worried about the lack of loyalty to tradition, but expressed doubt about the efficacy of teaching young people who would not listen: 'All this mob here too all these young fellows and some old people they get slack now. They are still lost now, too much drinking. Big mob of young boys at ceremony time, they don't listen. If we still look after them, try to teach them, keep talking to them, I think they might take notice, I don't know' (1991).

But for Hitler Katcherelli, anxiety about the law is understood in the context of continuing demands from whites:

> I don't follow white man. We've got to stay separate from white man and have our own ceremony separate in our own country. We can have it right way and teach the young people and women to do right things. They've got to follow our colour. White people change all the rules and we can't know what's going on. Not like blackfella, we don't change. We learn from our father, uncle and all that and we saw it with our own eye. We can understand white men's law; English, work, read and write and all that. White men can't follow our law, can't understand what we mean (1982).

Hitler is asserting the superiority of blackfella law which is being threatened by the vain attempts to follow the white man's law which is unstable and unreliable. He is identifying the failure of attempts to make *mununga* law work for Aboriginal people.

Stanner perceptively observed that: 'The unconscious, unfocussed, but intense racialism of Australians is *unnoticed*' (1979:93, emphasis added). This may no longer be quite true, and it should also be said that it was always noticed by Aborigines, though it may not be so named. Stanner was perhaps the most insightful commentator on the conditions of Aboriginality in the middle part of this century, yet he made no link between his observation of this 'intense racialism' and the assertion that 'after initiation, an Aboriginal youth responds but poorly to other possible worlds open to him' (1979:99). Young people are of course aware of exciting and competing possibilities outside

Bulman, but few want to permanently enter a whitefella world which is full of pain and shame. There are few ways in which to be black and also to be fully connected to the modern world outside. Hunting and gathering are major forms of employment, and while they entail much effort and pleasure, and provide valued nourishment, they lead to no dialogue with the rest of the world. The production of artefacts and bark paintings for marketing is a flourishing and significant industry in some communities, though at Bulman there are only a few basket makers. Participation in this art market has its own pitfalls (Michaels 1990). The only paid work available at Bulman is associated with the provision of services to the community. Thus young people are not being incorporated into the wider society but remain encased in unique political and economic conditions where ordinary bureaucratic practices reproduce their inability to manage themselves.

In another vein, the sense of inadequacy, of not measuring up, of being out of kilter, can be taken and celebrated as that idiosyncrasy which confers autonomy from the norm, the freedom to remake oneself, and this can include also the tragic recognition of a freedom to fall. Strehlow's harsh judgement of 'the younger "spivs" and lesser minds' (Rowley, 1972a:244) failed to recognise that being a 'spiv' may represent a deliberate dicing with cultural death. Similar bold assertions of an alternative identity are evident in relation to drinking sprees at Bulman and to the marathon card games which command the interest of many residents and which whitefellas alternately tolerate with amusement or view with various degrees of alarm or overt disapproval. These formerly forbidden pleasures have come to be practised openly. The discontinuities of personal experience involved cannot be captured in the language of cultural change and transformation. Further, the extent to which individuals are transformed is limited. Rather, people grow into a cultural domain with experience of different material, social and racial relationships. Shared concepts and emotional understandings of country have shifted somewhat. Those born at different times are subjected to different forms of subordination, which bring changes in cultural consciousness, and new ways of protecting and asserting the social self and avoiding the eroding experiences of humiliation and anger.

For young people at Bulman there is a world of painful ambivalence towards the identity of their parents, their history and thus themselves. Frightening 'bush blackfellas' can be mimicked in a game (plate 8). A more painful ambivalence was apparent in the agitation of a young man, Les Murphy, when he was describing the film

The Gods Must be Crazy. The African bushmen portrayed in that film, he said in aggressive tones, 'were really stupid'. Like his 'myall' forebears they did not even know what a Coke bottle was, and his sense of anger and embarrassment on their behalf was striking. Some young men refuse to participate in ceremonial dancing, and have been known to speak of it as 'blackfella rubbish'. Such powerful internalisation of the mores of the world outside Bulman does not signify a wholesale rejection of Rembarrnga traditions but rather a transference of conflict between competing cultural domains to the subjectivities of individuals.

Nelly commented on the ironies of being forced to vote for representatives in ATSIC and in Parliament:

> Ceremony, that's what we do. We don't vote for anyone. That election coming up. What that election for? We don't like election; that belongs to you mob. Whitefella might say: 'You too late now, you've got to come in my law.' If he says that, I've got to say: 'You can't change my mind; you've got your own mind, I've got my own mind. My own brains can tell me what to do.' My brains tell me which way I've got to go. I will vote but I'll never win. That's your law, we just vote, we don't get anything out of it. I can vote for that bloke, but maybe I vote for a bad man to bring war to Arnhem Land.
>
> I vote because I'm in *mununga* country now. I'm speaking *mununga* English now. If I don't vote, poor old lubra me, I get a summons letter, and I'm fined fifty dollar or whatever they call it. And if I don't pay I go to jail; that's your rule. So I have to vote while I'm here wearing your clothes and talking your English and smoking your tobacco, eating your sugar and tea, and talking in your tape recorder. It's not a blackfella thing that one. When we do election, we vote for all the *mununga* in Canberra.
>
> We silly I reckon, our way. But we've got to vote because we've got that police law. We're citizens now. We've got police all around the blackfella, but one in the middle there, our culture. We can't ever change our culture. You see? (1993).

Nelly accepts that aspects of her life are being shaped by *mununga* ways but is not fooled into thinking that, because Aboriginal people vote, they exercise power. The Aboriginalisation policy is a deceptive facade, for the dilemma that Nelly spells out faces all Rembarrnga and will not be dissolved by offering more Aboriginal people positions of authority.

It is tempting to argue that the stifling of initiative and the passivity brought about by the state's close surveillance in the past and present has created a social pathology at Bulman, and perhaps this is part of the truth. While many individuals seem healthy, humorous and happy, there are many organisational and institutional aspects of the community which lurch from one crisis to another, which seem subject to individual's whims or self-interest, and from which many members of the community are alienated. But there are aspects of the community that function well alongside the irresistible pleasures of the ubiquitous card games and the intermittent drinking sprees. Endless conflicts over the adoption of what the state considers proper bureaucratic practice seem destined to be played out as modernity is installed and resisted. Were it possible for the Bulman people to insist on systematic negotiation about the operation of the state's institutions, perhaps the alienation and internal conflict at Bulman could be overcome.

Conclusion

Palimpsest Processes

Palimpsest: manuscript . . . carrying a text erased or partially erased underneath an apparently additional text. The underlying text is said to be 'in palimpsest' . . .
—The New Encyclopaedia Britannica, *15th edition, volume 9*

It remains to explore some more general conclusions and ways of thinking about contemporary colonial and race relations in the light of this narrative. These ideas fall into three sections. I first discuss hybridity and develop the palimpsest metaphor, and then consider the continuing meaning and significance of race in an attempt to retrieve it from its status as a demonic or populist category, and reinstate it as an important and even positive form of social differentiation. The third section is a final plea for legitimising amateur, experiential knowledges of otherness, of difference, of blackfellas and whitefellas.

Metaphor: hybridity and palimpsest

I said in the introduction:

> Thus we can imagine Rembarrnga country as a space where the text, the images, the meaning of the space had to be covered over with other texts, images and meanings . . .
> Those being overwritten find that their images and texts, their

> relationships with their place, begin to merge with the imported ones . . .
> The new surfaces are moulded to what was already there . . . there is oil
> and water involved here; in some places the new surface will never 'take'.

The language used to elucidate vast social processes is laden with
metaphor, and one could trace the history of anthropology and popular
representations of Aborigines through the waxing and waning of a
series of metaphoric representations of the relationship between 'Us'
and 'Other'. 'Smoothing the dying pillow', once a popular phrase
spoken in sympathy, is now used with the heavy irony of those
embarrassed by their forebears, those who 'settled' Australia. 'Assimilation' can now be referred to contemptuously, as though it was only
an outdated government policy rather than the cultural process of
making similar, which characterises much intercultural experience.
Perhaps 'self-determination' was an ideal rather than a metaphor, but
whatever it was it is fast being forgotten, or remembered only with
sorrow or a cynical resignation. The current 'reconciliation' policy
means many different things, and nothing at all to the Bulman mob.
On the national stage it is subordinated to the divisive politics of the
late 1990s. The metaphor of hybridity is now gleefully employed in
critiques of colonial representations because it so thoroughly under-
mines the separation and essentialising of cultural domains.

The notion of hybridity may be a useful way of speaking about
the shifts and melding of cultural forms in these supposedly post-
colonial times and I do not deny that life at Bulman could be described
as thoroughly hybrid, replete with inbetween and undecidable categories. There is a sense of hybridity in Nelly's proclamation, 'I can go
blackfella way or whitefella way', because both these 'ways' are part
of her own identity. Social identities at Bulman are composed from
being stockmen and school kids as well as from being *dua* or *yirritja*;
all have common experience of those things claimed by whites as
theirs. But the term 'hybrid' carries other meanings that are relevant
here. While once a precise biological term, 'hybridity' lost its innocence when imported through the racialisation of human genes into
the domain of the social. Hybrids have often been deemed mongrels[1]
and hybrid cultural forms are not universally celebrated. If Aborigines
have a different form of English, a different manner of schooling, a
different kind of town, these are deemed inferior and attract sanctions
and tutelary plans.

These judgements rely on a pervasive racial binarism. Things—that
is, the materials and symbols of culture—belong either to 'us' or to

'them'. If they belong to 'us' then 'our' authority over these things remains. 'We' know modernity and claim ownership of it. However Aborigines have been socialised in both arenas and 'the forced antithesis of those domains is something their very being is evidence against' (Collmann nd:28). Yet the reality and force of the antithesis is evident in everyday life. There is no easy amalgamation of the experiences of being stockmen and being lawmen, as is evident for instance when people who usually speak English or Kriol when sober often speak Rembarrnga when drunk.[2] Pride is taken in being blackfella at one time and being whitefella at another. But shame can also attach to both in particular times and places, because the different cultural codes are vehemently despised or lauded according to circumstance. Aborigines recognise that they inhabit a social world in which whites judge them to be wanting. Primary socialisation occurs in a world of cultural tensions where the emotional valencies of the signs of culture are specific and sensitive, and the palimpsest repeatedly offers the cloak and peace of invisibility.

The metaphor of hybridity, whatever Homi Bhabha means by it,[3] stresses the choices and intentions of those who can take advantage of the messing up of racial and cultural categories and too easily bypasses the varied experiences of those who remain hidden on the margins. This theorising does not refer to the everyday, ongoing struggles, which are part of the always incomplete colonial project. The celebration of difference that is evident in notions of multiculturalism and hybridity has been experienced by the majority of Aborigines as a convergence towards *mununga* practices. Aboriginal people are forced constantly to make choices in the context of seemingly arbitrary changes in policy and personnel. If this is hybridity, its coerciveness is apparent in the problematising of identities which can no longer be unreflective. The confusion about social identity is the source of the longing for oneness, the romanticisation of an authentic, original, cultural form. In fact, it is difference itself which is reified in public and popular discourse as given, immutable, racial.

I introduced the palimpsest metaphor to draw attention to the active layering of cultural meanings in the material and habitual world of the everyday. It highlights the process by which the salience of those social forms which are enacted by one segment of society, continually obscure and contort the meanings generated among subordinate populations. What is hidden or undisclosed can remain powerful, although what is smothered may be dying unseen. At the same time, the palimpsest suggests that an active concealing and revealing of indigenous forms is used in the struggle for legitimacy and against shame, and can point to the way new shades of meaning can be attached to old indigenous and racial practices. Thus the palimpsest refers both to the hidden and to the process of hiding and exposing, as reflections and resonances from the indigenous and colonial past come to mean different things in the present. It also refers to the complexities of micropolitics, where the skins of blackfellas resist the penetration of whitefella meanings even as their minds embrace modernity. The palimpsest is a series of processes only some of which are visible on the surface. Other, older images and meanings lie underneath the membrane of modernity, ready to re-emerge, restored and realigned.

Social categories: race and culture

Culture is commonly thought of as an expressive, voluntaristic realm; 'cultural' difference ought to be celebrated. More embedded and recalcitrant differences are discomforting. Race cannot be named as a source of difference as race is an error to be expunged (Cowlishaw & Morris 1997). Yet a profoundly racialised set of ideas and practices surround Aboriginality and Aborigines. The ideas are racial in the sense that the characteristics which define traditional Aborigines are seen as embedded in the group, as belonging to the past and as inferiorising burdens. Kinship and clan structures, ceremonial practices, languages and complex attachments to land are associated with illiteracy, blackness and primitivity, none of which can be named or dealt with because to do so would imply the legitimation of racial difference which is thought to entail racial inequality. But there is a sense in which these impediments to modernity are also conceived of as cultural, to be recognised in limited ways, but neutralised, side-stepped or overcome in relation to programs for advancement. It was the newfound rendering of culture as malleable that allowed the self-determination era to proceed with such enthusiasm and confidence in its anti-racist mission.

How can the present so readily 'know' and 'abhor' the racism of the past? In the 1950s and again in the 1970s the state tried to expunge the official language of a previous racist regime in a truly remarkable series of discursive erasures. The righteous language of assimilation, introduced in the 1950s with education and training to lift Aborigines into a state of equality, suddenly appeared tainted with the taste of 'welfare' as the language of community autonomy began to be employed in the 1970s. Each stage seemed wonderfully non-racist in comparison with its predecessor, and there was, with each new policy, relief and a sense of liberation from the burden of dominating the Natives, the Wards, the Aborigines, and now the indigenous people who are instructed that they are now self-determining. With each change the preceding regime was denounced for its backwardness. But the preceding regimes were never really displaced; their practitioners were mainly retained and their practices were clothed in a new public rhetoric. The history of trying to abolish native culture is still present in the contemporary wish to reinstate it.

The inability or refusal of progressive state officials to deal with stark contrasts in practice, belief and social structuring is part of an anti-racism which turns out to be racist because it fears what might turn out to be 'racial', that is, ineradicable difference in the actual people it faces. Instead of recognising what are deemed racial differences, this anti-racism celebrates more superficial cultural expressions which can be learned about and mimicked, or read and displayed, in ways that assert tolerance and also offer the stimulation of difference without disturbance. Racial discrimination is abhorred and rejected as immoral and, with formal equality in place, no racial problem need be recognised except for isolated unfortunate incidents caused by aberrant remnants of the racially prejudiced.

This work has shown that, for all the popular and unpopular acceptance of otherness, difference and multiculturalism, the state and the nation have severe and unadmitted problems with other cultural practices and social institutions. The historical trajectory towards an imagined unified modernity still underlies attempts to recognise and celebrate cultural differences. Differences that make whole communities of people awkward and troublesome to institutions and public propriety are not so welcome. I am arguing that the place where Aborigines are remains a space of difference, but one where robust 'racial' difference is being inexorably squeezed out while a malleable, tractable kind of 'cultural' difference is encouraged. Thus the notion of culture as deployed by the state operates as a veneer under which people are being moulded into new harmonious forms. The surface difference can remain, its visibility giving the appearance of variety and hybridity, so long as nothing more recalcitrant and embedded interrupts the modernising thrust of the state's policies and the nation's blind trajectory.

Unlike some of the settlers in remote areas, the colonial state feared the threat to established authority posed by radical difference. They attempted to make over what was there, rather than enter a dialogue with difference that may not, after all, have posed a threat. The same process is evident today when Aborigines are depicted as inhabiting spaces bereft of the pleasures, desires and meanings of social life and emptied of the community's history and memories. This occurs when the 'third world conditions' of 'our Aboriginal people' in the outback are exposed, as in 1994 when the then Federal Minister for Health, Graham Richardson, visited Bulman, and was widely reported as feeling shock and dismay at the living conditions he saw there. Designed to highlight certain constructions of social disadvantage, the media images also represent Aborigines as pathetic suffering refugees who need help to take advantage of the modernised world we have installed in their country. Even the land claims process may force Aboriginal groups to represent themselves as mendicant, as when a group 'had to be established as a needy subject' (Sansom 1985:83).

This racialised social domain has the effect of transforming the voice of self-determination into a parody of the mendicant, with eternal cries for relief from suffering, more equality and proper respect. The parodic quality stems from its separation from any grounding in the complex and varied experiences of being Aboriginal. The cries emerge through the filter of public discourse, political argumentation, policy formation and journalistic reportage of various disputes, none of which recognise their own anchorage in the past. While racial categories are as real to Aborigines as they are to non-Aboriginal people, Aborigines were not privy to the foundation narratives of evolution and the myths of imperialism. They were not the constructors of the set of racially given, stereotypical barriers to common human forms of interaction, communication and cooperation which accompanied white settlement of the continent and continued throughout its colonial history. However, Aboriginal political actors have to use the race they were given as the anchor for their claims to specific rights as indigenous people. And race has come to structure the relationships among Aboriginal people themselves as the state continues to police the restructured racial categories.

Colonial authority has reproduced itself in new and ever more modern and progressive guises, and has tried to divest itself of the stigma of colonial rule. In Bhabha's words, 'its discriminatory identifications no longer have their authoritative reference to this culture's cannibalism or that people's perfidity' (1985:156); that is, to what could be called the 'bad habits of the primitive'. One reason is that, even in the remotest regions, old Aboriginal men no longer marry several young girls; bodies are clothed; everyone speaks some form of English; if people don't live in houses, at least they have come to want them. Another reason is that respect for cultural difference is now required, which means that certain exotic signs attract exaggerated enthusiasm or formal recognition. Yet, at the same time that racial and cultural hierarchy is denied, it is ever present, continuously reconstructed by the very presence and authority of whitefellas. This has been illustrated, not through differences in cosmology or epistemology, but as experienced more directly in the mundane and material characteristics of a dynamic lived social domain, and through the habitual and largely unconscious practices which express social identities in embodied action and interaction.[4]

The fear of racial categories which pervades the domain of social sciences and indeed of white liberal urbanity is often enunciated as a fear of fixity. Yet, as is clear from this book, race changes. That is, the conceptual and imaginative space inhabited by racial categories alters over time. It is not a particular theory of genetic or cultural inheritance which fuels racial hatred; any 'touch of the tarbrush', any claim to specificity, is sufficient for those who want 'the Aborigines' to be a target for racial hostility. Skin colour, like clothing, stance and eating habits, is a cultural matter. White and black skins have all-pervading cultural meanings and implications. I am arguing that it is not necessary to carefully exclude biology from consideration in order to avoid racial discrimination, but rather to render it in its proper place—as biology. The fear of speaking about black, brown or white skin, about particular hair or eyes, implies a fear that physical differences really are causes of racial inequality. Certain cultural practices are feared for the same reason. But silences about real differences enable political and economic inequality to be naturalised. It is a liberal discourse nervous of its own complicity which refuses to name racial categories, fearing racial terms, not because they are fixed, but because they are imbued with implications of racial hierarchy and white supremacy.

I have attempted to bring into view aspects of race relations which are seldom rendered into representations in social science. Studies on the cultural or racial frontier are beset with problems stemming from the difficulty of bringing a cool analytic gaze into an arena where our own scholarly identities are at risk and our political judgements cannot be hidden. Arguments that colonial power has been homogenised and that the active and positive responses to the colonial process must be recognised (e.g. Thomas 1994) have relied on art and texts to make their case. But only some elements of race relations are ever represented in mainstream art, and even fewer emerge into the public domain. Neither the vastly various guises of white power nor the contours of colonial destructiveness are available for such analysis. It is the hopeful, the brave and the complicit who will make such representations while other experiences remain unrepresented. This book is, in a sense, in the genealogy of those recounting the tragic colonial tale, but it also seeks to make explicit the process of bad faith where the colonising state continually displaces and reconstitutes its moral authority, both despite and because of its moral failures.

Apart from representations in theatres and art galleries, the discursive concept 'Aboriginal culture' contains few substantial images or realistic conceptions, but rather a plethora of phantoms and stereotypes. There are few popular characterisations of Aboriginal modes of sociality, styles of speech or humour, or of practices in relation, for instance, to privacy or authority, let alone knowledge of kinship and religious beliefs and practices. Until recently, only certain stigmatising characteristics and typifications occupied this space and were the object of public hostility and comment as well as liberal defensiveness.[5] On the national stage, Aboriginal leaders who recognise liberal goodwill, and who deploy the legal and social language of political debate, are celebrated with immense enthusiasm, gratitude and relief.

While these leaders may flatter or berate whitefellas, there are voices from the outback with other things to say. Nelly contrasted the selfish interests of mining companies in the country with her more innocent concerns:

All of us, we lived forty thousand years when we used to walk over pretty stone, with lead or diamond or all that. *Mununga* calls it lead or diamond or silver-lead and he knows there's money in there. But we, we used to find that stone, and we still know where that stone is. That stone, snake been makim, big kangaroo been makim, goanna been makim. Like we say, that been make out of our own body, our culture. And we still saying that, and we'll never lose it. Mining people wanting to come up and dig all that, but us lot, we going to lose our life. We going to die. If other people don't kill us we will get sick from that stone and die.

They say that mining can make a person come rich. Only the mining boss himself is rich. But mining is ruining our place. If that mining is in a ceremony area, that's our body they are busting up. They are digging our body and grinding it up in that machine and hurting our feelings. All that stone with the dots, that's our culture. That's the snake's *guna*. I'm snake dreaming too, and the mining makes us mob sick. *Mununga* does not understand that because *mununga* says that's money. He makes himself rich and he can't give anything to others, to blackfellas. Some of them will go fifty-fifty with the *mununga* (1993).[6]

At the same time that Nelly is hoisting whites on their own petard by commenting on their moral failures, she is using for her purposes the knowledge of time and of Aboriginality which is produced and socially affirmed by those whites. We can see here how people's self-knowledge comes to be mediated through constructions they have adopted from elsewhere. Nelly's voice also attests to the ambiguity and opacity of contemporary Aboriginal culture.

The opacity of culture

I said in the introduction:

> All representations of the world are partial, flawed, subjective and creative, and they are in competition. Representations which gain legitimacy do so not simply on grounds of an objective measurable kind of accuracy; rather they satisfy a query, touch a chord, support a structure or a dissatisfaction, or fulfil some other combination of functions.

This is a very different view of knowledge from that on which an earlier ethnographic enterprise was founded. Culture was assumed to be wholly observable and knowable, available to the sensitive, intelligent gaze of the western anthropologist in the form of behaviour and belief which could be rendered in English and understood by those who managed the colonised. The epistemology which rendered cultures as wholly knowable, and people as exemplars of their race or their culture, also led state officials to study a little anthropology before engaging more confidently in the modernising project. While anthropologists have been attacked for the flaws in their rendering of other peoples' cultures as timeless and archaic, they have in recent years been their own most effective critics. Yet they have not entirely divested themselves of the sense of the superior authority of anthropological renderings which is implied in the classic forms of ethnographic research and which is being bolstered by the use of anthropological knowledge of Aboriginal peoples in the courts (Dyck 1985). I want to argue for a recognition of the limits of such knowledge, and for an acknowledgment of the indeterminacy and opacity of culture for several reasons.

First there is the fact that there was an interdependence between the state's knowledge and its nescience concerning indigenous people. That is, while the colonial state is commonly depicted as intent on compiling systematic knowledge of the colonised (Said 1985a), this work has demonstrated that governing practices depended on a profound and determined refusal to know or engage with that otherness with which they were dealing. The paradox is that the production of the colonised 'as a fixed reality which is at once an "other" and yet entirely knowable and visible' (Bhabha 1983:23) depended on the lack of familiarity with the existential domain of those being governed. While a good deal of codifying took place, in the formal sense of recording information which was often inaccurate, such as lists of names and tribal affiliation, and more recently, collecting statistics on various forms of deprivation, the only systematic recognition, observation and recording of Aboriginal social life was by anthropologists and popular writers of outback tales. However, by authorising anthropological research, colonial authorities authorised themselves to manage Aborigines. That is, anthropological knowledge operates, as do other forms of scientific expertise, to authorise those who exercise power. Their experts can understand on their behalf and so the nation can legitimately encompass domains of difference.

Second, what was denied in Australia as in other colonies was that Indigenous people could represent a challenge to the West by demonstrating the possibility of a fundamentally different sort of society, with a radically different epistemology and ontology. The state's interest in the indigenous domain of difference was only in order to rule humanely. It could not afford to recognise the radical otherness which lay before it. Such a recognition could have threatened its own self-confidence and interrupted the process of domestication of the land and its inhabitants. Had these others been allowed to occupy the same linear time (Fabian 1983), the West would have no past to declare itself ahead of. We would have been forced to compare ourselves morally with these others rather than consider ourselves in the lead in the human race.

A third element is the confidence in the ability to know, to get to the bottom of everything, to classify, understand and explain, which is a general characteristic of the western intellectual scientific tradition.[7] Scientific, systematic western knowledge is seen as innocently enlightening and those who know are either politically neutral or else part of an inevitable and liberating thrust of modernity. But what is experienced as 'culture' resists comprehensive explanation and documentation, always retaining mystery and complexity which cannot be captured or exhaustively described. To recognise the limited knowability of a cultural universe is to destabilise the authority of ethnographic knowledge and render its authority problematic. My argument is not that differently acculturated people cannot understand one another, but that such understanding is obstructed by the hierarchy of knowledge which constructs one kind of people as the authority on the being of others. Neither the analysis of social processes nor the understanding of other human beings depends on the assertion of this wider authority.

The discipline of anthropology, which provided a compendium of authoritative accounts of other cultures, is treated sometimes with disrespect and sometimes with reverence, depending on the social context. For example, in Australia, the public comment on claims to sacred sites has led to anthropologists being subjected to contemptuous and derisive commentary on the one hand and lauded as experts on the other.[8] Anthropologists are sometimes seen as providing a magical key to exotic cultural experience. Since the Australian state's recognition, first of land rights and then of native title, anthropologists have been offered what Sansom (1985:73) calls an 'anthropological concession', allowing them ownership of the knowledge of Aboriginal ownership of land. The way this knowledge is deployed has the potential to constrict and confine the expression of Aboriginality by reasserting traditionalism and limiting Aboriginal culture to what are deemed authentic forms, thus further dispossessing many Aborigines who are deemed inauthentic and delegitimising the modernity of those deemed authentic.

While other domains, whether deemed primitive, oriental or marginal are difficult for the West to know because of their 'difference', white culture is difficult to know because of its familiarity. Its real opacity is disguised as normality and common sense. By emphasising the opacity of culture in general we can draw attention to the contours of our own. The understanding achievable by certain emissaries of the state and whitefellas in general is obstructed by particular kinds of 'information' packed in their western cultural baggage. The mediated knowledge which supposedly stems from racially specific experts implies an objectified cultural domain of Aboriginality which can only be approached through an arcane archive. It is elements and dregs garnered from that archive which informs the whitefellas at Bulman. This is not an attack on the intellectual work of recording and analysing social or cultural domains of any kind. But such studies cannot stand in for embodied interaction where knowledge of otherness is based on experiencing the specific rather than understanding the whole.

I am emphasising the opacity of culture as a strategy to reverse the arrogance which racially specific knowledge encourages. It is a means of resisting the reductionist tendencies of the rule of 'rationality', and parrying the avid and arrogant curiosity which pervades public interest in Aboriginality. It is intended to affirm the possibility of people understanding one another through experience rather than through typifications and generalisations. That is, by rejecting the notion that it is the white person's duty and right to know all about 'our Aborigines', and by delegitimising the tainted and outworn body of racial knowledge which has been inherited from the past, it might be possible to recognise that local Aborigines, with their particular historical experiences, are the final authorities on their own worlds. Meetings between whitefellas and blackfellas at Bulman could thus be realigned around the hitherto unexpressed priorities and political ambitions of Rembarrnga and other residents. The Gunabibi and Yabaduruwa, which are squeezed into the corners of Arnhem Land, could then re-emerge to enrich the country.

This book has turned out to be about the success of white colonists in establishing their hegemony. While much that Fanon wrote about the psychology and pathology of colonialism is echoed at Bulman, there is little evidence here of the decolonisation process he described (1967:27ff). Thus there is nothing 'post' about this colonial situation. Fanon asked 'What does a man want? What does a black man want?' I would have rather asked, 'What does a white person want?' An answer is encoded in earlier chapters, but I want to assert further that what would benefit the white men and women who work at the racial frontier is a casting off of old stale knowledge and entering into a dialogue with the black men and women with whom they interact. The past is a weighty barrier to setting up such a dialogue. Yet other possibilities are available both in personal relationships and in the land claims and joint commercial ventures where anthropologists, lawyers and miners are working with Aboriginal communities. These remain largely invisible in the public domain except as small, heavily edited and over valorised accounts of fantastic meetings between two cultures. While some claims are bringing into being new and deadly conflicts and rivalries, there are rare examples of negotiations and dialogues emerging which subvert the racial hierarchy and demonstrate that there are ever present possibilities for a creative and productive form of race relations in Australia.

Notes

INTRODUCTION

1 The primary identity asserted by nearly all of the people I knew well during my first period of field work was Rembarrnga, but they are not the only people whose words and views are recounted here. Annette Murray identified Ngalkbon, Rembarrnga, Djinank, Ngalakan, Jawoyn and Ritharrngu people at Mainoru, and these languages are all represented at Bulman today. Because the core group with which my original field work was conducted were Rembarrnga, and because most of the older people are multilingual and speak Rembarrnga though they may not primarily identify with that language, I use Rembarrnga to refer to the whole Aboriginal community at Mainoru and Bulman.

2 I have not capitalised the terms 'black' and 'white', 'blackfella' and 'whitefella' as these are generic descriptive designations rather than proper names. See also note 5 below and note 7 in Chapter one.

3 I use the term 'colonial' descriptively to refer to the whole system of relations between the imperial power and the colonised Indigenous people of Australia. This relationship did not end with Australia's independence from Britain, but continued as what has been called 'internal colonialism' (Beckett 1983).

4 In line with my attempt to evoke local colour I will use the vernacular term 'the Territory' where appropriate instead of 'the Northern Territory'.

5 I use the term 'whites' because it captures the objectification of difference

through skin, which was at the heart of the perceived facticity of race. While many authors prefer the term 'European', it is inaccurate when used to refer to what were mainly English people. The division I am referring to is between those representing modernity and the nation–state, and Aborigines who have been systematically excluded from these categories.

6 Even in the polyphonic contemporary world there is a price to pay for not fitting neatly into the proper academic canons, as I have found that many reviewers depend on clear signposts to direct theoretical traffic. Authors are expected to identify their arguments in abstract terms in the introduction. I hope that my work will be understood as systematic ethnographic interpretation which contests accepted representations and develops a series of arguments without anchorage in a single, global authorising theory to establish its validity.

7 'Ringer' is the local vernacular for a station hand, stockman or drover.

8 While linguists judge Kriol to be a language in its own right, its status and function, for instance in the educational institutions of the Northern Territory, are contentious and problematic. It is widely seen as a childish and limited language.

9 In Rembarrnga and related languages *dawero* is a form of organisation which can be glossed as patrilineal clan.

10 Physical anthropology and biological interest in evolution have not disappeared, for instance in the use of biological markers to trace prehistoric population movements. It is the search for a consistent basis for categorising contemporary human beings into discrete biological groups which has lost its legitimacy.

11 The critiques of Friedman (1997), Ahmad (1992) and others have exposed the weak political and conceptual underbelly of the flourishing literature on hybridity, the third world and indigeneity. These critiques also demonstrate the obstacles ready to trip up anyone who ventures into this realm of 'post-colonial' theorising, identity politics and even more into the arena I have boldly named 'race relations'. This discussion is developed in the conclusion.

12 This local specificity is a significant element in any understanding of the conditions of Aboriginal life throughout Australia's history. Not only were the early colonies and the later states subject to different laws and statutes, but local conditions varied greatly due to the virtual autonomy of managers of reserves, missions and government stations, local police and protectors and local white communities in their practices in relation to Aborigines.

13 This refers to state officials, reformers or members of a cosmopolitan elite from urban centres who are seen as meddling in the racial realities of the north.

14 I borrow the notion of aesthetics here from Eagleton where 'aesthetics

operates as a working replica of reason, a kind of cognitive under-labourer' (1990:16–17). This approach does not posit an opposition between emotions and reason, but is concerned with the emotional attractiveness and seductiveness of reason as well as the rationality and intellectual concerns that exist in all emotions. It is this combining of emotion and ideas that is central to the power of the aesthetic, and it is this which is evoked by our ideas and desires about the future and our place in its realisation.

CHAPTER 1—FIELDS OF ENQUIRY

1 Tidy Town competitions are held regularly all over rural Australia, funded and managed through the Keep Australia Beautiful Association, which relies on donations and volunteers.

2 The term 'settlement' was then used for these government-run institutions. In accord with 'post-colonial' practice, both are now towns run by their own councils, and the signposts at the turn-off identify them by restored Aboriginal names.

3 Dolly died in 1979. Though the names of deceased people are usually not spoken, at least for some years, Rembarrnga people have given permission for the names and the photographs of Dolly and others to be used in this book.

4 *Bunji* is a kin term, sometimes glossed as 'friend' or 'mate', which refers to individuals, male or female, who are in the same category as those eligible to be a spouse. Such relationships are characterised by a flirtatious warmth and humour.

5 *Ngaritjan* is one of the eight 'skin' categories of the subsection system which operates in parts of Arnhem Land as an alternative to kinship designations. Every member of the community is positioned in the network of real or putative kin connections. That is, everyone belongs to either the *dua* or *yirritja* moiety, and to one of the eight subsections, a position determined by one's parentage (Hiatt 1965; Maddock 1982) (figure 1).

6 'Mob' is an Australian vernacular term for any localised group of people. It presumably originated in the cattle industry and is especially common in Aboriginal English.

7 Despite its pejorative connotations in Australia, I use the word native without inverted commas to emphasise the normality of such a term in the world I am evoking. I refer to actual Rembarrnga people as such, and the general term 'Aborigines' for the wider category of indigenous Australians. Likewise the terms 'whitefellas', 'whites' and 'Europeans' are used for more or less general categories. I believe that the struggle over such language is significant, and I am trying to deconstruct a certain

common (non)sense which tries to combat racial inequality by expunging the notion and terminology of race, instead of analysing its social construction. The recent recognition of native title has led to a new acceptance of the term 'native'.

8   Such disjunction remains in the 1990s. Franca Tamisari, who conducted field work at Millingimbi in 1990–92 was ostracised by some of the resident white service providers for reasons which they did not explain, and in ways that echo my experiences in 1975. It seemed that close relations with Aboriginal residents, disloyalty to her own racial domain, and a sense that she was encouraging bad habits by sitting around and not 'working', were all part of the reasons. Some white service providers were, by contrast, interested in the Aboriginal people and open to learning from them (Tamisari, pers. com.).

9   At Malyanganuk I had my worst illness, with severe reactions to bites added to dysentery and the nearest water was the swampy billabong with leeches. When the mosquito dreaming tree was pointed out to me I bitterly and unanthropologically suggested that it should be cut down. Smiler gently pointed out that such an action would mean a far worse plague of mosquitos.

10 I had been research assistant to Dr Les Hiatt, Reader in Anthropology, University of Sydney. As a mature age student, I was not eligible for postgraduate scholarships and Dr Hiatt had managed to wrest the Norman Haire Fellowship out of the hands of the Medical Faculty to use it for its intended purpose; that is, research into human sexual behaviour, rather than into physiological questions. Thanks to his efforts I held that fellowship for three years.

11 My two children were left in the care of a friend in Sydney for three months in 1975 and four months in 1976, an insufficient period of time if I had wanted to complete research for a standard, holistic kind of ethnography. My thesis was to rely heavily on library research (Cowlishaw 1997a).

12 While police were feared, their only appearance at Bulman in 1975–76 was in bizarre circumstances which typify this cultural frontier. Alma Gibbs, loyal and long-term house worker at Mountain Valley, complained to the station manager that her nephew Eric from Bulman had taken the car she'd bought recently and had not returned it as promised. Alma could not drive. The manager reported the car stolen and the police set out from Katherine with an arrest warrant for Eric. They found that Eric had not reached Bulman before the car, one of the kind often sold by a certain dealer in Katherine to Aborigines from the bush, had broken down. He had walked miles before he got a lift to Bulman. The car remained abandoned on the road, and the police returned to Katherine.

13 The funeral itself was held at Bamyilli, and was a combination of Rembarrnga and Christian ritual (Cowlishaw 1983). The ceremonial

procession to the grave was followed by a sermon from the Christian Minister who preached passionately about the importance of death and Hell's punishments for heathens, a category which, by his definition, included most of the listeners. When the closed coffin was lowered into the earth someone whispered that maybe the body was not really in there, indicating an entrenched suspicion of whites, perhaps an echo from the days when Aboriginal corpses were stolen by men of science. Further funeral rites for Dorothy's husband occurred a few weeks later, but none of the whites recognised that these rites marked the re-burial of the bones of Dorothy's first husband who had died many years before.

14 Structural-functionalism, which had dominated Australian anthropology since Radcliffe-Brown's time, was being pervasively criticised in the 1970s but the major ethnographies still sought an understanding of Aboriginal social life through its institutions and structures which gave students little sense of living people despite attempts by some authors to show that individuals were not slaves to kinship and other rules.

15 Major sections of this entry have been deleted as this is a secret and sacred ceremony, not available for public knowledge.

16 For further discussion of religious ceremony and ritual in this region see Berndt (1951), Keen (1994), Maddock (1982), Tamisari (1998).

17 For more information on the skills of 'Aboriginal Men of High Degree', or 'medicine men' see Elkin (1977, f.p. 1945), Maddock (1982).

18 Parallel cousins are the offspring of same sex siblings, the children of two sisters or two brothers. Such children are classified as siblings. Readers who are unfamiliar with the meaning of these kin categories among Aborigines need only study any general anthropological text book to grasp the basic principles.

19 Promise marriages have become less common among Rembarrnga. A girl who was pressured to marry her promise husband in 1975 left him and was then allowed to 'choose' a husband. Parents and uncles say a girl and boy can choose, so long as they marry 'straight', that is from the correct kin category.

20 Silas Roberts recorded local amusement at a party of European's having supplies dropped in to them from a plane because they were ignorant of the wealth of food around the billabong where they were camped (Lockwood 1962:225–26). Despite the reliance on flour and other bought goods, many Rembarrnga view the country as a source of subsistence and thus have a sense of autonomy from dependence on money.

21 Once I went with some young men in the bull-catcher to get a 'killer'. We tore through the scrub after a buffalo and when it stopped and turned on us, Bruce shot it through the head at close range. It was still alive but he had no more bullets to finish it. Had it not been mortally wounded, we would have been in serious danger, and yet such lack of foresight was celebrated as a challenge and fillip to daily life. Careful

planning against the dangers of the bush by whitefellas seems, by comparison, over-anxious and petty.

22 Of course movement of workers is very much employer's, that is whitefella, business. A Ngalpon man came to Bulman for part of the funeral ceremony after being refused four days' leave by his boss; his head was subsequently shaved. Head shaving was traditionally a punishment for Aborigines on some pastoral stations and missions in the Territory (cf., Dewar 1992:12).

23 'Moiety' is the term anthropologists use for the classification of the world into two complementary and mutually exclusive domains; this classification permeates the whole universe and relates to both cosmology and cosmogony.

24 For a contemporary anthropological understanding of the principles of Aborigines' intricate but flexible system off relationship with country see Myers (1986a). For the specifics of kinship and country in Arnhem Land see Hiatt (1965), Keen (1994), Maddock (1982).

25 When Joanne had given birth to this baby at Bulman in 1975, Dolly, who was helping said, 'Don't call out, men over there playing cards', and Joanne had kept quiet through the birth. The baby Steve has since grown up healthy and strong.

26 The presence of a few lice was not viewed with horror because the skill of removing them was well developed and they were kept under control. A more extensive infestation indicated the victim was not well cared for and was considered disgusting. Increasingly chemical treatment has reduced both the lice and the grooming practices which their presence entailed. The disdainful white gaze has furthered this erasure.

CHAPTER 2—OPENING THE COUNTRY

1 I also found I had had a fleeting experience of Rembarrnga culture long before; the dancer Beth Dean had visited my country high school in New Zealand, and her performance of a variety of styles of 'ethnic dancing' had included an Aboriginal dance which she had learned from Nelly Camfoo at Mainoru. This thrilling performance of dramatic and expressive movements, and the glimpse of exotic and unimaginable people was immensely exciting to a teenage girl from a dairy farm in Awakaponga.

2 In this transcription of Minnie George's Kriol, I have retained as much of the original style and lexicon as possible while rendering it accessible to non-Kriol speakers. To avoid burdening the text with complex exegesis, I rely on the interest and attention of readers to seek the more complex meanings available (cf., Rhydwin 1996). For instance, the first line here emphasises '[H]im been bush', meaning 'it was bush'; that is,

there were no buildings then. In subsequent transcriptions I have trans-lated Kriol into standard English, as preferred by those I consulted, while trying to retain some of the rhythm and lexicon of Kriol.

3 This self-induced paranoia, generating extreme fantasies about the deadly threat from the bloodthirsty primitives, arose initially in NSW in the wake of unpredictable attacks on stock and stockmen. Morris shows that, in the 1830s when the Myall Creek massacre of a peaceful group of station dwelling Aborigines took place, there was no real threat of attack (1992:79–80).

4 'Pen-pusher: *colloq.* one who works with his pen, esp. a clerk, considered as menial or drudge' (Macquarie Dictionary). I use this term for the officials of the state whose pens were always busy trying to control the racial frontier.

5 People such as Xavier Herbert who continued to voice heresies on matters of race could find themselves held in public contempt, left with few supporters and even attacked in the street (McGrath 1987).

6 When the administration of the Northern Territory was transferred from South Australia to the Commonwealth in 1911, the first Administrator, Gilruth, set up his office in Darwin with a Chief Protector of Aborigines. The Chief Protector's position was subsequently the focus of a good deal of conflict centred on native affairs policy (Rowley 1972a:234–8). Along with Captain Cook, Gilruth has become a central figure in a number of Aborigines' mythic representations of white invasion (Rose 1984).

7 Many of the leases granted earlier had not been stocked or 'improved'. For example PL 821 was taken up in Rembarrnga country by John Costello from 1884 until it was cancelled in 1890 (Bauer 1964).

8 For further discussion of the conditions for Aborigines during World War Two, such as payment of wages and regular hours of work, proper housing and food, and the changed policies after the war, see Rowley (1972a) and Beckett (1988).

9 Farrar senior was first employed on Lake Nash station by John Costello whose biography, written by his son (Costello 1930), is aggressively contemptuous of Aborigines while indicating clearly the fearful threat he believed they posed to his family's pastoral endeavours.

10 'Lubra' is a term with a complex colonial history. Presumably originally taken from an Aboriginal language, it became a general term for an Aboriginal woman and accrued derogatory connotations.

11 Rowse gives a compelling and valuable analysis of the way 'Aboriginal insiders' became part of the station regime. He argues that black and white insiders 'enjoyed an accord that neither the critics with pens nor those with spears could share' (1988:82). While I concur with his assertion that urban critics have often misunderstood the cattle station communities, it seems quite misleading to take the 'convergence of white and black accounts', at face value.

12 These are 'skin' and kin terms, just three of dozens of terms which map the everyday discursive kinship universe.

13 Judy died in 1978.

14 I infer this from newspaper reports of the brothers and their families. His formal marriage to Judy seems not to have been reported. One brother took up another property and the third generation branched into the Darwin transport business.

15 Poddy-dodging refers to stealing poddys (calves)—or unbranded 'clean-skin' cattle—and branding them, a practice that was endemic in the outback cattle country of Australia.

16 A dogger is a man employed to catch dingoes and wild dogs on pastoral stations; they spend long periods travelling and camping in isolated areas.

CHAPTER 3—CIVILISING THE COUNTRY

1 This was Billy Farrar's first wife. The term 'half-caste', once widely used to describe people with both European and Aboriginal parents, is now considered a pejorative term, implying a fractional, inauthentic identity. This issue is dealt with in more detail in later chapters.

2 This is a reference to the practice of sorcery; to 'sing' someone is to cause their illness or death. Bandicoot's apparent acceptance that Boddington could have used sorcery against the Mainoru mob may imply that white men could have access to power located in the black man's domain, but it is rather a narrative device to enhance the drama.

3 The Native Affairs Branch of the Department of the Interior was established in 1934 replacing the Chief Protector and his designated Protectors of Aborigines. A Director of Native Affairs was appointed who became much more active after World War Two ended.

4 Peterson had replaced Boddington and Lena Ray remained a sleeping partner with a quarter share. By 1942 Farrar had gone and Jack McKay and Peterson bought Lena Ray's $\frac{1}{4}$ share for £500. In 1947 McKay bought Peterson's $\frac{3}{8}$ interest for £3000 and became sole holder of Pastoral Lease 157N and four grazing licences.

5 The Northern Territory was governed from South Australia until 1911 when the Commonwealth took over its administration.

6 The Ordinance of 1911 'included not only a "half-caste" child under 18, but a female "half-caste" not legally married to "a person who is substantially of European origin or descent and living with her husband" . . . The 1924 Ordinance . . . extended the definition to include "half-caste" males below the age of 21; it was extended again in 1927 to those males "whose age exceeds twenty-one years and who, in the opinion of the Chief Protector, is incapable of managing his own affairs

and is declared by the Chief Protector to be the subject of this Ordinance"' (McCorquodale 1985:28).

7 Many other reasons could be explored, such as the techniques of formal training and regimented practices, and the administration's constant complaint, still common today, that suitable staff were difficult to obtain.

8 Stanner saw the white settlers' material poverty as relevant in the case of the Daly River peanut farmers. He said, 'All of these men were hard on their natives, some brutally so, but perhaps not much more so than they were on themselves. They supposed their lives would be insupportable if they lost their physical dominance, and this may very well have been so. They and the Aborigines were mutually dependent, desperately so, and no love was lost in either side' (1960:73).

9 Such a view is supported by the fact that the Berndts were employed by the pastoralists Vesteys to assist them in enticing in to the station those Aborigines who remained outside, rather than to help them nurture and reproduce the community of those who had already come in (Berndt & Berndt 1987).

10 This story was related by Bandicoot Robinson (Bulman Oral History Series 4, 1995) and though plausible may be apocryphal. Tex (pers. com.) said that the Hood brothers got Billy Moore drunk and talked him into signing over the station to them. I was also told that Jack McKay had helped Billy Moore purchase the station.

11 I do not imply that the Rembarrnga people who came to the station were not hungry; after all everyone becomes hungry every day. I am arguing that they were not starving and would not have starved in Arnhem Land.

12 On one occasion when Aborigines' agency was recognised, it was at once forbidden. Patrol Officer Sweeney reported that some 'Arnhem Land natives' showed initiative and a 'growing sense of responsibility' in telling crocodile hunters to leave. He was told by the NAB to 'instruct the Aborigines not to take any direct action on trespassers but to advise the nearest missionary of the presence of any parties with as full a description as possible' (F1 52/493 1951). Initiative was apparently not to include telling white people what to do.

13 Lloyd Warner, the earliest field worker in Arnhem Land, spent eighteen months on the north coast in the 1920s and wrote a detailed ethnographic study entitled 'A Black Civilisation', which included a moving portrait of his friend Makarolla. Experience and training did not remove Warner from the world of fanciful predictions which relied on a standard view of other cultures as fixed in the past. In an interview at the end of his field work he was reported as saying, 'The Aboriginal is doomed to extinction. With the coming of whites his civilisation collapsed. [There is] no place where white rot cannot be found in black culture. The best

thing authorities can do is to expedite miscegenation . . . they are nearer whites than any other dark race' (NTTG 27 Nov. 1928).

14 Rowley observed that: 'Of the whole of the Australian frontier, the one area where there was a serious attempt to apply a colonial policy based in the law and on principle to the process of extending control, was Papua' (1972:147).

15 Perhaps it is necessary to point out that the notion of primitivity is problematic because it is not merely a description of a simple material technology of hunter–gatherers but carries implications of a generic simplicity and backwardness, counterposing this to sophistication and a higher rationality. This implicitly denies that modern humans are subject to impulses and emotions which are deemed primitive.

16 Later, patrol officers in PNG would often compare Aborigines unfavourably with Papua New Guineans who were seen as much more susceptible to modernisation and evolution (Lattas pers. com.).

17 Though some, such as Rowse, have repudiated the use of a Foucauldian analysis to understand the relationship between anthropology and the state, it seems to me that an 'intimate and mutually reinforcing relationship' (Rowse 1992:99) did exist between them, though a complex and indirect one.

CHAPTER 4—REFORMING THE PEOPLE

1 The Rembarrnga painter, Paddy Wainbarrnga, recognised the role of books in colonial power when he spoke of the exploits of Captain Cook in the film *Too Many Captain Cooks*. Captain Cook with his 'books' features as a culture hero and villain in mythic histories from many places (Smith, 1980; Rose, 1984).

2 In the 1990s, various pastoralists' and farmers' representative associations used similar strategies against the High Court decision in Mabo (native title) and in Wik (survival of native title on pastoral leases (Cowlishaw 1995b).

3 The barriers and limits to such regulations were made clear in Ronald and Catherine Berndt's study of pastoral stations in the 1950s (1987). In the 1970s further attempts were made to realise Aborigines' rights of access provided for in pastoral leases, but even today there are difficulties in enforcing the law in the outback.

4 This appears as a note in a sparse single box of C.D. Rowley's papers which are held at the Institute of Aboriginal and Torres Strait Islander Studies in Canberra.

5 The draft regulations from the 1947 conference provided for 'a cash wage of from 12/6d per week up to 1 pound for those with over three years experience . . . the draft was shuffled between Interior, the Attorney

General's Department and the Administration for two years' (Rowley 1972a:337).

6 Increasing anxiety and attention to townspeople, half-castes and what were called 'sophisticated natives' partly arose from the challenges to the racial categories which lawyers were taking to courts on behalf of their clients in the 1950s.

7 The trust fund monies became the subject of a vast array of bureaucratic discussions, memos, arguments, lists and accounts. One file was on the inheritance of monies from Aborigines who died, as the file stated, 'intestate'. The next-of-kin was decided in terms of the 'English system' and the worthiness of the beneficiary was determined by protectors and patrol officers (F1 54/821).

8 In response to Mrs Dodd's request for assistance to teach the adults at night, Harry Giese offered to fund such instruction, but nothing appears to have come of this suggestion.

9 While the bestowing of royal titles on Aborigines by whitefellas was common in some areas of Australia, and may have been attempted at some stage here, this is the only reference to the practice in this area that I have come across.

10 The apparent even-handedness entailed an inequity because the number in the 'natives quarters' far exceeded those in the 'homestead'.

11 Names are changed in response to deaths, as here when another woman called Mary had died so this Mary was renamed Dolly.

12 The names of people suffering from leprosy are expunged from archival records in an attempt to protect the individuals and their families from the shame which whites attribute to the disease. The secretiveness adopted by Aboriginal people has its source not in a sense of shame stemming from notions of pollution, but rather in the fear inculcated by the savage consequences that contracting the disease brought.

13 Genovese wants to confine the notion of paternalism to conditions where the master–servant system is considered the ideal form of social relations within the social system and its attendant hegemonic ideology (1974:661). Such relations characterised the slave regimes of the southern United States in the nineteenth century, and are, he argues, incompatible with bourgeois social relations.

14 McGrath (1987) and Rowse (1988) both argued that Aboriginal workers resisted proletarianisation, with the alienation and mobility it entailed, in favour of the established paternalistic system within which they had some control. Any such analysis must recognise the broader structural conditions under which such a preference was expressed, for instance as McGrath shows, there was seldom anywhere Aborigines could safely go if they left the station. See also Read & Read (1991). They had no independent rights and could be banished as 'troublesome natives' to a government station many miles from kin and country (F1 54/737).

CHAPTER 5—RACIAL INTIMACIES

1 Extensive cattle projects to the north of Bulman around the turn of the
   century had been abandoned, and Rembarrrnga country was subsequently
   protected from further European exploitation when the Arnhem Land
   Aboriginal Reserve was declared in 1931. But voluntarism is not a simple
   condition, especially when applied to a group of people; as material
   conditions change and new needs and desires are created, choices are
   shaped and limited and a series of contingencies established.

2 The constraints of language in this case force an equivalence upon
   practices that are fundamentally different. We have one term, 'marriage',
   to which anthropologists have added 'polygamy', which includes 'polygyny' and 'polyandry', but which retains meanings that are inappropriate
   to many institutions to which they are applied. For earlier anthropologists' views of Aboriginal practices in this area see Hiatt (1965),
   Maddock (1982), Warner (1937).

3 Again language can betray meaning. The term 'immorality' is a misleading reference to what Rembarrnga would see as creating disorder and
   conflict. The especially salient position held by sexuality in the sphere
   of European morals is not necessarily reflected among other peoples.

4 What anthropologists have called 'avoidance relationships' are common
   in many parts of Australia, though in different forms. For a discussion
   of some anthropologists' view of the practices in this area see Hiatt
   (1966), Meggit (1962), Cowlishaw (1980).

5 Specific struggles forced the national government into discussion with
   leaders in the 1960s, for instance in the cases of the Gurindji strike and
   the Yirrkala bark petition (Lippman 1994:35–7), but there was no system
   of political representation until the National Aboriginal Consultative
   Committee was established in 1973 (Weaver 1983).

6 In response to police intervention when a protesting young man was
   being forcibly taken to undergo initiation, the new Director of Welfare,
   Harry Giese, decreed that 'all male babies born of Aboriginal parents in
   hospital to be circumcised before their mother returns to her country'
   (F1 54/1013 1955). The initiation of young men was here placed within
   the realm of a primitive tradition that would be rendered obsolete by
   modern technology. Such autocratic over-riding of a domain of culture
   and meaning was easy for Giese, fired as he was by the fervent,
   progressive conviction that the natives must adopt rational modern
   practices. The fact that the young man resisted initiation was taken to
   mean that he concurred in this view.

7 Assimilation became the explicit policy of governments from the early 1940s
   and was welcomed as a positive policy both by anthropologists (Elkin, 1974,
   f.p.1938; Stanner 1979:205–6) and Aboriginal groups that had campaigned
   for relief from exclusion and legal discrimination. Contrary to many

interpretations, the stages of administrative policy display a remarkably stable underlying logic over time, an indication of the interdependence between government policy and other social forces.

8 The proto-anthropologist Baldwin Spencer may have instigated the policy of removing children in 1912, when, as Chief Protector, he recommended in that 'no half-caste children should be allowed to remain in any native camp' (HREOC 1997:132). He also foreshadowed contemporary arguments from 'sex workers' by recommending that 'using or detaining a female for immoral purposes should be classified as employment under the 1911 Aboriginal Ordinance' (cited in McGrath 1984:263). He presumably believed, as McGrath says, that this could bring such practices under some form of control, but the suggestion was deemed 'vicious in the extreme and strikes at the root of the great "White Australia" policy' (ibid.).

9 The widespread public demand in the 1950s and 1960s that Aboriginal women be protected from sexual exploitation, emanated largely from urban women's organisations. Such demands precluded the recognition of any expression of black women's desire, and legitimate inter-racial relationships. Most of the active anti-racist agenda wanted more protection, and also protested against the removal of children. The humanist concern to 'protect' Aborigines tended to operate as a facade for colonial paranoia about 'miscegenation' and could reinforce the oppressive effects of government surveillance.

10 Policies in relation to the future of Aborigines as a biological race varied across the colonies and states. The possibility of 'breeding out the colour' was promoted at one time (Jacobs 1986), but it was the existing population of 'half-castes' who were to intermarry with whites, while the 'full-bloods' would die out.

11 An example is the miner at Maranboy who had his licence to employ cancelled after several times being suspected of 'abducting' a woman and of 'associating with female Aborigines'. There was insufficient evidence to convict and anyway 'the girl may have been party to offence'. The police eventually found that the same girl had been involved each time and was what we would now call his *de facto* wife. This man was harassed for criminal and immoral acts on the basis of his loyalty and fidelity (F1 52/512 Oct. 1955).

12 This song by Ted Egan begins: 'They couldn't understand why the drover cried, As they buried The Drover's Boy, For the drover always seemed so hard to the men in his employ'.

13 Ted Egan (Egan 1997:94–96) spent a few days at Mainoru in 1958 and interpreted the relationships between whites and blacks as 'down to earth, real, superb'. He presents Jack McKay in typical Territory fashion as the rough diamond whose earthy, uninhibited language and sexual badinage were appreciated by the women. Egan's assertions that everyone had

access to all the goods in the house, that all swam naked, and that Jack McKay 'had balls like Paroo mailbags' which were 'a constant subject of discussion among the Aboriginal women', are a part of the continuing outback tradition of revelling in a certain type of rough humour which challenges the niceties of urban discourse. The embedded racial patronage is cloaked in the pleasure and humour of an exchange he records, in which Jack McKay jokes with a very old woman who is ill, 'Nothing wrong with you darling. All you need is a good fuck. I'll be down tonight.' This, Egan asserts, resulted in hilarity all round.

14 The Ordinance of 1918 gave the Director the power to issue permits to marry, but I found no records in the NT archives of applications being received and processed until the 1940s. Only about eight applications appear in the files between 1944 and 1948, more in 1948, and many more in the 1950s.

15 'Half-castes' and other 'part-coloured', who were normally deemed Aboriginal and came under the Ordinance, did not need special permission to marry others deemed Aboriginal, though a number of letters from such people requesting permission indicates considerable confusion. Those who applied for exemption from the Ordinance also had to run the gamut of official scrutiny.

16 'That [or this] old man' is a common affectionate term for husband and has little to do with age.

17 Several Rembarrnga women were without children and a number of different explanations were proffered. Nelly's comment that she was a 'dry cow' is an example of the refusal to separate the language of other living things from terminology used for humans (Cowlishaw 1981). There have been accusations that Aboriginal women were sterilised against their will in similar circumstances. I have found no documentary evidence of the practice, but the idea is quite plausible.

18 When public protest arose the NAB stated that the number of Aboriginal children removed in the Territory were as follows: 1911–1952 incl: 263 males; 320 females. Total 583. An average of 14 per year. 1946–1951 incl: 45 males; 65 females. Total 110. An average of 18.3 per year. (F1 52/250 Feb. 1952). These figures do not include unofficial and temporary removals. This file does not indicate how the figures were compiled.

19 In the Territory towns, as in the southern states, Aboriginal children deemed neglected were also removed from their kin. Other children were also taken, apparently unofficially and often illegally. Christine Lindsay told me the story of her younger sister having been taken away by a white man when she was about nine years old. She was 'a little bit light colour, that man really liked her. He asked me and I said yes. Then they left her at that school in Alice Springs.' That is, Christine believes her sister was abandoned after having been taken by someone who 'liked her'. The sisters have been in touch lately. Such fragments of loss, sorrow

and hope lie close to the surface in many of the oral histories of the Bulman mob.

20 In 1995 the Federal Government authorised the Human Rights and Equal Opportunities Commission (HREOC) to enquire into the removal of Aboriginal children but the Commission was granted limited resources and was not able to hear all of those who wanted to appear before it. Nonetheless it produced a comprehensive report (1997) of the evidence of 535 people it did hear, and of hundreds more who made written submissions. It documented the pain and ongoing distress caused in many lives by the various state laws in different parts of Australia.

21 Some of these assumptions were reproduced by such eminent people as the Minister for Aboriginal Affairs in 1996 after the report of the 'stolen children' was tabled (SMH 7 Oct. 1996). He and others stated that Aboriginal children had benefited from the experience, particularly those who had achieved public acclaim as activists. Rembarrnga people envy the circumstances of some of their 'half-caste' relations who are well educated and employed, but rather than condoning the cruelty and pain caused by the removals, they see themselves as having been wrongly deprived of the same educational opportunities.

22 The responses of Aborigines to light-coloured children was not fixed or invariable, and would have been responsive to local race relations. I have found nothing but a sense of sorrow, loss and anger concerning those children forcibly taken.

23 One ex-Mainoru white stockman told me with a smirk that homosexuality was common among Aborigines, an opinion based on his observation that stockmen often shared swags and 'not just for the warmth'. This lonely repressed Irishman may have been confused by the extent and ease of physical intimacy among close relations of the same sex, which may indeed have a sexual component. In my experience homosexual relationships are unknown or at least unrecognised in Arnhem Land.

24 Presumably Jimmy Dodd assisted Larry in a time of illness.

CHAPTER 6—A NEW MODERNISM

1 He claimed that 'Aboriginal education is largely directed towards developing attitudes and personal habits as well as knowledge that will make the Aborigines socially acceptable to Europeans. When that stage has been reached there will no longer be need for special schools' (F1 56/1331, 1955).

2 The printer who had agreed to publish the list found that changes were still being made when the list was long overdue and, after several years of continuing conflict and complaint, he sued the DNA for payment of

his firm's account. Despite the five years taken to complete the Register of Wards, many of the Mainoru residents were not entered on it and remained unlisted until it became obsolete in 1964.

3 Albert Namitjira had gained widespread recognition as an accomplished artist. His distinctive water colour landscapes had popular appeal and commanded good prices.

4 This Australia-wide department, formed when a 1967 referendum gave the Commonwealth government jurisdiction over Aboriginal affairs, replaced the Territory's Welfare Branch which had previously administered them.

5 In the past the AWU in Darwin had perceived its constituency as only white workers; Aborigines were unfair competition, though other unions in Australia had struggled against racial inequality.

6 The minimum weekly wage had been £2.8.3 for Aboriginal pastoral workers on top of their keep while the NT award for stockmen was £11.15.10 (Stevens 1984:19, 22). On government stations the weekly wage of £8.8.0 for an Aboriginal labourer was 54 per cent of the NT award, but only £2.0.0 was paid in cash. The rest was the cost of keeping the labourer, his wife and children on the settlement (Rowse 1998:173).

7 Counsel for the pastoralists told Rowley that he thought Vesteys would change to a 'progressive policy' and that they had listened to the argument for a 'real native labour' policy, in the interests of 'greater efficiency'. The real issue was what time the companies would have to adjust to the change (Rowley's papers).

8 The Commission observed that many Aboriginal workers were known as 'hose holders', who did simple tasks such as watering the garden to qualify for rations, and were not 'workers' in any real sense (CCAC, 1966:668). Their fate could not be the Commission's major concern.

9 The new era had begun to impinge on Jack McKay as is clear from a new and unfamiliar patrol officer's report that 'Jack McKay was waiting the result of the present "wages case" before increasing wages further', and that he planned to charge for meals and for accommodation. 'However, the station is not going to keep "manufacturing" jobs as it has done in the past; economics will also enter into the matter' (F941/0 64/256 1965).

10 A local stockman told me that one newcomer to the industry in the 1980s 'made his money by amalgamating and reducing management costs to almost zero using sixteen-year-old kids to manage a huge station. The cattle just run riot and he gets a mustering team to muster all the stations and then clear off and let the place go to rack and ruin' (1989).

11 One pastoralist boasted to me in 1975 that after he was required to pay equal wages he had applied for unemployment benefits on behalf of members of the 'blacks' camp' on his station and explained to them that the government was paying them to work for him.

12 One of the local whitefellas who was involved in these events, an outback stockman and drover whose responsibility in the past had been to cattle rather than men, was Paddy Cavanagh (see Chapter 3). He was reticent about his part in these events when I spoke to him in 1989, but asserted that he and Len Brodie had helped the people move to Bulman.

13 The 'difficulties' which the Gibb report deals with all concern barriers to Aboriginal assimilation; for instance they faced 'the task of developing an understanding of the relationship of work and monetary rewards' (1971:8) and would require 'special education to bridge the intellectual and attitudinal gaps between their present condition and that required for them to realise their potential in a great variety of fields of employment' (ibid.:22).

CHAPTER 7—BETRAYALS

1 Previously the state legislatures had responsibility for Aborigines; the Northern Territory has always been administered from Canberra as it was not a state.

2 The sensitivity surrounding the notion of selling ritual secrets or paraphernalia was evident in Elkin's anxiety after he was presented with a *rangga* at Mainoru (1961). Heather would only hint that the accusation about 'selling secrets' meant this man was paid for giving information to an anthropologist. Perhaps her perception was equivalent to that of Strehlow, whose sense of authority over the sacred life of Aranda stemmed from his belief that the young men were not worthy of their heritage (Strehlow 1947).

3 Peter Lee said, 'Afterwards we went to Mountain Valley. I was chucked out by another angry man a Yankee. Just loaded up all the kids, all the gear. Going now altogether. We wanted to go our own way now, get a place. Go back to our own country, Arnhem Land' (1989).

4 The change in policy direction began with changes at the top levels of the bureaucracy. Nugget Coombs (eminent economist) with Barry Dexter (public servant) and W.E.H. Stanner (anthropologist) ran this Council with a small team who developed policies based on the radically new notion that Aboriginal people could be given a say in the policies concerning their future. The NT administration (especially Giese) often pointed out that CAA (especially Coombs, Dexter and Charles Perkins) did not know anything about the pastoral/tribal population. Coombs made it his business to reverse this nescience by spending time in a number of Aboriginal communities in the centre and north of Australia.

5 Heather named the ten and claimed to know the causes of death: two genetic conditions; three alcohol related; two accidents; one pay-back;

one unspecified illness; one reaction to a drug treatment for another illness.

6 Since Heather died, the albums have been deposited in the NT Museum. While initially resentful, Nelly and others recognise that the photos are safe there and they have had copies made of many of the photos. However the obvious enthusiasm of the strangers at the museum to own and preserve their photos forever is somewhat puzzling.

7 Stories of travel always include detailed, extended and loving naming of places and the rhythm of travel, rest and subsistence, demonstrating the way memory is embedded in places. I have reluctantly omitted much of this detail in these transcriptions in order to concentrate on the historical narrative.

8 Years later the Director, Harry Giese, still believed that his programs had been wrongly terminated saying, 'I firmly believe that the way in which we were tackling the problem, the welfare, the education, the development, the self-reliance, the self-sufficiency, I believe that we were on the right track. There were some things that we might have qualified, but basically I believe that we had the support of the communities and particularly the leaders of the communities' (interview 1991).

9 Since 1970 there has been piecemeal and varied recognition of indigenous law and language. Heritage legislation and the recognition of land rights have occurred in some states. In 1977 the Law Reform Commission began an inquiry into the recognition of Aboriginal customary law, which reported in 1986. Now, part of Aboriginal law is recognised in Native Title legislation, and anthropologists have offered to mediate such knowledge (Sansom 1985). Two arenas where cultural expression have flourished are in the songs, literature and art produced by Aboriginal people, and in the recognition of land rights.

10 Gulperan Pastoral Co. was so named because, although the camp was at a place called Goinjimbi, that name was too difficult for use in radio telephone communication. There has been a re-emergence across the land of submerged place names, a re-affirmation of the meanings attached to Aboriginal places, and increased residence at outstations, all unequivocally positive consequences of the self-determination policies. Perhaps more significant is the requirement that visitors to Arnhem Land have a permit to travel, so that traditional owners authorise such visits and residents are informed of who is in the area and for what purpose.

CHAPTER 8—A VIABLE ENTERPRISE

1 A cattle enterprise at Ngukkur in the same period displayed many similar characteristics to Gulperan (Thiele 1982). Other publications which explore some aspects of these processes are Loveday 1982, 1985; Dyck 1985;

Altman 1987; Tonkinson and Howard 1990; Rowse 1993. Weaver (1985) analysed the problems of representivity were being grappled with at this time at a national level.

2 The Welfare Branch of the Commonwealth Department of Territories, presided over by Harry Giese since 1953, had been the enlightened descendant of the Native Affairs Branch which had administered the Aboriginal Ordinances, which in turn had been an advance on the earlier lack of policy.

3 One published account of this project identifies its failures and argues that recognising 'the Aboriginal decision making process' would overcome its problems. However this entails the assumption that the *Djungaii* would 'assess the spiritual compatibility of the brief [i.e. the cattle project] with the land' in the same way as a conservationist (Ledgar 1985). Another article rates the later buffalo farming a success (Roberts & Ledgar 1992), but subsequent events saw that project also collapse.

4 At this time community councils were being set up to run Aboriginal stations and some instigated the removal of their managers. I have been unable to clarify whether it was on the instigation of Beswick Council that Danny Watson ceased to manage Beswick.

5 I have paid scant attention to the matter of dissent among state officials. Arguments among whitefellas as to the better policies and about each other's inadequacies, especially as true believers in and knowers of the nature and needs of Aborigines, diverted them from acknowledging that they were silencing the Rembarrnga. Some of the state's employees who identified most fervently with Aboriginal interests were also the most critical of the government and other whitefellas (Sackett 1990; Stoler 1989).

6 After the Weemol town plan was abandoned, funding of $150 000 for three houses was eventually made available as part of the pastoral enterprise 'to ease the demand for housing in the area' (E460/51 74/2249 1975). When finally erected in 1977 they were badly built of poor materials and in the line of seepage of the septic tanks, which were wrongly built and had to be replaced. Such disasters were so common as to raise the possibility that projects were deliberately subverted. Later, the basis of funding was changed and Bulman became 'a community in its own right' (E460/64 76/25), which could be funded as a 'residential community' or a township, instead of an 'enterprise'.

7 Such practices were well-known locally and many accusations circulated. There were some prosecutions, but few convictions owing to the difficulty of proving fraud when the directors of companies were illiterate and innumerate. A local image of the Territory in the 1970s depicted the Aboriginal population as a huge sieve into which the government poured money and under which whitefellas congregated to collect the money that fell straight through.

8   In the 1970s von Sturmer considered that Aboriginal societies were in a state of crisis and his sketch of the conditions in the Alligator River region parallels some of the points made here (von Sturmer 1982). A more detailed analysis of these events can be found in Cowlishaw (1998).

9   These meetings increased in frequency over the years. By the 1980s a series of government departments and branches of departments were responsible for aspects of life at Bulman, and each department's representatives arrived for these meetings independently, causing a good deal of confusion and strain on those who were being pressured into attending.

10 An example is the suggestion that a written offer of shares in Gulperan Pastoral Company be sent 'to all localities where Aboriginals who have an affiliation with the Bulman area are known to reside'; that is, to largely illiterate and certainly not financially sophisticated communities who had no money anyway (E460 48/1972).

11 At an initial meeting about Gulperan a senior DAA official, new to the Territory, was so irritated by the advice of the old hands, one of whom was concerned to draw his attention to the fact that the community was requesting housing rather than a pastoral station, that he went into 'a closed session' without observers and visitors (Robert Smith, pers. com.). The rivalry among whitefellas to be the true friend of Aborigines, played out in the use of such a technique, would merit much more attention than I can give it.

12 These were a supportive neighbouring land-holder, a government agronomist and a Welfare division officer. Arguably their presence could have meant better liaison between the state and the Bulman community, and decisions that were more sensitive to local conditions and more responsive to the community needs.

13 It was assumed that Rembarrnga people shared the ordinary cultural capital of schooled whitefellas. For instance, a young Rembarrnga woman with two years of high school education was assumed to be able to run the store (E460 73/7229 1973). In fact many of the Europeans with considerably more schooling and more commercial experience were not competent at such tasks, though the lack of profitability of the Bulman store may be evidence of other less admirable skills.

14 The discourse authorised by scholarly work on welfare dependency and social disadvantage was another element in the state armoury. Theories of social dependency from right-wing American think tanks were being imported into Australia in the 1970s. Malcolm Fraser, whose government curtailed the funding for Gulperan and all other Aboriginal programs in 1975 pending review, admits to being deeply influenced by the work of that leading spokesperson for anti-welfare individualism, Ayn Rand. A conservative form of American anthropology and sociology blamed the poor for their own poverty, which stemmed from the lack of initiative systematised into a 'culture of poverty' fostered by welfare dependency

(Lewis 1966). This argument was used to redefine the relationship of the state to Aborigines who had to be self-motivating. The dependency which had been created by the state was now the problem to be cured by the state. Such theories circulate as a set of accepted diagnoses in public discussion of 'the Aboriginal problem', and 'Aboriginal health'.

15 Some anthropologists have argued that Aborigines deploy indigenous notions of mutual responsibility in relations with whites and governments, and try to reproduce relations of mutual responsibility, of 'caring for' or 'looking after' (Myers 1986a:35; Rowse 1989:21–22; von Sturmer 1982:99). The indigenous gloss which anthropologists put on such interactions can imply that Aborigines generally misperceive government intentions. Like the epithet 'Aboriginal time' this notion of 'looking after' is in danger of becoming another stereotype which positions Aborigines as people who misapprehend their obligations and the realities of the modern world.

16 As discussed earlier *Bunji* is a term used to refer to those male or female kin who are in the same subsection or 'skin' category as 'spouse', and with whom a warm and joking relationship is the norm. The 'skin', or subsection, refers to a system of categorisation which embraces the whole social universe in a kin-based network of relationships.

17 Von Sturmer speaks of the 'real consultation, the sheer grind and leg work necessary to establish the informed climate in which proper decisions can be made, the steady and systematic building up of knowledge of the protagonists, their inter-relationships, their stances, their goals, in order to understand not so much what is being said as what remains unsaid; the determination of conditions in which real decision making can occur locally (1982:88–89). A Yolngu man at Milingimbi speaking of white staff said, 'We've got to start from the beginning with each new one' (Franca Tamisari, pers. com.).

18 The common pattern, and values associated with distribution and exchange among Rembarrnga, cannot easily be translated into notions of investing capital, conserving value and profiting from sales (Povinelli 1993).

19 'Nephew' is a weak translation of the depth and significance of such a relationship. Florry and Chuckerduck were fully aware of the seriousness of Kenneth's transgression, but accusation and recrimination are not part of interpersonal relations here.

20 As Teresa Lea (pers. com.) has pointed out recently, there have now developed endless attempts at *consultation* by a bureaucracy which wracks its collective brains to improve its performance. She is in the process of analysing the cultural domain of the Aboriginal health bureaucracy in the late 1990s.

21 Sullivan recorded a case where the request that a modest pump be installed at a small outstation was countered by insistence that an

expensive large pump be requested. By the time it was installed the community had dispersed (1986). Such 'irrationality', in the sense of being counter to the proclaimed rationality of bureaucratic practice, is in fact commonplace and part of the confusion and tangle that is Aboriginal administration.

22 This is the text of Tex's letter:

We would like a grant from the ABTF. Our future for 73, 74

(1) We like a school as soon as possible this year. We would like Fencing Material to put up a Bullock Paddock 12 met square. To do that we would like a Dozer to clear lines all so a Tractor Post hole Digger and Post Drill Run off the Power from the Tractor.

(2) We would like 20 head of Broken horses so we could Muster and get some Cattle together in our Paddocks. Then we want (5) Boys to start work soon. Then we need more later on (4) Boys. When the wet starts we can run them back to Bamyilli settlement and only keep (2).

(3) We would like another Toyota also a Bull truck and we could use it to carry Rail Yard Post also lots of things around the station

(4) I would like to Run the Station for 2 or 3 years as long we find a man to run the Book work for me and Radio. I like to go Forward. The man who would be Book keeping would have a wife she can be the school teacher.

(5) [sic] My wife Nelly would like a little Dispensary so she can look after our sores and sore eyes She is capil [capable] enough to do it.

(6) we would like to Train our own Hygiene man or find one. That is our main start.

(7) we would like better houses

(8) we like a homestead at the Top Springs past the abortoirs where there's plenty of water.

(9) I would like to be Proud of Things and land that we owned.

(10) We would like the Lease and Brand for stocks and ear mark soon as Possible

(11) I would like to have a Pump to Boot up water to a 10,000 Gallon tank and all so a Licktricity so we could have lights. we would like to have it now we been waiting long time please help us.

T.J. Camfoo,
Director (E460 73/7229)

23 The man they requested was a DAA official and presumably could not or did not want to take up responsibility for Gulperan. They were careful not to criticise directly the man they were rejecting.

24 One manager sexually embarrassed and harassed women constantly, even in the presence of his wife, and this couple and another not only charged high prices but tried to run private retail businesses separately from the community store to make more money for themselves.

25 This manager had sent ten cartons of beer and a carton of scotch out to Bulman when Bruce Murray was manager (E460 75/25/2). Bruce was killed in a car accident in 1980 when he was under the influence of alcohol. Kevin Forbes died in 1995.

26 Rex Campion left the position after less than a year. He died of lung cancer in 1994.

CHAPTER 9—ENJOYING DEMOCRACY

1 Alma was only ever able to live at 'that place' Barapunta for brief periods as she suffered severe diabetes.

2 The pretensions of whitefellas are considered ludicrous rather than morally repugnant, but this needs to be seen against the background of a small-scale society where it is virtually impossible to sustain pretence and deception.

3 The changes cannot be subsumed under any single trajectory; there has been a resurgence of ceremonial activity and the government's heritage protection program has legitimised certain traditional forms of knowledge. All Bulman children have regularly attended primary school since 1980, though the level of literacy has varied with the skills of different staff. Voting for ATSIC councillors and in the Northern Territory and Commonwealth elections is routinely catered for. Besides the Gulperan scheme described above, various other programs have entailed visits from and interaction with many government officials.

4 ADC was formed to concentrate on development or what were called 'enterprises' in Aboriginal communities generally. But again the staff in the Katherine office lacked experience in business and none were trained accountants.

5 All Aboriginal people are entitled to register to elect the regional council of ATSIC.

6 There is constant political manoeuvring and struggle about these positions and appeals are made to rules stemming from both *mununga* and blackfella domains. Other Rembarrnga people who have been employed in skilled jobs include Nancy Murray and Annette Murray, both now fully qualified teachers. Trainee teachers' assistants include Joanne Forbes and Jill Curtis. Lorna Martin was the main health worker from 1982 to 1993, but when the new clinic was built and more staff employed, she retired. The difficulties of being a community health worker stem from having to learn and exert a foreign set of ideas and practices onto the intimate concerns of others. Especially with close kin, the complex relations of authority, avoidance, intimacy make this an arena of considerable danger.

7 On the national stage the elected body Aboriginal and Torres Strait Islanders Commission (ATSIC) was established. Other organisations

intended to serve Aboriginal needs such as the Land Councils, the Aboriginal Legal Service (ALS) and the Northern Territory's Sacred Sites Authority (later the Aboriginal Areas Protection Authority), incorporate Aboriginal people and interests into the state structures. The Northern Land Council (NLC), established in 1976 by the Commonwealth under the *Land Rights (Northern Territory) Act*, consists of a Council of traditional Aboriginal people, with a staff which was, initially, largely white. The public and virtually official hostility in the Territory to land rights in general and the NLC in particular meant that the organisation was characterised by defensive unity in the early years. There was no space for any critical consideration of how the NLC should best tackle the kinds of problems I am discussing here. Any breach of the united front was an invitation to hostile interests to pounce, and pounce they did, attempting to present the NLC as over-riding the varied wishes of its constituency. The potential of the NLC to develop an alternative discourse and a negotiating role was illustrated in a report on the economic options for Gulperan in 1985 which contained a rare recognition of 'inconsistencies between the pastoral operation and Aboriginal culture', such as restrictions on the use of hunting areas and the lack of availability of staff during ceremonies (E460/37 85/133 1985).

8 Eileen's cousins perceive her as now being in a fortunate position and argue that all Aboriginal people should have had the opportunities these 'stolen' children had. Annette said, 'All Aboriginal people were taken away—from their land.' The idea of monetary compensation for those that have materially benefited seems nonsensical to Rembarrnga people, though the taking of the children is seen as having been unforgivably cruel, especially towards the parents.

9 A common accusation made by whites was put to me that, 'a lot of the urban half-caste people are most racist towards the full-bloods. But you can't talk about that.' Since the post-Mabo attacks on 'political correctness', people can 'talk about that' and will pounce gleefully on perceived contradictions as people who were made racially ambiguous by changing legal, political and ideological conditions change their tactics and renegotiate their identities.

10 Some were retrenched station employees or refugees from some urban environment who were able to convince DAA of their knowledge of accountancy and interest in, or sympathy for, Aborigines.

11 In the early 1980s DAA held a conference on the subject of choosing staff for remote communities, and debated whether 'undesirables' could be screened out before being appointed or whether they develop on the job, and whether they should be forced to attend a course. One official worried about the manipulative power of the staff who might influence Aboriginal communities not to adhere to government policy and to undermine the authority of DAA. The process of Aboriginalisation made

this formulation of the problem redundant but the ability of communities to appoint and employ appropriate personnel remains fraught with difficulties.

12 Again the bias of the language must be negotiated, for to be 'unable' to fetishise goods has a very different moral implication from being 'unwilling'. Yet the inability may in fact entail a refusal to try, a refusal to deem oneself lacking because of the 'inability'. The presumed binarism of meaning has tricked us into an interpretative dilemma.

13 Likewise, Willy Martin's expression of pleasure in gaining independence from government funding echoed the standard discourse of the NLC. Referring to royalty monies he said, 'Now we don't need government— we have own money.' But the distribution of royalties is controlled by complex Commonwealth legislation and is managed and directed by the NLC bureaucracy. Willy had not only to adopt the language but to learn the operations involved in this form of self-determination.

14 In the realm of art and artefacts there is considerable respect for local knowledge, and workshops in printing and wax dying have had some success. Again this underscores western veneration for particular aspects of Aboriginal culture, particularly what in the west is seen as 'the arts' or high culture.

15 I take this phrase from Stephen Webster's work in New Zealand where, in contrast to the anthropological notion of culture as 'a whole way of life', he argues that, 'a culture is a people's whole way of struggle in the effort to regain control of [their] history' (1993:238).

16 For earlier discussions of the issue of what is widely known as 'two laws' see Maddock (1977), Williams (1987) and Austin-Broos (1996). These works seem to me to underestimate the sense of struggle and disturbance to the certainties of everyday life which are part of the hegemonic process of the introduced 'law'.

17 When I was at Mt Catt in 1997 Smiler wanted me to take him to Katherine to see a 'clever man' who would be travelling through from the west that day and who could diagnose the person responsible for the sudden death of his daughter two years before. Smiler said, 'They've got a way of doing it with the clothes.'

18 For example, the term 'cousin' in English refers to several different relationships: mother's, sister's and mother's brother's children as well as father's sister's and father's brother's children.

19 If a man has to address his sister he uses the term *biyangduyu'*, meaning 'rubbish', and my 'brother' old Billy Lukanawa followed the convention, calling to me, 'Hey Rubbish, give me twenty dollars. Or $3 or $2.' I was pleased to be recognised as a sister and, incidentally, chose the small price of $3 which he wanted for a stake in the card game. Annette expressed great pleasure in her uncle's public acceptance of me as a classificatory sister rather than as one of the whites who are hostile to

such avoidance practices. Here the inherited self-consciousness about Aboriginal lives and practices is reversed as both Annette and I take pleasure in the affirmation of meanings which had been muted by the scorn of past white regimes.

CONCLUSION: PALIMPSEST PROCESSES

1 A claim made publicly by the mayor of Whyalla in October 1996 about the offspring of 'racial' mixtures during the debate about the national origins of Australian immigrants.

2 Collmann argues that this is not a case of repressed pride in a black heritage emerging under the influence of alcohol, but rather that, where people experience 'acutely conflicting patterns of primary socialisation' a 'reserved self' develops which enables the 'social process which threatens to reduce them to nothing but the roles they play' to be negated (nd: 31, 23–29).

3 Bhabha uses hybridity, not simply to refer to the combining of different elements of cultures, but to discourse on the possibilities attached to in-between spaces created by hybridity and its power to subvert colonial representations through 'its mimicry, its mockery' (1994:115). The extensive critiques (e.g. Ahmad 1992; Werbner & Modood 1997) demonstrate at least that too much has been claimed for hybridity and at most that it is irrelevant to contemporary struggles of those deemed third world, hybrid or indigenous; that is, the majority of human kind. While a deconstruction of that segment of colonial thought which is located in western universities is being achieved, and this may have great significance in itself and in its effects, I would argue that there are revamped and new forms of racial segmentation, differentiation and hierarchy which are oblivious to such critiques and indeed are being legitimised on the basis that they do not partake of the older discourses and ideologies. This is not to deny that ambiguities and ambivalences of race relations and the complexity of meanings associated with representations of colonial relations have been elucidated by Fanon and Bhabha.

4 The most casual visitor to the Northern Territory is aware of the process of racialisation and the discourse it generates; it is an ordinary unremarked social background for those who are accustomed to it. The equivalent racialising processes in south-east Australia show some similar and some very different aspects (Cowlishaw 1988). Now that many Aboriginal people are state officials, the racial categories no longer conform to the structural domains of the state and the indigenous population. The criticism that the use of the racial categories is no longer appropriate, is based on a literal reading of these socially constructed domains. 'Aboriginal' and 'white' are discursive understandings of a relationship which is

constitutive of each; the discomfort which is generated on the racial frontier is evidence enough of the power of these constructions.

5 During the writing of this book there has been further amelioration of this condition with many Aboriginal authors publishing autobiographical accounts of their lives in vernacular terms which reveal something of the unique life worlds of Aboriginal people (Camfoo in press; Cummings 1990). There is also a literature about white experiences on the racial frontier emerging, both popular (Dingo 1997) and scholarly (Jackson 1995; Muecke 1997).

6 Other kinds of problems arise from the distribution of mining royalties as Nelly explained: 'And these mining people here, they only give to traditional owner. It's not fair. We all own that snake *guna* dreaming. That's everywhere. Coronation Hill, Jabiru, Pine Creek and Gove too and Groote Island, Cox river. We should all get the money. Whole lot of we Jungaii (1991).

7 Sartre claimed that none of man's diverse projects were wholly foreign to him: 'There is always some way to understand an idiot, a child, a primitive man or a foreigner if one has sufficient information' (1978:47), and he has been criticised for ignoring the way such imaginings consolidate the radical European humanist conscience at the same time as obliterating the history of its arrogance (Spivak 1991:155). I would argue that it is not the striving for understanding, or the confidence that it is possible which are faulty, but rather the implication, ironic in Sartre's work, that such understanding depends on 'sufficient information' rather than experience. This faith in the detached intellectual project needs to be subjected to a thorough critique given the kinds of complicity with global forces being exposed in recent works such as those of Werbner and Modood (1997) and Ahmad (1992).

8 For instance in relation to mining at Coronation Hill near Katherine and the Hindmarsh bridge dispute in South Australia (Bell 1998).

Bibliography

NEWSPAPERS

Northern Territory Times and Government Gazette (NTTG)
Northern Star
Sydney Morning Herald (SMH)

ARCHIVES

Northern Territory Archival Service (NTAS).
Welfare Board Annual Reports (WBAR) (in NTAS) 225.
Land and Survey Department (in NTAS).
Elkin papers. Fisher Library Archives. University of Sydney.
Rowley papers. Australian Institute of Aboriginal and
  Torres Strait Islander Studies.

Australian Archives, Darwin.

The following files in the F1 series are referred to:

23/254	36/592	38/536	39/408	40/203	42/367	42/461
43/24	45/150	49/113	49/532	49/574	52/250	52/493
52/512	52/519	52/574	52/579	52/759 (275–7)		52/775
52/778	52/1118	52/1160	53/184	53/307	53/659	54/111
54/737	54/821	54/984	54/991	54/1013	55/1126	55/414

56/1331   56/2209   57/145   57/981   59/3141   63/3200   66/635
66/809   66/3583

The following files in the F315 series are referred to:
49/189   49/265

The following file in the series F941 is referred to:
64/256 (511)

The following file in the series E242 is referred to:
5/K1/1/7 (299)
5/K14/3/32

The following are E460 files of the erstwhile DAA to which special access was granted by ATSIC:
T4/77/87   T65 73/8349
14 82/164   16 83/363   37 85/133   48/1972   51 74/180
51 74/2249   51 74/180   54 83/363 1&2 54 83/441
64 76/25   71/3516   72/622   72/1003   73/7229
75/25 1&2   133 83/103   79/11922   83/441

BOOKS

Ahmad, A. 1992. *In Theory: Classes, nations, literatures*. London: Verso.

Altman, J.C. 1987. *Hunter-Gatherers Today*. Canberra: Government Publishing Service.

Attwood, B. & A. Marcus. 1997. *The 1967 referendum or when Aborigines didn't get the vote*. Canberra: Australian Institute of Aboriginal and Torres Strait Islander Studies.

Austin-Broos, D. 1996. '"Two Laws", Ontologies, Histories: Ways of being Aranda today'. *Oceania* 7, 1–20.

Bachelard, G. 1969. *The Poetics of Space* (trans.) Maria Jolas. Boston: Beacon Press.

Barnett, S.A. 1988. *Biology and Freedom*. Cambridge: Cambridge University Press.

Barwick, D. 1972. 'Coranderrk and Cumeroogunga: Pioneers and policy'. In *Opportunity and Response* (eds) S. Epstein & D. Penny. London: Hurst & Company.

Bauer, F.H. 1964. *Historical Geographical Survey of Part of Northern Australia*. CSIRO.

Beckett, J. 1964. 'Aborigines, alcohol and assimilation'. In *Aborigines Now* (ed.) M. Reay. Sydney: Angus & Robertson.

——1983. 'Internal colonialism in a welfare state: The case of the Australian Aborigines'. Paper presented to the American Anthropological Association, Chicago, 1983.

——1985. '"Knowing how to talk to white people": Torres Strait Islanders and the politics of representation'. In *Indigenous Peoples and the Nation-State* (ed.) N. Dyck. Newfoundland: Memorial University, Newfoundland.

——1987. *Torres Strait Islanders: Custom and colonialism*. Sydney: Cambridge University Press.

——1988a. 'Aboriginality, Citizenship and the Nation State'. In *Aborigines and the State in Australia* (ed.) J. Beckett. *Special Issue of* 24, 3–18.

——1988b. *Past and Present*. Canberra: Aboriginal Studies Press.

Bell, D. 1998. *Ngarrindjeri Wurruwarrin: A world that is, was, and will be*. Melbourne: Spinifex.

Berger, J. 1975. *The Seventh Man*. Baltimore: Harmondsworth.

Berndt, R.M. 1951. *Kunapipi: A study of an Australian Aboriginal religious cult*. Melbourne: Cheshire.

Berndt, R.M. & C.H. Berndt. 1987. *End of an Era: Aboriginal labour in the Northern Territory*. Canberra: Australian Institute of Aboriginal Studies.

Bhabha, H. 1983. 'The Other Question'. *Screen*, 18–36.

——1985. 'Signs Taken for Wonders'. *Critical Enquiry*, 144–65.

——1994. *The Location of Culture*. London and New York: Routledge.

Biddle, J. 1996. 'Loss and the letter'. Paper presented to the Department of Anthropology, Macquarie University.

——forthcoming. 'Writing without ink: Methodology, literacy and cultural difference'. In *Culture and Text: Discourse and methodology in social research and cultural studies* (eds) A. Lee & K. Poynton, Sydney: Allen & Unwin.

Bloch, J.M. 1958. *Miscegenation, Melalukation and Mr Lincoln's Dog*. New York: Schaum Publishing Co.

Bulman Oral History Series, 1995. Numbers 1–13. Barunga, Northern Territory: Barunga Press.

Burbank, V. 1988. *Aboriginal Adolescence: Maidenhood in an Australian community*. New Brunswick: Rutgers University Press.

Camfoo, T. (in press) 'The autobiography of Tex Camfoo'. In *Love against the Law* (ed.) G. Cowlishaw, Canberra: Aboriginal Studies Press.

Carter, P. 1987. *The Road to Botany Bay*. London: Faber & Faber.

Castoriadis, C. 1992. 'Reflections on racism'. *Thesis Eleven* 32, 1–22.

Chase, A. 1984. *Anthropology and the Courts*. Brisbane: Griffith University.

Clifford, J. 1986. On ethnographic allegory. In *Writing Cultures* (eds) J. Clifford & G. Marcus. Berkeley: University of California Press.

Cole, T. 1988. *Hell West and Crooked*. Sydney: Angus & Robertson.

Collmann, J. 1979. 'Fringe camps and the development of Aboriginal administration in Central Australia'. *Social Analysis* 2, 38–57.

——1988. *Aboriginal Fringe Dwellers and Welfare*. St Lucia: University of Queensland Press.

——n.d. 'Drunkenness and the exploration of self among Central Australian Aborigines'. Department of Anthropology: University of Adelaide.

Conciliation and Arbitration Commission, 1965. Equal Wages Case. In

Commonwealth Arbitration Reports. 113, 651. Canberra: Commonwealth Government.

Costello, M.J.J. 1930. *Life of John Costello.* Sydney: Dymocks.

Cowlishaw, G. 1978. 'Infanticide in Aboriginal Australia'. *Oceania* 48, 262–83.

——1980. 'Women's realm: Socialisation, sexuality and reproduction in Aboriginal society'. PhD thesis: University of Sydney.

——1981. 'The determinants of fertility among Australian Aborigines'. *The Australian Journal of Anthropology* 31(1).

——1982. 'Socialisation and subordination among Australian Aborigines'. *Man (NS)* 17, 492–507.

——1983. 'Blackfella boss: A Study of a Northern Territory cattle station'. *Social Analysis* 13, 54–69.

——1988. *Black, White or Brindle: Race in rural Australia.* Sydney: Cambridge University Press.

——1990. 'Helping anthropologists: Cultural continuity in the constructions of Aboriginalists'. *Canberra Anthropology* 13, 1–28.

——1994. 'Policing the races'. *Social Analysis*, 71–92.

——(ed.) 1995a. *Bulman Oral History Series.* Katherine, NT: Barunga Press.

——1995b. 'Did the earth move for you?' *The Australian Journal of Anthropology* 6, 32–63.

——1996. 'White women held captive in Arnhem Land'. *Olive Pink Bulletin* 8, 17–22.

——1997. 'Race at work'. *Journal of the Royal Anthropological Society* 3, 95–113.

——1998. 'Erasing race and culture: Practising "self-determination"'. *Oceania* 68, 145–69.

Cowlishaw, G. & B. Morris (eds) 1997. *Race Matters.* Canberra: Aboriginal Studies Press.

Cummings, B. 1990. *Take This Child.* Canberra: Aboriginal Studies Press.

Dean, B. & V. Carrel. 1956. *Dust for the Dancers.* Sydney: Ure Smith.

Dening, G. 1988. *History's Anthropology: The death of William Gooch.* Lanham MD: University Press of America.

Dewar, M. 1992. *The 'Black War' in Arnhem Land: Missionaries and the Yolngu 1908–1940.* Canberra: Australia National University.

Dingo, S. 1997. *Dingo: The story of our mob.* Sydney: Random House.

Doolan, J.K. 1977. 'Walk-off (and later return) of various Aboriginal groups from cattle stations'. In *Aborigines and Change: Australia in the '70s* (ed.) R.M. Berndt. Canberra: Australian Institute of Aboriginal Studies.

Durack, M. 1974. *To Keep Him My Country.* Adelaide: Rigby.

Dyck, N. (ed.) 1985. *Indigenous peoples and the nation-state.* Social and Economic Papers No. 14. Toronto: Institute of Social and Economic Research, Memorial University of Newfoundland.

Eagleton, T. 1990. *The Ideology of the Aesthetic.* London: Basil Blackwell.

Egan, T. 1997. *Sit Down up North: An autobiography.* Marrickville, Sydney: Kerr Publishing.

Elias, N. 1984. *The Civilising Process.* Oxford: Basil Blackwell.

Bibliography

Elkin, A.P. 1932. 'The social life and intelligence of the Australian Aborigine: A review of S.D. Porteus's *Psychology of a Primitive People'*. *Oceania* 3, 101–18.

——1934. 'Anthropology and the future of Australian Aborigines'. *Oceania* 5, 1–18.

——1937. 'Native education with special reference to the Australian Aborigines'. *Oceania* 7, 459–500.

——1951. 'Reaction and interaction: A food gathering people and European interaction in Australia'. *American Anthropologist* 53, 164–86.

——1961. 'Maraian at Mainoru, 1949: I. Description'. *Oceania* 31, 259–93.

——1972. *Two Rituals in South and Central Arnhem Land'* (No. 19). Sydney: Oceania Monographs.

——1974. *The Australian Aborigines*. Sydney: Angus & Robertson.

——1977 (f.p. 1945). *Aboriginal Men of High Degree*. St Lucia, Queensland: University of Queensland Press.

Fabian, J. 1983. *Time and the Other: How anthropology makes its object*. New York: Columbia University Press.

Fanon, F. 1967. *The Wretched of the Earth*. Harmondsworth: Penguin.

——1986. *Black Skin, White Masks*. London: Pluto Press.

Forrest, P. 1989. 'A short history of the Bulman area'. Unpublished report.

Foucault, M. 1977. *Discipline and Punish: The birth of the prison*. Ringwood, Victoria: Penguin Books.

——1978. *The History of Sexuality*. New York: Pantheon.

——1980. *Power/Knowledge*. Sydney: Harvester Wheatsheaf.

——1991. 'Questions of Method'. In *The Foucault Effect: Studies in governmentality* (eds) G. Burchell, C. Gordon & P. Miller. Sydney: Harvester Wheatsheaf.

Friedman, J. 1997. 'Global crises, the struggle for cultural identity and intellectual porkbarrelling: Cosmopolitans versus locals, ethnics and nationals in an era of de-hegemonisation'. In *Debating Cultural Hybridity: Multi-cultural identities and the politics of anti-racism* (eds) P. Werbner & T. Modood. London & New Jersey: Zed Books.

Genovese, E. 1974. *Roll, Jordan, Roll: The world the slaves made*. New York: Vintage Books.

Gibb, C.A. 1971. *Summary of the report of the committee to review the situation of Aborigines on pastoral properties in the Northern Territory*.

Gillespie, D. 1982. 'John Hunter and Maningrida: A chorus of alarm bells'. In *Service Delivery to Outstations* (ed.) P. Loveday. Darwin: Australian National University Northern Australia Research Unit.

Goldberg, T. 1995. *Racist Culture: Philosophy and the politics of meaning*. Oxford UK: Blackwell.

Gould, S.J. 1981. *The Mismeasure of Man*. New York: W.W. Norton.

Gramsci, A. 1971. *Selections from the Prison Notebook*. London: Lawrence and Wishart.

Gray, G. 1994. '"Piddington's indiscretion": Ralph Piddington, the Australian National Research Council and Academic Freedom'. *Oceania* 64, 217–45.

Gsell, F.X. 1955. *'The Bishop with 150 Wives': Fifty years as a missionary*. London: Angus & Robertson.

Gunn, A. 1963. *We of the Never-Never*. Sydney: Angus & Robertson.

Hall, V.S. 1955. *Walkabout*, 15–17.

Hamilton, A. 1972. 'Blacks and whites: The relationship of change'. *Arena* 30, 34–48.

——1975. 'Aboriginal women, the means of production'. In *The Other Half: Women in Australian society* (ed.) J. Mercer. Ringwood, Victoria: Penguin.

——1981. *Nature and Nurture*. Canberra: Australian Institute of Aboriginal Studies.

——1990. 'Fear and desire: Aborigines, Asians and the national imaginary'. *Australian Cultural History* 9, 14–35.

Hartwig, M.C. 1972. 'Aborigines and racism: An historical perspective'. In *Racism, The Australian Experience* (ed.) F. Stevens: ANZ Book Co.

Hasluck, P. 1988. *Shades of Darkness*. Melbourne: Melbourne University Press.

Heppel, M. (ed.) 1979. *A Black Reality: Aboriginal camps and housing in remote Australia*. Canberra: Australian Institute of Aboriginal Studies.

Herbert, X. 1977 (1959). *Seven Emus*. Melbourne: Fontana Books.

Hiatt, L. 1965. *Kinship and Conflict*. Canberra: Australian National University.

——1966. 'A spear in the ear'. *Oceania* 37, 153–4.

Hill, E. 1985 (f.p. 1951). *The Territory*. Sydney: Angus & Robertson.

Howard, M.C. 1982. 'Australian Aboriginal politics and the perpetuation of inequality'. *Oceania* 53, 82–101.

Human Rights and Equal Opportunities Commission, 1997. *Bringing Them Home: Report of the national inquiry into the separation of Aboriginal and Torres Strait Islander children from their families*. Human Rights and Equal Opportunities Commission.

Jackson, M. 1995. *At Home in the World*. London: Duke University Press.

——(ed.) 1996. *Things as They Are*. Bloomington: Indiana University Press.

Jacobs, P. 1986. 'Science and veiled assumptions: Miscegenation in West Australia, 1930–37'. *Australian Aboriginal Studies*, 123–45.

Johnson, C. 1987. 'Captured discourses captured lives'. *Aboriginal History* 11, 27–32.

Kapferer, B. 1988. *Legends of People, Myths of State*. London: Smithsonian Institution Press.

Keen, I. 1994. *Knowledge and Secrecy in an Aboriginal Religion*. Oxford; Clarendon Press.

Langton, M. 1997. 'Rum seduction and death: "Aboriginality" and alcohol'. In *Race Matters* (eds) G. Cowlishaw & B. Morris. Canberra: Aboriginal Studies Press.

Lattas, A. 1996. 'Humanitarianism and Australian nationalism in colonial Papua:

Hubert Murray and the Project of Caring for the Self of the Coloniser and the Colonised'. *The Australian Journal of Anthropology* 7, 141–65.

——1997. 'Aborigines and contemporary Australian nationalism'. In *Race Matters: Indigenous Australians and 'our' society* (eds) G. Cowlishaw & B. Morris. Canberra: Aboriginal Studies Press.

Lea, T. 1988. '*48–88' Northern Territory Women's Register*. Status of Women Committee and the Australian Bicentennial Authority.

Ledgar, R. 1985. 'The pastoral industry on Aboriginal land. Its impact; its legacy; the future'. In *The application of science and technology to Aboriginal development: Workshop Proceedings*. Alice Springs: Central Land Council and Technical Advisory Group on Aboriginal Lands.

Levi-Strauss, C. 1966. *The Savage Mind*. Chicago: University of Chicago Press.

Lewis, O. 1966. 'The culture of poverty'. *Scientific American* 215, 19–25.

Lindsay, D. 1884. *Mr D Lindsay's Explorations Through Arnhem's Land*. Adelaide: South Australian House of Assembly.

Lippmann, L. 1994. *Generations of Resistance*. Melbourne: Longman.

Lockwood, D. 1962. *I, the Aboriginal*. Adelaide: Rigby.

Lockwood, R. 1964. *Up the Track*. Adelaide: Rigby.

Long, J. 1992. *The Go-Betweens: Patrol officers in Aboriginal Affairs Administration in the Northern Territory 1936–1974*. Canberra: Australian National University.

Loveday, P. (ed.) 1982. *Service Delivery to Remote Communities*. Darwin: Australian National University North Australian Research Unit.

Loveday, P. & D. Wade-Marshall. 1985. *Economy and People in the North*. Darwin: Australian National University North Australian Research Unit.

Macknight, C.C. 1976. *Voyage to Marege: Macassan Trepangers in North Australia*. Melbourne: Melbourne University Press.

Macleod, C. 1997. *Patrol in the Dreamtime*. Kew, Victoria: Mandarin.

Maddock, K. 1977. 'Two laws in one community'. In *Aborigines and Change* (ed.) R. Berndt. Canberra: Australian Institute of Aboriginal Studies.

——1982. *The Australian Aborigines: A portrait of their society*. Ringwood, Victoria: Penguin.

——1983. *Your Land is Our Land*. Ringwood, Victoria: Penguin Books.

Marcus, J. 1997. 'Journey out to the centre'. In *Race Matters: Indigenous Australians and 'our' society* (eds) G. Cowlishaw & B. Morris. Canberra: Aboriginal Studies Press.

Markus, A. 1990. *Governing Savages*. Sydney: Allen & Unwin.

May, D. 1994. *Aboriginal Labour and the Cattle Industry*. Melbourne: Cambridge University Press.

McCorquodale, J. 1985. 'Aborigines: A history of law and justice 1829–1985'. PhD thesis, University of New England.

——1987. *Aborigines and the Law: A digest*. Canberra: Aboriginal Studies Press.

McGrath, A. 1984. 'Black velvet'. In *So Much Hard Work* (ed.) K. Daniels. Sydney: Fontana/Collins.

——1987a. *Born in the Cattle*. Sydney: Allen & Unwin.

——1987b. 'Mirror of the north'. In *Australians 1938* (eds) B. Gammage & P. Spearitt. Sydney: Fairfax Syme & Weldon Associates.

Meggit, M. 1962. *Desert People*. Sydney: Angus & Robertson.

Merlan, F. 1978. 'Making people quiet in the pastoral North: Reminiscences of Elsey Station'. *Aboriginal History* 2, 70–106.

——1998. *Caging the Rainbow*. Honolulu: University of Hawaii Press.

Michaels, E. 1990. *Bad Aboriginal Art: Tradition, media and technological horizons*. Minneapolis: University of Minnesota Press.

Millis, R. 1992. *Waterloo Creek*. Ringwood, Victoria: McPhee Gribble.

Montagu, A. 1972. *Statement on Race*. New York: Oxford University Press.

Morris, B. 1985. 'Cultural domination and domestic dependence: The Dhan-Gadi of New South Wales and the protection of the state'. *Canberra Anthropology* 8, 87–115.

——1989. *Domesticating Resistance*. London: Berg.

——1990. 'Making histories/living history'. *Writing Australian Culture: Special Issue of Social Analysis* 27, 83–129.

——1992. 'Frontier colonialism as a culture of terror'. In *Power, Knowledge and Aborigines* (eds) B. Attwood & J. Arnold. Victoria Australia: La Trobe University Press.

——1997. 'Racism, egalitarianism and 'Aborigines'. In *Race Matters: Indigenous Australians and 'our' society* (eds) G. Cowlishaw & B. Morris. Canberra: Aboriginal Studies Press.

Muecke, S. 1997. *No Road (Bitumen All The Way)*. Fremantle: Fremantle Arts Centre Press.

Myers, F. 1986a. *Pintupi Country, Pintupi Self*. Canberra: Australian Institute of Aboriginal Studies.

——1986b. 'Reflections on a meeting'. *American Ethnologist* 13, 430–47.

——1988. 'Burning the truck and holding the country: Property, time, and the negotiation of identity among Pintupi Aborigines'. In *Hunters and Gatherers? Property, Power and Ideology*. (eds) T. Ingold, D. Ricks & J. Woodburn. New York: St Martins Press.

Nandy, A. 1983. *The Intimate Enemy: Loss and recovery of self under colonialism*. Delhi: Oxford University Press.

Paine, R. 1977. *The White Arctic: Anthropological essays in tutelage and ethnicity*. Social and Economic Papers No. 7. Toronto: Memorial University of Newfoundland.

Palmer, K. 1990. 'Government policy and Aboriginal aspirations: Self-management at Yalata'. In *Going It Alone* (eds) R. Tonkinson & M. Howard. Canberra: Aboriginal Studies Press.

Peterson, N. 1985. 'Capitalism, culture and land rights: Aborigines and the state in the Northern Territory'. *Social Analysis* 18, 85–101.

Pike, G. 1975. *Frontier Territory*. Darwin: Pike & Stringer.

Poignant, R. & A. Poignant. 1996. *Encounter at Nagalarramba*. Canberra: National Library of Australia.

Povinelli, E. 1993. *Labor's Lot: The power, history and culture of Aboriginal action.* Chicago: University of Chicago Press.

Powell, A. 1988. *Far Country: A short history of the Northern Territory.* Melbourne: Melbourne University Press.

Pratt, M.L. 1986. 'Fieldwork in common places'. In *Writing Cultures* (ed.) C.G.G. Marcus. Berkeley: University of California Press.

Pritchard, K.S. 1975. *Coonardoo.* Sydney: Angus & Robertson.

Read, P. & J. Read. 1991. *Long Time Olden Time: Aboriginal accounts of Northern Territory history.* Alice Springs: Institute for Aboriginal Development.

Reid, T. 1990. *A Picnic With The Natives: Aboriginal-European relations in the Northern Territory to 1910.* Melbourne: Melbourne University Press.

Reiger, K. 1985. *The Disenchantment of the Home.* Melbourne: Oxford University Press.

Reynolds, H. 1981. *The Other Side of the Frontier.* Townsville, Queensland: The History Department, James Cook University.

——1990. *With the White People.* Ringwood, Victoria: Penguin.

Rhydwen, M. 1996. *Writing on the Backs of the Blacks.* Queensland: University of Queensland Press.

Roberts, E.Y. & R. Ledgar. 1992. 'A pastoral project on Aboriginal savanna lands'. In *Ecology and management of the world's savannas* (eds) J.C. Tothill & J.J. Mott. Canberra: The Australian Academy of Science.

Robinson, G. 1995. 'Violence, social differentiation and the self'. *Oceania* 65, 323–46.

Rosaldo, R. 1989. *Culture and Truth.* Boston: Beacon Press.

Rose, D. 1984. 'The saga of Captain Cook: Morality in Aboriginal and European law. *Australian Aboriginal Studies* 2, 24–39.

——1991. *Hidden Histories.* Melbourne: Cambridge University Press.

——1996. 'Whose confidentiality; whose intellectual property'. *Native Title News.*

——1997. 'Australia Felix rules OK!' In *Race Matters* (eds) G. Cowlishaw & B. Morris. Canberra: Aboriginal Studies Press.

Rowley, C.D. 1972a. *The Destruction of Aboriginal Society.* Ringwood, Victoria: Penguin.

——1972b. *Outcastes in a White Australia.* Ringwood, Victoria: Penguin.

——1972c. *The Remote Aborigines.* Ringwood, Victoria: Penguin.

Rowse, T. 1988a. 'Middle Australia and the noble savage: A political romance'. In *Past and Present: The construction of Aboriginality* (ed.) J. Beckett. Canberra: Aboriginal Studies Press.

——1988. 'Were you ever savages? Aboriginal insiders and pastoral patronage'. *Oceania* 58, 81–99.

——1989. 'White Flour, White Power'. PhD thesis: Sydney University.

——1992. 'Strehlow's strap: Functionalism and historicism in colonial ethnography. In *Power, Knowledge and Aborigines* (eds) B. Atwood & J. Arnold. Melbourne: La Trobe University Press.

——1998. *White Flour, White Power.* Melbourne: Cambridge University Press.

Rumsey, A. 1989. 'Language groups in Australian Aboriginal land claims.' *Anthropological Forum*, 69–79.

Sackett, L. 1990. 'Welfare colonialism: Developing divisions at Wiluna'. In *Going It Alone* (eds) R. Tonkinson & M. Howard. Canberra: Aboriginal Studies Press.

Said, E. 1985a. *Orientalism*. Ringwood Victoria: Penguin.

——1985b. 'Orientalism reconsidered'. *Race & Class* XXVII, 1–15.

Sansom, B. 1980. *The Camp at Wallaby Cross*. Canberra: Australian Institute of Aboriginal Studies.

——1985. 'Aborigines, anthropologists and the leviathan'. In *Indigenous Peoples and the Nation State* (ed.) N. Dyck. Social and Economic Papers No. 14. Toronto: Institute of Social and Economic Research, Memorial University, Newfoundland.

——1988. 'A grammar of exchange'. In *Being Black* (ed.) I. Keen. Canberra: Aboriginal Studies Press.

Sartre, J-P. 1956. *Being and Nothingness: An essay on phenomenological ontology* (trans.) Hazel E. Barnes. New York: Philosophical Library.

——1978. *Existentialism and Humanism*. London: Eyre Methuen.

Schaffer, K. 1988. *Women and the Bush*. Melbourne: Cambridge University Press.

Smith, B. 1980. *The Spectre of Truganini*. 1980 Boyer Lectures. Sydney: The Australian Broadcasting Commission.

Smith, B. & T. Smith. 1991. *Australian Painting, 1788–1990. Bernard Smith with three additional essays on Australian painting since 1970 by Terry Smith. 3rd Edition*. Melbourne: Oxford University Press.

Spivak, G.C. 1991. 'Theory in the margin'. In *Consequences of Theory* (eds) J. Arac & B. Johnson. London: The Johns Hopkins University Press.

Srivastava, S. 1996. 'The garden of rational delights: The nation as experiment, science as masculinity'. *Social Analysis* 39, 119–48.

Stanner, W.E.H. 1960. 'Durmugam, a Nangiomeri'. In *In the Company of Man* (ed.) J.B. Casagrande. New York: Harper and Brothers.

——1979. *White Man Got No Dreaming*. Canberra: Australian National University Press.

Stevens, F.S. 1974. *Racism; The Australian Experience*. Sydney: ANZ Book Co.

——1984. *Aborigines in the Northern Territory Cattle Industry*. Canberra: Australian National University Press.

Stoler, A. 1989. 'Rethinking colonial categories: European communities and the boundaries of rule'. *Comparative Studies in Society and History* 31, 134–61.

Stoler, A. & F. Cooper. 1997. 'Between Metropole and Colony: Rethinking a research agenda'. In *Tensions of Empire: Colonial cultures in a bourgeois world* (eds) F. Cooper & A. Stoler. Berkeley: University of California Press.

Strehlow, E. 1947. *Aranda Traditions*. Melbourne: Melbourne University Press.

Tamisari, F. 1998. 'Body, vision and movement: In the footprints of the ancestors'. *Oceania*, 68, 249–70.

Taussig, M. 1980. *The Devil and Commodity Fetishism*. Chapel Hill: University of North Carolina Press.

——1987. *Shamanism, Colonialism and the Wild Man*. Chicago: University of Chicago Press.

Teece, C. 1978. *Voice of the Wilderness*. Rockhampton: Teece.

Thiele, S.J. 1982. *Yugul, an Arnhem Land Cattle Station*. Darwin: Australian National University, North Australia Research Unit.

Thomas, N. 1994. *Colonialism's Culture*. Cambridge: Polity Press.

Thomson, D. 1935. 'The joking relationship and organised obscenity in north Queensland'. *American Anthropologist* 37, 460–90.

Todorov, T. 1982. *The Conquest of America*. New York: HarperPerennial.

Tonkinson, R. & M. Howard (eds) 1990. *Going It Alone? Prospects for Aboriginal autonomy*. Canberra: Aboriginal Studies Press.

van der Heide, F. 1985. 'Murwangi: A history of the attempts to establish a pastoral industry in North East Arnhem Land 1883 to 1983'. PhD thesis: University of New England.

von Sturmer, J. 1982. 'Aborigines in the uranium industry: Towards self-management in the Alligator River region?' In *Aboriginal Sites, Rights and Resource Development* (ed.) R.M. Berndt. Perth: University of Western Australia Press, for the Academy of the Social Sciences in Australia.

Warner, L. 1937. *A Black Civilisation*. New York: Harper.

WBAR. 1960–1. *Welfare Branch Annual Reports*. Welfare Branch, NT Government.

Weaver, S. 1983. 'Australian Aboriginal Policy: Aboriginal pressure groups or Government advisory bodies?' *Oceania* 54, 1–22 85–108.

——1985. 'Political representivity and indigenous minorities in Canada and Australia'. In *Indigenous Peoples and the Nation State* (ed.) N. Dyck. Newfoundland: Memorial University, Newfoundland.

Webster, S. 1993. 'Postmodernist theory and the sublimation of Maori culture'. *Oceania* 63, 222–39.

Werbner, P. & T. Modood. 1997. *Debating Cultural Hybridity*. London: Zed Books.

Willey, K. 1964. *Eaters of the Lotus*. Brisbane: Jacaranda.

Williams, N. 1986. *The Yolngu and their Laws: A system of land tenure and the fight for its recognition*. Canberra: Aboriginal Studies Press.

——1987. *Two Laws: Managing disputes in a contemporary Aboriginal community*. Canberra: Australian Institute of Aboriginal Studies.

Wise, T. 1985. *The Self-Made Anthropologist*. Sydney: Allen & Unwin.

Young, R.J.C. 1995. *Colonial Desire: Hybridity in theory, culture and race*. London: Routledge.

Index

Printed in the United States
by Baker & Taylor Publisher Services